Consumer Skills
Revised

Consumer Skills

Revised

IRENE OPPENHEIM, Ph. D.

Formerly Consultant, Consumer Education
and Home Economics,
New Jersey Department of Education

Bennett Publishing Company

Peoria, Illinois 61615

Copyright © 1977, 1982

By Irene Oppenheim

82   83   84   85   86   KP   5   4   3   2

ISBN 87002–344–6

Library of Congress Catalog No. 80–69440

Printed in the United States of America

Preface

The purpose of this book is to help you learn to navigate the complicated maze facing today's consumer, to sharpen your shopping skills, to learn to use resources wisely, to get the most for your time, energy, and dollars. It doesn't mean penny pinching, but just a businesslike approach to getting your money's worth. If, as a young person, you start learning to use your resources for the things that you really want, you will have this ability for the rest of your life. It's a little like learning to swim or to drive a car—you don't forget how to do it. You just have to keep practicing.

This book has five sections: *Managing Money, Sharpening Your Shopping Skills, Protecting Yourself, Looking Ahead, and The Environment and the Economy.* Each section deals with topics that are important if you are to get the most satisfaction from using your money and other resources.

It is not necessary to read this book in sequence. If one chapter interests you more than others, you might study that one first. However, all the chapters in this book deal with topics that young people starting off on their own would find very helpful.

To make them interesting and easy to understand, many chapters include short anecdotes about people. You can probably use your imagination and put yourself in the situation of some of the young people who are discussed in this book.

At the end of each chapter there are some additional tools to help you. First, you will find a *Review* section. This has two parts—a list of the most important ideas from the chapter, and a list of the terms which have been discussed. Next is a section on *Problem Solving,* which contains ideas for you to consider. Finally, there is a section, *To Do in Class,* which has both topics for class discussion and activities to do in class.

Acknowledgments

I would like to thank the many people who have helped in the preparation of this book. Ideas and suggestions came from a variety of sources, including some people whom I know only through correspondence or a chat on the phone. Most of all, I would like to thank my publishers, whose patience I tried, and my family, who lived with me through the process.

Table of Contents

PREFACE.. 5

ACKNOWLEDGMENTS... 5

SECTION 1: Managing Money....................................... 9

Chapter 1: The Spending Game................................ 10
The Meaning of Money, 10; Influences on Spending, 15; Young People and Spending, 19.

Chapter 2: Making Money Behave............................ 26
Pocketbook Problems, 26; How Will You Manage?, 29; The Envelope System, 34; A Monthly Spending Plan, 36; Looking Ahead, 36; Sharing Responsibility for Money Management, 39; The Working Woman, 41; The Scope of the Job, 41.

Chapter 3: Using Credit....................................... 44
The Use of Credit Goes Back a Long Time, 44; Credit Has Helped Change American Life, 45; Who Uses Credit?, 46; When Should You Use Credit?, 47; Debt Limits, 48; Types of Credit, 48; Credit Costs, 54; What a Credit Contract Must Tell You, 57; Your Credit Rating, 57; When You Can't Meet the Payments, 60.

SECTION 2: Sharpening Your Shopping Skills.................. 63

Chapter 4: The Shopping Game............................... 64
The Difficult Art of Shopping, 64; Prices, 64; Using Advertising Constructively, 66; Where Can You Shop?, 67; The Bargain Hunt, 72; Guarantees and Warranties, 77; Securing Product Information, 79; Labels, 79; Consumer Problems, 87; Converting to the Metric System, 95.

Chapter 5: Looking Your Best................................ 104
How Important Is Fashion?, 104; Planning Your Wardrobe, 105; Selecting Clothing, 110; Caring for Your Wardrobe, 118; Packing a Suitcase, 123; Grooming: The Finishing Touch, 123.

Chapter 6: Getting Around 130

The Automobile and Mass Transit, 130; Your Own Car, 130; Buying a Car, 131; When Is the Best Time to Buy or Sell a Car?, 141; Paying for Your Car, 141; Buying Insurance, 142; Your Responsibility as a Driver, 154; A Driver's License, 154; Renting a Car, 154; Leasing a Car, 155.

Chapter 7: Having Fun 158

The Growth and Distribution of Leisure, 158; The Use of Leisure Time, 160; Cutting Costs for Recreation, 177.

SECTION 3: Protecting Yourself 179

Chapter 8: Protecting Your Health 180

The Miracles of Medicine, 180; Your Responsibility for Good Health, 180; Teenagers' Rights as Patients, 189; Prepaying Medical Expenses with Health Insurance, 190; Cutting the Cost of Medicine, 194; The Government's Role, 195.

Chapter 9: Social Insurance 200

The Social Security Program, 200; Retirement, Survivors, and Disability Insurance, 200; Unemployment Insurance, 210; Worker's Compensation, 212; Public Assistance to the Needy, 213.

Chapter 10: Your Legal Rights and Responsibilities 218

Contracts, 219; Criminal Law, 229; Protecting the Consumer, 230.

SECTION 4: Looking Ahead 241

Chapter 11: Investing in Yourself 242

A High School Diploma Improves Your Chances for a Job, 242; Education May Help You Earn More Money, 242; Career Planning, 242; Preparing for the World of Work, 245; If You Are Considering More Education, 248; Job Trends, 250; An Overview of Some Occupational Areas, 252; Looking for a Job, 257; Keeping Up-to-Date, 262.

Chapter 12: Bank Services 266

Types of Banks, 267; Assets Invested in Mortgages, 267; Getting Paid by Check, 268; Paying Your Bills, 271; Checking Accounts, 274; Saving Money, 279; Safeguarding Valuables in a Safe-Deposit Box, 285.

Table of Contents

Chapter 13: A Roof Over Your Head............................ 288
You Have Several Choices, 288; Your Needs Will Change, 288; What Should You Spend on Housing?, 293; To Rent or Buy, 295; Renting a Home, 295; Cooperatives and Condiminiums, 297; So You Want to Buy a House, 298; Have You Considered a Mobile Home?, 306; Financing Your Home, 311; Closing Costs, 314; Insuring Your Home, 314; Taxes in Brief, 315; Moving: The Big Day, 316.

Chapter 14: Buying Life Insurance........................... 320
How Does It Work?, 320; The Basic Types of Life Insurance, 320; Forms of Life Insurance Contracts, 325; Shopping for Insurance, 325; Life Insurance Features, 332; Types of Insurance Companies, 336; United States Government Insurance, 336; Tax Advantages of Life Insurance, 337; Women and Life Insurance, 337; Switching Policies, 337; Method of Payment, 338.

Chapter 15: Other Investments........................... 340
Fixed-Dollar Investments, 340; Equity Investments, 340; Collections, 340; Real Estate, 345; Stocks, 347; Bonds, 349; Selecting Stocks and Bonds, 351; Investment Funds, 356; Government Securities, 357; Investment Clubs, 358; Lotteries and Gambling, 358.

SECTION 5: The Environment and the Economy..................... 361

Chapter 16: Protecting the Environment......................... 362
Population Pressure, 364; The Use of Land, 365; Water, 367; A Growing Mound of Household Trash, 370; Energy, 371; Air, 373; Noise, 376; The Economics of Improving the Environment, 377; Unresolved Issues, 378; The Need for Cooperative Efforts, 379.

Chapter 17: You and the Economy........................... 382
Your Role in the Economy, 382; Types of Economic Systems, 382; The U.S. Economy, 383, Equalizing Opportunities: The Government's Role, 394.

INDEX... 398

SECTION 1

Managing Money

CHAPTER 1

The Spending Game

Today everyone is in the spending game. From the little toddler who picks out his favorite crunchy cereal to the senior citizen buying medicine, we all share in the desire to have some of the goods and services available in modern society. Each person's attitude toward money affects the way he or she participates in the spending game.

THE MEANING OF MONEY

Money means different things to everyone. For some it means a sense of power. With money they can better control their world. Some early industrialists accumulated far more wealth than they needed. More than money, it seemed they wanted to control an industry.

For others money is security. Such people feel a great need to hang onto money, to save it for future needs.

Still others feel that money is for spending—that it is the avenue to fun. People with this attitude usually feel that unless they can enjoy money when they

Even today people in less developed countries struggle for survival.

FAO Photo

have it, there is no point in working hard for it.

All of these attitudes go back many years in history.

The Judeo-Christian Ethic

The *appreciation of thrift and hard work* grew out of a time when even the most necessary things were scarce. In biblical days men farmed with crude tools, often in areas where it was hard to make things grow. Garments were fashioned of skins that the family tanned or cloth that had to be spun or woven. It took tremendous effort for a family to get the necessary food, clothing, and shelter. People had to work hard. The lazy and the weak had great difficulty in surviving.

Until the dawn of the age of industry—about the mid-1800's—most people had to work very hard to stay alive. Early immigrants to this country, such as the Puritans of New England and the colonists in Virginia, struggled hard for survival. As you know, Thanksgiving Day originated as a feast of the Pilgrims of the Plymouth Colony to celebrate the harvest and the fact that there would be food for the winter. As recently as the last century, the pioneer

Poor housing is still a problem in many cities.

families of the Midwest and Far West worked from sunup to past sundown for just the basic necessities. The obvious need for hard work in order to survive became part of the religious attitudes of the times. Hard work, thrift, and frugality (making do with bare essentials) were considered virtues.

Even today many people preserve these attitudes. Some may use money carefully to conserve it for an unforeseen emergency or for the retirement years. Others feel they should spend sparingly for some items in

High productivity usually results in larger incomes.

International Harvester Co.

Today many people in industrialized countries can choose to spend money on things that they enjoy.

order to have money for more important things. Many parents, for example, make personal sacrifices for the sake of their children—a week at camp for the kids comes before a new coat for Mom. For those who have retained this general attitude of their ancestors, money is to be used with purpose, not carelessness.

The Money-is-for-Spending Attitude

A second attitude toward money has historical roots too. Certainly as far back as biblical days there were people who felt that wealth should be used *for pleasure-giving activities and comforts, rather than just necessities.* This has been true in every age. For centuries it was expected that rulers and chiefs would live in a luxurious manner.

Today, with a large middle-class population in the industrial nations, many more people have an opportunity to choose how they will use assets. A great many feel that with the built-in security of old age pensions, unemployment insurance, and other programs, they can use much of their income in ways that they enjoy. Still others feel that they have worked hard for money, and therefore it should be used in ways that give them pleasure.

The Attitude of Indifference

In contrast to the second philosophy is the attitude of people who are unconcerned about living as their fellow men do, who do not care whether they have all the comforts that society can provide. Their *indifference toward money and what it can buy* is reflected in a life style that emphasizes feelings—love, understanding, happiness, appreciation of nature—rather than things. Over the years, this philosophy has been pursued in different ways and degrees.

Many of the early prophets led the way to new styles of living. In fact, almost every man who founded or greatly influenced an important religious group scorned the usual pattern of living of his contemporaries—Jesus, John the Baptist, John Calvin, Isaiah, and many others. Monks and nuns of the Middle Ages spent their lives in seclusion and self-denial but preserved much of the literary heritage of the Western world. Also, monks of such Eastern religions as Buddhism, who to this day often serve as the educated leaders of their society, lead lives with little or no material comforts.

History contains many more examples of people who cared little for material things.

In the 1900's George Washington Carver worked as an agricultural chemist and educator but didn't cash his paychecks for years. You may be able to think of other examples.

Today the pattern is no different. There are still those who view life differently from the rest. In recent years, for example, many people have placed more emphasis on the pollution problems caused by an industrial society than on the material goods produced. Many are also concerned about the depletion of our natural resources, such as forests and oil. For them, as well as those who had similar attitudes throughout history, money is far from first on their list of values.

How Do You Feel?

Have you ever imagined that you were in someone else's shoes? Try it now as you read about three young people with different attitudes toward money.

Case Study. A high school senior, Brad Smith lives with his parents, two sisters, and one brother in a large city in Michigan. Brad's father is a foreman at a ball bearing plant and his mother is a part-time clerk in a dry cleaning business. Although they have no serious money problems, family expenses are high.

Brad enjoys school, both academically and socially. He keeps his grades up and still has time to play basketball with the team.

On weekends he is a checker in a supermarket. With the money he earns, Brad pays for many of his personal expenses but not most of his clothing. Brad's parents feel that the money he earns is his to use as he chooses. Often he buys on a whim—like the time he drove to the shopping center to buy shoes and came home with three record albums instead.

Brad's plans for the future are uncertain. After graduation, he has thought about training at a nearby technical school. That way he could still live at home. When Brad's father suggested that he save some money for the training program, Brad answered, "Why? If I need it, I can always work part-time."

From this brief introduction to Brad, can you guess what his attitude toward money is? What part of his attitude do you support? What would you criticize? Do you think Brad will face any financial problems in the future?

Case Study. For as long as she can remember, Maria Juarez's parents have preached to her about saving money. "A penny saved is a penny earned," her mother repeatedly points out. Maria sighs wistfully each time she puts away the remainder of her weekly allowance for safe keeping.

As a junior in high school, Maria has no close friends. Because of her parents' feelings about "frivolous" spending, Maria has never been encouraged to participate in activities. In fact, her parents have often prevented her from taking part. When she was younger, she used to beg to do things, but the usual response was, "You know that's a waste of money, Maria."

Although the desire is there, Maria can't find a way to make friends. The last time a chance for friendship came along, she was too frightened to accept it. A neighbor girl invited Maria to go to a movie with a group of girls. "Oh, no, I . . . I can't," Maria said. "I'm saving money for . . . for college." Maria had lied. She had no plans for college. It was just another of the excuses she had learned to make. Now Maria's parents worry about her. They worry about her shyness and troubled outlook, but they do

not understand and they don't know how to help.

What attitudes toward money do you find in Maria's story? Why do you think Maria could not easily adjust to her parent's attitude? How did Maria's problem become more than just a money problem? Do you think that attitudes toward money often cause more serious problems in families?

Case Study. Strangely enough, Mark's situation is similar to Maria's, but by his own choosing. A serious-minded, studious, young man, Mark Mannheim devotes nearly all of his time and energy toward the achievement of one goal—going to college. He has been saving money for this ever since he was old enough to have a paper route. Mark knows that his parents' income will not support a son in college.

As a result, Mark does not socialize much. Studying and working take up most of his time. Every now and then, however, he hears friends talking about a good party or an exciting basketball game, and for a moment he regrets what he is missing. Yet in a short time his thoughts return to that single ambition that means so much to him.

How do you feel about Mark's attitude toward money? Have you ever wanted anything enough to make great personal sacrifices? Do you think Mark will regret his actions in later years?

Now that you have read and thought about the three general attitudes toward money, think about your own outlook. Do you fit into one of the three classifications? You may have a difficult time deciding. Your attitude could be a combination of two categories or might even fall somewhere in between. No doubt you could find a variety of opinions among the members of your class. What accounts for these differences? Actually, many factors influence attitudes toward money and the spending game. A close look at some of these could help you understand why you may feel one way and your best friend or members of your family feel another.

INFLUENCES ON SPENDING

What makes us buy? Why do we want so many different things? Should we get them now or wait? Many factors influence our spending.

The Family Situation

The family plays an important role in establishing spending attitudes. A key factor is how the family feels about money and its management. For example, a family may lose its income when the father becomes ill. This could cause the members to become bitter over their losses, or they might compensate with love, understanding, and cooperation. The child of a well-to-do family may not be given everything he requests. Instead he may be required to earn an allowance or hold a job to buy what he wants. Whatever the situation, each child in a family will watch, listen, and learn. As the child grows older, he or she combines family attitudes with new influences.

Values

Over the years man has developed ideas about what is right, desirable, and proper. We call these *values.* Values are an important part of our culture, representing what we favor, what we strive for, and what we reward.

Why do we need values? They give us guideposts. They help us make decisions, to pick one thing before another.

Institute of Life Insurance
What influences will affect this woman's purchase?

Values are very personal. It is unlikely that any two people have exactly the same values. Even within a family a husband and wife may disagree. You and your best friend will probably not agree on everything. Perhaps there are some matters on which your views differ from those of your family.

We strive to place our values concerning our wants and needs in a hierarchy, from those we must have to those of little importance.
Margaret Jacobson, Cooperative Extension Service, Michigan State University

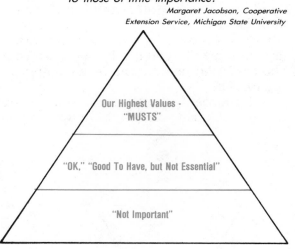

Our Highest Values - "MUSTS"

"OK," "Good To Have, but Not Essential"

"Not Important"

Values greatly influence how we use time, energy, and money. Is it better to spend money on entertaining friends or on a nice vacation trip? Should a person be generous to religious and charitable groups, even if it means driving an older car? These are just a few value judgments that affect the way people live. As you can see, these judgments are based on personal values.

Today the consumer is hard to predict. What he or she buys depends, to a large extent, on individual values. Often young people buy unusual combinations of things. One young man in college had a new sports car, cowboy boots, and one pair of very patched dungarees that he had worn almost every day for six months.

WHAT ARE YOUR VALUES?

Have you ever thought about your own values concerning time, money, and other people? Try answering the following questions and consider your priorities. Think through the question, "What is important to me?"

• If you had some free time, what would you do? How would this reflect your values?

• If you were given $20 for your birthday, how would you use it? What are your choices? Why would one be most appealing to you?

• Suppose that you need some extra money for spring clothes. How would you handle this situation? Make a list of all the alternatives available to you.

• Assume that this Friday evening you want to invite your friends to your house? What are some of the things that you will need to consider? Will your plans have any effect on other members of your family? If so, how?

• Assume that Sunday is the day of the class picnic, and you want to go. It is also your Grandmother's sixtieth birthday. Therefore your family expects you to go to a party for her. What would you do and why?

The Group Influence

Most of us want to *belong,* to be accepted as part of a particular group. Many people feel the need to find a small group in which they can feel they have an important part.

Think about how much belonging to a group affects spending. Because the individual has a desire to be accepted by others in the group, he or she is likely to adopt many of their ideas. Consequently, he spends money in similar fashion to the rest.

In some groups, such as exclusive social clubs, much emphasis is placed on financial success. This is also true in certain neighborhoods, among executives of some companies, and in other formal and informal groups. Members of such groups may feel they must use money in a showy way—for a luxurious car, fancy home, styl-

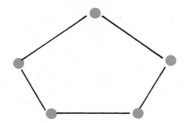

Margaret Jacobson, Cooperative
Extension Service, Michigan State University
Members of a group hold some values in common. A person who does not share the important values of a group may find himself on the outside.

ish clothes. Items which are purchased mostly to show financial success are called *status symbols.* (Of course, not everyone who drives an expensive car or joins a country club is a *show off* or a social climber.)

Appearance is probably one of the primary links among people in a group. Part of the desire to dress in a certain way—whether with blue jeans or expensive furs—stems from the fact that people feel they may be considered odd or different by the rest of the group if they don't.

Think about some groups you are familiar with, both organized and informal. In what ways do the members share similar values? Some groups you might consider are school clubs, sororities and fraternities, businessmen's organizations, street gangs, political organizations, and protest groups.

Changing Social Patterns

Changing social patterns also influence spending. For one thing, Americans are working fewer hours. The typical working week for a person employed in an office or factory is between $37\frac{1}{2}$ and 40 hours and is often less. Paid vacations and single holidays are increasing.

As a result, people have more time for recreation and vacations. More money is now spent for sports, hobbies, and travel. Many of us spend for such activities as attending movies and games, bowling, golf, skating, skiing, and boating. As a typical young person, you probably want to go places and do things that your parents may not have been able to see and experience when they were younger.

In addition, our national desire to eat out has affected spending for food enormously. Food is no longer considered to be just

What do you suppose the members of this group have in common?

U. S. Department of Labor

Young people contribute to the large volume of snacks and beverages sold.

something essential to health and growth. Although this is very important, most people think that eating should also be pleasant. Snack foods have created a booming industry. Quick-service eating places are much more popular than they used to be. People want to eat out in a casual manner and can afford to do so. Easy-to-fix foods, like frozen dinners or macaroni-and-cheese packages, make popular home meals for young and old, although they are often more expensive than meals made from scratch.

Mood

Sometimes *mood* can influence spending. Many people have been known to buy a new garment because they felt lonely or depressed. Some people eat when they feel blue. Certainly we all have times when we need to do something to lift our spirits, but we don't care to waste money either. The solution is in planning. If you are prone to impulse or mood buying, perhaps you should set aside a specific amount of money just for those occasions.

Credit

"Buy now, pay later." Briefly, that is what credit means. If we can use credit, buying becomes much easier. Many of us want to have things now and will make purchases if we can spread the payments over a period of time. Credit is used widely today, allowing people to buy articles they might not otherwise obtain. Although this is a wonderful help for some, it is a serious problem for those who charge beyond their ability to pay. (Credit is discussed more fully in another chapter.)

Advertising

Advertising is an important device for helping people become aware of what is on the market. In particular, many new products are widely advertised because manufacturers want people to know and desire their product as soon as possible. Television, newspapers, magazines, billboards, and store displays are ways of influencing the public. To encourage people to buy, many advertisements go beyond the mere telling of facts, since facts alone do not adequately sell products. By adding a little emotional appeal, profits can be increased. Even the most cautious person may be persuaded to buy something he doesn't really want or need by relating it to his desire for success, popularity, good looks, or independence. Wise shoppers know this. Therefore they consider their real needs and their emotions before buying.

The State of the Economy

Most people feel prosperous and freer to spend when the economy is booming and jobs are plentiful. Generally, when there are many job openings, women find it easier to get better-paying jobs and young people can find part-time work. More people working means more money to spend.

Few people today would call themselves rich; still, many have enough for some of their *wants* as well as their needs. Today the basics—food, clothing, and shelter—take a much smaller proportion of a typical family's income than they did about one hundred years ago. The result is that people now have more *discretionary income*—that is, money for more than just basic needs.

Attitudes about the Future

Optimism and pessimism—these both influence personal spending. We tend to spend more freely if we feel good about the future. If your father thinks that he might be out of work tomorrow, he is apt to be more cautious about spending money today. A young man or woman just starting in the working world is usually more optimistic about future earning power than the person approaching retirement, so he or she may spend more freely.

YOUNG PEOPLE AND SPENDING

Now that you have read about those things which generally influence spending by people of all ages, let's focus only on young people to see how they participate in the spending game.

Young People Set New Trends

The trends started by young people cover several areas. Some of these are fashion, sports, travel, and social concerns.

Until recently *fashions* were generally set by and for people thirty and over. In women's fashions, high-priced designers would sell to the wealthy who, in turn, set the styles which were copied by the mass market. However, this is no longer true. Leading fashion designers are youth oriented. The older person wants to look and feel young. Men's and women's clothing is designed for the youthful look. The real test of whether a fashion will be accepted by the country depends on whether or not

Advertising is all around us. What examples do you see in this drawing?

Skiing has boomed in popularity.

Canadian Government Office of Tourism

Lack of finances does not deter many of today's ambitious young people. Travel expenses are often cut by camping and backpacking. Can you think of some drawbacks to this mode of travel?

the young people will adopt it. Present-day fashions tend to be set by young people and copied by the older age groups. The stylish length for women's skirts is now largely determined by what the young accept.

Trends have also been started in *sports.* Skiing, for example, was once an exclusive sport for the few who lived near mountains or who were rather wealthy. Then young people in general became interested. Many people in their teens or early twenties had the money to spend for the necessary clothes, equipment, travel, and accommodations, and they wanted to ski. Now skiing is popular with nearly all age groups.

Young people are *travel-minded.* Neither the length of a trip nor how it is financed seems to deter youth. Backpacking, bike riding, going by car, train, or plane—the young people of the nation are on the move. One airline estimates that 330,000 college-age students will soon cross the Atlantic by air in a year's time.

20

Do-it-yourself projects are very popular. Teen business accounts for about one-third of the growing $3-billion home sewing market. Crocheting and knitting are also popular. Home hair care and styling have been adopted by many. Electrical appliances for hair care, such as dryers and rollers, are selling fast, and some of them are used by men.

Young people have a more active interest in *social concerns*—drug abuse, women's rights, ecology—than ever before. As a result, one leading cosmetics company recently changed the focus of its sales program from dating and makeup to social issues.

Young People Have Money to Spend

Since 1945, young people have become a rapidly increasing segment of the consumer market. They have more money to spend and a desire to use this money for their own activities. One estimate is that in just one year teens spend about $20 billion on personal items and leisure activities. This money comes from several sources but mostly from jobs and allowances.

Not many years ago teenagers were expected to help provide for the family. They were needed on the farms to help produce food. Youths were also an important part of the labor force in factories as late as the early 1900's. However, conditions changed as laws were passed restricting child labor and requiring more schooling.

Still many young people are working, even while in school. After-school and weekend jobs are common. Summer vacations are work periods for many.

A great many teens, even those who also work, get a regular allowance from their families. The allowance is often for such specific things as school supplies, lunches, or clothes. Generally, though, there is con-

Eastman Kodak Co.

Young people are active in sports. Tennis is just one example.

siderable freedom in how young people use their money. If you are typical, you probably buy some of your own clothes and decide how much of your own money to spend.

What Young People Spend On

Spending is heavy on certain things. The young have helped put across a booming market for *music.* They feed the juke boxes and buy radios, record players, tape recorders, and cassettes. The record market is determined largely by what the teenagers want; they make or break record sales.

Sports equipment is bought in great quantities by teenagers and people in their early twenties. Golf clubs and shoes, bowling balls, tennis rackets, skis and ski gear,

Today young people are big spenders on clothing. Stores supply special departments like this one to meet their needs.

camping and boating equipment—these are just a few of the items which can make sports an expensive pastime.

Young people are big spenders for *cosmetics and personal grooming items.* Girls often experiment extensively with cosmetics, which means that they buy a great many. It is widely recognized that a large part of the market for women's cosmetics is girls in their teens and early twenties. Young men are taking an increasing interest in grooming. Consequently, expenditures for shaving products, deodorants, and hair care preparations for men have grown tremendously.

Most young people cannot afford a new car, much as they might like one. Therefore a large part of the market for *used cars,* particularly older models, is sustained by young people.

Young People Influence Family Spending

Even when they aren't spending money directly, youths influence family spending. Many parents buy frozen dinners, pizza, snack foods, and soda because the young people in the family want them. Sometimes the force behind a big family purchase comes from the younger members. The choice of a car, TV set, or stereo is often strongly influenced by the teenagers in a family. Parents, for example, may buy an extra TV set for their children. A second or third car may be purchased to avoid a series of parent-teenager conflicts over who gets "the wheels."

The initial impetus to buy many other things often comes from the young people in the family. They are sensitive to what is current and want to be part of the contemporary trend.

Young People Influence the Business World

Members of the business world have recognized that young people are important consumers and have increasingly *geared their selling efforts* for certain goods and services to the youthful market. Many changes have come about as young people have been recognized as an important market. Clothing stores cater to the tastes and desires of the young market with special sizes, departments, and specialty stores. Thirty years ago teenage sizes, junior departments, and boutiques were unknown. Now most stores that carry clothing for the teenager stock fashionable, attractive styles in a range of sizes, reflecting the desire of the younger person to be dressed in the current mode. Often these clothes are more highly styled than the clothing for adults.

Considerable *advertising* is aimed at the youth market. A glance at *Cosmopolitan, Redbook,* or *Sports Illustrated* will suggest the range of items advertised for the young person who is buying now and will be buying more soon. In *Seventeen,* which is largely geared to the high school girl, one can find ads for silverware, furniture, and dishes. One of the reasons why producers advertise to a group that is not yet ready to purchase their items is to stimulate interest in these goods as part of the "good life." Another reason is to develop brand loyalty. Advertisers often feel that young people have not yet developed strong preferences for any brand. Their hope is that if young people start buying their brand early, they will continue to buy it for many years to come.

For similar reasons, *charge accounts* are offered to teenagers in many places. Stores want young people to develop the habit of buying from them at the stage when preferences are determined. It is widely believed that people of all age groups tend to patronize a store more readily and to buy more freely if they have a charge account there. Moreover, retailers want a share in the $20 billion annual teenage income. They know that young people alone spend billions of dollars a year on apparel, footwear, cosmetics, and toiletries. Therefore, in hopes of building loyal customers and cashing in on the market, stores offer charge accounts to young people.

FOR REVIEW

Points to Remember

- Money means different things, such as power, security, or a source of fun, to people.
- Some of the most important factors which influence an individual's spending are: the family situation, values, the peer group influence, changing social patterns, mood, the availability of credit, advertising, the state of the economy, and whether or not one is optimistic about future earning power.
- Young people are big spenders, especially for music, sports equipment, cosmetics, personal grooming items, and used cars. They also exert an important influence on family spending.
- Today many trends are set by young people through their use of money, especially in fashions, sports, travel, and do-it-yourself projects.
- The business community has responded to young people as consumers with specially designed merchandise and promotional techniques.
- Although using money is an important way of getting goods and services that you want, many other resources are available, such as time and energy.

Terms to Know

advertising	optimism
attitude	pessimism
decision	resources
discretionary	social patterns
income	thrift
frugality	value
life style	

PROBLEM SOLVING: TRY MAKING DECISIONS

How would you handle these situations? Assume that you are a senior in high school and have saved $600 from summer work.

Linda Petroski has been accepted at two colleges. If she lives at home and attends a community college, the $600 will cover a major part of her school expenses for a whole year. However, she wants to go out of town to a school where room, board, and tuition are over $2,000 a year. She can't get much scholarship help, so she will have to borrow some money and work to go away to school.

Joe Cohen wants a car. He can use the money as full payment on an older car or as partial payment on a more recent model. If he buys the newer car, he will have payments to make for three years. The older car, however, needs some repair work.

Kathy O'Shea plans to be married a year from now when her fiancé gets out of the Army. He is stationed overseas. If she sends him the money, he can buy tableware and china at bargain prices. Kathy's friend thinks she should keep her money in a savings account, where it will earn interest, until she and her fiancé are together again.

John Cabrini wants to travel, and he has a month of free time. His parents are going to the same old place at the lake for a two-week vacation with the younger children. He could go along. Some friends of his, however, are going on a backpacking trip that sounds like fun. If he goes to the lake, his folks will pay all the expenses, but if he goes hiking he will have to use his own money.

TO DO IN CLASS

Discussion

1. How are your values and goals related to something you recently acquired?
2. How do you feel about the following situations?
   a. Sue gets paid for every top grade on her report card.
   b. Judd's father punished him for staying out late by taking away his allowance for a few weeks.
   c. Since Mike started delivering newspapers, his mother feels that he should not receive his allowance.
   d. Mary, age 14, and her sister Jan, age 17, receive the same amount of money for an allowance because their parents want to be fair.
3. How do you think the trend toward a shorter working week is likely to affect the use of time and money by individuals and families?
4. What is the role of advertising in creating *wants*?
5. Ask several class members to tell what they would do with an unexpected windfall of $25.

Activities

1. Summarize the following on an unsigned sheet:

a. How much money is in your pocket or purse now?

b. When will you get more?

c. What do you have to pay for between now and then?

d. What big items do you have to plan ahead for?

Ask a committee to compile the results and present them to the class.

2. Debate the following: A family's level of living is determined by values and goals more than by the size of income.

3. Display illustrations and clippings from magazines or newspapers of situations that show different values.

4. Figure the total cost of what you are wearing or carrying right now.

5. Divide into groups and act out the following family situations. Add details or characters to develop each situation the way your group feels appropriate.

a. You want money to buy a new outfit, but your parents say no because your sister needs a new coat.

b. Your father has held a high-pressure job for many years. The strain has pushed him close to the breaking point, mentally and physically. Your mother wants him to leave his job to open a small business in another community where the pressures will be much less. He would like to do this but fears the family would have to sacrifice too much if he did so.

c. Your parents agreed to loan you the car for Friday night. However, the tank is almost empty, and you haven't enough money for both gas and going out.

d. You are saving money to buy a birthday gift for a very special friend. A week before the birthday, you discover the money has been taken from its hiding place in your drawer. Later your mother tells you she took it to pay the electricity bill. Her income, your family's only means of support, was not enough to pay the monthly bills.

6. Analyze some popular TV programs or movies.

a. Was the story based on a situation that involved money?

b. Where did the people get the money they spent?

c. What kind of problems did people get into because of money or the lack of it?

d. Were there any expressions that indicated someone's financial status? (Loaded, filthy rich, poor as sin)

e. What situations upset an individual's or family's financial security?

f. Was money connected with happiness or unhappiness?

7. Read Vance Packard's *The Status Seekers* (New York: David McKay) and prepare a report for the class. Describe what he says about status symbols and include your own opinions.

CHAPTER 2

Making Money Behave

POCKETBOOK PROBLEMS

It was the week after Christmas and Bob was broke. Although he had shopped carefully, presents for everyone had cost more than he had figured. So there he was with a vacation and no money.

Bob's problem is quite common. It's so easy to spend just a little more than you had planned or to get caught short because of an unexpected expense. You tear your slacks, your best friend is having a birthday party and you need to buy a present, or the tire on your bike is cut by a piece of glass and you need a new one.

A young person on a first job or going away to school might have unexpected expenses for clothing, transportation, social activities, or a new pair of glasses.

Your parents may have a big bill for repair of a leaky roof or medical expenses because of illness. Perhaps your younger brother has grown like a weed and needs new clothes.

That Poor Feeling

The United States looks like a rich and wonderful place to people in many parts of the world. The African or Asian student who comes here is usually amazed by the vast number of goods people own. However, very few Americans *feel* so prosperous. Many have trouble making ends meet.

Obviously, a family can't manage well if there isn't enough money for the necessities. There is a *minimum subsistence level*—that is, an amount of money which an individual or family must have in order to manage adequately. This varies, of course, with such factors as family size, health, and locality. However, even when people get above the minimum subsistence level, many still find that their desires outrun their income.

How much is enough? The members of a family with a $10,000 annual income may think they would be very happy if only they had $12,000, but the family with $12,000 feels just as sure that they could get everything they want with $15,000 or $18,000. According to Z. A. C. Spectorsky in *The Exurbanites,* a study was done of executives who work in New York City but live in lavish homes located on several acres beyond the suburbs. Although many of this group were earning very large incomes, they were heavily in debt and looking forward to having a bigger income too.

Often that poor feeling that people in nearly all income brackets experience is brought on for very real reasons. People who cannot properly manage the money they have will certainly feel that they need more. If they can learn ways to become better managers, at least part of this problem should be solved.

Impulse Buying

One habit which contributes greatly to management problems is impulse buying. If you have some money and see something you like, do you buy it? Many people do. It's very tempting to buy something you might enjoy having when you have a little money in your pocket. Stores take advan-

This family in Tennessee lives below the subsistence level. The husband has a low-income job. The roof of the 22-by-20-foot, one-room shack is cardboard, and there is no electricity.

tage of impulse buying by placing counters where they will catch the eye and entice us to buy.

Most impulse items are not very expensive. A girl might decide to try a new lipstick because it looks unusual. A boy might feel the same way about a gadget for his bike or a new poster for his room. Your Dad may have a weakness for gourmet foods, or your Mom for scarves. Although they are usually inexpensive, items bought on impulse can ultimately cost a great deal.

Think about what you bought last. How did you decide upon it? Was it an impulse item, or did you go shopping just to buy that particular article?

For most people, the more expensive the item, the more carefully they consider the purchase. Your parents probably spend more time deciding on a car or washing machine than on shirts or underwear. You probably select your coats more carefully than your socks. However, this isn't always the case. Many a family has had money problems because they really went overboard on something expensive.

For many people, managing money is as difficult as finding their way through a maze.

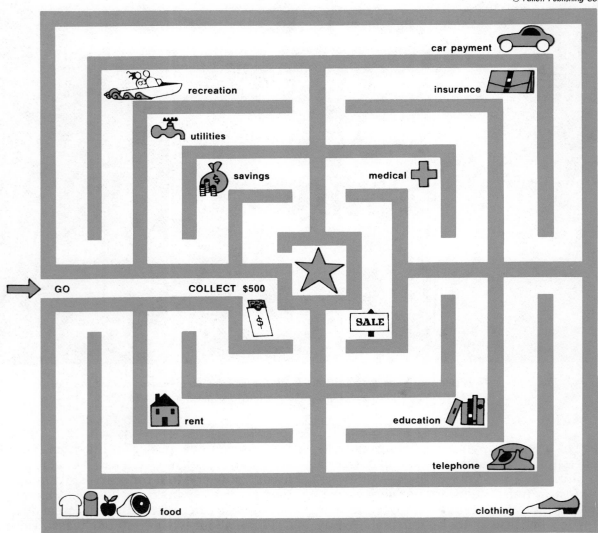

Overuse of Credit

In addition to impulse buying, overuse of credit often contributes to that poor feeling. Handling money today is much more complicated than it used to be. It's quite easy to know where you stand if you have an allowance or job and pay for everything in cash. It's much more tricky when you use credit, particularly if the temptation to say "charge it" has placed you in debt beyond your ability to pay.

Whatever the cause, money problems are a great source of unhappiness to many people. Moreover, such problems often lead to marital troubles. The people who can't make ends meet are usually worried about money or unhappy because they can't do the things they would like. Much of their distress could be eliminated simply through better management.

HOW WILL YOU MANAGE?

Although it is simple to talk about good management, it is not as simple to put it into practice. How can you manage? You can't buy everything that looks interesting. But you probably can get the things you need and perhaps some of the ones you want. People manage money in different ways. You may have friends who seem to make their allowances or salaries go far. Others are always broke. The kind of manager you become will depend on how well you learn to use money and other resources to secure what you need and want.

Part of this young woman's job as a part-time clerk in a clothing store is to handle customers' purchases. How might this help her understand the wise use of money and credit?

IBM

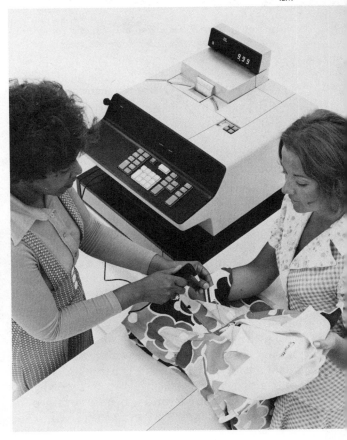

The effort Ann gives to each purchase varies with the importance of the purchase. If much money is involved, she plans carefully.

Institute of Life Insurance

Bethlehem Steel Corp.
These young people are saving the cost of a car wash by doing the job themselves.

USDA Photo
Here a professional painter works on the exterior of a house. How might young people help cut family costs for such work?

Look for Other Resources

Although money is the primary way of getting goods and services, many other resources are available. Frequently, you can spend more time and energy and less money or no money to get something. You can make a shirt or go to a sale, press your own pants, or repair the car yourself.

Community resources can be used. You may go on a picnic or camping trip instead of to the movies or for a vacation at a hotel. Public health facilities are available in many areas. You might go to a clinic instead of a private doctor. The charge will probably be less at the clinic than at the doctor's office.

Trading or sharing is another way of using resources other than money. Many girls lend each other clothing for special occasions. You might swap records or tapes with your friends. Some young people share the cost of driving to school or for recreation.

Reusing something is still another way of using resources other than money. A girl might make a skirt from an old dress. You might fix your punctured bike tire again instead of buying a new one. Schools regularly collect scrap materials to use for art projects such as collages and mobiles. Some outstanding modern sculpture is made from old metal parts. Reusing is also a way of buying something with less expense. Many people get parts for car repairs from junk yards or use retreaded tires.

You can probably think of many other ways to use available resources.

Determine Your Wants and Needs

Today individuals and families make many more decisions about how to use

A playground is a community resource.

money than people did one hundred years ago. In the late 1800's the essentials for survival—food, shelter, and clothing—took almost all of a family's income. Now these things take a much smaller proportion. Because of this, some families are able to define their needs as more than just the essentials. In fact, it is probably true that as incomes increase, so do the family's wants, many of which may be thought of as needs.

The list of "needs" grows longer when the family members see what others have. Moreover, with new developments, the list of "needs" expands even more. Television, for example, was unavailable to families years ago. Today TV sets can be found in poor as well as affluent homes. Through the mass media, people stay well aware of

what is available to add to their needs and wants.

Not all people, however, are able to secure more than the essentials, nor will everyone desire the same things. The poor people in India, for example, and the poor in the United States see their needs differently. In India, where so many of the people live very meagerly, food, shelter, and clothing are the real needs. Here in the United States, where so many people have so much, needs may include such things as adequate medical care, education, and possibly such labor-saving equipment as washing machines and dryers.

You can see how difficult it is to determine what is a need or want and how easy it is to classify too many things as needs.

CUNA Mutual Insurance Society and
Credit Union National Assoc., Inc.

Our list of wants keeps growing.

Now think about what *you* want and need. Perhaps you would like to make two lists. How will you decide what to put on each list? Compare your lists with the ones Sue Lehman made.

SUE LEHMAN'S LISTS

NEEDS
1. **Tuition for business school**
2. **Senior prom dress**
3. **New shoes**
4. **Electric curlers**

WANTS
1. **Stereo**
2. **New coat**
3. **Makeup mirror**
4. **Hope chest**

EVALUATING YOUR WANTS AND NEEDS

When you think in terms of needs and wants, you will begin at the same time to evaluate them even further. In other words, you might ask yourself: "What do I *want* the most?" And more important: "What do I *need* the most?"

Two principles may help as you analyze your needs and wants. The first is the principle of *diminishing marginal utility*. Another way of saying it is that the extra satisfaction or value derived from getting another unit of the same product decreases with each successive purchase of the same kind. For example, you might enjoy the first ice cream cone very much and even the second, but a third, fourth, and fifth would probably be more than you want—

or need. If you already have six sweaters and you buy a seventh, you will probably get less use and enjoyment from the new one than if you had only two or three. Perhaps you are familiar with this situation. Have you ever gotten something for Christmas or your birthday that was just like something you already owned? Maybe you have an oversupply of shirts and don't really use all of them. Can you name other examples?

The second principle is that of *opportunity costs.* If you buy one thing, you can't get something else.

Just as your parents cannot get all that they want, you cannot buy everything you want either. If you want one item, often you must sacrifice something else. If you get new shoes now, you may not be able to get slacks for a while. Perhaps you decide to get new tennis equipment instead of clothing. Because they are limited, resources should be allocated by applying the principle of opportunity costs.

Establish Goals

When you are able to distinguish clearly between your wants and needs, you are ready to set up goals.

You might want to save for a car, buy some new clothes, go to school, or get a new TV. A young couple may want to think about things they both want—better jobs, a home, or furnishings. Your parents probably have many things they want or need to spend money on—new brakes on the car, nicer carpeting, or a holiday trip.

In the business world setting up goals is called long-range planning. Usually a committee develops plans for a period of several years. Maybe they want to enlarge their overseas business, mechanize to make their products at a lower cost, or develop a new way of shipping without breakage.

By setting up goals, you supply an incentive for saving and a basis for developing a spending plan. Later, when you attain your goals, you will have the satisfaction of securing something you need or want very much.

Use a Plan

With goals in mind, you can develop a spending plan. There is no ready-made plan that can tell you how to spend your money. Your friend's plan won't fit your needs nor will yours fit his. People differ. Therefore you must evaluate your own situation to determine just what will work best for you.

There are several steps to follow in making a spending plan. As you read, decide how you would change Ann Hudson's plan, shown on page 35, to fit your own requirements.

DETERMINE YOUR INCOME

Do you get an allowance or paycheck every week, every two weeks, or once a month? Whichever it is, plan accordingly.

A newspaper route offers a fairly stable income.
Institute of Life Insurance

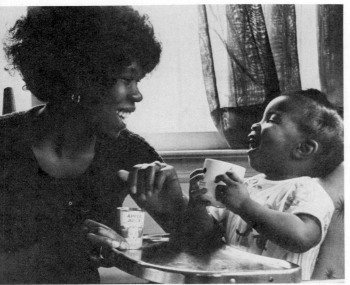

Gerber Products Co.

Income from baby-sitting is often irregular. Irregular earnings must be estimated in order to plan spending.

If you get money on an irregular basis, by baby-sitting or yard work, for example, try to estimate what you average per week and use this amount in your plan.

KEEP A RECORD OF YOUR SPENDING

This record will be helpful in determining what expenditures to include in your plan and how much you need to allow for each. It is a good idea to keep this record for several weeks. By recording all your spending over a period of weeks, you can determine the average amount you spend on different items.

MAKE A SPENDING PLAN

By looking at your spending record, you can now estimate expenditures. Decide what items you will allow in your plan and enter a reasonable amount to spend for each. Perhaps you will see areas where you can cut down spending in order to allow for more in other areas.

In Ann's plan provision has been made for savings. Later this money could be used to buy something she wants or for an unforeseen expense. If any money is left in other categories at the end of the week, it too can go into savings.

REVISE THE PLAN IF NECESSARY

Your first try at planning probably won't be perfect. In fact, most things take practice. You can't learn to swim in just one try, so don't expect to be a great money manager the first time. If your plan doesn't work the first time, make some changes and try again. If your income changes or your needs change, you will also need to make changes in your plan.

STICK TO THE PLAN

This may be the most difficult part, requiring awareness and self-control. You must be aware of how much you are spending from day to day and be able to control the desire to buy beyond your limits. If you succeed, you will know the satisfaction of having money to spend for what you really want plus a reserve of savings. Also, you will probably feel secure about your financial situation.

THE ENVELOPE SYSTEM

Case Study. Kim Swenson, a high school junior, used an interesting method to handle her money—the *envelope system*. First she figured her average income per week. Next she made a plan, allocating money for each important expense. Then she prepared an envelope for each expense category. As she received money every week, she filled the expense envelopes.

This system can enable you to save money for a special purpose. For example, Kim wanted a pair of skis but never had the money to buy them. Therefore instead of following her usual spending plan she made a new one allowing only a minimum for the necessities and all the rest for savings. On an extra envelope she wrote *skis.* As Kim received money every week, she filled the expense envelopes first and placed the rest in the envelope marked *skis.* At the end of each week anything left in the expense envelopes also went into the *skis* envelope. Because of her goal, Kim

found herself giving up many extras. In a relatively short time, however, she had her skis and a new realization about money. In order to have one thing, she had learned to give up others, a principle that would serve her all her life.

Kim's method, of course, will not be suitable for everyone. There are other ways

ANN HUDSON'S INCOME PER WEEK

Allowance	$ 3.00
Babysitting	$ 5.00
Library work	$ 3.00
Total	$11.00

ANN'S SPENDING PLAN

Per Week
(Income Averages $11 Per Week)

Expenditures	Amount
Lunches	$ 4.25
Snacks	.70
Entertainment	2.55
Grooming and clothing accessories	1.50
Miscellaneous	1.50
Savings	.50
Total	$11.00

ANN'S RECORD OF SPENDING

First Week

Lunches	$4.25
Snacks	1.25
Movie	1.50
Notebook	.59
Money owed to friend	2.00
Total	$9.59

Second Week

Lunches	$2.55
Snacks	.89
Bowling	5.00
Makeup	1.37
Total	$9.81

Third Week

Lunches	$ 3.05
Snacks	.75
Gift	4.25
Haircut	6.00
Ticket to ball game	1.00
Total	$15.05

Fourth Week

Lunches	$4.25
Snacks	.35
Club dues	1.00
Hose	2.95
Ballpoint pen	.49
Total	$9.04

Note: You may want to keep a day-to-day record in order to keep close track of such expenses as lunches and snacks.

to handle money. You will probably want to experiment to find the system that works best for you.

A MONTHLY SPENDING PLAN

Case Study. If you prefer a more businesslike system for handling money, you might like to try Joe Perone's method. Joe is a senior in high school and lives at home with his parents. He works part-time in a hardware store to earn enough money to buy a car. From his job he averages $30 a week in take-home pay. In addition his parents give him a $5 a week regular allowance plus $20 a month for clothing. With this he must purchase all his clothing during the year.

Joe's spending is planned on a monthly basis. When he first began using this plan, Joe figured his average monthly income at

$170. He then allotted a certain amount for each of his expenditures per month. Now every month he enters the expenditures and the amount he can spend for each in a notebook with the pages divided into two columns. Throughout the month, he enters his daily purchases. By adding the figures in each column, he can quickly determine whether or not he is within his budget. Any money left at the end of the month can be added to savings.

LOOKING AHEAD

Managing money becomes more complicated as you take on more responsibilities. Living away from home means that there is more to manage. Have you ever thought about what it will cost just for rent, utilities, food, and clothing when you are on your own? As you read about the people described on the following pages, look for good management ideas. Perhaps you can also offer suggestions for better management.

A Young Working Woman

Case Study. Nineteen-year-old Betsy Greenwalt moved to a nearby city in order to take her first full-time job as a telephone router for a trucking company. Betsy, who works with other young people and enjoys her job, has a take-home pay of $130 per week. She shares a furnished apartment with her roommate, Barbara Jameson.

Betsy has a steady boyfriend who is in the management training program of a large retailing company. Since they plan to marry in a year, they are each saving for furnishings for their home. Betsy's boyfriend comes to dinner at least one night a week. Often other friends drop in to visit in the evenings.

The girls need dishes, pots and pans, and linens for the apartment but have decided

JOE'S SYSTEM*

January	
Plan to Spend	Actual Expenditures
Lunches $20.00	Jan. 2 $ 1.25 Jan. 3 $ 1.50 Jan. 4 $ 1.00
Snacks $10.00	Jan. 3 $ 0.42 Jan. 5 $ 0.15
Entertainment & Misc. $25.00	
Clothing $30.00	Jan. 4 $12.00 (Shirt)
Gifts & Contributions $10.00	Jan. 7 $ 2.00 (Church) Jan. 13 $ 5.00 (Birthday Gift)
Savings $75.00	Jan. 5 $20.00 (Deposited in bank) Jan. 12 $25.00 (Deposited in bank)

*Joe uses a separate notebook page for each category of expenditure every month. For example, lunches would have a whole page. However, to save space all the categories are put on one page here.

to buy them individually rather than jointly. (Betsy hopes to use hers after she's married.) In addition, they would like to buy a stereo and a TV set. Arrangements for these purchases haven't been made as yet.

On Saturday mornings the girls share in cleaning the apartment. There is a laundry room in the building so the girls use the coin-operated machines for washing their clothes. Betsy takes her dry cleaning to a coin-operated dry cleaner.

Some of Betsy's money management is handled for her by her employer through *payroll deductions.* Federal and state income taxes, as well as social security payments, must be taken out of her salary before she is paid. In addition, she has $10 a week deducted from her check and deposited in her savings account at the credit union. By doing this she does not have to make the savings deposit herself, thereby reducing the temptation to spend the money intended for savings elsewhere. If she wanted to, she could also have some money taken out for a government bond. Many employers also permit deductions for United Fund pledges, union dues, insurance payments, stock purchases, and installment payments.

From this description, what evidence can you find that Betsy is a good manager? Could you offer her any suggestions for the future?

A Freshman at College

Case Study. In September Steve Wischnevsky will attend a state university where he plans to study architecture. His parents will pay for his room, board, and tuition, but he will provide clothes, transportation, and personal expenses. During high school Steve saved a little money and now he has a summer job. Hopefully, he will have enough money so that he won't have to work during his freshman year.

Steve plans to open a checking account at college since this seems like the best way to handle his money. His parents will send him monthly checks of different amounts. In September, for example, they will give him $420 to cover his tuition, room and board, and books. But in October they will only send $120 for room and board. He plans to deposit his parents' checks and some of the money that he has saved for college expenses in this account. (The rest of the money that he has saved for college expenses will be kept in a savings account that earns interest until he needs it.) Then, as he needs to pay expenses, he will write checks. In this way he will have a record of his expenses and keep his money secure until he needs it. (The use of a checking account is discussed more fully in another chapter.)

What do you think about Steve's ability to manage money? If he had no one to take

STEVE'S ESTIMATE OF SCHOOL EXPENSES

$1,100	Tuition—half in September and half in February.
1,575	Room and Board—$95 per month for room and $20 per week for food.
200	Transportation—5 round trips at $40 each: to college in the fall; home for Thanksgiving, Christmas, semester break, and spring vacation; and back home in June.
475	Miscellaneous—clothes, personal expenses, and minor school expenses.
175	Books—half in September and half in February.
$3,525	*Total* (Steve will have to provide $750 of this amount.)

WHEN STEVE WILL NEED THE MONEY

	Sept.	Oct.	Nov.	Dec.	Jan.	Feb.	March	April	May	Totals
Tuition	$550	—	—	—	—	$550	—	—	—	$1100
Room and Board	175	175	175	175	175	175	175	175	175	1575
Transportation	40	—	40	40	40	—	—	40	—	200
Miscellaneous	75	50	50	50	50	50	50	50	50	475
Books	100	—	—	—	—	75	—	—	—	175
Monthly totals	$940	$225	$265	$265	$265	$850	$225	$265	$225	$3525

care of some of the costs, do you think he would still find a way to attend college?

A Young Married Couple

Good money management is important to a successful marriage. Love and hope won't buy food or pay the landlord, nor can two live together as cheaply as one. Still, there are some ways to economize in sharing a household. This is one reason why so many young people, whether on their first job or in school, team up with a roommate if they are living away from home.

Case Study. Meet Carmela and Bob Ortiz—a struggling young couple. Both are eighteen and were married last summer after graduation from high school. Bob works as a gas station attendant and repairs cars on Sundays and in the evening to earn extra money. Carmela works three days a week as a hospital aide. Bob's take-home pay is $120 per week, and Carmela's is $80, a total of $200. When Bob repairs cars in the evenings or on weekends, he is paid extra.

Carmela and Bob have many friends and enjoy seeing them. They get together with friends almost every week at someone's house.

Bob and Carmela are not always in agreement about money matters. Bob gives Carmela his paycheck to pay the bills. His extra earnings are divided as a personal allowance for each of them. He feels that they should not make any more purchases until all their bills are paid. Also, he would like to start saving money so that he can buy a franchise for his own service station some day. However, Carmela is unhappy because she doesn't have enough money to buy clothes the way she did before they were married.

Shortly after their marriage Carmela and Bob bought some furnishings for their apartment on credit. Now they must plan their spending around these installment payments—$40 each month for the car, $12 for the living room furniture, and $10 for the refrigerator. Unfortunately, too many people buy first and plan later, thinking only about the monthly cost of an item rather than the total cost. This is a backwards approach to planning which is avoided by the smart money manager.

If Carmela and Bob are serious about leasing a gas station, they must save for the initial deposit required by most companies. Because of their modest income and installment payments, spending will have to be planned carefully in order to save. Perhaps a plan like the one shown on the next page could be worked out.

Barring any big emergencies, the couple should have the $2,500 down payment within three years, providing they follow a rigid spending plan. If Bob gets a lot of overtime work, this could speed it up. Should their plans change in the future, they will still have their savings available for some other use.

The spending plan shown does, however, have some weaknesses. Trying to save such a large percentage of their income may be difficult, particularly when all of those common but unexpected expenses arise. Although Bob's employer does provide medical insurance that covers the couple to some extent, their spending plan doesn't include anything for certain medical and dental expenses, as well as contributions, gifts, and miscellaneous items. With a larger income, Carmela and Bob might be able to manage and save money more easily. Can you think of ways they might increase their income?

Now evaluate both Carmela and Bob individually, giving thought to their readiness for marriage, maturity, and money management abilities. What do you think will be ahead for the young couple if they have a child in the next year or two? Do you believe that as long as a couple share love, they can remain happy and content through difficult financial situations?

A POSSIBLE WEEKLY PLAN FOR CARMELA AND BOB*

Rent	$ 50.00
Household Operation (Utilities and Phone)	10.00
Food	60.00
Gas and Car Expenses	20.00
Household Supplies	2.00
Clothing (Includes Laundry Expense)	10.00
Recreation and Entertaining	10.00
Car Payments	20.00
Furniture Payments	10.00
Refrigerator Payments	5.00
Savings (For Franchising Service Station)	40.00
Total	$237.00

*Monthly expenses have been divided into four weekly ones. This means that for those months with an extra payday there will be a little left over for savings or emergencies.

SHARING RESPONSIBILITY FOR MONEY MANAGEMENT

Today more families are sharing the management job. You are probably handling more money as you grow older. Perhaps your parents share with you the responsibility of handling the money for your various needs. Maybe you earn money and feel that you can decide how to use it.

Who should manage the household's money? Maybe you are living alone and that settles it, but perhaps you are married or planning to be married soon. Then you need to decide together on the best way to handle your money.

Some people feel that the only right way is the way their parents managed. Others have strong feelings about men's and women's roles in managing money. In some families one person can make money go farther than another.

It really doesn't matter who handles the money in a family. The important thing is to make it work well for you. If the husband can make the money last longer, let him do it. On the other hand, maybe the wife is better at stretching dollars.

Case Study. Some families divide the job. Mr. Sanders pays the rent and takes care of the car. Mrs. Sanders buys the food, household supplies, and clothes for the children. They go together to make major purchases like a suit for Mr. Sanders or a new TV.

HOW FAMILIES AT THE MIDDLE-INCOME LEVEL USE THEIR MONEY

Form **5695**
Department of the Treasury
Internal Revenue Service

Personal Taxes
Energy Credits

▶ Attach to Form 1040. ▶ See Instructions on back.

29

Name(s) as shown on Form 1040

Your social security number

Enter in the space below the address of your principal resid... ...claimed if it is different from the address shown on Form 1040.

Part I Fill in your energy
energy credit car...

Was your principal resi...
If you checked "N...

1 Ener...

Total Building Systems, Inc.
Housing

Gerber Products
Food

D. Schaffer South; Barry Schaffer, Owner
Clothing and Personal Care

Hewlett-Packard Co., Medical
Electronics Div.
Medical Care

Recreation and Other Consumption
USDA Photo

Transportation

APPLICATION
Term Insurance to Age 25

SINGLE PAYMENT LIFE INSURANCE FOR CHILDREN
(Children from 1 through 23 years old are eligible)

1. Proposed Insured:
(Child's Name)

Social Security, Pensions, Insurance, and Contributions

40

Case Study. In the Anderson family, Mrs. Anderson handles the money. She is very good at making it cover the family needs. Her husband has a regular amount which he uses for gas, lunches, haircuts, and other incidentals. Mrs. Anderson buys everything else for the family except the costly items. The Andersons go together when they are buying such things as a new dinette set or a living room sofa.

THE WORKING WOMAN

Today, most women work. Single women need to support themselves. A married woman may be the sole supporter of a family. A married woman also may provide additional income.

In some families, making ends meet with only one income is very difficult. Thus, the wife takes a job to help make things easier. Sometimes families have special goals that encourage mother to work. Her salary may be used for Christmas gifts, a vacation, putting a child through college, or any of countless other objectives. On the other hand, some married women work because of the personal satisfaction involved. It gives them an opportunity to keep in regular touch with the outside world, to make new friends, to escape from what some consider the daily routine of housework, or to pursue a career. In many homes the woman is the sole supporter of a family due to illness or for some other reason, a husband and wife may reverse the traditional roles. Thus, the husband may manage the home and the wife may take an outside job.

The work pattern for many married women begins with a short work period right after marriage followed by a longer work period after the children are older. Still, many mothers work during most of their pregnancy and return to work shortly after the baby is born. Other mothers, however, would not think of leaving their little ones with child care workers during the early years. As with most issues, there are two sides to this controversy. Can you think of reasons to support both sides? Is it possible that what is right for one mother is not right for another? What are your feelings about working mothers?

Occasionally, when both husband and wife work, problems arise over how the wife's income should be handled. Here are some suggestions that have helped many families avoid arguments:

• Talk over the details of handling both incomes before the wife goes to work. This may mean discussion even before marriage.

• Plan for the personal expenses of both husband and wife. A working wife has extra expenses—transportation costs and lunches, for example. Her clothes may need cleaning more often. She may need to spend a little more on haircuts, having her hair set, and clothes for work. If there are young children at home, there may be baby-sitting expenses.

• Consider the wife's income as part of the family income. Plan together for the use of the money that is left after she pays for expenses connected with working. If the wife doesn't expect to work very long, try to pay all the basic living expenses out of the husband's income. Then when the wife stops working, the cut in income won't be such a hardship.

• When problems come up, try to talk them over calmly. Everyone gets in a tight spot now and then. We all make mistakes. Getting angry at each other doesn't help.

THE SCOPE OF THE JOB

Money management is a big job. It includes keeping records of expenses, knowing the dates when outstanding bills are due, and arranging payment of bills. It also involves keeping other important records that pertain to family finance, such as bank books, cancelled checks, checkbooks, social security numbers, safety deposit box numbers and keys, securities, insurance policies, records of income, and receipts for major purchases.

Is it any wonder that so many people are overwhelmed by money management problems? Yet they need not be. With planning and organization as well as a sound knowledge of good management techniques, most families will be able to manage quite well.

FOR REVIEW

Points to Remember

- Money problems are a great source of unhappiness to many people.
- The widespread use of credit has complicated the job of money management for most families.
- Effective money management requires planning.
  - Establish goals.
  - Make a spending plan.
  - Revise the plan as needed.
  - Try to stick to the plan.
- As you take on more responsibilities, money management becomes more complicated and requires more skill for successful results.
- Good money management is important to a successful marriage. Both partners need to work together on planning and using money. Try to:
  - Plan together.
  - Allow for personal spending.
  - Be realistic about needs and also about how much the family has to spend.

Terms to Know

diminishing marginal utility
goals
impulse buying
minimum subsistence level
money management
monthly expenses
needs
opportunity costs
payroll deductions
plan
responsibility
wants

TO DO IN CLASS

Discussion

1. What would you do if you could not quite afford something that you considered very important?

2. Often a family has to decide which member should get something because there isn't enough money to satisfy everyone. What is the fairest way to make such decisions?

3. What problems can money solve? Are there things which it will not solve?

4. How should the size of one's allowance be decided?

5. Why do some families manage wonderfully on a small income, while others can't get along on a much larger one?

6. What are things worth?
   a. Is a new TV set worth overtime work?
   b. Is new furniture for the living room worth giving up the family vacation?

Activities

1. Make a bulletin board to show some typical goals of teenagers and the values on which these goals might be based.

2. Keep a record of your income and expenses for two weeks. At the end of two weeks summarize the results on an unsigned sheet of paper. Have a committee make a chart to show how people in the class used money.

3. Make a possible spending plan that you could use after you graduate from high school. Choose one item from each of the following three lists and base your plan on the situation created by your three choices.

Jobs or School: secretary; store clerk; bank teller; factory worker; student.

Living Arrangement: at home; apartment with kitchen; room in a dormitory, without kitchen; sharing an apartment with kitchen.

Transportation: your own car; bus; walk; carpool.

4. Write a brief history of a family you know. Indicate the times when they probably had peak expenditures. What are some of the ways they could have met these?

5. Where do you expect to be five years from now? Refer to the *Occupational Outlook Handbook* (published by the U.S. Dept. of Labor) and find out approximately how much money you and/or other wage earners in the family might be earning.

6. In making spending decisions, you must make choices and consider *opportunity costs.* As suggested by Dr. Thomas Garman in *Consumer Education Forum,* select advertisements from magazines and newspapers and talk about the products or services in terms of the principle of opportunity costs. Look, particularly, at recreational and leisure time ads.

CHAPTER 3

Using Credit

What is credit? Buy now; pay later. Credit is a promise to pay later. Its use is based on trust. You agree to pay later, and the person selling goods or rendering services has faith that you will.

THE USE OF CREDIT GOES BACK A LONG TIME

The simple idea of buying now and paying later has been part of man's life since ancient times.

More than 10,000 years ago man began to settle in the long valley ribboned by the Nile. In the swamps of the Delta there grew in profusion the tall reed called papyrus—the bulrushes that Moses' mother used to make a boxlike float for her baby.

The Egyptians taught themselves to fashion an excellent type of paper from the reed. Among its many uses, papyrus provided a means of recording an obligation—the first promissory note or I.O.U. (In hieroglyphic symbols it's true, but binding nonetheless.) The ancients had found a means of buying now and paying later. The Egyptian equivalent of the term 'charge it' came into being.

The Greeks came along a bit later with their belief in the worth of the individual citizen. A freeman was an exalted thing—someone to be trusted

in all aspects of life, including commercial transactions, and the use of credit began to spread.

. . . As Rome grew from a collection of prehistoric villages to an empire, there also arose a strong sense of order, and legal institutions developed. Among other things, Roman law established credit procedures and set penalties in case of default or failure to pay.

Thus, the ancients provided a means of recording credit transactions, . . . and created laws which regulated the relationship between debtor and creditor.*

The use of credit continued down through the centuries but in very limited

Writing a credit contract in hieroglyphic symbols.
Federal Reserve Bank of Philadelphia

Truth in Lending—What It Means for Consumer Credit, Series for Economic Education, Federal Reserve Bank of Philadelphia.

ways. Business and government used credit, but very little credit was available to the average person, the man or woman who worked for wages or a salary. However, in the last few decades all this has changed. Today Mr. and Mrs. John Q. Public and their families can and do make extensive use of many forms of credit.

This dramatic turnabout was the result of a variety of factors. Most important was that with modern know-how factories could turn out vast quantities of consumer goods—automobiles, appliances, household articles, and clothing. Still, there was no point in making these things unless people could buy them. The widespread use of credit was one of the developments that came with industrialization.

Under the old system few people had enough cash in their pockets or purses to buy "big-ticket" items. Consumer credit enabled them to buy. For a small sum down families could have a washing machine, dishwasher, or TV instead of waiting to save the entire purchase price.

Today consumer credit is so widely used that more than half the families in America owe somebody for something. It is generally recognized that consumer credit is an important factor in keeping the economy going. If many people buy things, other people are employed making them.

As the use of consumer credit has grown, there has been a sharp decline in the old prejudices against buying on credit. In fact, we are moving toward a cashless society, using credit for more and more of our purchases.

The government even encourages the use of credit by allowing people to deduct interest charges in computing their federal income tax.

CREDIT HAS HELPED CHANGE AMERICAN LIFE

Credit has made a difference in the way we live and manage our lives. Just compare two families, one living today and the other fifty years ago.

Case Study. The Crandalls lived in Minnesota half a century ago. Mr. Crandall was a druggist in the local store. He had a long week. The store was open Monday through Saturday and some evenings. Mrs. Crandall did the family shopping for food at Brown's grocery store. During the week she would charge her purchases and settle the bill every Saturday when Mr. Crandall was paid. Except for this charge account and a small bill that they still owed the doctor, the Crandalls had no debts. They hadn't bought much on credit. Neither did they own very much. They rented their house on South Street and paid the rent monthly

Many people could not buy without credit.

DESIRE   NO CREDIT   NO DEMAND

in advance. Some of the furniture in the house belonged to the landlord—the dining room furniture and two of the bedroom sets. The rest they had bought over the years, except for the big old piano, which had belonged to Mrs. Crandall's mother. They wanted to save enough money to be able to buy a mechanical refrigerator to replace their old icebox.

Case Study. Compare the Crandalls with a young family today. Bob Markham is also a druggist, but he lives in a house which he owns jointly with the bank. That is, he has a mortgage held by the bank. The house is equipped with not only a refrigerator but also a washing machine and dryer. These came with the house, and their price was included in the purchase price of the new ranch house.

The Markhams have two cars. One is for him to get from the suburbs to his job in town. The other enables Mrs. Markham to get around for shopping, errands, and her part-time job.

The Markhams' way of life, which is partly dependent upon having things like cars and certain household equipment, would not be possible if they had to pay for it all with cash. Right now in addition to the mortgage, they still owe on one of the cars and the power lawn mower.

A new era has dawned with the widespread use of credit. Today we buy homes, automobiles, washing machines, dryers, TV sets, clothes, college educations, and a host of other things with credit. Peter Drucker, a noted economist and writer, labeled this new way of life as the "rental economy." He and many other people feel that buying on credit is much like renting, and so it is, with one exception: When the last payment is finally made, you are really the owner.

WHO USES CREDIT?

Most people use credit for some reason. Middle-income families are the biggest users of installment credit.

Young families are heavy users of credit. One study showed that in families where the husband was under forty-five, four out of five families were buying one or more items on credit.

As you have read, even young people use credit today. Along with the right to vote, many eighteen to twenty year olds gained other legal rights of adults, including the use of credit. Over a third of the states have now passed legislation lowering the age of majority from twenty-one to eighteen or nineteen. Thus, many young people can be held legally responsible for their credit dealings.

In states where the age of majority is still twenty-one, however, it is very difficult to collect a debt legally from those who are younger. Still, many stores in these states, recognizing the available market, will offer

Young families are heavy users of credit. Do you think it is wise to buy a television set on credit?

459. *Easy Terms*

accounts to teens. Some require that the parents already have an account at the store, that the parents co-sign the account, or that the parents give permission. (Co-signing means that if the teenager doesn't pay, the store can collect from the parents.) Some teens simply use their parents' cards. In case of problems, stores, either informally or legally, count on parents to stand behind teen accounts. Many stores, however, feel sure that young people will try to meet their payment responsibilities for two reasons: (1) in order to keep the accounts; (2) because their reputations are involved.

Generally, accounts for teenagers are limited to $50-$90 of credit, with monthly payments scaled to income through allowances or part-time jobs. The retailer tries to supply the kind of account a teen can handle. This, however, does not mean that the youthful buyer will not encounter certain opportunists. In fact, teenagers have often fallen prey to expensive credit dealings over insurance, jewelry, encyclopedias, dancing lessons, and others. In the past, many of these credit contracts could be voided. Now, however, with the lowered age of majority in many states, more young people are legally bound to such contracts, whether fraud is involved or not, pointing up the real need for credit awareness by people in their teens.

WHEN SHOULD YOU USE CREDIT?

People use credit for different reasons. Most people use it because they want something *now* and don't have enough money to pay for it. Many young people find that their needs and desires outpace their available income. Students going on to a technical school or college may have to borrow to meet expenses even if they have some savings. The young person on a first job may have to borrow to buy a car if no other transportation is available. Newlyweds may need some basic furniture and equipment.

During peak spending periods, families may turn to credit. Christmas is a big spending time. Graduation time is another. The cost of a ring or pin, yearbook, and party expenses can eat up a lot of money. If you are working, overtime pay or a bonus might help out. However, most people meet these expenses in one of two ways— by saving money ahead or using credit and paying later.

In addition to these, there are still other good reasons why people use credit. For one thing, simply establishing a good credit rating can be quite helpful. Moreover, many people who travel—students who go away to school, vacationers, and businessmen—like to have a convenient way to get money while away from home. Since it is often difficult to cash personal checks when you are not well known, a credit card may solve the problem.

A housewife buys a washing machine on the installment plan from a department store. If the machine fails to work correctly, the housewife feels she will get better service if the washer is not fully paid for. In case of serious problems with the washer, she could withhold payment. A businessman uses a credit card for his business expenditures because the receipts will be accepted both by his employer and the Internal Revenue Service when tax time comes around. Also, he doesn't have to carry cash to meet expenses. Finally, many companies borrow when they feel that they can earn enough money to pay the credit charge and have a profit too.

Obviously, there are many reasons for using credit. No hard and fast rules on

Cooperative Extension Service,
Washington State University

We use service credit every day. Electricity and water for this laundry equipment are two types of service credit.

when to use credit can be applied to everyone. Still, a few suggestions may be helpful. Use credit:

- To meet emergencies.
- For necessities rather than luxuries.
- For major items and durable goods that have benefits after payments are completed.

With these guidelines in mind, decide whether you think any of these expenses merit the use of credit: surgery or other medical care; a college education; a guitar; a good-quality refrigerator; and a week's vacation.

DEBT LIMITS

Before buying on credit, one more factor should be weighed. How much debt can you afford to carry?

This is not a simple question for most people to answer. A young man with good reason to expect a rising income might be justified in using more credit than a man who is going to retire soon. A small family would be able to manage bigger payments than a large one with the same income. You might have to ask yourself some important questions: Will I be able to handle an added expense? Can I cut down on some other things in order to pay for something new? Should I wait until I have a little more cash or until something else is paid off?

Some financial experts suggest a debt limit of 10-15 percent of your income after taxes. For example, if your income after taxes is $12,000, you shouldn't owe more than $1200 (10 percent) to $1800 (15 percent). Many people feel that some big expenses, such as a home mortgage or car payments, should be considered as a regular part of the budget. Thus, they do not include these two items in the recommended debt limit.

TYPES OF CREDIT

Once you decide that you can afford the additional cost of credit to be used for a good reason, you are ready to do business. Your credit dealings may take any of several forms.

There are three basic types of credit—*service credit, sales credit,* and *cash loans.*

Service Credit

A bill from a doctor or dentist may be sent to the patient's home. If a plumber fixes a leaky faucet in the kitchen, he may send a bill, rather than expect to be paid immediately. This is service credit. Often we aren't even aware that we are using it. Did you talk to a friend on the phone recently? Then you used a telephone that is available on credit. Did you raise the thermostat because your room was cold? Possibly your family hasn't paid the heating bill yet, or if you live in an apartment, the landlord hasn't paid it. (Heating bills usually come periodically if you use gas or electric heat and after delivery if you use oil or coal.)

Most service credit is available without any extra charge—if it is paid on time. Failure to pay can result in the addition of late payment charges to a bill, discontinuation of service, and sometimes legal proceedings.

Service credit is vitally important because it provides a systematic method for supplying necessary services. Though often taken for granted, such credit is a big part of our everyday lives.

Sales Credit

Perhaps your family is buying a house with a mortgage. Maybe the family is still paying for a new TV, or you have a charge account at a department store. This type of credit, when you get the goods now and pay for it later, is called sales credit.

Sales credit is available from retail merchants in several forms: regular charge accounts; revolving charge accounts; credit card accounts; and installment accounts.

With a *regular charge account,* purchases are paid for within a specified length of time, usually 30, 60, or 90 days. Generally, no extra charge is added unless payment is made after the specified time. Billing is usually monthly.

With most 30-day accounts, sometimes called open accounts, to keep from paying a service charge, each month's bill must be paid in full before the next billing. For example, Marla bought a pair of jeans and a shirt on September 16 on a 30-day account. The store's billing date is the 27th. Marla received her bill on September 28. If she pays the bill before the next billing date (October 27), there will be no service charge. Perhaps your family has a charge account like this at a drug store or department store.

When charging on a 60- or 90-day account, the cost of an item can sometimes be divided into two or three payments, with no extra charge. For example, you might pay $40 a month for a $120 chair on a 90-day account with no extra charge. Since accounts in different stores are not always handled exactly the same way, it is best to ask about the store's policies when opening an account.

Revolving credit, extended by many retail stores is another type of charge account. Generally, a customer is given a maximum amount that he or she may charge. This limit is based on credit record and income. Monthly payments must be made on a portion of the outstanding debt, with a monthly service charge (interest) on the unpaid balance. The added charge, of course, makes the cost of items more than just the purchase price. As you reduce or pay off the debt, you may buy something else up to the credit limit.

Suppose that you have a credit limit of $200 with Carvel's Department Store. First you buy a coat for $90. In two months, you have paid off $27. Now, owing a balance of $63, you can buy a cassette player for $120 and still be within your $200 limit. Your monthly payments will continue to be the same. As with regular charge accounts, all stores do not follow identical procedures on revolving accounts, so get the facts clear in your mind if you decide to open one.

Burroughs Corporation

The use of credit cards has grown rapidly.

Think of how many things you and your family buy and use with charge accounts. When do your parents have to pay an extra credit charge? You may find that the total amount of extra charges is surprisingly high.

A very popular form of sales credit is the *credit card account.* These small plastic squares are revolutionizing our use of money and credit. Your parents may have one or more credit cards. Perhaps you already have a card to pay for gasoline. Air travel cards are widely used by students who go away from home to school.

With a credit card you can buy many goods and services that you want. There is the story of a young woman who lived for a month using credit cards instead of cash. One of the few things that she couldn't buy with them was a hot dog at a stand.

No one knows how many people carry credit cards. There are several different kinds available and many people carry more than one. You may be familiar with some of these kinds of credit cards:

- Retail store cards.
- One-purpose cards.
- Bank cards.
- Travel and entertainment cards.

Retail store cards are the most widely used type of credit card. Stores issue these cards to customers without charge.

Generally, they combine the features of a 30-day charge account and a revolving credit account. If a customer pays his bill within the stated period, usually 10-30 days, there is no extra credit charge. If he does not choose to pay his full bill, he must pay a portion of the money owed each month and a monthly service charge on the unpaid balance.

One-purpose cards are issued by businesses so that you can charge their products or services—gasoline and automobile service, air travel, hotel and motel use, or car rentals.

Many one-purpose cards are free. However, sometimes you have to pay for one, such as an air travel card.

Bank cards such as VISA or Interbank cards are issued free by banks. They are one of the newer types of cards but are now widely used. Bank cards can be used at a wide variety of places such as stores, hotels, and restaurants.

Travel and entertainment cards, such as American Express, Diners Club, and Carte Blanche are used largely by businessmen, although others may apply. There is a yearly fee for their use, about $25-$35.

Credit cards often serve as instant identification, so if you lose one, someone else may be tempted to use it. A federal law now limits your liability to $50—the most that you will have to pay—if someone uses your lost credit card. However, if you do lose a card, notify the issuer promptly in writing, and you may avoid paying anything at all, even if someone else uses the card.

Credit cards are also used in other ways. The existence of credit cards and lists of them has made it easy to compile mailing lists for various purposes. Sales organizations and politicians sometimes use them to get lists of people with special interests.

An *installment account* is still another type of sales credit. It is generally used for large purchases like appliances, furniture, and automobiles.

The user of installment credit signs a contract and agrees to make regular payments over a definite period of time. Often a certain amount of money, called the *down payment,* is paid at the time of purchase. Payments include a portion of the outstanding balance, interest, and any other charges that may be involved. Sometimes such fees are called service or carrying charges. The seller or lender usually holds a chattel mortgage on the purchased goods. This means that he has the right to sell them if the payments are not made according to agreement.

Often the store that sells you something does not have enough money to keep selling on credit, so they sell your credit contract to someone else, such as a bank or

When you apply for credit, you will probably be asked to fill out an application form like this one.

Credit Application

(Please Print)

Full Name	Social Security Number	Birth Date	My Total Indebtedness at this time is	Are You An Endorser or Guarantor for Others?	Have You Ever Gone Through Bankruptcy?
Home Address	Home Phone	☐ Own or ☐ Rent	How Long There	$ _____	☐ Yes ☐ No	☐ Yes ☐ No

List Below all of Your Bank Accounts. Name of Bank and Office | TYPE | ACCOUNT NO.

Marital Status	Spouse's First Name	Number of Children	Previous Address	How Long
Your Employer or Name of Business if Self Employed	Position		How Long There	Yearly Salary
Business Address				Business Phone
Name & Address of Previous Employer		How Long There	Other Income	Source of Other Income
Name & Address of Spouse's Employer		Spouse's Salary	How Long There
List Below All Present Debts Including the Name and Address of the Creditor or Company Owed		Unpaid Balance	Monthly Payment
Mortgage or Rent			
Auto Loan or Other Creditor:			
Other Creditor:			
Other Creditor: Other Real Estate Owned:			

I/We authorize you to obtain such information as you may require concerning the statements made in this application and declare that all replies to the above questions are true and accurate in every respect and agree that this application shall remain the sole property of The First National Bank of Princeton whether or not the loan is granted. An investigation may be made, of my/our character, general reputation, personal characteristics and mode of living. Upon written request, the nature and scope of this investigation, if one is made, will be disclosed to me/us. I/We further authorize you to disburse information concerning any obligations heretofore discharged, presently liquidating or hereinafter incurred when you have reason to believe said information will be used for credit granting purposes.

Signature of Applicant (Ink Only)
_____

Signature of Spouse
_____

Date

finance company. Sometimes this is even arranged before you sign the contract, although you may not be aware of it. A retail store with limited capital might arrange for a bank or other organization to finance its customers on a regular basis. The sales of new automobiles are often handled this way; a sales finance company gives the credit, although your local dealer may make all the arrangements.

Holder in due course is the term that describes a sales contract that has been sold by a retailer to someone else. This is not a problem to the customer unless he has a complaint. In the past some retail merchants have tried to avoid handling complaints by saying that they are no longer involved since the credit contract is owned by someone else.

However, under the Fair Credit Billing Act, if the item was purchased on a credit card other than the store's, the credit card company is also responsible for the merchandise. Thus, a purchaser of defective merchandise could withhold payment from the credit card company under the following conditions:

- The item purchased cost more than $50.
- The store is less than 100 miles from the purchaser's home.
- The consumer makes a real attempt to get the matter settled with the store.

Also, consumers now have the right to sue the purchaser of an installment loan or contract.

Cash Loans

Have you ever forgotten to bring money to school for lunch and then had to borrow from a friend? This is a cash loan. Your folks, if caught short at income tax time or during the Christmas season, might borrow some extra money.

As you can see, a cash loan does not involve the purchase of goods. With this type of credit, the credit seeker goes directly to a lending agency and borrows money. The borrower, however, may use the money to make a cash purchase if he wishes.

Two types of cash loans from commercial lenders are available—installment and single-payment loans. An *installment loan* is handled the same way that an installment account is. You sign a contract agreeing to pay back the amount borrowed plus a specified amount of interest, also called the loan fee, in a certain number of periodic payments. With a *single-payment loan,* you agree to pay back the entire amount plus interest in one payment on a particular date. The installment loan is used more often by individuals and families because it is easier to pay back than a single-payment loan.

WHEN YOU NEED A CASH LOAN

If you need a cash loan, where can you go to borrow? Actually, you have several options.

Commercial banks grant loans with or without collateral. A *collateral,* or *secured, loan* is one in which you put up your bank account, stocks, life insurance policy, or other securities which can be used to pay off the loan if you cannot make the required payments. Businessmen frequently use loans with collateral. They pledge merchandise, accounts which are due to them, and other securities. Your parents may have used stocks or bonds as collateral. A home mortgage pledges the house as security. Car buyers generally use the car as collateral. A loan without collateral is called a *signature,* or *unsecured, loan.*

Generally, banks like to take care of their established customers. Therefore, if you are looking for a bank loan, apply where you have an account, where your family has done business, or where your loan can be endorsed by your employer or another person who will stand behind you. Some banks, as well as other lending agencies, require a co-signer on certain loans. The co-signer, who signs the contract with you, is responsible for the loan if you fail to pay.

If you have a savings account, you may be able to get a passbook loan at a bank. Your savings account serves as collateral. If you pay back the loan, then your savings account is not disturbed. However, if you have a problem paying it back, the bank will take the amount you owe from your account. Usually they will not lend you more than you have in savings.

Suppose you don't have a savings account to borrow against, but you need money for school or a car. Don't be afraid to ask at a bank. Some people are timid about going to a bank, but this may be where you can get the lowest interest rate.

Banks are fussy about the people they will lend to. You need a good credit record. Also, their decision will depend on the size and length of the loan and whether or not money is in short supply. This changes from year to year. Sometimes one bank will give you a loan and another won't. Even if you aren't known at the bank, the bankers may decide you are a good credit risk and give you the loan. Remember, it never hurts to ask.

Savings and loan associations are similar to banks. They operate under federal and state laws. Originally, one of their chief purposes was to help members buy and build homes. Now, however, they make loans for other purposes as well. The interest rates on deposits tend to be a little higher than at commercial banks. Also, savings and loan associations generally

U. S. Department of Labor

Companies often have credit unions to serve their employees. The company credit union would be a good source of credit for this radio announcer.

will lend a higher percentage of the appraised value of a house than a bank.

Life insurance companies loan money to policyholders on the cash surrender value of their life insurance policies at relatively low interest rates. Not all life insurance policies, however, have a cash surrender value. (This is discussed more fully in the chapter on insurance.)

Credit unions loan to members only. Large loans may require collateral or a co-signer. Interest rates are lower than those of finance companies and sometimes lower than bank rates.

Consumer finance companies, also known as loan companies, specialize in making loans. They take greater risks than banks, credit unions, and life insurance companies and often lend smaller amounts. Consequently, their interest rates are higher.

Borrowing from *pawnbrokers* is simple, quick, and often expensive. The borrower puts up some item of value, such as jewelry, a camera, or a musical instrument, as collateral. If the amount borrowed plus the interest is repaid within the specified time, the article is returned. If not, the pawnbroker sells it. Charges are high because many people are not able to redeem their goods.

Loan sharks prey upon desperate people. They are unlicensed lenders who charge very high rates and often use high-pressure tactics to collect. Usually the frantic person who turns to them for help only makes his or her situation worse.

CREDIT COSTS

The cost of credit, whether for a purchase or a loan, varies, depending partly upon the amount of credit and how much of a risk the businessman takes. Large loans, such as to big businesses, generally cost less per dollar borrowed than small loans to individuals. You may have heard the term, *prime rate.* This is the rate charged for loans to big and well-established companies.

Credit rates also vary with fluctuations in the economy. When money is in short supply, credit costs more. Some very careful people try to time major purchases like a house for a period when the money supply is large in order to get lower rates. However, most people buy when their needs are greatest.

What you will have to pay for credit depends on the rate of interest, how long you take to repay, and whether there are additional charges for getting the credit.

Higher interest rates raise the cost of credit.

Longer time payments raise the cost. Although you may not realize it, time can cost more than interest. Long-term credit adds so much that a three-year plan at 12

Stay away from loan sharks.

When you borrow money, you usually have to pay a charge for its use, just as you pay rent for the use of a house.

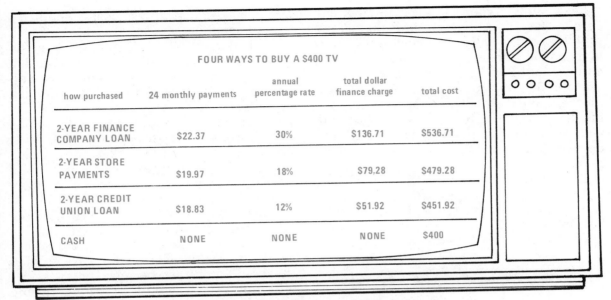

FOUR WAYS TO BUY A $400 TV				
how purchased	24 monthly payments	annual percentage rate	total dollar finance charge	total cost
2-YEAR FINANCE COMPANY LOAN	$22.37	30%	$136.71	$536.71
2-YEAR STORE PAYMENTS	$19.97	18%	$79.28	$479.28
2-YEAR CREDIT UNION LOAN	$18.83	12%	$51.92	$451.92
CASH	NONE	NONE	NONE	$400

Compare these four ways to buy a $400 television set.

percent costs more than a one-year plan at 24.6 percent.

Some credit plans have extra costs. For instance, you may have to take out credit life insurance on a loan so that if anything happens to you, the lender will get his money. Moreover, you might have to buy high-priced auto insurance from the lender or pay for a credit investigation.

In summary, credit costs increase with . . .

- Higher interest rates.
- Longer time payments.
- Extra charges.

Because of all the costs involved, you should shop carefully for credit. Often you can save as much (or more) by shopping for credit as you do by shopping around for an item you want to buy.

*Board of Governors of the
Federal Reserve System*

What extra credit costs do you see in this segment of a contract?

1. Amount Financed:
   (a) Cash Proceeds .... $ **445.80**
   (b) Lien Fee .... $ **1.50**
   (c) Other Charge(s)
   CREDIT LIFE INS. $ **2.70**
       (describe)
                       TOTAL $ **450.00**

2. FINANCE CHARGE:
   (a) Interest $ **45.00**
   (b) Other **SERVICE FEE** $ **5.00**
       (describe)
                       TOTAL $ **50.00**

3. Total of Payments (Total 1, 2) .....
                       TOTAL $ **500.00**

Case Study. When buying a sewing machine, Mary Lou Taylor found that shopping for credit really was worthwhile. She had looked and looked for a sewing machine. Mary Lou knew that she could buy one for $89.95, but she really wanted a more expensive one that she had seen at the sewing center. It did both straight and zigzag stitching and a number of embroidery stitches. The machine was $149.95 plus tax.

The only problem was that Mary Lou didn't have that much money. She could wait and buy it in the fall with money from her summer job. On the other hand, she needed summer clothes for her job, and she

Shop for credit as well as goods and services.

could make them at less cost if she had a sewing machine.

With the store's credit plan, she would not have to make any down payment but would pay $7 a month for 36 months. This comes to a finance charge of $102.05 at a rate of $1\frac{1}{2}$ percent per month on the unpaid balance, corresponding to an annual percentage rate of 18 percent. As another possibility, she could make a down payment which would reduce the number of monthly payments and result in a lower credit charge.

Since Mary Lou is eighteen, the store will extend credit to her, and she can sign the contract herself. If she were under eighteen, her parents would have to sign the credit contract because many stores will not extend credit to young people under legal age.

There are a number of other ways that Mary Lou could finance the sewing machine, but her father and/or her mother would have to borrow the money and sign for it because she doesn't have a regular job and a credit rating. Here are some of the lower cost ways to borrow:

• Her parents could borrow against their savings account at a rate of 11 percent. (Rates usually vary, depending on the economy.) At the same time the savings account would continue to earn interest at $5\frac{1}{2}$ percent.

• Her mother could borrow from the credit union at the factory where she works for 10 percent. (Credit union rates also vary.)

• Her father could borrow against his life insurance for 7 percent. (Of course, his life insurance would be reduced by the amount of the loan until it was repaid.)

• Since her family has well-established credit, her father could probably borrow from the bank at 11 to 14 percent. With stocks as collateral, he could get a slightly lower rate.

These are also some ways to finance that would probably cost more than buying the sewing machine on the installment plan from the store:

● Her parents could borrow from a small loan company, such as the ABC Finance Company, at a rate of about 36 percent.

● Her mother could pawn her ring. She would probably get only a little over a hundred dollars, even though it is worth much more, and pay a high interest rate besides.

What do you think Mary Lou should do? These are some factors that she should consider:

● *What will it cost?* Consider both the cost of the goods or service and the credit cost.

● *Will the size and number of payments fit* into her spending plan?

● *Are there other services* that make one credit plan more desirable? For example, does she have the option of prepaying without a penalty?

WHAT A CREDIT CONTRACT MUST TELL YOU

Whenever you buy on a time payment plan or take out a loan, the store, finance company, or bank must tell you in large print on the front of the contract what you are paying for the use of credit. The federal Truth-in-Lending law requires that credit contracts state this cost of credit in two ways. The first is the actual dollar amount. The second is the annual percentage rate.

Use this information to compare the cost of credit from various sources. Be sure to read it before you sign. Never sign a contract before all the blank spaces are filled in.

The Singer Co.

Mary Lou knew just which sewing machine she wanted.

(Credit contracts are discussed more fully in Chapter 10.)

YOUR CREDIT RATING

If you are a good credit risk, you can get credit more easily than someone who is not. Also, with a good credit rating, you may be able to get credit at a lower cost. This applies to businesses as well as individuals. A large store that is part of an

American Telephone and Telegraph Co.

Automated equipment allows this young lady to check the customer's credit standing with the company before issuing additional credit.

When you apply for credit, the business may phone the credit bureau about you. Without the services of credit bureaus, many businesses could not supply credit to so many in such a short time. In one call the credit bureau can relay information that would take the businessman many calls to find on his own. Imagine the difficulties involved with hundreds of stores in a large city calling each other repeatedly to learn of each other's credit experiences with specific people. The credit bureau solves this problem by keeping a central file to serve all member businesses. Each time a business inquires on John Doe, the inquiry is recorded on John Doe's file. Regularly, the file is updated by checking with the inquiring businesses to see if credit was extended and how the experience with John Doe has been. This information is posted in the file and supplied to other businesses who inquire. Not anyone who calls, of course, can secure information on a person. Only members of the bureau who can accurately identify themselves are allowed verbal credit reports.

When the credit bureau secures information from businesses, they are interested in answers to these questions:

- Do you pay your debts on time?
- Do you work where you say you do?
- Where do you live? Do you rent or are you buying?
- What is your family status?

Generally, the credit bureau does not actually *rate* a person's credit. They simply pass on the information they have received, and the inquiring business makes its own evaluation.

Sometimes credit bureaus make mistakes. You may have trouble getting credit although you know your record is good. Under the *Fair Credit Reporting Act,* if your application for credit, insurance, or a

established chain can usually borrow at better rates than a small store owned by one man or woman.

How do credit managers decide whether or not they will give you credit? More and more are using a scoring system. The scoring method used by one bank is shown on page 59. How do you think you would score with such a system now? Will you be likely to total more points in a few years?

Protect Your Credit Rating

A good credit rating is an asset. It enables you to get credit when you need it and from sources that cost less.

Protect your credit rating by meeting your payments regularly. An occasional late payment won't ruin your record, but a habit of being late may be reported to the local credit bureau.

job is rejected because of a bad credit bureau report, you must be given the name and address of the bureau. Then, although you will not be allowed to read your own file, the credit bureau must tell you the "nature and substance" of the information in it, except for medical information. They must also tell you the source of most of the information except for hearsay information about your character and personal life. In addition, they must tell you who was given your credit record during the previous six months and who was given information for employment purposes during the previous two years.

There is no charge for obtaining this information from the credit bureau if you go within thirty days of an official rejection.

You can correct a false or misleading report, also without charge, by doing the following:

- Having the credit bureau reinvestigate the disputed information.
- Filing a statement of 100 words or less, giving your explanation of the prob-

Take this sample test to see how you rate. Decide how many points you should get for each item and total them to find your score.

CAN YOU GET A LOAN?

Previous Loans with Same Bank	No previous loan: No points given or deducted.	Satisfactory loan: 40 points.	Unsatisfactory loan: Subtract 40 points.
Residence	Less than a year: No points given or deducted.	One to four years: 15 points.	Five or more years: 25 points.
Telephone	Home telephone: No points given or deducted.	No phone: Subtract 25 points.	
Job	Less than a year: No points given or deducted.	One to four years: 15 points.	Five or more years: 25 points.
Salary (Gross Monthly)	$0-1000: No points given or deducted.	$1000-1200: 10 points. $1200-1500: 20 points. Above $1500: 30 points.	
Bank Accounts	Special checking: 20 points.	Regular checking: 30 points.	Savings account: 20 points.
Purpose of Loan	Car: 25 points. (No points given for anything else.)		

40 points or less: Applicant is a poor risk. (If the loan is granted at all, applicant must have a co-signer to guarantee the loan.)
41-79 points: Applicant is considered.
Over 80 points: Loan is granted except in unusual situations.

lem, which will become part of any future reports about you issued by the bureau.

• Ask the credit bureau to send your statement to people who have already received copies of the disputed record.

WHEN YOU CAN'T MEET THE PAYMENTS

No matter how hard you try, there may be times when credit is a problem. Why does this happen? For one thing, some people find that getting and using credit is easy—for a while. The rude awakening comes when the bills suddenly add up to more than the income can cover. Bills are in default—not paid on time. Tempers flare and the credit record rapidly deteriorates. The overextended credit user spends many anxious hours trying to figure out a solution to the problem.

Most people realize that they are using too much credit before they get into serious trouble. Although things may be a bit tight, they do manage. However, sometimes unexpected things happen that really make it impossible to keep up payments. A serious illness or job loss can cause credit difficulties if insurance or other compensation does not make up for the reduced income.

A most important thing to remember in times of difficulty is this: Don't compound the problem. Some lending agencies offer cash loans which are designed to pay off your other debts. These are known as consolidation loans or bill payer loans. Granted, a single loan may be simpler to handle than several accounts. However, you must remember that the new loan will have to be large enough to cover all or most of your debts; it must extend over a longer period of time than your other debts in order to keep the payments down to an amount you can manage; and the interest rate will be an added expense to what you already owe. Such loans should be undertaken only if the borrower understands the full implication of what he or she is doing.

Credit problems, as difficult as they may seem for some, can be cured. The first step is to stop using credit. If this means destroying a credit card or closing a charge account, then do so. Next, remain calm. There is nothing to be gained by yelling at family members and creditors or by making quick and foolhardy decisions.

Contact your creditors. A letter may help with minor problems, but a personal interview may be needed to straighten out a bad situation. Above all, be honest with them. Most reputable firms would rather help you work out a plan for repayment that you can meet than take severe action. They may allow you to pay just the interest for a while or refinance over a longer period of time, thereby maintaining your good credit record.

If you get behind on your payments and don't do anything about it, your creditors may do any of several things. They may keep bothering you for the payments or turn the account over to a collection agency. In either case, you may be contacted at home or work by mail, phone, or in person until a settlement is reached. They may also take back the merchandise (repossess it). Moreover, in some states they might go to court and get your employer to garnishee (give them) part of your wages if you have a job. Federal law prohibits firing an employee the first time this happens. Some employers will fire the employee if it occurs again.

All of these actions can lead to embarrassing and frustrating ordeals. How much better it is to seek help before any of these steps are taken, or better yet, learn the principles of good management now so that credit problems will be less likely to occur in the future.

Next, seek help if the problem is serious. Many communities have agencies which counsel families with money problems. Reputable credit bureaus can also provide help. They may be able to advise you or refer you to someone else who can help.

Bankruptcy is a legal procedure designed as a last resort for people who cannot meet their debts. There is a court hearing presided over by a Referee in Bankruptcy. Following the hearing a trustee is appointed to divide the assets of the person who has filed for bankruptcy among the creditors listed in the petition.

The debtor then has no further obligation to these creditors. However, he can reinstate a debt after bankruptcy by signing an unconditional promise to a creditor that he will pay the debt. Sometimes people do this so that they can again get credit from a company to whom they owed money before the bankruptcy proceedings.

Certain debts are not discharged through bankruptcy proceedings—government taxes, debts not listed on the bankruptcy form, and debts incurred by fraud on the part of the debtor.

An individual can only file for bankruptcy once in six years.

With counseling, you may be able to avoid filing a bankruptcy petition or having to work out a plan for repayment with the help of the court. These procedures should be last resorts because of their impact on your credit record.

FOR REVIEW

Points to Remember

• Credit is a promise to pay later. Its use is based on trust, one's promise to pay.

• The widespread use of credit grew with industrialization. As it became possible to produce goods in quantity, it became necessary to find ways to enable people to buy these things.

• Most families use several forms of credit.

• Credit costs vary with different lenders. It pays to shop for credit as well as for goods and services.

• Your credit rating is an important asset.

• Credit can be a useful tool, but many people find it easy to overbuy with credit.

Terms to Know

annual percentage rate
bankruptcy
collateral
contract
co-sign
credit
creditor or lender
credit, finance, or service charge
credit rating
credit union
debt
default
dollar cost
finance or small loan company
garnishee
holder in due course
installment
interest
loan shark
pawnbroker
prime rate
refinance
repossess
revolving credit

PROBLEM SOLVING: HOW DO YOU HANDLE CREDIT?

Are you happy-go-lucky, very careful, or in between? Answer these questions and then ask yourself how you really feel about borrowing:

1. You need $5 and you don't have it. Where would you try to borrow it?

2. Would you rather borrow from your family or your friends? Why?

3. Suppose you are going to trade school, junior college, or college and need a loan to help pay your tuition. Where would you try to get it? Are you opposed to borrowing for tuition? If so, why?

4. When you borrow money from your family or friends, do you always repay it on time? If not, what do you do about the situation?

5. Your friend wants to sell his 10 speed bicycle for $90. It's a good buy and you want it. But you only have $45. What would you do?

6. Imagine that you are out of school, working, and living away from home. There are some things you need, a car and furniture for your apartment. How would you handle this situation?

7. What do you do when people want to borrow from you? Is your response different if the loan is for lunch money instead of a record or clothing?

TO DO IN CLASS

Discussion

1. What do you think are some acceptable uses for credit?

2. Look ahead to some specific expenses that you anticipate in the next three or four years. How do you plan to handle these?

3. Do you think that young people should postpone buying until they can pay cash or buy what they want now on credit?

4. What kind of person is a good credit risk? What kind is a poor one?

5. It is usually harder for people to get credit if they have no credit rating. How do you plan to establish your credit rating?

6. What is the difference between a regular charge account and a revolving account?

7. What would you expect to happen if you do not repay a loan; that is, you are in default?

8. Do you think businesses have a right to know about your income, debts, and character?

Activities

1. Invite a bank officer to discuss loans and the risks involved to both borrower and lender.

2. Find out about the laws governing loans in your state. What is the maximum permissible rate for various types of loans?

3. Visit a credit union to see how it operates and serves people.

4. Make a bulletin board display of the principal sources of credit in your community.

5. Visit a local court that handles bankruptcy cases.

6. Prepare a bulletin board illustrating the changing needs and uses of credit by a family at different stages of the life cycle.

7. Find out where one could borrow $300 in your community. Compare these sources as to collateral needed, the services offered, repayment plans, and the cost of credit.

8. Find out whether a creditor can garnishee your wages if you are in default on a credit contract. (In some states this is not permitted.) Also, if it is allowable, how much can be taken out?

9. Invite someone who works with low-income families to discuss some of the problems these families have in using credit.

SECTION 2

Sharpening Your Shopping Skills

CHAPTER 4

The Shopping Game

THE DIFFICULT ART OF SHOPPING

Susie Campbell was going to camp as a junior counselor and needed a trunk. She had used her cousin's last summer when she was a camper, but this year her cousin would be using it. Susie thought that she could probably use a trunk for storage so she decided to get one that would last. She and her mother looked around for a small sturdy trunk that wasn't too expensive. They found one that seemed just right at a shopping center. It even had a removable tray to hold small articles.

With some difficulty, they fitted the trunk in its carton into their car and took it home. It stayed in the carton until the day Susie was ready to pack for camp. To her dismay, when she opened the trunk, she found that the tray was broken. There was nothing to do but put it back in the box and take it back to the store. She exchanged it for another one, which she opened up and examined before taking it home. Back home again, an hour and a half later, Susie finally started to pack for camp.

What happened to Susie is just one example of the many frustrations that confront consumers every day. Even though she had tried to shop carefully for the right trunk, she had neglected to check at the store to be sure that it was in good condition.

Shopping isn't easy. It takes time, effort, knowledge, and skill to remember and apply all of the techniques that smart shoppers use. Just as people aren't born track stars or ballerinas, they are also not born canny shoppers. You can, however, become a wise shopper by learning the right skills and putting them into practice. This chapter will help you master the difficult art of shopping.

PRICES

Price is a yardstick that we use to state the cost of an item. The careful consumer uses knowledge about how prices are set in shopping.

Pricing the Product

When you buy an item, many people get part of the money you spend. Some people get paid for making the product, and others get paid for packaging, transporting, selling, and wrapping it.

To find out who gets your money, let's assume that you have just bought a $4.00 bottle of cologne in a department store. First the company that made it will get some money to pay for the cost of manufacturing the cologne, bottling it, packaging it attractively, shipping it to the store, and their profit. The manufacturing company will probably get about 40 percent of the $4.00, or $1.60.

Next the department store that sells the cologne needs some money to pay its expenses and make a profit. They will probably get 45 percent of your dollar, or $1.80 from your cologne purchase. This percentage is called their *markup*. Rent, lights and furnishings, electricity, paper bags, and protection service are some of the expenses that must be paid by the store.

Did a saleslady sell you the cologne? Her pay may depend, at least in part, on the amount she sells each day if she gets a commission on her sales. Generally, store personnel get a base salary plus a commission on the sales they make. The saleslady probably gets an additional 10 percent of what you spend, or in this instance 40¢.

You can be sure that the advertisers get some of your money too. Many of us try different products because they are advertised so much. When you bought the $4.00 cologne, advertisers probably got 5 percent, or 20¢. This pays the high cost of putting ads on TV, in magazines, flyers, and other places to catch your eye and ear and pays for the advertiser's profit.

You can see that when you buy cologne you are paying for much more than just the cost of the materials to make it. This is true of other products as well.

The Pricing System

According to the traditional economic theory, prices are a measure of the value of goods or services. If prices are very high, many consumers cannot buy. When prices are very low, suppliers may go out of business. In periods of high demand and limited supply, prices rise. When the demand is low and supplies are great, the prices fall.

In an industrial society, such as the United States, things do not always work so simply and smoothly. Sometimes producers try to get retailers to sell only at high prices by establishing minimum resale prices. Consumers may boycott stores because of high prices. Often consumers do not have enough information to make wise choices. If they cannot judge quality, they may think a high price is an indication of quality. Strange as it may seem, a number of studies have shown that sometimes goods sell better at a higher price.

Prices are also influenced by many other factors. People expect to select a new Lincoln in a far different atmosphere than a five-year-old, used Chevrolet. Part of the price for the car reflects the showroom costs.

Comparing Prices

Most people want good value for their money. Comparing prices is one way to do this—buy at the best price. Many people use advertisements for some of their comparisons. Newspapers, magazines, TV, and radio all advertise. Often you can get some idea of how prices differ at stores and other outlets.

You can go from store to store to compare the same or similar items. When you are in a store, you can compare prices too.

National Canners Assoc.
Advertising helps us distinguish between similar products.

Advertising strives to appeal to all people.

Would two sweaters on sale, such as two for $30.00, be a better buy than if bought singly?

To facilitate comparisons some supermarkets have adopted *unit pricing.* Unit pricing means that the cost per unit of weight or measure is given on the shelf where the product is located. If Marvel flour is selling for 95¢ for a five-pound bag, the unit price is 19¢ per pound. This enables the customer to compare prices on similar items of different brands and sizes with greatest ease.

Many people use the telephone for comparison shopping. With a phone call you can find out if a store has the product and the price. This technique is useful for ser-

vice as well. How much does the dry cleaner charge to clean a winter jacket? What will it cost for new rear wheel brakes on your car?

USING ADVERTISING CONSTRUCTIVELY

Advertising is all around us—on billboards and signs; in newspapers, magazines, and circulars; and on radio and television. Through advertising, information is relayed from manufacturers to consumers. With the increased growth of self-service stores, advertising has taken over part of the salesperson's role—to provide information about products, brands, and services.

When men lived in caves, they had nothing to sell and no need to advertise. As trade developed, people needed a way to tell about the things they wanted to sell or swap. Advertising grew to be big business when the vast fruitfulness of industrial technology began to shower us with an abundance of goods and services.

Advertisements tempt us to buy in many ways. Some appeal to emotions—the need for love or acceptance by others. TV commercials, magazine ads, and even subway posters extol the virtues of this or that product to make us lovelier, more handsome, or younger looking. Can an iron pill make a middle-aged woman feel younger? Will a shampoo that highlights your hair make you more alluring? Well, many people seem to think so because the products sell.

Not all advertising sells products. You may have seen advertisements telling you to stay in school, to join the Army, or fight pollution.

Advertisements furnish information. Often this is useful. You can tell which toothpastes have fluoride added to prevent tooth decay. Has a wool sweater been treat-

Catalogs contain advertisements for many different products.

ed so it can be machine washed and dried? This information may attract your attention through an advertisement.

Often people plan their shopping with the help of advertisements. Your parents may compare the prices of food as advertised in newspapers or flyers. You may study the ads to see who is selling shirts on sale.

Many critics of advertising condemn it as a means of creating economic waste. They feel that people are encouraged to buy things they don't really need. For example, we do tend to buy more new clothes because of changes in fashion. People often remodel their kitchens because they want to keep up with the times, although some of the equipment may still be usable. Can you think of other examples that might support this view?

WHERE CAN YOU SHOP?

The item you want may be available at several stores or retail outlets. What is the best place to shop? Answers to these questions will help you decide: How much do you want to spend? Where is the store located? How long do you expect to use the item? Is a difference in quality important? Will you need service or a guarantee? Can you return the article if you change your mind when you get home?

You can probably find your shirt size without any help. However, suppose you want a new pair of ice skates. You may want to shop where the salespeople can help you get the right size. Suppose you are buying a tape recorder. You may want to buy where the lowest possible price is offered. The chart on pages 68 to 70 compares some of the advantages and dis-

SHOPPING FACILITIES

Outlets	Descriptions
RETAIL STORES Business establishments engaged in selling goods and services to consumers. *CHAIN*—member of a group of stores with the same or similar goods and policies. *True Chain*—owned and operated by one company. *Voluntary Chain*—independent stores associated for common buying and promotional activities. *INDEPENDENT*—operated by the owner.	*DEPARTMENT*—chain or independent store which sells a large variety of goods and services and is divided into departments for purchasing, promotion and selling. *SPECIALTY*—chain or independent store which specializes in a limited type of merchandise, such as children's wear, shoes, clothing, books, gifts, furnishings or groceries. *VARIETY*—chain or independent store which sells a variety of consumer goods usually in a low price range and with a high amount of self-service and open-counter display. *DISCOUNT*—chain or independent store which attempts to undersell other merchants on some known lines and types of merchandise.
NONSTORE RETAILERS Business established to sell goods to consumers on a nonstore basis.	*DIRECT DOOR-TO-DOOR*—selling in the consumer's home. *MAIL ORDER*—selling by mail or telephone. *VENDING MACHINES*—providing goods through a coin-operated machine on a self-service basis.
COOPERATIVES Associations created and jointly owned by their members.	*COOPERATIVES*—formed by a group for the purpose of buying merchandise jointly at reduced prices. They may sell to members only or to the public as well.

This information taken from pages 22-23 of the booklet titled YOUR SHOPPING DOLLAR, copyrighted by the Money Management Institute of Household Finance Corp., Chicago, Illinois

SHOPPING FACILITIES (Continued)

Advantages	Disadvantages
Department stores usually offer: • a wide selection at different price levels • a variety of customer services • return privileges • one-stop-shopping facilities • some night shopping	*Department stores may be:* • too large to find what you want easily • too far from your home for convenient shopping • too large to offer personalized service
Specialty shops usually offer: • a wide selection within the specialty • services of well-trained, experienced salespeople who know their merchandise • different price levels • personal attention	*Specialty shops:* • sell only one type of merchandise • may charge higher prices than stores that sell many lines of merchandise
Variety stores usually offer: • open display of merchandise • low priced goods • many types of merchandise	*Variety stores usually:* • offer few customer services • hire few salespeople and give them only minimum training
Discount stores usually offer: • convenient parking facilities • lower prices on some products • night shopping	*Discount stores may:* • fail to display merchandise attractively • offer few customer services • limit return privileges • hire few salespeople • fail to mark prices on merchandise
Door-to-door selling usually offers: • convenience of shopping at home • opportunity to see or try products in your home before buying	*Door-to-door sellers usually:* • limit return privileges • provide little or no opportunity for comparison shopping • offer limited selection and price range • call without an appointment and may come at an inconvenient time
Mail-order shopping usually offers: • convenient arm-chair shopping • return privileges • reasonable prices • accurate and helpful catalog descriptions	*Mail-order houses:* • offer no opportunity to see and compare merchandise before ordering • usually charge for delivery • require time to fill orders and ship merchandise—delivery is faster in urban areas

(Continued on page 70)

SHOPPING FACILITIES (Continued)

Advantages	Disadvantages
Vending machines offer: • quick and easy self-service • reasonable prices • 24-hour availability *Cooperatives offer:* • profit sharing for members—often in the form of refunds on purchases • sometimes lower prices than in competing retail stores	*Vending machines:* • offer little opportunity to inspect goods • permit no returns • provide no customer services *Cooperatives may:* • provide only a limited amount and type of merchandise • offer few customer services • employ inexperienced personnel and management

advantages of the major types of shopping facilities.

Get to know the retail outlets in your area. There are probably a variety of types near you.

Trends in Shopping

MAIL-ORDER BUYING

A steadily growing number of people have become armchair shoppers. Mail-order buying, which had its roots in rural America, is a multibillion-dollar operation. Giant mail-order catalog houses offer a wide selection of goods at competitive prices. The tremendous buying power of these companies enables them to compete in price and quality.

Many people find mail-order buying convenient.

Institute of Life Insurance

Sometimes mail-order shoppers aren't familiar with how it works and run into problems. Eager to place her first catalog order, Marsha took a quick glance at the copy about the desk she wanted and filled out the order blank. For weeks she had looked in the stores for a desk but couldn't find the right one. This was it. A few weeks later the desk arrived, and Marsha found that her new desk was made of unfinished wood and came unassembled. Moreover, she owed an additional $4 in shipping charges. In her haste Marsha had not noticed that the desk could be ordered this way. What mistakes did Marsha make? What should she do now?

HOME PARTIES

Case Study. A dozen guests were obviously enjoying themselves in Jane Donohay's living room at 11 o'clock one morning. After playing a few games, they were talking and laughing over coffee and cake. If you happened to look in, you might think it was just a neighborhood get-together.

Actually, it was a kitchenware party. One kitchenware manufacturer has built a

The old-time peddler brought his wares to the customers.

Some items, such as automobile and motorcycle parts, are most easily obtained from a local dealer.

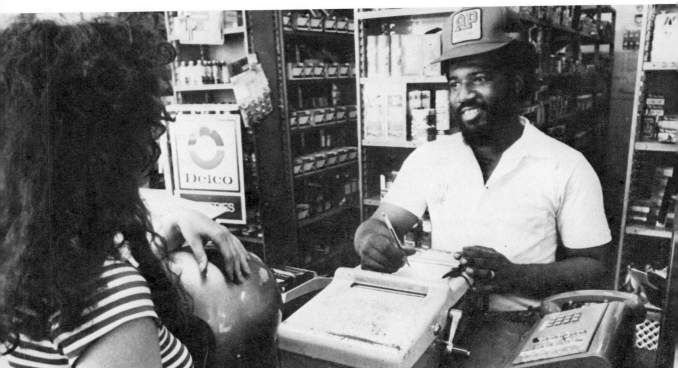

booming business by combining sociability and spending. Some people enjoy shopping this way. The popularity of this selling technique is evidenced by the number of different goods sold in this manner. Parties are held to sell kitchen items, makeup, jewelry, toys, clothing, household supplies, and accessories for the home.

Buying at a party can be fun. It can also be a waste of money if you purchase something you don't need or want because of a feeling of obligation to the hostess. Try not to be put on the spot. If you have no use for the items to be sold, simply decline the invitation. If you decide to go, set a spending limit in advance. This will help you keep a level head in spite of the party atmosphere.

THRIFT SHOPS, RUMMAGE SALES, AND GARAGE SALES

Some young people and others who have to manage on small budgets have learned to use thrift shops and rummage sales to buy clothes and household goods. Many towns have a thrift shop run by a volunteer organization or charitable group. Churches and schools run rummage sales in many communities. Often garage (basement or yard) sales are held at private homes. One or more families may gather items they no longer want for sale to the public. Sometimes you can find a useful article for very little money. Imaginative people may be able to fix up something used so that it looks like new.

AUCTIONS

Buying at auctions can be done in the city as well as the country. Just read the newspaper advertisements and you may find an auction nearby. Sometimes you can get a bargain. However, it is easy to get carried away by the excitement and pay too

much. Regular auction goers usually set a limit that they will bid before the sale starts.

SHOPPING IN THE FUTURE

There are some interesting projections about how retailing will help consumers satisfy their wants and needs in the future. For example, drive-in stores (some are already in business) may be just as common as drive-in banks are. It may be possible to shop from home by telephoning an order to automatic order-taking equipment. Cars now in the developmental stages may feature telephones and TV screens which permit shopping while traveling.

The retail store of today will not disappear, but it will be quite different. Electronic devices will speed up many transactions. More stores will use computerized credit checking. When a purchase is made, the clerk inserts the customer's charge card into a card-dialing telephone and is connected directly to the store's computer. The computer responds to the clerk regarding approval on the proposed charge purchase.

Some shopping centers will probably be part of complexes including hotel-motel facilities and entertainment and recreation facilities. As the working week continues to decrease, shopping will probably become more of a social activity, another way to use leisure to help express one's individuality.

THE BARGAIN HUNT

Many people try to cut costs by looking for bargains. *Coed* looks at the way it might have started:

Bargain hunting! Sounds like fun— but is it?

A matron of ancient Rome may have been the first to find out—the hard way. At any rate, some Roman lady strolling down the Appian Way may well have seen a sign like "Great Cloak and Tunic Sale—Especially Designed to Wear Under Armor. Buy a Set and Get a Laurel Wreath Absolutely Free!" . . . She may have bought one or two, for her husband or sons, only to discover later that they just weren't all that great, especially to wear under armor. Then, on trying to take them back, she may have found out they were "final sales" and she was stuck with them.

At any rate, some ancient Roman invented the phrase, "Caveat Emptor" (let the buyer beware).

Teachers Insurance and Annuity Assoc.
Enclosed shopping centers have become popular.

Saving at Sales

You can save money and bag real bargains when prices are cut. Why do stores have sales? A store may run a sale simply to get people to come in. The management may want to introduce you to new products. A manufacturer may be overstocked. Surplus or shopworn goods are sold to make room for new goods. If the economy is tight and people aren't buying, a sale can help promote business.

Many stores try to turn over merchandise in no more than two or three months. If a product doesn't sell quickly, the store cuts the price. Often they follow the rule, "Sell it, move it, or get rid of it." The first markdown may be small. If this doesn't work, they may reduce it again. Finally, it might go to the basement store or an outlet that specializes in selling at cut prices. Often these outlets cut out the labels because the prestige stores don't like to advertise that some of their expensive clothes turn up in cut-rate outlets.

The best sales are held by well-established stores. They want your good will and your regular business. By watching the ads, you may discover that reputable stores in your area offer good buys at all sorts of sales throughout the year. Are you familiar with any of these sales?

Seasonal sales usually come at the end of a season. When a final clearance on bathing suits is held after the Fourth of July or in late summer, you might get next summer's suit at half price. Spring clothes cost less after Easter, as summer approaches. Fall and winter clothes are often reduced in price for special sales just about the time that it really turns cold. Sometimes it's hard to get in the spirit of buying during seasonal sales. After all, money seems better spent in August for a lightweight jacket rather than a swimming suit. Summer is almost over and the jacket can be used all through the fall. On the other hand, the money saved by buying the lightweight jacket in November and the swimming suit in August could be used to buy a third item. Don't you agree that planning

73

ahead for this kind of buying can be worthwhile?

Timing is important when buying, but not only during seasonal sales. Toys are generally cheaper the last few days before Christmas and just after Christmas. Last year's new cars cost less in the fall when new models are coming out. Can you think of other occasions when good timing might help you save money? The buying calendar on page 75 may give you some ideas. It shows a schedule that stores often use to plan sales, promotions, clearances, and special events. Not all stores, of course, follow this exact schedule.

Private sales are usually held several days before the public announcement. Generally, charge account customers and other people who buy regularly at the store get announcements in advance.

For *special purchase sales* store buyers pick up goods from manufacturers or wholesalers at cut prices. The saving is passed along to the customers. These sales are worth watching for. Many special purchases are goods of regular quality that were in oversupply elsewhere.

Anniversary sales are store-wide promotions. There may be many bargains. Stores use these promotions to help you get acquainted with them.

Just because an item is on sale does not necessarily make it a bargain. These guidelines will help you get the most from your investment when you buy at sales:

- Consider the costs—time, energy, and money—of getting there.
- Shop at the beginning of the sale for the best selection.
- Be sure the sale price is really less than the regular price.
- Watch for damaged articles.
- Check styles. Something that will go out of style quickly may be a poor buy.

- Remember, it's not a bargain unless you need it.

Shopping Ahead of Need

Clothing is probably one of your big expenses. Planning and buying ahead, often a season at a time, is one good way to help manage clothing expenses. This enables you to buy better quality or more items for less money. If you wait until the week before a party and then discover that you don't have anything to wear, the pressure is on. You haven't much time for shopping, and you will probably have to pay full price for what you buy. (If you are growing fast, of course, you can't buy very far ahead.) Note how the young people in the following examples plan ahead for certain buying. Do you have such foresight?

Case Study. Barb buys panty hose as she needs them. When one pair runs, she buys another, generally for the regular price. Betty, on the other hand, watches for sales. She buys several pair when they are on sale, often saving 15 to 20 percent on each one. (Hosiery sales are usually held in the fall and spring.) Can you think of anything that would make Betty's shopping technique difficult for some people? How could this problem be overcome?

Case Study. Pete also watches for sales. If he can, he buys expensive items like jackets and coats at special sales. Columbus Day and Election Day sales are only two of the many sales which are prompted by holidays and events in the community. Since Pete outgrows clothes quickly, he is careful about buying ahead. For example, during the after-Christmas clearance of winter clothes, he bought a jacket but made sure it had extra length in the body and sleeves so it would fit next winter.

Case Study. It is June, and Jill has $50 in her checking account. She wants to make

CALENDAR OF SALES

January	**April**	**July**	**October**
For people with money left over after Christmas there are sales of winter clothing and lingerie. This is also a favorite time for sales of linens and housewares.	Just after Easter most stores slash the prices on spring clothes.	After the fourth, summer clothes are cut in price drastically. Air conditioners and sporting goods are usually on sale. July is a traditional time for sales of colognes and perfumes.	This is the end of the fishing season in most areas, and you can find great bargains in equipment. Some stores also have sales to lure early Christmas shoppers.
February	**May**	**August**	**November**
Stores want to reduce stock on winter items. Skis, ski clothing, skates, sleds, and long sleeved shirts for men are usually available at cut prices. Many stores also feature bedding, glassware, and silver. Some luggage makers have their annual sales.	Some stores offer pre-season bargains in summer clothes. This is also spring cleaning month. Household supplies may be on sale.	This is clearance time on cars. New models come out soon and dealers want to unload. Also, any summer clothes and sporting goods still left will be at clearance prices.	There are a surprising number of sales on winter clothes. Stores want to cut their inventories and get people in for holiday shopping.
March	**June**	**September**	**December**
Pre-season sales of spring clothes are held.	Summer clothes may be on sale later this month, particularly in the cities. This is bargain time for new furniture. The semi-annual new models come out in July, and stores want to sell the old styles. Frozen foods are usually cheaper because new packs will be ready soon, and it is expensive to refrigerate a big supply of frozen foods in the summer.	Many stores feature promotions on back-to-school clothes and supplies. These are even cheaper at the end of the month.	Before Christmas there aren't many good sales. But the week after you will begin to find great buys. Car sales are usually slow in December, and dealers will often cut prices to make a sale.

good use of this money. Invested in a savings account at 5 percent interest, the money could earn about $2.50 in a year. Jill knows, however, that in the fall she will need an all-weather coat. She can buy one right now at a clearance sale for $50 (regularly $75). What should she do?

Buying at the right time is not, of course, the only way to save money when buying clothes. Another way is to sew garments yourself if you have the ability and the facilities. Home sewing isn't always a bargain, but it can be. The real trick is knowing when it is worthwhile. Investing $15 and two days' work to make a pair of slacks that you can buy for $16.99 doesn't make economic sense. Investing $20 plus the work involved in a dress that you might have to pay $40 for is another thing. The wife of a New York Congressman made the gown that she wore to a presidential inaugural ball. She probably spent much less than the ladies who bought theirs.

Before you leave the house on a shopping trip, plan what you are going to buy. Decide what you want and how much you can spend. This will help keep you from spending too much for one item.

Remember that the newest fads or fashions are usually more costly when they first appear on the market. It takes a while for manufacturers to copy them at lower prices or for sellers to become overstocked. Also, of course, when the fashion cools, there will be great reductions in price.

Sales Promotions

Have you ever accumulated a pile of food product coupons or licked 1200 stamps to fill a trading stamp booklet? Perhaps your family has bought a set of dishes at the supermarket—one piece a week.

Stores try to build shopper loyalty with a variety of promotions. With mass production and large-scale commercial growers, the merchandise and food may be very similar in stores in the same area. Thus, they turn to other means of enticing customers into their stores.

One type of promotion has been trading stamps. Generally, the shopper gets 2½ cents in stamp purchasing power for every dollar spent.

Do these extras raise prices? It is very difficult to measure. To pay for themselves such bonuses must produce at least a 12 percent increase in sales. The first store in an area with a new plan may increase its volume tremendously and not have to raise prices to pay for the bonus. However, the stores that follow with similar plans probably won't increase their volume so much and will have to cover the cost with higher prices.

Why are these promotions popular? There are two theories. One is that people feel they are getting something for nothing. If there are few differences between stores, a bonus is an obvious extra. The other theory is that getting extras gives people a feeling of thrift, like the Christmas Club plan.

Generally, trading stamps are redeemed for merchandise. Some states, however, require that the stamps be redeemed for cash. Or, you can choose between merchandise and cash. A few states have banned trading stamps completely.

Other promotions give cash or merchandise. Some supermarkets play bingo. With each purchase you get a letter. The more often you buy at the store, the more letters you will get, increasing your chance of winning a prize. According to the Federal Trade Commission your chance of winning $1,000 in a supermarket game is 1.2

in a million. Can you think of other promotions businesses use to boost sales?

GUARANTEES AND WARRANTIES

Case Study. As a salesman, Jim puts a great deal of mileage on his car every year. Understandably, he sought the best buy on the market when replacing four tires. About eighteen months after purchasing the tires, Jim noticed the tread on all of them wearing very thin. He drove back to the store only to be told by the salesman that the guarantee period had expired. The salesman also said that the guarantee would not have been good anyway, because the tires were used for commercial purposes.

Guarantees are easily overlooked when buying merchandise. The item is new. It works now. Why worry? Later on, however, if something goes wrong, an ignored guarantee becomes important. You may ask yourself questions like: "What did I do with that guarantee? Was there one? Why didn't I read the guarantee before buying? Now, after only two months, I've got to spend more money for repairs."

No doubt, Jim had similar afterthoughts about the guarantee for his tires. A lack of concern for the guarantee could cost him or his company money that might have been saved if he had read the guarantee before buying. Had he known that the tires would not be covered because of commercial use, he might not have made the purchase.

A guarantee and a warranty are basically the same thing—a promise in writing to replace, repair, and/or service the article for a specific period of time.

Most appliances—TV sets, electric toothbrushes, alarm clocks, hair dryers, irons, sewing machines—come with warranties. Many other items do too. Some

Monsanto Co.

The Monsanto WEARDATED hangtag means that the garment is "guaranteed for one full year's normal wear, refund or replacement when returned with tag and saleslip to Monsanto."

Many appliances have guarantees.

Zenith

Product information is available from a number of sources.

roofs are guaranteed not to leak. Some carpets are guaranteed to be mothproof. Guarantees on clothing and fabrics are usually limited to such characteristics as "shrinkage less than a percent," "color fast," or "mothproof."

Compare guarantees when you shop. Will the store repair the radio free for the first six months, or do you have to pay for labor? Another manufacturer may guarantee both parts and labor.

Suppose you buy a record player in September with this guarantee: Service charges for labor and all the parts in your new Rock Music record player are guaranteed for three months. The motor is guaranteed for one year.

Situation 1. In October the arm comes loose. The guarantee covers repairs because you are within the three-month period.

Situation 2. The following April the turntable gets stuck. The guarantee doesn't cover the repairs because it is over three months.

Situation 3. In May you plug in the record player and nothing happens. You don't know if the guarantee will cover the repairs. If the motor is defective, it will. For other parts, you must pay for the repairs.

Be sure to get a copy of the guarantee when you buy products with one. Other-

wise you may not know when repairs, like those for the record player, are covered. You might want to file the guarantee or put it away for safe keeping. Sometimes the guarantee is on the label of the box. It may be in the instruction booklet. Large appliances often have a separate guarantee certificate.

Requests may be made to return a card, which you fill out, to the company in order to register your purchase. If you fail to do so, the company often will not honor your warranty.

Many consumers have been critical of warranties and guarantees. They feel that producers often limit their liability with them. For example, if you fail to return the guarantee card is the manufacturer no longer liable for defective parts? The same is true of automobile guarantees. If you do not service your car for the guarantee period at an authorized service station, which may be higher priced, will you lose the guarantee coverage? In test cases the courts have held that manufacturers are clearly liable for dangerous parts, and in recent years automobile companies have called cars back to replace defective parts.

Under the Warranty Act a guarantee must say what it means. The law does not require that manufacturers give a guarantee. However, if they do so, they must comply with the Warranty Act.

The warranty for any product that costs more than $5 must include:

- What is covered.
- Who is covered.
- The name and address of the company giving the warranty.
- The procedure for getting the warranty honored.

If the product costs more than $10, the warranty must also plainly state whether it is a *full warranty* or only a *limited warran-*

ty. A full warranty is one that meets minimum federal standards.

SECURING PRODUCT INFORMATION

Today there are so many brands, makes, models, and styles that it is difficult to choose wisely, so get all the help you can before you buy. Sometimes you can decide on a purchase by seeing what has worked well for your friends or considering what is available in several stores. Often, however, you can't get enough information that way to make a decision.

Additional information is available from a number of sources. Three magazines are very useful for buying a wide range of products and services, *Consumer Reports, Consumers Research Magazine,* and *Changing Times.* The first two of these regularly test a limited number of a wide variety of products. Why not get acquainted with all three? They are available on newsstands, in many libraries, and by subscription. You can get useful information about cars, insurance, tennis balls, raincoats, watches, sewing machines, and many other products. Specialized magazines such as *Popular Mechanics* and *Popular Science* are also helpful for some items.

The United States government produces a wide variety of booklets for consumers. Some include the government's tests of products that they buy for the armed forces, government offices, and hospitals. The main source for government booklets is the Consumer Information Center, Pueblo, Colorado 81009.

LABELS

According to federal laws, certain information must be on the labels of products. (Clothing labeling is discussed in the next chapter.)

Consumer Reports

Identification of contents of frozen pizzas underway at Consumers Union food lab.

Personal Products

Personal products are big business. Mountains of cream, perfume, shampoo, deodorant, hair coloring, and other products are sold to the American public. In fact, foreigners visiting the U.S. often comment on what an important place these products seem to have in our lives.

How can you decide what to buy? Clearly, some things are useful—a shampoo that works well in the water in your area, a deodorant, and some others. Much money is spent, however, on beauty products that simply bolster egos. Are you looking for an instant miracle, something to make you look like a movie star or your favorite hero?

Young people are often tempted to spend a great deal of money for preparations to improve their skin, particularly things to clear up or hide acne. If you have a problem, you would be wise to discuss it with a doctor before trying self-medication.

Read the ratings of some personal products in *Consumer Reports* or *Consumers Research Magazine.* See if there is any important difference between the high-priced product and the less expensive ones. Often low-priced items are very similar to high-priced ones. Supermarkets, discount stores, and variety stores usually have low-cost personal products.

It's easy to overbuy; don't be tempted to get more than you will use. If you want to try something new, see if you can try a sample in a department store or one that a friend has purchased.

The safety of cosmetic and personal products is watched over by the Food and Drug Administration. However, although they try to keep harmful products off the market, you may still have difficulties.

Some people are very sensitive to the chemicals used in such things as dandruff remover shampoos and long-lasting deodorants.

Often you can avoid products that are irritating by reading the label. If you know that a particular deodorant gives you a rash, check the label before you buy a new one to see if it has the same active ingredients.

The label must tell you:

● *What is in the package.* The law requires an identity statement in bold type on the main display panel in a size and position that is easy to read. A statement of ingredients must appear somewhere on the label.

● *How much is in the package.* This must be stated on the front of the package.

● *Who makes or distributes it.* This must be on the label but not necessarily on the front.

Which sleeping bag would better suit your needs? Often you can find out what is the best product by reading published results of tests.

Consumers Research Magazine

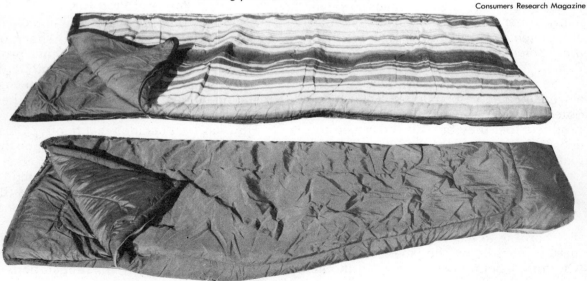

Use this information when you shop. What one toothpaste advertises as their special tooth-saving ingredient may also be contained in other toothpastes. The label will tell. Does the family-size bottle of shampoo really save you money? Compare the price per ounce or millilitre.

Foods

Starting back in 1906 a series of laws have been concerned with food labeling. The Fair Packaging and Labeling Act was passed to require more complete and prominent labeling information so that the customer could make product value comparisons more easily.

What information is required on the label of food packages?

• *The identity of the food.* This must be stated as the common or usual name of the food. If the food is offered in a variety of forms, such as whole, sliced, or chopped, the particular form must be a prominent part of the statement of identity—unless shown by a vignette or visible through the container. Also, this statement of identity must be on the principal display panel.

• *The net quantity of the contents.* For most packages, this statement must appear

LABELS ON PERSONAL PRODUCTS GIVE THESE FACTS

What's in the package? How much is in the package? Who makes it?

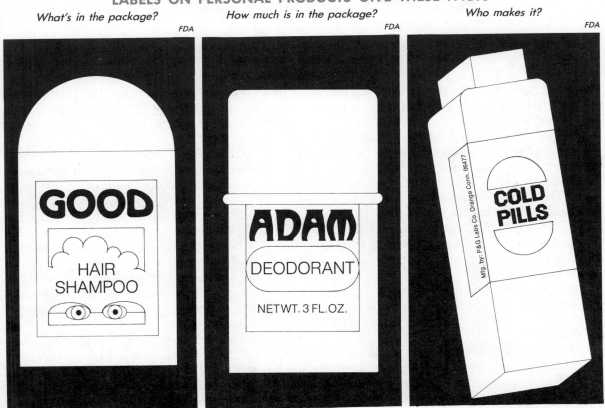

81

Del Monte Corp.
What information can you find on this label?

in the lower 30 percent of the principal display panel. It must be printed in bold-face type and separated from other printed information so that it may be easily read. The use of exaggerated terms like *full gallon, jumbo pound,* and *giant quart* is prohibited.

• *The name, address, and zip code of the manufacturer, packer, or distributor.*

• *The ingredients* must be stated if the food does not have a *standard of identity* established for it. A standard of identity is a recipe filed with the Food and Drug Administration (FDA). Catsup, mayonnaise, and a number of other mixed foods that are in common use have standards of identity.

There are some other important provisions regarding food labeling:

• The manufacturer does not have to put the size and number of servings on the label. However, if he does, the size of each serving must be stated in the same type in immediate conjunction with the serving statement.

• Food labels may contain additional information that is not required by law:

  • A brand name to identify the product.
  • Recipes that suggest how to use the product.
  • Storage and cooking recommendations.
  • A statement of grade.

• *Cents off* promotions may be used only when they represent a real savings to the consumer.

• The number of different package sizes in which a food may be sold is not restricted by law. However, the Department of Commerce is authorized to seek voluntary agreement from manufacturers so that a

NUTRITION INFORMATION
(PER SERVING)
SERVING SIZE = 1 MUFFIN
SERVINGS PER CONTAINER = 12

	MIX	MIX + 1 EGG + ½ C. MILK
CALORIES	120	130
PROTEIN, GRAMS	2	3
CARBOHYDRATE, GRAMS	20	20
FAT, GRAMS	3	4

PERCENTAGE OF U.S. RECOMMENDED DAILY ALLOWANCES (U.S. RDA)

PROTEIN	2	4
VITAMIN A	0	2
VITAMIN C	0	0
THIAMIN	4	4
RIBOFLAVIN	2	4
NIACIN	2	2
CALCIUM	8	10
IRON	2	4

FDA

This is the minimum information that must appear on a nutrition label. All fortified foods and all foods for which a nutrition claim is made must display nutrition information on the labels. Nutrition information is per serving. The label gives the size of a serving (for example, one cup, two ounces, one tablespoon) and tells how many servings are in the container. Listing of cholesterol, fatty acids, and sodium content is optional.

USDA

Consumer demand grows for open dating of food products, especially perishable and semiperishable items.

single commodity will not be offered in a confusing array of package sizes. Also, the FDA has the authority to define the range of package sizes—for example, small, medium, large, and extra large. Thus, the large size of one manufacturer's product will not be the medium size of a competitor.

Open dating, used on some products, tells you the date by which food should be sold.

FOOD GRADES*

Product	1st Grade	2d Grade	3d Grade	4th Grade
Beef	USDA Prime	USDA Choice	USDA Good	USDA Standard
Veal	USDA Prime	USDA Choice	USDA Good	USDA Standard
Calf	USDA Prime	USDA Choice	USDA Good	USDA Utility
Lamb	USDA Prime	USDA Choice	USDA Good	USDA Utility
Poultry	U.S. Grade A	U.S. Grade B	U.S. Grade C	
Eggs	U.S. Grade AA	U.S. Grade A	U.S. Grade B	U.S. Grade C
Butter	U.S. Grade AA (U.S. 93 Score)	U.S. Grade A (U.S. 92 Score)	U.S. Grade B (U.S. 90 Score)	
Cheddar Cheese	U.S. Grade AA	U.S. Grade A	U.S. Grade B	U.S. Grade C
Swiss Cheese	U.S. Grade A	U.S. Grade B	U.S. Grade C	U.S. Grade D
Nonfat Dry Milk	U.S. Extra Grade	U.S. Standard Grade		
Processed Fruits and Vegetables	U.S. Grade A (Fancy)	U.S. Grade B (Choice or Extra Standard)	U.S. Grade C (Standard)	

USDA

*There are lower grades of meat, but these grades seldom appear in the retail market. They are generally used in processed meat items such as frankfurters.

GRADES

Grade labeling is very useful in the intelligent selection of food, but it is not required by law. Although foods are often graded at the wholesale level as an aid to purchasing agents, they are rarely graded at the retail level, except for meat, butter, and eggs.

Grades are a measure of quality. If a food has been graded by a government grader, it may carry the official grade mark, shaped like a shield. Grade marks are put only on foods that are clean and wholesome.

MEAT INSPECTION STAMPS

The law requires that all meat and poultry shipped in interstate commerce must be inspected for wholesomeness by the U.S. Department of Agriculture. Meat inspection stamps are put directly on the carcass of the animal, except for poultry. Poultry generally is stamped on the box in which it

Choice meat usually has more fat marbled in the meat.

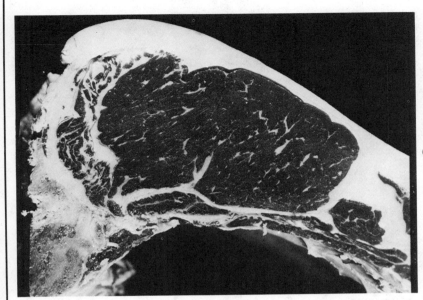

CHOICE

USDA Photo

GOOD

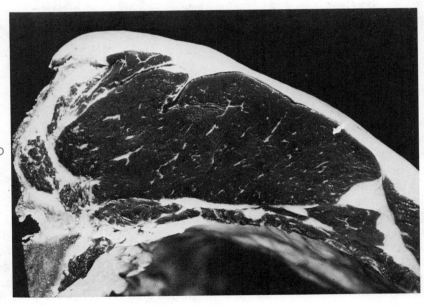

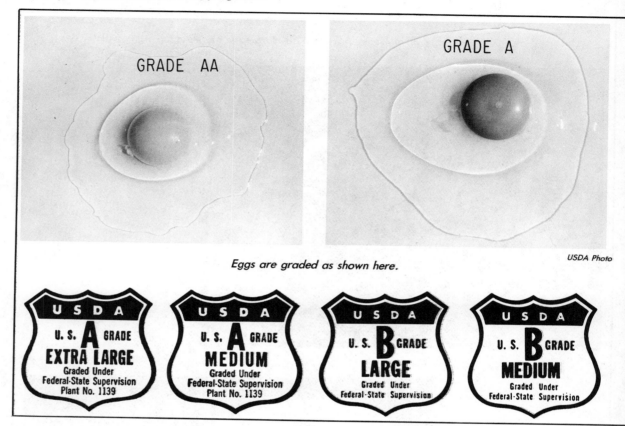

Eggs are graded as shown here.

USDA Photo

is shipped, and the stamp is not visible to the consumer. For canned or packaged meat an inspection stamp must be placed on the label.

Meat and poultry that are not shipped across state lines must be inspected by the state according to federal standards. If this is not done satisfactorily, the U.S. Department of Agriculture can step in, inspect the meat, and charge the state. Some states have elected to have the U.S. Department of Agriculture inspect meat and poultry

within the state because the cost is less than doing it themselves.

Seals of Approval

A number of organizations have seals for use on products. These are some of the most widely used:

The *Underwriters' Laboratories' seal* on appliances and equipment indicates that the designs of the products have met UL standards for safety.

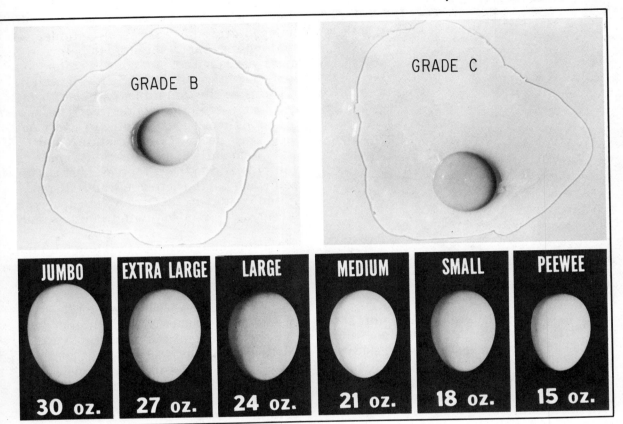

The *American Gas Association Label* indicates that the appliance has been tested by A.G.A. and conforms to standards of the United States of America Standards Institute.

The *Good Housekeeping Consumers' Guaranty Seal* is used on products advertised in the magazine. *Good Housekeeping Magazine* agrees to replace or refund the purchase price if the product is defective.

The *Parents' Magazine Guaranteed Seal* may be used on products advertised in the magazine, and which the magazine considers suitable for use by families with children. *Parents' Magazine* will refund or replace the product if it is defective within 30 days of the purchase. (See page 89).

CONSUMER PROBLEMS

Hardly a week goes by for most people without experiencing some problem associated with consumerism. One girl bought a blouse, only to have it shrink a complete size after the first washing. A young couple

U. S. Department of Labor

Large companies employ a consumer complaints manager.

paid $300 for a vacuum cleaner (plus several "free" gifts) from a door-to-door salesman and later saw a comparable one advertised at half the price. Have you, like these people, experienced buying problems? Whether you have or not, you probably will in the future. A familiarity with the kinds of difficulties people have should help you avoid some of the frustration.

Dealing with Salespeople

It takes skill to deal with other people. Are you skillful in dealing with salespeople? Many young people feel very insecure. They wonder if the salesperson is treating them fairly. Occasionally, customers are rude and demanding. In this day and age salespeople are pretty scarce. Why is it that sales clerks are always around when you don't need them and never when you do? Although exaggerated, this shopper's lament points out part of the frustration that many people feel in connection with salespeople. In order to keep costs down, many stores are using less help today. During busy times, the problem of finding someone in the store to help you is compounded. Tact and courtesy often go a long way in getting help when you need it.

Occasionally, an unpleasant clerk is encountered. Is it any wonder that salespeople sometimes become irritable? Every day they must deal with complaining, indecisive, demanding, and irate customers. If you only add to their troubles, chances are you won't get the help you want. Therefore you must find an effective way to deal with salespeople. The following pointers may help:

- If possible, come to the store with the information you need to make the purchase (correct sizes; fabric samples when matching).
- When in doubt about something, ask questions. Most clerks would rather help you make the right purchase the first time to save difficulties later.
- Try to be decisive. Much time can be wasted in making up your mind. You may be wise to skip the purchase when in doubt or to come back later after giving it some thought.
- If you have a problem, approach the salespeople with tact and courtesy. People are more likely to go out of their way to help you if your attitude is positive.

The "Fixit" Problem

The radio is broken. The alarm clock doesn't ring at the right time. The hair dryer keeps shorting out. How do you go about finding a person or place to fix them? "With difficulty," remarked one wag.

I can't get it fixed properly. It isn't worth fixing. These are typical comments concerning the repair problem. Large stores and major manufacturers are very much aware that difficulties exist. Many have their own repair services for the products they sell under warranty. In addition, some service companies will also make these repairs. Repairs that are not covered by guarantees are often expensive in relation to the purchase price of an item. It may cost almost as much to replace the heating element of an iron as to buy a new one on sale.

For a big item like an air conditioner or dishwasher, it may take several weeks for a repair service to get to your house.

Because repairs can pose problems, it is smart to consider the repair service available when buying. Does the store have a good service department or agency? If you can't carry the item in for repair, will the store make home repairs? Is there a repair shop or a dealer close to you who can service the make you want to buy?

What is a reasonable price for repairs? This is a difficult question to answer. Unless you really know what the problem is, you aren't in a good position to know what needs replacing. Unfortunately, some repair people are not as knowledgeable as

American Gas Assoc.

American Gas Association Label.

Parents' Magazine

Parents' Magazine Guaranteed Seal.

Good Housekeeping Consumers' Guaranty Seal.

Good Housekeeping Magazine

Underwriters Laboratories Seal.

Underwriters Laboratories Inc.

89

they should be about new models and features that are on the market.

Some repair services take advantage of customers. In one large eastern city, some people took a TV set needing a $2.95 tube to seventeen repair shops in their area. Seven shops gave honest appraisals of the trouble, but the other ten quoted repair prices that ranged from $8 to $156.95.

Occasionally, people have been charged for repairs never made and parts never installed. You should be aware of what repairs are to be made on automobiles and appliances and request a written estimate of the cost. You may want to ask that the faulty parts be saved for you. Check your itemized statement of parts and labor to see that it is correct and that the work was actually done. Often friends can recommend repair people who do satisfactory work, taking some of the risk out of choosing a service agency yourself.

Returning Merchandise

There are times when you just have to return something. Even with careful shopping, you do make mistakes or purchase an item that is defective. You may have carefully selected a red sweater to go with your red tweed slacks. However, later you find that the colors don't match. In the store you looked at them together under fluorescent lights, but in daylight the colors look different.

One woman bought a new canister vacuum and had a problem. The floor sample in the store worked beautifully. However, when she made the purchase, she received the vacuum in a sealed carton which she didn't examine until she got home. When she opened the box at home, she found that the hose was missing.

How do you go about returning the sweater or the vacuum? Whether you plan to return it in person or have it picked up by a store's delivery service (many large department stores have this type of service), you need to consider several things:

• Was it bought at a sale? Often sale merchandise cannot be returned, even if you have made a mistake. A sweater that is sold at a "final sale" is yours for life—even if you are sorry about it when you get home.

However, a vacuum that is defective or incomplete may be returnable if it is in the original carton and guaranteed by a reputable manufacturer. In some cases the store will take back a defective or incomplete appliance and give you another one. In others they will send for the missing part or send the whole thing back to the manufacturer, and you just have to wait for it. Still other stores will refer you to a factory authorized service center where it will be repaired or the part replaced without charge. If it is a repair, you will probably have to make a second trip to pick it up when it is ready.

• Have you worn it? Stores usually will not take back anything that has been worn.

• Have you waited more than a week before returning it? Generally, stores accept returns within a period of five days to a week. After that they are reluctant to take something back.

After you have considered these points and feel that you should be able to return the item, you are ready for the next step—decisions:

• Will you return the item in person or do you want to have it picked up?

• Do you want your money back? Would you like to exchange the item for something else? Will you take a credit slip to use for something else? Many stores will not give refunds.

Remember that most reputable stores are reasonable about taking things back for good reasons. They may not like the nuisance, but they feel that they have a reputation to protect.

Before you buy, consider the problem of returning the item. It might be wise to buy a toaster where you know you can exchange it for another one in just one trip if it is defective. On the other hand, you might as well buy your bathing suit wherever you can get the best buy since stores will not take swimsuits back under almost any circumstances.

Don't Be Fooled

Changing Times says, "Maybe *you* wouldn't buy a bottle of snake oil, but there are plenty of people who would. Only it's not called snake oil anymore, or even High Popolorum (a "cure" for everything from cold feet to palpitating heart that once sold for $2 a bottle).

"Nowadays, the medicine wagon spiel has been supplanted by gimmicks more sophisticated and far more profitable than the wildest conjurings of the itinerant peddler of the past. . . . Every year the public is gulled out of hundreds of millions of dollars through a variety of fraudulent sales tactics."

Misleading ads and glib salesmen can sound very convincing. Time taken to check their claims is time well spent. The careful consumer avoids trickery, yet attempts at deception are often so cleverly devised that even an alert consumer can sometimes be fooled. Would you be sharp enough to see through the fraudulent schemes described here?

BAIT AND SWITCH

The ad looks enticing, but when you get to the store, they say, "It's all sold out." Then they try to sell you a higher priced model. Used cars, vacuum cleaners, and many other items are promoted this way. Look in the for-sale column of a city newspaper. There may be an ad for a rebuilt, unclaimed, or repossessed sewing machine. This could be a come-on for the bait-and-switch tactic. Some stores have

The appliance which is advertised or on display may be used as a bait to convince you to buy another model at a higher price.

only a few bait items for sale. The object is simply to get you in the store. Once there, you might make a purchase. Sometimes bait items are damaged, seconds, or mismatched. After seeing the low-quality, advertised items, the advertiser hopes that you will decide to buy something better at a higher price.

PHONY CONTESTS

Nearly everyone enjoys the thought of winning a prize. This is what makes the phony contest a successful gimmick for selling merchandise. You may be notified that you have won a contest, but when you try to claim the prize you are subjected to a long session with a high-powered salesman who wants to sell you something. You might see a puzzle in a magazine or newspaper. All you must do is solve the puzzle, generally quite simple, and you win the "prize." Along with the "prize," however, comes an overpriced item to buy or articles for you to sell. Your best protection against

techniques of this sort is to investigate thoroughly before you sign anything. If no signature is required, think carefully before you invest much time and energy in a contest that is not likely to be worthwhile.

SPECIAL SALES

Although many sales are legitimate, some are misrepresented. Businesses may have fake "selling out" sales to get you into the store. If the store is really closing, you may be able to find a good buy. It is wise, however, to be sure they are really selling out. Think carefully before you buy at such events.

DOOR-TO-DOOR SELLING

Buying from door-to-door salespeople can be risky. Some reputable companies have sold door-to-door for years. If you are familiar with the company and sure about the representative, you can probably feel safe about buying. On the other hand, many people who sell door-to-door charge

When a stranger knocks on your door, he or she may be a salesperson. Remember, don't be afraid to say no.

a lot for very little. Often prices of merchandise are very high compared to what you would have to pay at a store.

Salespeople who come to your door may use a variety of techniques to get into the house. A common one is the survey technique. The salesperson tells you that he is taking a survey and would like to ask you a few questions. Ask these callers what the subject of the survey is and whether they have something to sell before you let them in. Insist on seeing their identification to find out if they are really taking a survey.

The sympathy approach is used by some salespeople to get you to buy magazines or books. A common story is that the person is working his or her way through college and needs your help.

If you are buying magazines from someone who sells door-to-door, be sure you don't sign an order form for more magazines than you want or at a higher price than you had agreed upon.

There is a Federal Trade Commission regulation that gives consumers a three-day period to reconsider a purchase of more than $25 from a door-to-door salesperson. (Some state laws allow reconsideration of purchases that are even smaller.) This means that you are entitled to return the merchandise, or break a contract, if you change your mind during the three days. You must notify the seller in writing.

SERVICE FRAUDS

Certain outfits "specialize" in making home repairs—blacktopping; furnace, chimney, and roof repairs; or tree service. The offer of a "free inspection" may sound good but may also lead to the phony discovery of problems. For a fee, which may be quite high, the caller will supply the required service. A reputable service agency, however, might charge a more reasonable rate for repair or tell you that no problem exists.

Automobile service can be a source of trouble, particularly if the car owner knows little about cars. A common tactic is to advertise low-cost repairs for specialties like the brakes or transmission and then strip down the customer's car, "discovering" that it needs major repair. On the other hand, many reputable companies specialize in such things as brake and muffler repairs. Ask your friends or your local Better Business Bureau about other people's experience with a repair service that you want to use.

EASY MONEY

Is there an easy way to make money? Probably not. Yet you may have seen advertisements that make such claims. You can raise animals, write songs or stories, or sell greeting cards, according to these ads, as an easy way to make money. Many of these promotional schemes require you to buy something in order to get started. Selling the product to you is how the promoter makes money. How you make yours once you have the materials is left up to you.

Not all selling programs are frauds. Some well-known, large companies sell personal and household products this way. Their dealers, who sell door-to-door or at home parties, do make money. Before you consider a plan, check carefully into the reputation of the company.

CORRESPONDENCE SCHOOLS

There are many worthwhile correspondence courses. For example, many people in the service have earned a high school equivalency diploma or college credit this way. Some state universities offer correspondence courses, and there are a number of private companies who offer worthwhile courses.

However, there are also some companies who offer courses of little value. Some promise employment after graduation or suggest that a particular field is in need of people trained by them. Before you sign an agreement to take a course, check with people in employment and personnel offices to see if the course will really help you get a job. Otherwise, your time and money may be wasted.

IMPROVING YOUR HEALTH

Just as there is no easy way to earn money, there is no quick and easy way to cure all health problems and to change certain body features. Medical problems need the attention of a physician, not quack medicine or mail order cures. Problems with acne, baldness, wrinkles, and weight cannot be overcome with simple products or services. The temptation to buy may be strong. The results are likely to be disappointing.

PERSONAL IMPROVEMENT CONTRACTS

The attractive offerings of dance and charm schools and health clubs have encouraged people to sign contracts far too expensive for their incomes. A thorough reading of the contract will tell you what you are getting and the cost involved. When in doubt, the safest procedure is not to sign at all.

ABSOLUTELY FREE

You have probably seen an advertisement for something that is "absolutely free." Perhaps a book club is giving away a free book, if you sign up to buy several more. One retailer offered a 32-piece stainless steel tableware set free for buying a set of dishes. However, when the Federal

Trade Commission investigated the tableware offer, they found that the price of the dishes was high enough to include the cost of both the tableware and the dishes.

Don't be fooled by offers of free things. Generally, you can't get the "free" item without paying for something else. Check the price of the items in the offer elsewhere before considering a "free" offer.

Combatting Fraud

Some unscrupulous people will do almost anything to make money at another's expense. The list of known gyps has been reported to be as high as 800. In addition to those frauds just described, you may be familiar with some of these:

- Selling out-of-state land tracts or lots under false pretenses.
- Sending widows bills for nonexistent debts.
- Selling fake fuel-saving devices for cars.
- Collecting money for leading people to unexpected inheritances.

The consumer cannot expect to know about every type of fraud that has been used. He or she can, however, be wary and look for these warning signs of a gyp:

- An offer of something for nothing.
- A salesperson who runs down his own or another's product.
- A contract with vague or tricky wording.
- Pressure to sign right away.
- Offer of a kickback to you for referring friends to a salesman.

The average person can best combat fraud by not becoming a victim. If the swindler cannot find people to deal with, he cannot stay in business. You can help by following these guidelines for avoiding fraud:

- Be skeptical.
- Buy from legitimate merchants.
- Don't pay until you're sure.
- Never sign until you've slept on it.
- Compare prices first.
- Read all contracts before signing.
- Never sign a blank contract or one with blank spaces.
- Get guarantees in writing.
- Check with the Better Business Bureau, your local Chamber of Commerce, or a consumer agency if in doubt.
- Report cases of fraud to the above agencies and government consumer protection agency, if there is one in your area. If there is not a consumer protection agency, try the State Attorney General's Office.

Consumer Complaints

In one large city, the following consumer complaints were reported to the Better Business Bureau during a three month period: unsatisfactory service or repair—26 percent; nondelivery of merchandise ordered—17 percent; misrepresentation—14 percent; problems over credit terms, interest rates, and billing—11 percent; defective merchandise—10 percent; overcharges and exorbitant prices—7 percent; guarantee or warranty not fulfilled—5 percent; nonrefund of deposits—4 percent; and high-pressure selling—1 percent.

Certainly all of us have complaints from time to time. Most of these can be handled by direct contact with salespeople. More difficult problems, however, may need to be taken to a higher level. Department heads and store managers can be consulted, or a letter to the president of the store or company may get action. If your problem is still not resolved, some additional avenues of help are provided in the chart on page 96.

CONVERTING TO THE METRIC SYSTEM

The United States was one of the first nations to base its currency on a decimal system. However, it has been among the last to convert weights and measures to the metric system, which is also based on a decimal system.

One major reason for changing the measuring system is that the nation's manufacturers do much business with other countries. Buying and selling goods is much easier when all of the nations use the same measuring system. Even before the Congress considered metric legislation, many industrial products and household goods were made or labeled in metric measurements, in order to be more acceptable abroad.

Some metric measurements have been commonly used in the United States for years. Sports fans know that many swimming races have long been measured in metres. Film, skis, and camera lenses have commonly been sold in metric sizes. The labels on many packaged foods give the weight of the contents in both grams (a metric unit) and ounces. Drugs are prescribed and sold in milligrams and millilitres.

In the modern (SI) metric system there are seven base units. They are:

- The *metre,* for length.
- The *kilogram,* for mass or weight. (Many scientists and metric experts prefer the term "mass," but "weight" will probably continue in everyday use.)
- The *second,* for time.
- The *kelvin,* (and the *Celsius*) for temperature.
- The *ampere,* for electric current.
- The *candela,* for the amount of light.
- The *mole,* for the amount of substance.

IF YOU NEED TO COMPLAIN

1. Start where you purchased the item or service. Explain your problem in a factual manner. Most reputable stores, agencies, and service providers will try to help you.

2. If the problem is related to an item, write to the manufacturer. (Most libraries have references with the addresses of large manufacturers.) Address your letter to the service department, a particular official if you can find the name of one, or just to the president of the company.

3. If this is not successful, try some of your local agencies and organizations.
   - A local consumer agency.
   - State or local consumer organizations.
   - Better Business Bureau.
   - Chamber of Commerce.
   - Action lines sponsored by local newspapers, radio, or TV.

4. If your problem is related to:

	Contact
Deceptive advertising	The regional office of the Federal Trade Commission
Mail fraud or theft	Your local post office
Food, drugs, or cosmetics	The regional office of the Food and Drug Administration
Water, sewer, or pesticides	Your local department of health
Professional services	The ethics committee of the professional association, licensing agency, or other appropriate state agency

5. For legal assistance in resolving a problem:
   A. Consult your own lawyer or a legal aid group.
   B. Use a small claims court, if one is available in your area.
   C. Take your problem to a city, county, or state prosecutor (usually located in the attorney general's office).
   D. Ask for help from a local or state department or agency of consumer affairs.
   E. Consult appropriate state or federal regulatory agencies.

Note: If you do not know the appropriate government agency to contact, your local or state government can help you.

In addition, the federal government publishes a list of agencies and organizations periodically. This is available in many libraries and for purchase from the federal government.

What You Will Need to Know

Most people will never use several of the base units. They are mostly for scientific usage: for instance, candela, the amount of light; or mole, the amount of substance. However, measurement of temperature, for instance, will be used more commonly. There are two base units for temperature.

The kelvin is for scientific work, and the degree Celsius for everyday use. In previous years Centigrade was used rather than Celsius.

Since some of the base units may seem unfamiliar, perhaps a good way to learn about the metric system is to study its most common units and terms.

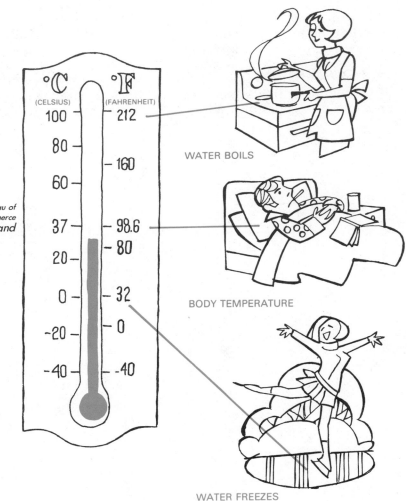

"Metric Counter," National Bureau of Standards, U. S. Dept. of Commerce
Here you can compare Fahrenheit and Celsius temperature scales.

WATER BOILS

BODY TEMPERATURE

WATER FREEZES

MOST COMMON UNITS

metre (m): a little longer than a yard (about 1.1 yard)

litre (l): a little larger than a quart (about 1.06 quarts)

gram (g): a little heavier than a paper clip

COMMON PREFIXES (used with many units)

milli: one-thousandth (0.001)

centi: one-hundredth (0.01)

kilo: one thousand times (1 000)

For example:

1 000 millimetres = 1 metre
100 centimetres = 1 metre
1 000 metres = 1 kilometre

OTHER COMMON UNITS

millimetre (mm): 0.001 metre—about the diameter of a paper clip wire

centimetre (cm): 0.01 metre—a little more than the width of a paper clip

kilometre (km): 1 000 metres—somewhat more than a half mile

kilogram (kg): 1 000 grams—a little more than 2 pounds

millilitre (ml): 0.001 litre—five of them make a teaspoon

OTHER USEFUL UNITS

hectare: about 2½ acres

metric ton: about 1 ton

TEMPERATURE

degrees Celsius (°C) are used

Changes in Sizing Household Products

Conversion to a metric system of weights and measures will take time. However, in

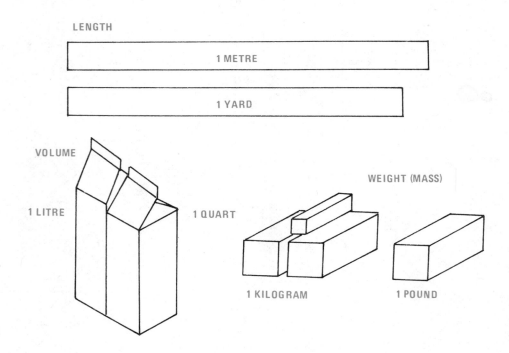

LENGTH

1 METRE

1 YARD

VOLUME

1 LITRE 1 QUART

WEIGHT (MASS)

1 KILOGRAM 1 POUND

the future most articles in the United States will probably be made and sold in metric units.

For a while, both traditional units and metric units will probably be used. As was mentioned, for some products both types of units have been used for quite a while. Many thermometers and measuring utensils carry both Celsius and Fahrenheit scales.

CLOTHING AND TEXTILES

Some clothing sizes will be in metric units. For example, men's shirts will probably continue to use a dual number system for collar and sleeve sizes. However, the numbers will be in metric units. A collar size of 16 (inches) will be expressed as 41 (cm). Sleeve lengths will also be in metric units.

Familiar dress sizes will probably be replaced by body measurements expressed in centimetres. Many clothing patterns now state body measurements, fabric requirements, and seam allowances in centimetres. Textiles will probably be sold in square metres.

Shoes may be sized by length and width, expressed in centimetres. However, another method, called the *mondopoint system,* has been proposed as an international system of shoe sizing. It involves two numbers, such as 240/95. The first is the length of the foot. The second is the distance around the foot at the ball. Both are given in millimetres.

FOODS

Some people prefer to measure by weight and others like to measure by volume when preparing foods. Weight is more accurate and is widely used in Europe. However, American recipes for home use have traditionally been expressed in volume, and this practice is expected to continue when recipes are metric.

A one-cup measure translates to millilitres as shown here.

National Bureau of Standards, U. S. Dept. of Commerce

Compare miles per hour to kilometres per hour in this drawing.

National Bureau of Standards, U. S. Dept. of Commerce

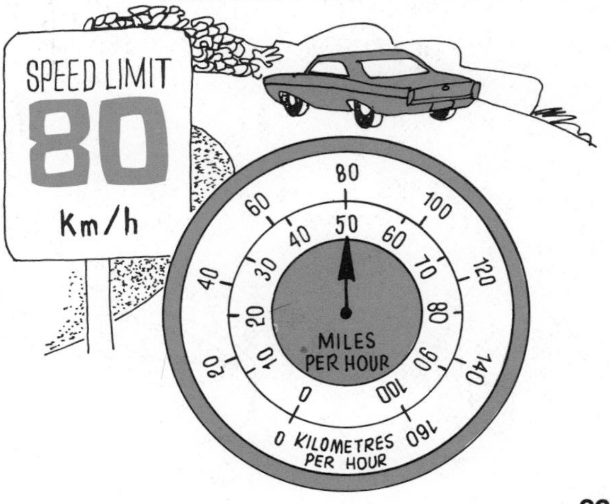

A shift to the metric system will result in changing package sizes to standard metric sizes. Milk will be sold in litres rather than quarts. Meat will be measured in grams and kilograms.

Metric units make the price comparisons of products much easier. This is a great advantage to the consumer.

OTHER HOUSEHOLD PRODUCTS

Nearly all containers and packages will probably be sized in metric units. For example, toothpaste will probably be marked in millilitres as is done now in Canada.

FOR REVIEW

Points to Remember

- Skillful shopping takes time, effort, and knowledge.
- Some technical information may be needed for intelligent decision-making. This type of information is often available from several sources.
- Pricing policies are not the same in all stores or retail outlets. Shopping around can save you money.
- Usually the purpose of advertising is to persuade you to buy.

As the United States converts to metric, more and more products will be sold by metric measures.

National Bureau of Standards, U. S. Dept. of Commerce

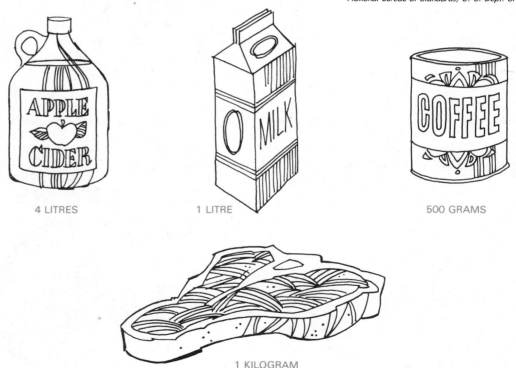

4 LITRES   1 LITRE   500 GRAMS

1 KILOGRAM

- The skillful shopper can find bargains but is wary of gyps and frauds.
- Sometimes service is more important than buying at the lowest price.
- Food, clothing, and personal products must be labeled in ways prescribed by law. Use these labels when you shop.
- You can get action on many complaints if you know where to address them.
- The metric system of weights and measures is based on a decimal system.

Terms to Know

advertising
bait and switch
bargain
brand
cooperative
degrees Celsius
grading
gram
guarantee
ingredients
litre
markup
meat inspection stamps
metre
model
net quantity
price
private sale
retailer
service charges
special purchase sale
standard of identity
trading stamps
warranty

PROBLEM SOLVING: CHECK YOUR UNDERSTANDING

1. Mary bought a red nylon print shirt to go with her new slacks. The label said that it was machine washable in warm water. She was very careful to wash it according to the directions. Then she put it in the dryer with some other things. When she took it out, it was all wrinkled. Can you explain what might have happened?

2. Pete bought a pair of jeans at the discount store. They were labeled "sanforized." Would you expect them to shrink when he washes them?

3. Susie bought a battery for her car which came with an 18-month guarantee. After three months, she found that there was a dead cell in the battery. What steps should she take?

4. Jane bought a tape recording of the latest popular songs. When she got home, she found that the sound on the tape was very poor. How could she have avoided this problem?

5. Mary wants to buy a steak for a surprise birthday party for her mother. What can she do to assure that she will get a good steak?

6. John's family wants to buy a new TV set, but they don't know what to get. Where can they get information that will help them make a wise decision?

7. What are some of the advantages of the metric system for the consumer?

TO DO IN CLASS

Discussion

1. What is a bargain?
2. When should you return merchandise?
3. What features are important in buying a:
   a. Stereo?
   b. Sweater?
   c. Mouthwash?
4. What are some of the biggest problems you have in shopping?

5. Where can you get help and information to aid you in shopping?

6. Many people have complained that advertisements intrude too much, that TV commercials interrupt programs, big billboards clutter scenic highways, etc. How do you suggest that we keep advertising within reasonable limits?

7. What are some of the problems that consumers are likely to encounter during the conversion to the metric system of weights and measures?

Activities

1. Conduct a survey to find out what services are offered by the stores in your area: the hours they are open and least crowded; who may have a charge account; etc.

2. Collect labels, tags, warranties, guarantees, and seals. Describe what information they contain.

3. Role play the following situations: returning merchandise; getting information from a salesperson; a "hard sell" versus a "soft sell."

4. Buying a watch:

a. Bring to class watch advertisements which you think will be helpful in deciding which one to buy.
b. List the brands of watches owned by the members of the class. Are these the same ones that are in the ads brought to class?
c. Use whatever information you can obtain to decide on a make and model to fit a particular individual's needs.
d. Divide into groups to shop for the watch in *c.* Be sure to shop at the following: a large department store, a reputable retail dealer such as a jewelry store, and a discount store.

e. Discuss in class where it would be best to buy the watch and why.

5. Cut out at least five different sale ads for articles. Figure out how much you could save by buying each item on sale. You may need to price the items in a store or a large mail order catalog.

6. Consider this problem. Laura is trying to decide whether to join a book club. If she does, she will get four books free. Then during the next year she will have to buy four more books for about $9 each. Unless she notifies the company in advance each month not to send it, she will receive the monthly selection in the mail. What are the advantages and disadvantages of joining this club? If possible, get several book club brochures and compare prices. Check the cost of these books in stores. Are the books available in your local library? Are they books that you would reread or refer to after you have read them?

7. Find advertisements with appeals to health, beauty, and economy. Make a bulletin board of these indicating how the appeal is made.

8. Divide into teams. After each team selects a product—shaving cream, toothpaste, cologne, shampoo, deodorant, or other—go to a drugstore, supermarket, health and beauty department, or discount store to find out:

a. How many brands of this product are available?
b. How many sizes are available for each brand?
c. Which size and brand is the "best buy?"
d. What information is on the label? What other information would be useful? If possible, bring samples of these products to class.

Study the newspaper advertisements for these products for several weeks. Compare the prices.

Try different brands of these products. (Class members might loan some of these to their teams.) Report the results to the class.

Look in *Consumer Reports* and *Consumers Research Magazine* to see if any of the products have been evaluated by them. If so, you might compare your results.

9. Using a metric tape measure or metre stick, measure objects around school.

10. Collect food products that are presently giving the contents in metric units. Consider how these products might be packaged.more simply using even metric measures.

11. Calculate the heights and weights of class members in metric measures.

CHAPTER 5

Looking Your Best

Has there ever been a disagreement over clothing in your family? If your answer is yes, be assured that you are not alone. Clothing causes problems for many families in all walks of life. Often young people feel that they need to spend more on clothing than the family can afford. Also, parents and young people frequently disagree about what is appropriate dress. This situation, however, is nothing new. As long ago as 700 B.C. the prophet Isaiah was disturbed because some people longed for fine linen and veils, tinkling ankle bracelets, and nose jewels. Today the desired fashions may be different but the problem is the same.

HOW IMPORTANT IS FASHION?

Fashion is whatever is popular at the time. There are fashions in housing—see pre-Civil War mansions of the South, the gingerbready decorations of the Victorian period, and the low ranch house of today. There are fashions in food. Hamburgers only recently became popular in Europe; pizza was hardly known in the United States before World War II; and the popularity of yogurt and natural foods boomed in the seventies. New car models appear on the market each year. There are even current styles in bicycles. Above all, however, clothing fashions probably capture the most attention.

Who are the first to adopt fashion trends in clothing? It depends partly on the time. One hundred years ago girls put on bustles to mimic the style their mothers followed. Thirty years ago clothing fashions were started by the wealthy and later picked up by the less affluent. Today young people are often the most responsive to new fashions. Young women are more likely to adopt new skirt lengths before their mothers do. Young men try new hair lengths before older men. Young people are eager to try the new things they like, opening the way for others to follow. They are the ones who influence fashion now. Who do you think will set the fashion trends in the future?

With the help of the mass media a new fashion can sometimes sweep across the country very quickly. Often these fashions last only a short time, but others become part of the culture. For example, slacks have become part of the accepted way of dressing for women and girls. Can you name other clothing fashions that have been popular in the last few years? What is the latest clothing fashion among your friends? How long do you think it will last?

When you buy clothes, it is important to think about fashion. New styles are tempting. You will probably want some clothes that are fashionable, but will you be happy with a closet full of perfectly good clothes when styles change? If not, you will be wise to limit yourself when buying faddish clothing. Some careful shoppers buy fairly basic separates and then adapt to fashion with the latest in vests, belts, and other accessories. You can read newspapers and

Pendleton Woolen Mills

This outfit probably will not be outdated as quickly as some styles.

magazines to find out what is new and then try to decide what is fad and what will be around for a while.

PLANNING YOUR WARDROBE

It takes know-how to keep your clothes in super shape, especially when you have very little time and limited money. A good wardrobe has to be worked on regularly, replacing, repairing, and maintaining. Planning will help. Keep your overall

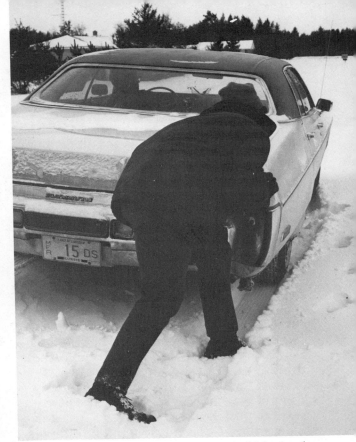

National Safety Council

Climate will influence your clothing needs.

clothing plans in mind when you shop. Try not to fall for something that looks great in the store but doesn't fit into your plans. In addition, think about your needs. This is an important part of planning.

What Do You Need?

You can save money and have a more useful and attractive wardrobe by planning around your activities. If you're a sports enthusiast, you'll probably need plenty of durable sportswear. Climate may also influence your needs. You don't have to buy a great deal. In fact, you are probably wise not to overbuy. Clothing isn't a good long-term investment. You may grow, styles change, and your activities and needs may change. It is much smarter to buy or make only what really fits your needs, as long as it looks good on you and feels comfortable. (There are "lemons" in clothes as well as cars. They are those things you don't enjoy wearing, which are permanently tucked away in your closet or drawer.)

To help you decide what clothes you need, start by trying on everything that you have now. Some people like to do this regularly every spring and fall. As you take inventory of your clothes closet, your clothes can be sorted into three groups: those that you wear and are in good shape; those that you wear but which need some repairs; those that you no longer wear. By asking yourself questions like these, sorting becomes easier: What do I enjoy wearing? What do I hate? Can I revive some things?

What will you do with clothes you haven't worn for a year or more? There are several possibilities. It may be that a garment simply doesn't match anything else you own. Perhaps a new pair of slacks would make an outfit if combined with a seemingly useless blue shirt. A new sweater might enable you to make use of a pair of brightly colored corduroy jeans that get little wear. Do you see how one wise purchase can expand your wardrobe?

LOOK AT YOUR NEEDS

Items	Have	Need	How Much Will I Need to Spend?
Shirts			
Slacks			
Sweaters			
Shoes			
Others			

Another alternative for those seldom-worn garments (and also for those that need repairs) is alteration. People today are very concerned about recycling goods. Can you do this with clothing? Why not? Your old slacks can be shortened or lengthened, or otherwise altered to fit the current style. You might not wear them at all the old way, but with a new look, they may become the most popular article in your wardrobe. You may be able to think of many imaginative ways to restore the clothes in your closet. What do you think of these? Children's clothes can be made from adult garments. An out-of-style skirt can be converted to shorts. Old hosiery can be used to stuff pillows. Dresses can be shortened by hemming or lengthened with a border of complementary fabric. Colorful patches can be placed over worn spots on jeans.

You may have some garments that are out of style and cannot be altered, but they are still in good condition. What can you do with them? Some people hate to part with these, thinking someday they will find a use for them. Since styles often do return if you wait long enough, sometimes people do use garments that they have saved for a number of years. This, however, presents problems of space for storage and preservation of the clothes over the years. In families with children, certain clothes that are no longer usable could be placed in a box or trunk and kept for dress-up occasions if space permits.

When all other possibilities have been exhausted, clothes that are no longer wanted can be thrown away. Before you add to the growing quantity of waste in our country, however, consider giving the clothing to others who might make use of it. The Salvation Army takes old clothes. Churches and other organizations in your community may do the same.

Your wardrobe is now reduced to those items which you wear and which are in good condition and those that need repairs or alterations of some kind. If at all possible, don't put off making the repairs. Small problems have a way of becoming larger.

Now you are ready to decide what new clothes you need. It may help you to make a chart like the one shown on page 106.

Be realistic when you think about your needs. It is so easy to confuse what you *want* with what you actually *need*. Do you really need more dress-up clothes or are most social events very casual? If you only ice skate once in a while, is it worth buying a special skating outfit that can't be used elsewhere? Chances are you could manage with something you already own.

Everyday things will probably be high on your list of needs. After all, these get the hardest use, and you are seen in them the most. Allow a little money for special occasions if you can. If the budget won't allow for both everyday garments and a special outfit, however, you will probably be happier if you buy the everyday outfits so you look nice more of the time.

Have you ever noticed how little luggage an airline attendant or traveling business-person carries? They have learned to dress smartly with very few clothes. You can too. Double-duty clothing helps. People who travel a lot and have to be well dressed know this trick. They choose clothes that will coordinate to make several outfits when combined different ways. One shirt or blouse can go with several slacks or skirts. A girl might get a print blouse that can be worn with either slacks or a long skirt. A boy might get a shirt that he can use for dress, school, or as a top with

USDA

In buying summer clothing, look for cottons.

Comfort in shoes depends on a good fit.

Institute of Life Insurance

swimming trunks. You may find that your list of needs is much shorter when you plan this way. A good wardrobe can be compact yet versatile. That's why it can be achieved on a student's budget.

How Much Should You Spend?

Most people are limited in how much they can spend for clothing. Money will go just so far. Talk with your parents and find out how much help they can give you with clothing purchases. If you have a job, you may be able to work out a plan where you help pay for some of your clothes yourself.

You can look attractive without spending a fortune. Some people spend money for clothes that are not becoming. Buying a few things that feel comfortable and look just right is more important than paying a high price or having an abundance of clothes.

Statistics tell us that most American families spend less than ten percent of their income on clothing and personal care. Women spend about one-third more than men. At the beginning of the century it was just the reverse. One reason for this changing trend is probably the exodus of women from the home and kitchen to outside jobs. (In 1890 only 18 out of every 100 adult American women were employed away from home. Today about 50 out of every 100 are.) Also, women are less likely to use the same clothing for work and leisure activities than men. (Is this fashion or personal taste?) A man could wear a jacket and slacks to the office and also out for the evening. Although many women can and do wear the same dress or slacks outfits for work and play, often they choose to change to something else.

Although figures tell us about broad trends in spending, they don't tell us much about individual people. Many people feel that the well-dressed look is very important. Others couldn't care less. How much your family spends on clothes will depend on how important the family feels clothes are. It is also influenced by income, where you live, clothing needs for the jobs of family members, social and recreational activities, and whether or not there are other pressing financial needs, such as medical care, or a long term goal like a new car, vacation, or college.

Today, many young people work part-time or on an irregular basis. Often much of their earnings is used for clothes. Some parents supplement regular clothing expenditures for young people with birthday and Christmas gifts.

YOUR WARDROBE BUDGET

In planning how to spend your clothing dollars, it helps to turn to the budget. If you can determine how much money you will have available for clothes throughout the year, you can go one step further and decide how that money should be spent. The guidelines that follow, of course, will not fit every situation. They will, however, give you ideas on how to budget your money so that you can have a complete wardrobe.

Have your foot measured every time you buy shoes.
Sears, Roebuck and Co.

Many people start their budgeting with the "must haves" like warm outerwear and shoes. Do you need a winter coat or jacket? Warm outer clothes are the most expensive part of your wardrobe. Build your plans around a versatile coat or jacket. In areas where winter is long and cold you will naturally need to spend more than if you live in a warm area such as Florida or Southern California.

Shoes are another big item. Skimping doesn't usually pay here. Shoes that are made well last noticeably longer.

Allow for maintenance—cleaning and repairing—if you will have to pay for this. Heels wear down and a stain on slacks may require a professional dry cleaner's efforts.

Once you have allowed for outerwear and shoes, use the rest of your money on the other things you need and want.

Case Study. Let's look at how Barbie Thomas planned her clothing budget. Barbie, a junior at Danesville High in Minnesota, had moved there in July from Arizona. Her father had been transferred. By the time the family was settled in their Minnesota home, it was August. School would start just after Labor Day in September, and Barbie was anxious to look her best. Eager to make new friends, she felt that the right clothes would help her put her best foot forward.

For the last year, Barbie's parents had been giving her $30 a month for clothing. This was supplemented with occasional earnings from babysitting jobs. A trip to the Youth Employment Service run by the community where the Thomas family now lived made Barbie feel confident that she could get babysitting jobs here too. Thus, she felt that she could allow herself $35 a month for clothing. A little money that she had saved early in the summer would help her get started.

Barbie knew she had to have a winter coat or jacket. In Arizona she hadn't needed a very warm one. Also, she would need a gym uniform at the new school, but she already had a pair of sneakers from last year that she could use.

BARBIE'S FALL CLOTHING EXPENDITURES

August		
3 pairs of panty hose @ $3.00 each— 1 red, 1 blue, 1 tan		$ 9.00
School shoes—dark blue		25.00
2 new short-sleeved tops to wear with slacks (She made them. One was a cotton madras from a long skirt that she didn't wear anymore. The other was made of a mod-print, polyester fabric that she bought.)		4.00
New medium-blue slacks		19.95
	Total	$57.95
September		
Gym uniform		$15.00
Gym socks		3.00
Bulky, white, wool, cardigan sweater		25.00
	Total	43.00
October		
Red ski jacket (on sale)		$24.95
	Total	$24.95

Fortunately, she hadn't changed size since last year and could use most of her old school clothes, several pants and tops, and a few skirts.

How Barbie planned her expenditures for the first three months is shown in the chart on page 109.

Barbie tried to plan around what she had. Most of her skirts and slacks would go with a red ski jacket and a bulky white sweater and blue shoes.

She really felt that she needed a couple of turtleneck shirts for cool days and a new purse, but she couldn't manage these until at least November.

Also, she wanted a medium-weight navy blue pullover sweater to wear under her ski jacket. There were other clothing items she would like to buy—winter boots to wear without shoes, a new slacks suit, a long skirt, and a new raincoat. These purchases, however, would have to wait until she could afford them.

SELECTING CLOTHING

Naturally, you want to look your best. Therefore you will want to be sure that everything you make or buy is becoming.

What are your best features?

Replacement Lens, Inc.

Some lines carry your eyes upward. These can make you look taller or thinner.

See how it works with clothes.

First, you have to be very objective about your figure or build. What are your best features? What would you rather cover up? Study yourself carefully in a long mirror.

The Style for You

Clothes can help you look taller, shorter, broader, or thinner if you know how to choose the right shapes, lines, colors, and fabrics.

The outside lines, or silhouette, of a garment can reveal or hide much of the stature underneath. A very trim, narrow silhouette makes you look smaller. A full, loose one can add to size.

Some outlines of clothing draw attention to particular areas. Choose your best feature and accent that area to draw attention away from those you'd rather hide. Are your hips too large? Then choose a silhouette that doesn't draw attention to them.

If you want to look taller and thinner, choose styles that have vertical lines. To look shorter and heavier choose styles with horizontal lines. Horizontal lines worn low have the greatest shortening effect.

Stripes can be used to make you look taller and thinner or shorter and fuller, depending on the direction and width.

Horizontal lines and contrasting colors can make you look shorter and fuller.

Printed fabrics and textured materials add to the appearance of fullness.

Diagonal lines are versatile. Depending on where they are placed, they can make you look thinner or fuller.

The placement of lines is important. Consider the effect of the important lines in an outfit.

Two dresses with vertical lines can give very different effects. A narrow front panel can give a slimming look, whereas a wide one causes the eye to move from side to side, which makes the person look bigger.

Strong patterns can have the same effect as the lines of the outfit in giving the appearance of length or width. A jacket with vertical stripes will make you look taller than one with crosswise stripes.

Costume details can change the effect because of the way they break up space. For example, big buttons, set far apart, horizontally, tend to carry the eye across.

You can use space to play tricks. The way in which an outfit is divided into areas can add or subtract from your apparent size.

Small buttons, set close together in a column act like vertical stripes and carry the eye up for a slimmer look.

Is the Color Becoming?

There is an old joke about the very fat lady who tried on dress after dress but couldn't find one in a color that she thought flattering. Finally, the exasperated saleslady said, "Madam, the Good Lord clothed the elephant in gray."

Color, like line, can make you look larger or smaller. Generally, bright, warm colors—red, yellow, orange—will make you look larger. Cool, dark ones—navy blue, dark green, gray, and black—have the opposite effect.

Light values increase size; dark ones tend to decrease it. A light blue will make you look bigger than a dark blue.

A shiny color will make you look larger too, whereas a dull one is slimming. A satin blouse will make you look fuller than one in a dull finish.

This doesn't mean that everyone who wants to look thinner should only wear dull, dark colors. That would be very uninteresting. However, it does mean that those who have flaws in figure or build need to consider carefully how much color to use and where. A simple, dark outfit with a colorful scarf or tie helps draw the eye up and gives a longer look. A row of bright colorful buttons would have the same effect. Stand in front of a long mirror and experiment. Go into a clothing department and try on clothes with color used in various ways to see what is flattering for you.

Does It Fit?

The most expensive garment won't be becoming if it doesn't fit. Good fit is very important to your comfort and enjoyment

Everyday clothing should be versatile and sturdy enough for all kinds of wear.

of clothing. Look at the things you own, but never wear. Some probably don't fit well, so you don't like to wear them.

What clothing sizes do you take? Measure yourself carefully in your underclothes and compare your measurements with a chart of sizes, such as is found in most mail-order catalogs.

When Is Quality Important?

Obviously, better-made clothes cost more money, but quality does not go up proportionally with price. A dress or suit that costs $100 probably has better fabric and workmanship than one that costs $30. However, it may not be more than three times better. You may be paying partly for a name brand, newness of style, and the snob appeal of the label.

Poorly made clothes quickly become unwearable. They droop, shrink, discolor, split apart at the seams, and the buttonholes pull out. In brief, they soon look terrible. Do you want one good blouse, slacks, or jacket or two cheaper ones? The answer probably depends on how you intend to use the garment. A girl probably won't give a long dress hard use. A boy may need a suit for only a few occasions. Perhaps you are growing quickly and there is no one in the family to inherit your clothes. Then there's no reason to spend extra for something that will last and last.

On the other hand, if you expect to wear the garment often, buying good quality may pay off.

Fibers, Fabrics, and Finishes

Nowadays most people seem to want to spend as little time and money on clothing upkeep as possible. Clothing which can be washed and worn has boomed in popularity, and spot-repellent fabrics are in great demand.

The care required for a garment depends on the kind of fiber in the material, how it is woven, what sort of finish is applied to the fabric, and how it is made. To learn how to care for an item be sure to read the label that is attached.

The charts on pages 115–117 tell about the use and care of the most commonly used fibers.

Knit fabrics have become popular because they are so easy to care for. More and

Ship 'N Shore

What to look for when you buy a shirt:

1. Collars should be evenly cut so that both sides match, and sewn smoothly without any puckers.

2. Be sure all the buttons are of fine quality, stitched on securely.

3. The tag should tell you that the shirt won't shrink, colors won't fade.

4. All seams should be fully cut and closely stitched, so they won't "pop."

5. Tails should be tapered evenly and stitched smoothly, with a neatly turned-up hem.

6. All extra details—such as plackets, pleats or tucking—should be sewn smoothly and evenly.

7. Buttonholes must be firmly stitched, in order to avoid fraying.

8. Sleeves must be fully cut and set in smoothly to assure good fit. See if cuffs are even all around and sewn neatly.

9. For crisp, lasting "body," features like the collar, neckband, placket and cuffs should be lined with an inner-facing that's soft and pliable for comfort, and shrink-proof to stay smooth and flat after laundering.

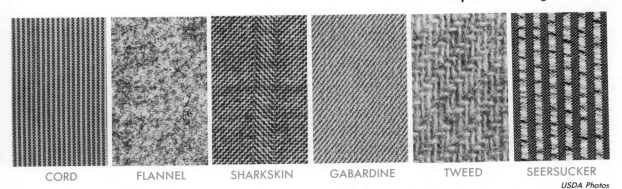

CORD   FLANNEL   SHARKSKIN   GABARDINE   TWEED   SEERSUCKER

USDA Photos

Here are some common fabrics. What garments might you expect to find made from these fabrics?

USE AND CARE OF NATURAL FIBERS

Fiber	Use	Care
Cotton	A very versatile fiber used for heavy-duty clothing like denim as well as sheer blouses. Can be made with a pile like corduroy and combined with other fibers for lightweight wash and wear garments such as shirts & dresses.	Most cotton fabrics can be machine washed and dried. A few, like velveteen, need more gentle care.
Wool	Largely used for warm clothing—sweaters, slacks, shirts, and outer wear. The label *wool* means that the garment is made of all new wool fibers. *Reprocessed* refers to wool fabric that has been made from another wool article that was never used. Felt, for example, may be made from reused or reprocessed fibers. *Reused* wool is a fabric made from used articles.	Wool generally needs careful treatment to avoid shrinkage—hand washing or dry cleaning. However, there are some new ways of treating wool so that wool garments can be machine washed **and dryed**.
Linen	A strong, yet brittle, fabric which is generally quite expensive. Some of the most common uses are for tablecloths and handkerchiefs. Some dresses are still made of linen or a mixture of linen and another fiber.	Linen can usually be washed in hot water and dried in a machine. However, linen dresses are not always pre-shrunk and usually need more gentle care.
Silk	A very expensive fiber generally used for scarves and ties. However, some silk is used for dresses and shirts.	Most silk articles need dry cleaning. A few, particularly solid color items such as shirts or stockings, are hand washable.

USE AND CARE OF MANUFACTURED FIBERS

REGENERATED FIBERS: Made from natural materials, such as wood pulp or cotton linters.		
Fiber	**Use**	**Care**
Rayon (Made from cellulose materials)	Can be made to look like the natural fibers and is often used in combination with natural or other man-made fibers. May be used in a sheer fabric, as a pile (like corduroy), or blended with other fabrics.	Strong unless wet; generally, rayon can be machine washed in a short cycle and machine dried at moderate temperatures. Some fabrics, such as a sheer blouse may require hand washing. Velveteen, taffetas, and some other decorative fabrics may need dry cleaning.
Triacetate and Acetate (like rayon, made from cellulose materials, but the manufacturing process turns out a fiber that is chemically different from rayon.)	Stronger than rayon, can withstand higher temperatures, and is less likely to stretch. Widely used in knit garments.	Triacetate garments can be machine washed and dried at moderate temperatures. Acetate is more fragile and usually needs hand washing. Some articles require dry cleaning.

SYNTHETIC FIBERS: Made from chemicals.		
Fiber	**Use**	**Care**
Nylon (General name for a whole group of fibers)	Used for lingerie and hosiery as well as light weight, windproof garments such as shells and ski jackets. Also used for swimwear because it dries quickly.	Generally needs very little special care unless it is used in a delicate item such as stockings or pantyhose. Most nylon articles can be machine washed and dried at cool temperatures.
Acrylics (Orlon, Acrilon, and Creslan are some acrylic fibers.)	Used for sweaters and carpets. A few are used in fabrics that resemble silk.	Fabrics made of acrylics are usually soft in feel. Many can be washed in a short cycle and machine dried at a cool temperature.

USE AND CARE OF MANUFACTURED FIBERS (Continued)

SYNTHETIC FIBERS: Made from chemicals.

Fiber	Use	Care
Modacylics (Verel and Dynel are modacylic fibers.)	Similar to acrylic fibers but particularly useful in long-pile garments like coats and linings. Most wigs are made of Dynel.	Very sensitive to heat. Some can be machine washed, such as pile coats, but most need hand washing.
Olefin (Herculon and Marvess are olefin fibers.)	Used in hosiery and carpeting as well as other items.	Absorb no water, and stains can often be wiped off.
Spandex (Includes Lycra, Vyrene, Spandelle, and other fibers)	Have an unusual amount of stretch; lighter than rubber. Used for girdles, swimsuits and as the elastic on many garments. Spandex is blended with other fibers to make stretch fabrics.	Many Spandex items can be machine washed and dried at moderate temperatures. If they are blended with wool, as in stretch ski pants, they may need hand washing or dry cleaning.

3M Co.

Spills do not penetrate fabrics with a stain-resistant finish.

more are machine washable and dryable. Also, they take little or no ironing. If you want or need to dry clean them, coin-operated machines work well, and cost less than professional dry cleaning.

Many fabric finishes add to the ease of caring for clothes. Stain-resistant finishes reduce stains and often make it easier to remove those that do occur. Many garments have finishes that reduce wrinkling.

A flame-resistant finish can be added to fabrics. This makes the fabric burn much more slowly to improve safety. Children's nightclothes are no longer treated with flame-resistant finishes because of possible health problems.

Read the Label

Clothing and fabrics for home sewing must be labeled to tell two things: (1) what the fabric is made of and (2) how it is to be laundered or dry cleaned.

Sometimes this information is combined on one label which is permanently fastened to the garment. In others, the label that tells about the fabric may be fastened on with a removable label. However, the permanent care label must be attached for the reasonable life of the garment. The permanent care label must clearly explain laundering or dry cleaning instructions. The chart on pages 120–121 will help you understand the terms used on care labels.

CARING FOR YOUR WARDROBE

After you buy clothes, time and money are needed to keep them in good condition. Is it worth paying extra for a shirt that needs no ironing? Will a new ski jacket have to be cleaned? Would dark colored shoes be less bother? You have to decide what you are willing to do in the way of upkeep—how much time, money, and energy you are willing to spend.

Keep in mind that if you can care for your clothes at home, they will probably

New garments and fabrics sold by the yard must have fiber content and care labels. On clothing, the care label must be permanently attached. The seller of yard goods must give you a label.

Blouses, Dresses, Jackets, Robes, Knit Tops, Loungewear, Vests, Nightgowns, Undershirts, Slips, Shirts, Sweaters.

Coats, Jackets

The label should be affixed to righthand front facing below waistline or at the neckline.

Reprinted by permission of Jerome Schapiro and Drycleaning World, May, 1972

Care labels are generally placed as shown here.

Pants, Skirts, Pajamas, Shorts, Tights, Half Slips.

The label should be affixed at center back waistline so that it will be permanent, except that for pants having a back seam, the label should be affixed at the side or upper surface of the back pocket.

Federal Trade Commission

Compare care labels. Which item will be easier and less costly to care for?

CONSUMER CARE GUIDE FOR APPAREL

	WHEN LABEL READS:	IT MEANS:
MACHINE WASHABLE	**Machine wash**	Wash, bleach, dry, and press by any customary method including commercial laundering and dry cleaning.
	Home launder only	Same as above but do not use commercial laundering.
	No chlorine bleach	Do not use chlorine bleach. Oxygen bleach may be used.
	No bleach	Do not use any type of bleach.
	Cold wash Cold rinse	Use cold water from tap or cold washing machine setting.
	Warm wash Warm rinse	Use warm water or warm washing machine setting.
	Hot wash	Use hot water or hot washing machine setting.
	No spin	Remove wash load before final machine spin cycle.
	Delicate cycle Gentle cycle	Use appropriate machine setting; otherwise wash by hand.
	Durable press cycle Permanent press cycle	Use appropriate machine setting; otherwise use warm wash, cold rinse, and short spin cycle.
	Wash separately	Wash alone or with like colors.

CONSUMER CARE GUIDE FOR APPAREL
(Continued)

	WHEN LABEL READS:	IT MEANS:
NON-MACHINE WASHING	Hand wash	Launder only by hand in luke warm (hand comfortable) water. May be bleached. May be dry-cleaned.
	Hand wash only	Same as above, but **do not** dry-clean.
	Hand wash separately	Hand wash alone or with like colors.
	No bleach	Do not use bleach.
	Damp wipe	Surface clean with damp cloth or sponge.
HOME DRYING	Tumble dry	Dry in tumble dryer at specified setting—high, medium, low, or no heat.
	Tumble dry Remove promptly	Same as above, but in absence of cool-down cycle remove at once when tumbling stops.
	Drip dry	Hang wet and allow to dry with hand shaping only.
	Line dry	Hang damp and allow to dry.
	No wring No twist	Hang dry, drip dry, or dry flat only. Handle to prevent wrinkles and distortion.
	Dry flat	Lay garment on flat surface.
	Block to dry	Maintain original size and shape while drying.
IRONING OR PRESSING	Cool iron	Set iron at lowest setting.
	Warm iron	Set iron at medium setting.
	Hot iron	Set iron at hot setting.
	Do not iron	Do not iron or press with heat.
	Steam iron	Iron or press with steam.
	Iron damp	Dampen garment before ironing.
MISCELLANEOUS	Dry-clean only	Garment should be dry-cleaned only, including self-service.
	Professionally dry-clean only	**Do not** use self-service dry cleaning.
	No dry-clean	Use recommended care instructions. No dry cleaning materials to be used.

Produced by the Consumer Affairs Committee, American Apparel Manufacturers Association, and based on the Voluntary Guide of the Textile Industry Advisory Committee for Consumer Interests

last longer. Usually, buttons break and zippers melt more often at a commercial laundry or dry cleaner.

One way to stretch your clothing budget is to take care of your clothes so they will last longer. A winter jacket that costs $48 and lasts for three years has an annual cost of $16 per year. On the other hand, if it only lasts two years, it costs $24 a year. Are you getting maximum use out of the clothes you buy? The chart shown on this page will help you decide.

If your clothes are not lasting the way they should, perhaps the problem is improper care. The suggestions that follow should help you stretch the life of your clothes:

• *Suit the clothes to your activity.* Change to old clothes for rough use. Cover up with an old shirt or apron for messy activities like painting.

Clothes last longer and look better if given proper care.

U.S. Department of Labor

• *Protect your clothes from the weather.* Wear a raincoat and boots in wet weather. Keep your shoes polished so a puddle or sudden rainstorm won't ruin them. Dry out wet clothing carefully, away from radiators.

• *Rotate your clothes.* Rest and air everything between wearings. Studies have shown that fabrics last longer if allowed to rest between use. Don't wear the same thing day after day.

• *Make small repairs promptly.* Catch the small rip before the whole pocket tears. Sew the loose button before you lose it and need a whole new set.

• *Wash and clean clothes according to the directions on the label.* You can't wash a wool sweater the same way you wash dirty socks and expect it to look nice. Keep your clothes clean; they will last longer and look better.

• *Store your clothes neatly.* They will look better, and you will be able to find them when you want to wear them.

• *Store out-of-season clothing carefully.* Protect winter woolens against moths by putting them away clean. Many neighborhoods now have self-service cleaning machines at the laundromat or in dry cleaning stores. This is an inexpensive way to clean garments. Most clothes cleaned this way do not need pressing if you take

HOW LONG SHOULD IT LAST?

	Number of Years
Coats and jackets	2–4
Slacks and skirts	2
Shirts	2
Sweaters	3
Shoes	1–2

National Institute of Drycleaning

them out of the machine promptly when it stops. Store summer clothes in a dry place or airtight packages to avoid mildew. If you have enough room, you can just leave clothes in the closet, but be sure they are clean at the end of each season.

PACKING A SUITCASE

Experienced travelers know that it is an art to pack a suitcase correctly. Whether you are spending the weekend with a friend or going to college, you need to know how to pack a suitcase so that your clothes are ready to wear as soon as you arrive at your destination. It is simple if you plan carefully and follow these guidelines.

Travel light. Make it a rule never to take more luggage than you can carry yourself. There are times when you will have to do just that. This means you can't take everything you might like to take, but you might be amazed at how much you can get into one suitcase if you pack carefully.

Plan your travel wardrobe. A minimum number of clothes will serve several purposes. One sweater might be worn with a casual slacks outfit, party clothes, and even over a tennis outfit. Don't take things you expect to wear very little. Consider the season and your activities. Take clothes that travel well—knits, wash-and-wear clothes, and dark colors and prints.

Pack with care. It takes a little practice but you can learn to pack like a pro.

Pack the things that you will need first on top. If you are going to arrive late at night, it's handy to have your nightclothes on top.

Pack your suitcase full enough so that clothes won't slide around. Corners and spaces should be filled. Underwear, socks, and other small articles can be tucked into spaces and corners. Don't stuff the bag so much that the hinges and locks are strained. (If you have to sit on the suitcase to close it, it might break while you are traveling.)

Put heavy items at the bottom near the hinges so that when you stand the bag up they will rest on the hinges. Otherwise, they might crush lighter weight items, causing them to wrinkle.

Use a plastic bag or waterproof kit for anything that might break or spill. Plastic bags are also useful for wrapping shoes and boots which might soil other clothes and for wet bathing suits.

Many people take a small tote bag for things they might want en route—a sweater, raincoat, book, or overnight things. This way they avoid repacking the whole suitcase if they stop someplace for just one night.

In packing the smaller items put your shoes in plastic bags, the toe of one touching the heel of the other, and place at the hinged side of the case. Other heavy belongings, such as a toilet kit, can be placed at the hinged side also. Fill the center with rolled underwear, socks, handkerchiefs, and other items, keeping them level with the shoes. Lay belts flat against the sides of the suitcase. Next fold the shirts and place with the collars up, overlapping them to each collar. Place ties on top of the shirts or on the tie bar. Pack robe and pajamas last.

GROOMING: THE FINISHING TOUCH

People usually get their first impression of you by your appearance—hair, face, figure or build, and clothes. If they are put off by that first look, they may make no effort to know you better. Who do you think is more likely to get the better job or be chosen for a leadership position at

PACK LIKE AN EXPERT

Remove protective curtain from case and spring bars from rack. Place on bar resting on sides of case.

Replace second bar in lower holds of rack. Long dresses may be placed over this second bar at waistline. (Do not use a hanger.)

Remove hanger from fixture. Place garment on hanger. Replace hanger on fixture. Fold sleeves neatly to center.

Grasp spring bar resting on sides of case and, with upward lifting motion, raise bar with garment draped over it to the top of the rack and insert in upper holes of rack. Replace protective curtain.

PACK LIKE
AN EXPERT

American Tourister Luggage

Unlatch and fold back protective curtain. Remove folding rack and hangers. Place trousers in case with legs extending beyond sides, alternating each pair. Smooth out.

American Tourister Luggage

Replace folding rack on center post, pressing down firmly against coats. Fold trouser legs back over folding rack and eliminate any wrinkles.

Arrange coats and jackets on hangers and attach to hanger post, permitting lower portions of coats to extend beyond edge of case. Fold coat fronts over each other so that the sides of the coats fall in a straight line. Place sleeves neatly over coat fronts.

American Tourister Luggage

Fold sleeves and coats individually over trousers. Smooth out. Replace and latch protective curtain. Pack remainder of case in normal manner with heaviest objects at hinged base and lightest ones toward the top.

American Tourister Luggage

U.S. Department of Labor

Good grooming enhances your appearance.

Du Pont

What makes this fellow appear well groomed?

school—the brilliant, but sloppy, person or the one who presents a pleasant appearance? Even in this day of more informal clothes there is a vast difference between a casual appearance and a messy one.

Your Hair

Your hair can be a great asset to your appearance if it is well cared for. Whatever style you choose—casual, long, or short, start with a good haircut. Most people are wise to have a good hairdresser or barber cut their hair. If you are skillful at working with your hair, you can do some trimming between regular cuttings, but get a good basic cut.

To keep your hair at the same length, you will need to have it cut at least every two months. Six weeks is better. Short hairdos may need attention every three to four weeks.

In choosing a style consider your personality, the type of hair you have, the shape of your face, your features, your size, and the amount of upkeep involved. Some hair just doesn't look right in certain styles. Thin, limp hair may appear skimpy if it is long and straight. It will probably blend nicely into a short- or medium-length smooth style. On the other hand, you can't get a smooth, sleek look with coarse or curly hair unless you are willing to straighten it or blow-dry it every day.

Hair on your forehead, such as bangs or waves, can shorten a long face and help round out an angular one. Fullness on the side can add or detract from the fullness of your face, depending on where it is placed. If you have an angular nose or a receding chin, choose a style that draws attention away from these features. If you are a large person or have large features, a very short, close-cropped hair style may look out of proportion. Consider your hair style as part of your total look, in proportion to the rest of you.

If you choose a style that needs setting, do this often enough to keep it in shape.

You can minimize work by choosing a style that takes less upkeep.

Your Face

People tend to worry about their faces. Are my freckles too obvious? (Actually, other people usually think freckles are attractive.) Is my nose too large? Will everyone notice this skin blemish?

What makes someone good looking? Look around at the people you know. What really makes some of them attractive is more than just their physical features. Chances are we react more to their expressions, their ready smiles, and the way they listen with interest to what others are saying. If you look carefully, you will probably discover that often their features aren't perfect.

Even though it is not good to worry about facial features, we still want to make the best of what we have. Proper facial care begins with the skin. Good health habits will do more for your skin than a fortune in creams and cosmetics. The right foods, regular exercise, adequate rest, and cleanliness can help your skin glow. When you feel well, your appearance is usually at its best. (Those people with serious skin problems need the help of a doctor. The cost of a visit to the doctor is usually a better investment than drug store creams.)

Cosmetics and Grooming Aids

Cosmetics and grooming aids are big business. You can spend a great deal of money on these products. Often it is difficult to distinguish between needs and wants. Here are a few suggestions to guide you.

Start with cleanliness. Remember that perfume was originally used to hide body odors in a period when people had only the most primitive washing facilities.

U.S. Department of Labor

A relatively simple hair style is preferred by some. Many people are not happy with an elaborate style that requires much care.

Today it is possible to bathe daily, brush your teeth regularly, and wash your hair often enough to keep it clean and shiny. Deodorants, mouth washes, and colognes or perfumes may enhance your attractiveness to others but are not needed as a cover-up if you are clean and fresh.

Use a minimum amount of cosmetics and grooming aids—just enough to make you look your best. Don't be tempted by things that are widely advertised or promoted by a movie star. Remember that entertainers have to look good under different conditions. A movie star's face may require layers of cosmetics to hide every minor blemish or wrinkle because it will be magnified in a screen blow-up or photograph. Try looking at yourself in a magnifying glass. This is how TV performers and movie stars are often seen. However, you will be seen under natural light without magnification, and minor imperfections won't be noticeable.

Often young people are big purchasers of cosmetics and grooming aids because they want to experiment—to see what is most becoming. Try to do your experimenting in low-cost ways. Some cosmetic departments, particularly in large department stores, have a place where you can try various colors and brands. This gives you an opportunity to experiment with different grooming aids. Look in chain stores, discount stores, and cut-rate drug stores for cosmetics and grooming aids. You can probably find some of the expensive brands at lower prices. Also, large chain stores often have cosmetics packaged under their own label. Frequently, the private label brands are very similar to the better-known brands.

FOR REVIEW

Points to Remember

- Fashion is whatever is popular at the time.
- A good wardrobe takes planning and effort as well as money.
- Buy only what you need. Clothing is not a good long-term investment.
- Owning a few things that feel comfortable and look just right is more important than having an abundance of clothes.
- People who travel a lot on business have learned how to be well dressed with very few clothes.
- Most American families spend under ten percent of their income on clothing.
- The color and line of a garment can make you look larger or smaller.
- If you expect to wear an article often, it pays to buy good quality.
- Easy-care clothing is in great demand today.
- It requires time, effort, and money to care for clothing.

- Permanent care labels must be attached to all clothing and to fabrics for home sewing.
- One way to stretch your clothing budget is to take care of your clothes so that they last longer.
- Careful packing helps keep your clothing in good condition when you travel.
- Good grooming is very important if you want to look your best.

Terms to Know

diagonal lines	quality
fabric	reprocessed wool
fad	silhouette
fashion	style
fiber	synthetic fibers
finish	trends
harmony	vertical lines
horizontal lines	

PROBLEM SOLVING:
CHECK YOUR UNDERSTANDING

1. What are some of the things a careful shopper can do before starting off on a shopping trip?

2. How might your clothing needs differ from your friend's?

3. What are some of the ways that you could save in buying cosmetics and beauty aids?

4. When is it wise to buy clothing at the end of a season?

5. What are some of the ways in which you can use the lines of clothing to enhance your figure or build?

6. Separate into wants and needs the clothes that you hope to get for the coming season?

7. When should you spend more for quality? When would quality be less important?

TO DO IN CLASS

Discussion

1. What is the most satisfactory clothing purchase you have made recently? Why was this a happy choice?

2. What clothing misfits do you own? How and where did you get them?

3. What effect do fashion changes have on the economy?

4. Some people have compared the consumer to a professional purchasing agent. In what ways are they similar? In what ways are they different?

5. Why is teenage clothing so often a subject of family controversy?

6. Consider the psychological effect of clothing. How do we express ourselves in clothing? What do we communicate through clothing? Describe ways in which clothing is used to make adjustments from one role to another. Have you ever formed an initial opinion of another person by his or her appearance?

7. Assume that a family of four has $1,100 a year to spend on clothing. Dad is a salesman; mother works in an office; Bob is 15; and Susie is 13. How could they allocate this money fairly?

8. In what ways might the clothing needs of older people differ from yours or your parents?

Activities

1. What fashions will last? What clothing will be in style for more than one season? Collect advertisements from newspapers and magazines to illustrate your views. Make a bulletin board of your predictions.

2. How much does it cost to clean or launder these garments at different places in your community: a warm jacket, slacks, sport coat, wool sweater, suit, raincoat, dress? Consider home laundering and coin-operated dry cleaning among the places. How much will it cost to keep these garments clean over the expected time they will last? Bring clothes from home to illustrate costs.

3. Develop a skit on each of the following situations:
   a. two friends shopping for clothing;
   b. a mother and daughter shopping for clothing;
   c. a young man and his family discussing a clothing purchase.

4. Invite the buyer from a clothing store or a clothing department in a large store to talk about how he or she decides what to buy.

5. Divide into teams to shop for specific items: a new winter coat, a younger sister's snowsuit, socks, or any article for a family member. If possible, try to bring the final selection to class. Prepare a report that explains what considerations were involved in making the purchase.

6. Have a white elephant swap of clothing and accessories that class members are willing to discard. Give each person one or more credit units on slips of paper for each item contributed. Have a committee price the items—a certain number of credit units for each item. Then select an auctioneer and take bids. People may bid with their credit slips. (Any leftovers could be given to a charitable organization.) It will be interesting to note how one person's white elephant can be of use to someone else. After the auction, have the buyers tell how they plan to use the articles.

7. Invite a social worker to class to talk about the clothing problems of low-income families.

CHAPTER 6

Getting Around

THE AUTOMOBILE AND MASS TRANSIT

A recent article related the following exchange:

"Gosh!" a teenage girl said, "They expect to build more cars this year. Where are they going to put them?"

"Well," said her father, "at least half of them will be in front of me going to the office!"

Transportation in urban areas has become a national headache. Cars bog down in rush-hour jams; the air is polluted by millions of exhaust systems; and getting around is often an ordeal.

As one writer pointed out, "A smooth ride to the moon was possible when a smooth ride to work often was not."

Proposals for improvement abound, and yet most of our major cities are still bottled up with cars. There is little question that new forms of mass transit are needed in densely populated areas.

Mass transit uses less space than the automobile. According to one source, an automobile which travels at 20 mph generally uses 6 to 45 times the land space per person that a transit bus uses. Moreover, compared to a rail car, automobiles consume 10 to 90 times more land space per person.

However, our present mass transit system often doesn't solve the problem of getting from less densely populated areas, such as suburban homes, to locations like bus stops, railroad terminals, and shopping centers. Cars do. Many people feel that it is more convenient to drive, even if public transportation is available for part of a trip.

Cost is another factor. Public transit facilities have raised their rates rapidly to meet growing expenses. People who now own a car may feel that driving doesn't add much expense. Others now car pool.

Cars not only present problems of using up space and polluting the atmosphere, scarce resources are used to make them and keep them going. To conserve oil it has been proposed by some that only vehicles with four-cylinder engines be built. Other types of engines might also be used more widely. The electric engine, for example, does not need gasoline and pollutes the atmosphere far less than the gasoline engine.

Mobility has become an integral part of our social structure, but imaginative solutions to the problems are needed to make it possible for people to get around in a way that is healthful, comfortable, and efficient.

YOUR OWN CAR

Wheels! Wheels! Wheels! Who wants mobility? Almost everyone it seems—from the toddler riding a tricycle to people old enough to sit happily behind the wheel of a car.

Mobility has become part of our way of life. Men and women commute to jobs at considerable distances from their homes. Young people often go many miles to school, even when they live at home. As our sprawling suburbs continue to grow, the need to have a way of getting around becomes even more critical.

Except for some central cities, public transportation hasn't kept pace with community needs. Maybe a school bus arrives every morning or afternoon, but what do you do if you stay for baseball or choir practice? Suppose you need to go to the shopping center for new shoes. How do you get there? Often, the answer is by car. To many people a car, like a television set, is considered a necessity.

You probably share with others a desire for better mobility. Young people are often willing to work hard to get a car. Many young men and women want the independence and mobility that a car can give. Perhaps you look forward to having a car when you get your first regular job.

BUYING A CAR

In 1916 a Model T Ford cost $360. Today $360 is not enough to buy a fender for some cars. Cars are expensive, even used ones.

Because a car is a big investment, most people want to get the best automobile possible for their money. How do you tell a bargain from a lemon? Enticing ads with low prices suggest that you can buy a lot for very little. Overwhelmed and confused, many people buy hastily with the help of a persuasive sales person. The results can be disastrous. The car may cost too much. It might not be right for their needs. Furthermore, it may need constant repairs.

Many pitfalls can be avoided with careful planning. Let's look at this step-by-step guide to car buying that can save you time and money.

Start Your Shopping at Home

Decide how much you can afford to spend. If you are financing the car, how much can you manage to spend for the down payment and for monthly payments? Be realistic. When you are buying a used car, figure that you may need at least $150 for unexpected repairs.

Figure out what you can buy for the money you have. There are a number of places to get help. Two paperback books are available on newsstands. The *NADA Used Car Guide* is published monthly and gives used car prices. *Your Price Authority Blue Book* lists wholesale prices for all makes and accessories of new cars.

New cars are expensive. Buying them on credit may take a large percentage of your monthly income. You may want to buy a good used car instead.

U. S. Department of Labor

WHAT ARE THE ADVANTAGES, DISADVANTAGES, AND SEATING ACCOMMODATIONS OF THE SIZES? GENERALLY:

Size	Advantages	Disadvantages	Seats
Subcompact	Lowest-cost available in U.S. Extremely easy to handle, park, garage. Excellent fuel mileage.* Low operating, maintenance costs. Uncomplicated engines, usually 4-cylinder. Good second, or son-and-daughter car.	Slightly stiffer ride, usually because of short wheelbase and light weight. Limited space for passengers, cargo. Luxury interiors and some optional equipment not available on all models.	Two front, somewhat crowded. Two rear, crowded.
Compact	Low initial cost. Low operating, maintenance cost. Good fuel mileage.* Easy to handle, park, garage. Fair cross-country car. Excellent for commuting. Good size for family of two adults, two small children.	Less-smooth ride than next sizes up. Less comfortable than larger cars for frequent long trips. Passenger and cargo space somewhat limited. Instruments, option choices somewhat limited.	Two to three, front. Two, rear.
Intermediate	Good room and comfort at low cost. Not as bulky as full-size cars. Easy to handle in traffic, to park, to garage. Relatively low-cost operation and maintenance. Well balanced for long-trip road car; gives good ride. Adequate passenger and cargo space. Good choice of engines, options, etc. Fairly good on fuel mileage.*	Not as spacious for big families or those with lots of luggage. Not as well suited for heavy loads or heavy-duty trailer towing. May need V-8 engine for hill-country operation.	For normal trips Three, front. Three, rear. For long trips: Two, front. Two, rear (or three children).
Full size	Most stability and riding comfort. Widest choice of options and equipment. Best long-trip car. Hauls heavy loads. Tows trailers easiest. Excellent for bigger families. Provides most space for passengers, cargo.	Costs more to buy, operate, maintain. Lower fuel mileage.* A bigger size to handle, park, garage. More complicated and heavier.	Three, front (bench seats). Three, rear in comfort.

Car Buying Made Easier© (Dearborn, Michigan: Ford Motor Co.)

*It's not surprising that larger cars consume more gasoline than smaller cars. However, the size and weight of a car are not the only factors that affect fuel economy. Other factors that influence the number of miles you will travel on a gallon of gasoline include the size of engine you select, as well as the type of transmission, tires, rear axle ratio and optional equipment you buy. Also, your own driving skills, terrain and weather can affect gas mileage. Moderation in acceleration, driving speed, quick stops and passing can significantly improve the efficiency of your engine's performance. It is equally important to provide appropriate maintenance for your car, as specified in the Owner's Manual. The result of all these factors is that it is virtually impossible to provide representative miles-per-gallon numbers for the various car sizes.

Station wagons are usually available in most of the sizes above. Small specialty/sports cars, economy-type buses and vans, and specialty light trucks are not specifically classified in the four size categories. Each is built to its own specialized or market-designated size for its particular purpose.

Consider your needs. Will you use the car largely for local driving or will you be using it for long trips? Generally, the older the car, the more likely it is to need frequent repairs. A clunker that barely runs may be fine if you only go a few miles a day, but if you are commuting a long distance to school or work, you need something more reliable.

The best car for you is very much a matter of personal choice. A used luxury car often has been maintained better by its original owner than a low-priced one. However, it will cost more to operate and be much more expensive to repair if the need arises.

A middle-aged used car can give relatively low-cost transportation. Of course, the car has to be chosen carefully, but in most cases the necessary repairs are likely to cost less than the yearly depreciation on a new car or one-year-old car. The exception would be having to make major repairs on a badly rusted body.

Another consideration as you think about buying a car is the size. What size car will best suit your needs? It is helpful to have this in mind before you talk to a dealer. The chart on page 132 tells about the advantages, disadvantages, and seating accommodations of the different sizes of cars.

Car Buying Made Easier,© (Dearborn, Michigan: Ford Motor Co.)

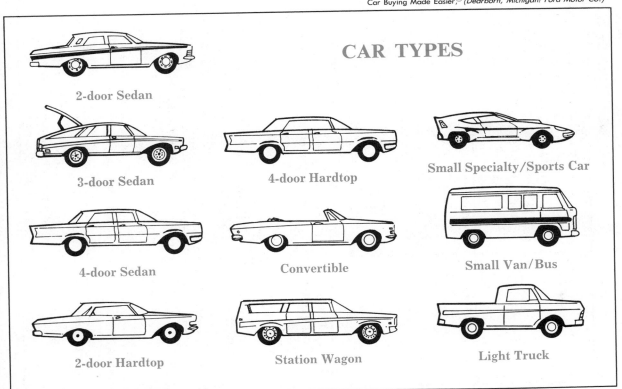

CAR TYPES

2-door Sedan

3-door Sedan

4-door Hardtop

Small Specialty/Sports Car

4-door Sedan

Convertible

Small Van/Bus

2-door Hardtop

Station Wagon

Light Truck

WHAT KIND OF CAR TO BUY

Type	Advantages	Disadvantages
Sedan, 2-door	Lowest-cost in a given line. Good family car for those with small children (no doors in rear). Sturdy, least subject to body squeaks as it ages. Rigid body-and-pillar design.	Awkward getting in and out of, or loading rear seat. Wider doors make it somewhat more difficult to get in and out of car in tight parking places.
Sedan, 3-door	Combines benefits of sedan and station wagon. Rear seat can be folded down to provide cargo area approaching that of a station wagon while retaining the body lines of a sedan. Often comes with "sporty" fittings and trim as standard.	Approximately the same as 4-door sedans. Usually available only in intermediate, compact, and sub-compact sizes.
Sedan, 4-door (pillared hardtop)	Good family car; 4 doors make easy entrance and exit to both front and rear, especially for older people. Sturdy because it has between-side-windows pillars. Narrower doors make it somewhat easier for you to get in and out of car in tight parking places.	More doors may subject car to more squeaks, drafts, as it ages. More doors and windows to lock for secure parking. Children in rear have access to rear-door locks and handles.
Hardtops, 2- and 4-door	Side views unobstructed by body pillars, with all side windows down. Hold resale value better than sedans.	Least rigid structure of all the metal-roof cars. Cost more. In 4-door models, children in rear have access to rear-door locks and handles.
Convertible	Unique design, compared to metal-roof cars— "different." Provides full open-air-and-sunshine driving.	Least rigid roof structure of all cars. Upkeep of fabric roof and raise-lower mechanism required.

Type	Advantages	Disadvantages
Convertible (continued)	Usually has heavier, lower-center-of-gravity construction to compensate for lack of metal-roof rigidity and bracing.	More subject to theft and vandalism by slashing roof. Depending on design, rearward visibility limited with top up. Most squeaks and rattles, as car ages. Few models available.
Station wagon	Highly useful all-purpose vehicle. Most states recognize as car and avoid "commercial vehicle" taxing on private family car use. Carries most passengers and cargo of all car-line vehicles. Versatile, rugged, adaptable. Has good resale value.	Slightly noisier than sedans. Larger interior with big window area takes longer to heat in cold weather, or cool in hot weather. Subject to more rattles and squeaks than sedans, as it ages. Higher-priced than sedans.
Small specialty/ sports cars	Good eye appeal. Options offered in wide range. Usually has more horsepower per pound of vehicle to give greater performance.	Higher-priced, compared to more conventional models. Higher-cost insurance probable if it has a high-powered engine. Limited number of passengers, up to four, with crowded rear seat. More subject to theft.
Vans/buses	Most space enclosed in least amount of body. Versatile, all-purpose passenger and cargo carriers. Low-cost operation, maintenance. Good forward visibility.	Noisier than passenger cars. More subject to wind forces. Subject to rattles, squeaks and drafts, as they age. Not the best road performers. Require care to guard from overloading.
Light trucks	Versatile, multiple-purpose design. Good rural-area type of transportation. Good stability and performance with loads. Good "second car" for rural-area family. Good commercial vehicle for contractors, others who work from job-site to job-site.	Limited to three passengers, in cab. Commercial or farm licensing normally required. Open-box type exposes uncovered cargo to all weather. No cargo security when parked and left unattended.

Car Buying Made Easier, © (Dearborn, Michigan: Ford Motor Co.)

Look Around

What's a good buy? Used cars are on the market because their owners wanted to get rid of them for some reason. Some status conscious owners trade as soon as they can afford a more expensive car. Others trade regularly only because they prefer the performance of a newer car. Many owners simply decide that the cost of repairs and the inconvenience involved make it undesirable to keep the car any longer.

The problem of getting a good buy is most difficult if you have very limited funds. If you only want to spend a few hundred dollars, one former used car dealer suggests that you will do best at a late model used car dealer. These dealers have to take some old cars as trade-ins on newer models. A few of these old cars may need only small repairs.

If you want to follow this suggestion, make a list of the five or six largest late model used car lots in the area. Call each one on the phone and ask to speak to the sales manager. Tell him what you can afford to spend. If the sales manager is not available, call back when he is. Don't talk with one of the salesmen. They can't earn a commission on an inexpensive car. Often the salesman will try to get you to buy a more costly car by borrowing the down payment from a small loan company. If the used car salesman negotiates the loan for you, he gets an extra fee from the small loan company. You, however, are saddled with an unwanted loan to repay.

The sales manager, however, is anxious to get rid of his old cars. If he tries to wholesale them, they won't bring much. Also, he knows that if he sells you a good old car today, you will probably be a customer for a later model in the future.

As you look around for the right car, you may hear some terms that are unfamiliar to you. Here are some terms that you ought to know in connection with your shopping:

As is means that the dealer takes no responsibility for the condition of the car. You will not get any kind of guarantee.

The term *under warranty* indicates that the car is still covered by the manufacturer's original warranty.

A *demonstrator* is a car which has been used to show prospective customers how the model operates. New car agencies often have demonstrators.

An *executive car* is one which has been used by an official of a company. Many large companies and some automobile agencies provide cars for some high-level employees. Sometimes the car is used in connection with their work.

Rebuilt, remanufactured parts have been dismantled, cleaned, and put together again. Badly worn pieces have been repaired.

A *factory rebuilt* engine has been taken apart, cleaned, and put together with the badly worn components replaced. This is usually done in a factory that specializes in rebuilding engines.

An *overhauled* or *reconditioned* engine has had some parts replaced or repaired, but it has not been taken completely apart.

Open and close the doors to check them.

Full power indicates that both the brakes and steering are power assisted.

Factory air means that the air conditioning was installed at a factory, usually by the company that manufactured the car.

Four-wheel drive is a vehicle that has power to both front and rear wheels. Four-wheel drive is particularly useful in snow and on rough terrain.

Mounted snow indicates that there are snow tires on extra wheels.

A *manual transmission* requires that you shift the gears yourself. With an *automatic transmission* the car shifts automatically as you start, stop, and change speeds.

Check Out the Car

Used car guarantees are not always dependable. If there is a guarantee at all, it is usually limited to thirty days. Many dealers won't give you that. Your best protection is to check the car thoroughly before buying.

First, find out the repair history of the make and model. Periodically, *Consumer Reports* publishes these. Then go over the car carefully. There are some simple things you can check yourself. Use the following checklist as a guide.

THE OUTSIDE

Does the paint match all over? Examine all sides of the car in a good light to see if there are repainted or ripply areas. If the paint doesn't match, what has been fixed? Has the car been totally repainted? Is there paint on chrome moldings and rubber seals? These suggest that the car may have been in a major accident and could be structurally unsound.

Open and close the doors without slamming. Try the hood and trunk. Do they work well? These things are hard to fix,

and worse yet, may indicate that the car has a bent frame. A car with a bent frame does not drive properly.

Check the tires for uneven wear. Uneven wear can be caused by a number of problems: wheels that are not properly balanced; a front end that is not properly aligned; or a bent frame. Balancing the wheels is simple and inexpensive; fixing the other problems is not.

Rock the car by pushing down hard at each corner or jumping on the bumper. If the car continues to bounce after you have let go, the shock absorbers are worn.

Look for signs of rust—paint blisters at the bottom of the door and the edge of the hood and fenders. Rust is difficult to remove, and once started it usually continues to eat away the body.

Another check, usually included as part of the vehicle inspection by the states that inspect cars, starts by jacking the front wheels slightly off the ground. Then bend down, grasp a wheel at the top with both hands, and shake it to and from you vigorously. Considerable free play or a clunking sound can indicate loose or worn wheel bearings or worn suspension joints.

Look at the tailpipe area. A black sticky deposit inside the pipe or a black film on

Check the wear on the tires.

the bumper or around the pipe indicates that the car is burning too much oil.

THE INSIDE

The car's interior is the best indicator of how the car has been used. Don't be fooled by a late model car. It may have been driven hard by a salesperson. Also, don't be mislead by low mileage. Although it is illegal to tamper with the odometer some unscrupulous people do turn them back.

Look at the accelerator, brake pedal, and clutch if there is one. These will show wear if the car has been driven a lot. A brand new pedal may indicate that the dealer is trying to fool you.

Other indications of hard wear are the upholstery and carpets or mats, especially on the driver's side.

Does the steering wheel look worn?

Rock the car by pushing up and down.

Try everything—the lights, windshield wipers, windows, radio, heater, glove compartment, and anything else that is inside.

Does the steering wheel turn more than a few inches without moving the wheels? Too much play might be a sign of problems—with the front end or the steering mechanism.

Press your foot down hard on the brake pedal for a minute. If it continues to sink after your initial pressure, there may be a leak in the hydraulic system.

UNDER THE HOOD

Are there signs of leakage—gas, oil, or water stains around the carburetor, oil filter, radiator hoses, or valve cover? These can indicate problems.

Open the radiator cap. Is the water or water and antifreeze mixture clean?

Check the battery. Is it fairly new or still covered by a guarantee? Most batteries last two to three years, less in extreme temperatures.

Start the engine with the hood open. Keep the motor running while you continue to look and listen. Are there any unusual noises which could suggest problems?

ROAD TESTS

Amazingly, many used car buyers never try the car on the road before they buy. However, a road test can tell you a great deal about the condition of the car. If a car looks good to you after making the on-the-lot tests, take it out on the road. While you are driving, listen for rattles, knocks, or squeaks.

Accelerate briskly a few times from 10 or 15 miles per hour to 40 or 45 miles per hour. Use high gear or the drive range of an automatic transmission. The engine should pick up speed smoothly. If not, it may need work.

Check the transmission. A manual transmission (stick shift) should shift quietly and smoothly through the gears. Watch for slipping clutch or gears that don't engage easily.

An automatic transmission should shift from gear to gear without hesitation. Noises in the transmission are a sign of trouble.

Pick a quiet street or road with a line down the center and very little curvature to the road surface. While driving very slowly, let go of the steering wheel and see if the car pulls to the right or left. Pulling can be caused by a number of things, some of which require major repairs. If the car pulls, have a mechanic check the cause.

On the same quiet road check the brakes by a series of stops from 40 to 45 miles per hour. The brake pedal should remain high and feel solid, not spongy. If the brake pedal feels soft, the car pulls to one side, or the brakes chatter, the brakes may need some expensive repairs.

Watch the oil pressure gauge. It should remain high when you are driving and fall when you idle. Some cars have a warning light instead of a gauge. In these cars the light should go off and stay off when you start.

Check the temperature gauge after driving for a while to be sure that the car doesn't overheat. If the gauge seems to fluctuate greatly during driving, have a service station check the water temperature with a thermometer.

Does the generator light go off soon after you start the car? It should remain off

Check the brakes.

Check to see if the car pulls to the side.

Does the car overheat?

except when you are idling. If it stays on, there may be a problem with the generator, voltage regulator, or possibly the gauge. A good way to check is to drive with all the electrical equipment on—lights, radio, windshield wipers, etc.

If there is an air conditioner, try driving in stop-and-start city traffic to see if the car overheats. This is when you will need the air conditioner most.

TAKE IT TO A MECHANIC

If the car passes all these checks, get the help of a reliable mechanic. He can spot things you may have missed.

Ask him to check the frame for damage or indications that the car has been in an accident.

Are there any leaks in the brakes or transmission? The transmission fluid should be clear and the brake lines in good condition.

How is the engine compression? Uneven compression is a sign of trouble. The engine may need anything from a valve job to a complete overhaul.

ADDITIONAL SUGGESTIONS

Ask about a warranty. Is there still a warranty in effect from the manufacturer? If you are buying from a used car dealer, will he provide a warranty? Sometimes a dealer will guarantee that the car will pass inspection—in those states where there is motor vehicle inspection. Be sure the guarantee is stated in writing.

Look for service stickers on the door or under the hood of a car. These sometimes give a clue as to the car's maintenance. If you are buying from the owner, ask if he or she has the service bills. Many people keep these for tax purposes. Sometimes you can find out where the car has been serviced and talk to the mechanic who has worked on it.

What Extras Are Worth Having?

Many extras can be added to a car to make driving easier and more pleasant. However, these are often an additional maintenance headache for the buyer of an older car.

Automatic transmission. Today most new cars are sold with automatic transmissions. Many people never learn to drive a car with a manual transmission, which requires changing gears by hand with a stick shift. If you don't know how to drive a stick-shift car, you may want an automatic, unless you are willing to learn to shift.

Extra powerful engines. Super-powered engines eat up high-priced gas and aren't really needed for smaller cars, unless the car will be used to tow loads, such as a boat or trailer.

Power steering. Some people find this a great help, particularly in parking medium- and large-sized cars. It isn't needed on most small cars.

Power brakes. For heavier cars these make it possible to brake more easily and quickly. They are generally unnecessary on light cars.

Remember, any extras you get may need additional or more costly maintenance. The more you get on a car, the more there is that can go out of order. Also, an extra like an automatic transmission is more expensive to repair than a manual one. The same is true of power brakes and other extras.

Getting the Lowest Price

Case Study. Here's the story of how one man purchased a car. Sy Wallington knew just the used car he wanted to buy. He had read ratings and reports on various makes and models carefully to decide on just the make, model, and accessories of a two-year-old car. He had also checked used car prices in *The Auto Red Book of Official Used Cars' Value.* The bank where he was planning to get his car loan had a copy.

The problem was how to get the lowest price. He had shopped around and found that the car he wanted was available at a number of places in his area. Also, he had checked each of these cars out himself and three seemed in good shape. Before taking any of the cars to a mechanic for additional checking, he decided to see what he could do on price.

He was quite frank with each salesman. He said that he had seen three cars in good condition that he was considering, and the price would be the deciding factor. What was the best they could do? One salesman was very anxious to make the sale. He quoted a price that was $150 less than the other two. This sounded very good to Sy, but he arranged to have a mechanic check the car before he made his final decision.

Sy knew that salesmen will cut their commission on both new and used cars if they are under pressure to sell. Sometimes salesmen are extra anxious to make a sale at the end of the month to meet a quota or earn a bonus. When business is slow, new annual models are due, or Christmas shopping is competing with car sales, car dealers may be particularly willing to shave the prices a little more. Some dealers build a reputation for slightly lower prices. Often they can do a larger volume of business this way, which they feel is more profitable. Occasionally, claims like this are made falsely. Judge for yourself in case the dealer is misrepresenting their way of doing business.

Buying a car is basically a bargaining operation. Automobile salesmen are very good at bargaining; they do it all day long. Remember, don't accept the first price quoted as the price the dealer necessarily expects to get. Most dealers will come down a little. A new car dealer might do this with a higher price for your trade-in car, if you are trading. Compare the costs of several cars. Don't be taken in by a sales pitch on the wonderful features you will get. You might not need them or want to spend the extra money for such features.

WHEN IS THE BEST TIME TO BUY OR SELL A CAR?

Although studies have been made by government and businesses on the average life of fleet-operated cars, similar information on privately owned cars is not available. Generally, the first 15,000 miles of operation are trouble free, and the next 15,000 require only a small amount of repairs. After 30,000 miles of driving, the cost for repair and replacement of tires begins to go up, and between 45,000 and 60,000 miles big repairs may be necessary. However, there are many variables which influence this, such as the care given to the car and how and where you drive, as well as how that particular car stands up.

PAYING FOR YOUR CAR

Cash is the cheapest way to buy a car, but car buyers often don't have enough cash, so credit is needed. Most new cars are sold on credit.

When you purchase a car on credit, two possible methods for financing are available: financing through the dealer or borrowing the money from a separate agency. Although some dealers may be financially able to handle their own accounts, you will recall from Chapter 3 that others often make the arrangements with the customer themselves but allow a bank or finance company to handle the account. As you shop for the best package—of car and credit—at different dealers, don't forget that you might find a lower interest rate at one of the cash loan sources discussed in Chapter 3. If so, the extra time it takes to make arrangements with both the dealer and a credit agency may be worthwhile.

Once you find the best priced car and credit for your needs, arrange terms at the highest monthly payment that you can afford. A fast payoff usually cuts the cost of credit. However, don't assume that if you agree to one set of terms initially, deciding later to pay it off faster will cut your cost. Many car purchase contracts require you to pay the full credit charge originally agreed upon even if you pay your loan off early. If you think that you might want to pay off your car loan early, be sure that your contract states that you can reduce your credit charge by doing so.

BUYING INSURANCE

How does it work? You pay the insurance company a fee. In return the insurance company agrees to pay for, or *cover,* certain accident expenses.

Know Your Insurance Terms

Knowing insurance terms will help you when you take out your own insurance. Are you familiar with the terms listed here?

- *Policy.* This is a written contract from the insurance company. Be sure to keep it. It tells you about the insurance you have purchased.
- *Coverage.* The dollar amount that your policy will pay in case of an accident

is called coverage. For example, a policy may pay $100 for a leg injury as a part of your coverage.

- *Premium.* Your payment to the insurance company for their service is called a premium. Premiums may be paid once, twice, or several times a year, depending on the policy.
- *Deductible.* The car owner agrees to pay the first $50 or $100 (or more) of damage to his car in any one collision, and the insuring company agrees to pay the remainder. The more you agree to pay, the less your premiums will be.

What Insurance Do You Need?

You need enough insurance to cover what you would have to pay if you had an accident. Many states require that you carry a minimum amount of insurance or pay to join a pool for uninsured motorists. This money is used to pay for injuries or damages caused by uninsured motorists. Car dealers and agencies that finance cars are anxious to protect their investment, so they usually require you to carry some insurance to protect them. If you drive in connection with a job, your employer may also require you to have certain kinds of insurance.

The Insurance Information Institute describes the following six basic coverages included in automobile insurance.

BODILY INJURY LIABILITY INSURANCE

This coverage applies when your car injures or kills pedestrians, persons riding in other cars, or guests in your car. It is in force as long as your car is driven by you, members of your immediate family, or others who drive your car with your permission. You and all members of your family are covered even while driving someone else's car if you have the owner's permission. When claims or suits are brought against you, bodily injury liability insurance provides protection in the form of legal defense, and if it is agreed or judged by a court that you are legally liable for the injury, the insuring company will pay bodily injury damages assessed against you up to the limits of the policy.

Coverage is generally sold with two limits: (1) the maximum amount of payments to one person in an accident and (2) the maximum amount of total payments for any one accident. Many states that have insurance requirements have a minimum of $15,000/$30,000 (bodily injury to one person/maximum payment for one accident). Some states require higher minimums. In light of recent court awards, many prudent people carry higher amounts.

PROPERTY DAMAGE LIABILITY INSURANCE

This coverage applies when your car damages the property of others. More often than not the property is another car, but it also covers damage to other property such as lamp posts, telephone poles, or buildings. It does not cover damage to *your* car. It is in force as long as your car is driven by you, members of your immediate family, or others who drive your car with your permission. You and all members of your family are covered even while driving someone else's car if you have the owner's permission. When claims or suits are brought against you, property damage liability insurance provides protection in the form of legal defense, and if it is agreed or judged by a court that you are legally liable for the damage, the insuring company will pay property damages assessed against you up to the limits of the policy.

MEDICAL PAYMENTS INSURANCE

Under this coverage the insuring company agrees to pay, up to the limits of the policy, medical expenses resulting from accidental injury. It applies to you and your immediate family whether in their car, someone else's, or if struck while walking. It applies to guests while they are occupying your automobile. Payment is made regardless of who is at fault, or if no one is at fault.

COMPREHENSIVE PHYSICAL DAMAGE INSURANCE

This coverage provides protection against financial loss resulting from breakage of glass, falling objects, fire, theft or larceny, missiles, explosion, earthquake, windstorm, hail, water, flood, vandalism or malicious mischief, riot or civil commotion, or collision with a bird or animal. It does not cover damage resulting from collision with other vehicles or objects.

COLLISION INSURANCE

This coverage applies when your car is damaged as a result of colliding with a vehicle or other object, or as a result of turning over. Damages are paid by the insuring company regardless of who is at fault. Most collision insurance is sold on a $100 or $200 deductible basis. Collision insurance does not cover injuries to people or damage to the property of others.

PROTECTION AGAINST UNINSURED MOTORIST

This coverage applies to bodily injuries for which an uninsured motorist or a hit-and-run driver is legally liable. It applies to the policyholder and family whether occupying their car, someone else's, or while walking. It also applies to guests occupying the policyholder's car. The insuring company agrees to pay damages to injured persons to the same extent that it

Insurance Information Institute

AUTOMOBILE INSURANCE
A Summary Chart — Six Basic Coverages

TYPE OF COVERAGE	WHERE COVERAGE APPLIES				
	persons		property		
	The Insured Including Family	Persons Other Than Insured	The Insured's Car	Cars Other Than Insured's	Property Other Than Cars
Bodily Injury Liability		🧍			
Property Damage Liability				🚗	🏠
Medical Payments	🧍	🧍			
Comprehensive Physical Damage			🚗		
Collision			🚗		
Uninsured Motorist Protection	🧍				

would if it had carried insurance on the uninsured or unknown motorist.

Generally, if a state or your employer requires you to carry insurance, they want you to have bodily injury and property damage liability, so that if you injure someone or destroy property, you will be able to pay for it. Agencies that finance cars may only care about collision insurance so that if you damage or destroy your car before it is paid for, they will get their money.

How Are Rates Determined?

The more risk involved in driving, the higher your insurance rates. Insurance companies, by studying past accidents, determine the levels of risk they take when insuring different groups of people. A high-risk person will be charged a higher price for insurance.

Here are some of the important factors insurance companies consider in determining how much you will have to pay.

RATING TERRITORIES

The states are divided into rating territories according to the accidents in the area. Rates are highest in cities, lower in suburban areas, and drop even lower for rural and semirural areas, where one is less likely to be in an accident.

AMOUNT OF COVERAGE

More insurance means you pay more. The driver with $100,000 of liability insurance generally pays more than the one with $10,000.

DRIVER CLASSIFICATION

Insurance companies generally consider your age, sex, marital status, how much you use your car, and your driving record.

Rates generally are highest for single male drivers between ages 17 and 24. This is the group with the highest accident rate. The Insurance Information Institute notes that under one classification plan the rates are highest for young unmarried men who own or are the principal operators of their own cars, but the rate decreases year by year from age 17 through 29. Under this plan there is a separate classification for the young unmarried female driver. She too pays more than the base rate but not as much as the men, with the cost decreasing each year from age 17 through 23.

Why do young people pay more for insurance? Take a look at the charts on pages 146 and 147 and see why. What reasons can you give for the large number of accidents that young people have?

In determining your driver classification, most companies will give a reduced rate if you have had driver education which includes behind the wheel training, and some give lower rates to students with good scholastic records.

THE AGE, MAKE, AND MODEL OF THE CAR

It costs more to repair or replace a Cadillac than a Chevrolet, so it will cost more to insure it. A sports car will be more expensive to insure than a sedan of the same size. Insurance records show that small cars are involved in more serious accidents than larger cars. This may be partly due to the fact that small cars are not usually as heavily built. Also, some small cars are very low, making them hard to see in heavy traffic.

Financial Responsibility Laws

Today all states have laws which are intended to keep drivers who cannot pay damages off the roads.

Here is how the laws work in some states. If you have an accident involving bodily injury or a large amount of property damage, you must file a report with the state agency and present proof that you can pay the damages up to the minimum required in your state, whether you are at fault or not.

You can satisfy the requirements by:

• Purchasing bodily injury and property damage liability insurance of the minimum amount set by the state in which the car is licensed.

• Putting up money in cash or other assets to prove that you can pay for the injuries and/or damage.

If you do not have insurance and cannot put up the money, your right to drive will be taken away until you can provide proof of financial responsibility.

Prudent drivers carry bodily injury and property damage liability whether required or not. Juries award large sums to people who have been injured in accidents. If you are at fault, you may have to pay a great deal. Without insurance, you would suffer a heavy financial loss. Even small accidents involving property damage only can be quite costly. Therefore carry the greatest amount of coverage you can manage. The cost for $50/100,000 worth of coverage is not much more than for $25/50,000.

Insurance Information Institute

RATES GO DOWN AS YOUNG DRIVERS GROW OLDER

AGE

17 18 19 20 21 22 23 24 25 26 27 28 29

Unmarried male operator under age 30 who owns or is a principal operator of the automobile

AGE

17 18 19 20 21 22 23 24

Unmarried male operator under age 25 who is not the owner nor principal operator

AGE

17 18 19 20 21 22 23 24

Married male operator under age 25

AGE

17 18 19 20 21 22 23

Unmarried female operator under age 24

BASE RATE

MOST DRIVERS PAY THIS

BASE RATE

Assigned Risks

All states have an assigned risk plan to provide automobile liability insurance for drivers who are unable to purchase it through regular channels. This group of drivers includes older motorists and people who have a poor driving record.

Each insurance company in a state has to accept people in the assigned risk group in proportion to the volume of automobile insurance business it does in the state.

Under the assigned risk plan the insurance company must provide at least the minimum liability coverage required in the state. However, they may charge higher rates than for drivers who are in a better classification.

A driver can get out of the assigned risk classification by driving for a period of time without an accident or traffic violation.

Automobile insurance rates have gone up rapidly in the last few years. More cars on the road means more accidents, injuries, damage, and deaths.

The states regulate automobile insurance rates. They decide whether the rates proposed by a company are equitable in relation to insurance claims. This doesn't mean, however, that all companies in any area within the state charge the same rates. Some companies are better managed, passing the savings on to their customers in the form of lower rates. Others are very selective about whom they will insure. They may accept primarily drivers who have good driving records. As a result, they can charge lower rates and still come out ahead. Some insurance companies, owned by the people they insure, do not try to make a profit. Therefore, *shop around for automobile insurance* to find the best rate possible.

WHY YOUNG DRIVERS PAY MORE FOR INSURANCE:
ACCIDENTS BY AGE OF DRIVERS

Age Group	Percent of Total Drivers	Percent of Total Accidents
0–19	10.3	16.6
20–24	11.3	18.4
25–29	10.2	12.0
30–34	9.6	9.6
35–39	9.6	8.5
40–44	9.9	7.4
45–49	9.8	7.4
50–54	8.7	5.8
55–59	6.8	5.1
60–64	5.3	3.5
65–69	3.9	3.0
70–74	2.7	1.3
75 and over	1.9	1.4

National Safety Council

Automobile insurance purchased from the car dealer often seems attractive because it can be included in your monthly payment package. The rates, however, are often cheaper and the service better from an outside agency. Compare cost, coverage, and what you can find out about service on a policy elsewhere before you take insurance from a car dealer.

Big repair bills can come from little crashes.

No-Fault Insurance

There has been considerable public controversy about automobile insurance and how it can be improved. Under the traditional method compensation to victims has often been far short of their needs; and frequently awards were made only after a prolonged court case.

The Commonwealth of Puerto Rico tried a plan which has since been adopted by some states, no-fault insurance. Under this plan an accident victim is compensated for medical costs and lost income or the survivors receive a death benefit without trying to establish who was at fault in the accident. The amount that will be paid for each kind of accident is set in advance and not determined by a court case.

The time-consuming and expensive legal procedure of establishing who is liable for the accident costs is avoided. Also, payments are made more quickly to the injured. Automobile insurance costs have not been lower in all states where the no-fault plans have been adopted.

Motorcycle Insurance

Basically, motorcycle insurance is similar to automobile insurance. However, there are wide differences in the policies of different companies, so be sure to check the details carefully. The Insurance Information Institute lists the following as some of the usual restrictions:

- Insurance does not apply when the cycle is engaged in speed or riding contests.
- Persons who operate a borrowed cycle are not covered by the owner's insurance.
- Passengers are not insured, even if they are riding with the owner.
- Medical-payments coverage for injuries to the operator is excluded.
- The automobile insurance carried by a father would not, in most cases, extend to a son or daughter while riding a borrowed motorcycle, even if the owner had given permission.

Weight and horsepower are important factors in determining the cost of motorcycle insurance. The bigger the cycle, the higher the cost. Otherwise, the cost of cycle insurance is determined by the same factors—such as age, driving record, and area—that apply to automobile insurance.

KEEPING YOUR CAR ON THE ROAD

American motorists spend billions of dollars a year for automobiles. Although most people recognize that it takes money to buy a car, they probably don't think about how much it costs to run it. The purchase price is only the first expense in a long list of costs involved in maintaining the car during the 100,000-mile, 10-year trip from the assembly line to the junkyard. A vehicle usually passes through two, three, or even more owners during its useful life.

The Costs

If you buy a new car or a nearly new one, the biggest single cost is the depreciation, that is, the loss in value of the car. Many automobile owners overlook depreciation costs because they aren't paid directly the way gas and oil are. When you drive a new car out of the showroom, it immediately becomes a used vehicle and is worth at least several hundred dollars less. The chart on page 149 shows how quickly a new car loses value.

While the depreciation costs reduce each year, other maintenance costs tend to increase. Parts wear out; tires need replacing; rust and weather spoil the body and paint.

AUTOMOBILE DEPRECIATION

If you keep your car for:	You lose the following approximate percentage of its original cost per year:
1 year	30%
2 years	25% (50% for both years)
3 years	22% (66% for three years)
4 years	19% (76% for four years)
5 years	16% (80% for five years)
6 years	14% (84% for six years)

U. S. Department of Labor

Regular maintenance can help you avoid costly repair bills.

A variety of factors can affect the service life and costs of operating a car. Some of these are individual driving habits, climate, garage facilities, type of road used, purpose for which the car is used, and plain luck. Some people are very rough with a car. In cold climates, where salt is used on the road, rust eats away the body more quickly than in warmer areas. In New York City one can pay $100 a month for a garage. Dirt roads may bounce the car around a lot, wearing parts out at a faster rate. A car used for business or long commutes will need more maintenance than one driven just a few miles a day. Also, some cars are better constructed than others of the same make and model.

Car costs can be cut in a number of ways. A small car costs less to operate than a large one. Not only is the initial cost less, but operating costs are too. (Such figures are published yearly by the Dept. of Transportation.) Financing the car over a shorter period of time or saving and paying cash can cut car costs. Keeping the car longer is another way to cut costs; the depreciation per year is less. Careful driving and proper maintenance are also ways to save.

Maintenance

Regular maintenance keeps a car run-ning well and often reduces the need for bigger repairs. You can find out when to service the car from the manual that comes with it. If you buy a used car that doesn't have a manual, try to get one from a new car dealer who sells the same make. By servicing your car regularly, you can avoid some big problems. It's like taking care of your teeth—regular care is important.

Servicing a car is usually one of the big headaches of car ownership. How do you find a good service station? How do you know that their prices are fair? You can ask around. Find out who your family and friends have tried. Get estimates from different service stations on a job, particularly if it is a big one. Check car dealers and department stores that service autos to see what they charge. Have the serviceman call you before doing any work that will cost more than the original estimate.

There are also many little things that you can do yourself to keep a car running well:

- Check to be sure that there is water in your battery and radiator.
- Watch for signs of trouble. Is the car hard to start? You may need new points, spark plugs, a new battery, adjustment of the timing, or something else.
- Does the engine knock when you accelerate? You may need a higher octane fuel. If this doesn't help, perhaps you need a tune-up.

Careful Driving

Acquire good driving habits that will help you get the most mileage for your money. The following are some suggestions:

- Let the engine warm up briefly before driving. Then drive slowly until the temperature is up to normal.
- Accelerate slowly and smoothly to save gas.

3M Company

To cut commuting costs many people are forming groups and commuting by van.

• Brake gradually when possible to reduce excessive brake wear.

Buying and Caring for Tires

As you drive, some parts will wear out and need replacement, such as the battery, spark plugs, and tires. Tires are particularly important because they can improve the safety and performance of the car, increase your enjoyment in driving, and help you cut operating costs if they are carefully selected.

To get the most from your tires, you need to match the tires to the car, the load, and the use, as well as your driving habits. Also, you will have to give them proper care.

Here are some suggestions from the National Bureau of Standards.

If you primarily drive short distances between home, work, school, and shopping, you don't have to worry too much about heat buildup, and you don't need heavy-duty construction. You do need long mileage, and protection against everyday hazards. For your purposes a bias tire with a medium to heavy tread will probably give you adequate service, though a belted bias or radial would give you longer wear.

If you do a lot of cross-country driving at turnpike speeds, you need a tire strong enough to withstand road shocks but with a medium depth of rubber in the tread to avoid heat buildup. The thicker the tread, the higher the heat buildup at high speeds. For your purposes a high-quality bias tire is acceptable, but you would get better traction, less heat buildup, and longer mileage from a belted bias or radial tire.

If you are a sports car buff or want optimum performance and handling, the belted bias or radial tire will give you the most satisfaction. It offers superior cornering and greater safety at sustained turnpike speeds. Of the two, the radial probably has a slight edge in precise handling, though it gives a somewhat harder ride. You may also want to consider a lower, wider profile tire. Generally speaking, the wider the tread, the better the grip on the road.

If you plan to carry heavy loads or drive on rough or rocky roads, you will want a tire with a heavier tread and a sturdy construction. Ask about heavy-duty tires when you make your purchase.

In many areas you will need snow tires for winter driving. It is just as important to select snow tires that fit your driving needs as it is to buy the right regular tires. If you will be driving in an area where the snow fall is light or it melts often, the best tire is one with open channels in the tread to minimize water buildup. On the other hand, if you will be driving in heavy snow, you will need a tire with a deep open tread.

Like conventional tires, snow tires also come in three basic types. *Mixing types of tires is dangerous and should not be done with either regular or snow tires. A good*

What type of tire should you buy?
NFCU Consumer Annual

BIAS

BELTED BIAS

RADIAL

National Safety Council

You may need snow tires for winter driving.

National Safety Council

Keep your distance in winter weather. You need much more room to stop.

rule is to buy the same type of snow tires for the rear wheels as the ones on your front wheels. For example, if you have regular radial tires on the front, you should have radial snow tires on the rear.

Studded snow tires increase traction on ice. However, on snow they are no better than regular snow tires, and in wet rainy conditions they give less traction than ordinary snow tires.

Tires don't come with studs. They are put in by the store when you purchase the tires and studs. Generally, it is recommended that each tire have about 100 to

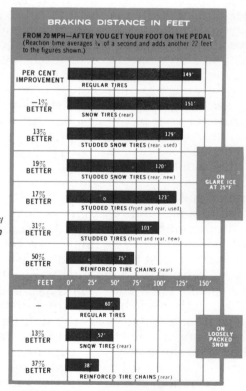

BRAKING DISTANCE IN FEET

FROM 20 MPH—AFTER YOU GET YOUR FOOT ON THE PEDAL
(Reaction time averages ¾ of a second and adds another 22 feet to the figures shown.)

	Distance	
PER CENT IMPROVEMENT REGULAR TIRES	149'	
−1% BETTER SNOW TIRES (rear)	151'	ON GLARE ICE AT 25°F
13% BETTER STUDDED SNOW TIRES (rear, used)	129'	
19% BETTER STUDDED SNOW TIRES (rear, new)	120'	
17% BETTER STUDDED TIRES (front and rear, used)	123'	
31% BETTER STUDDED TIRES (front and rear, new)	103'	
50% BETTER REINFORCED TIRE CHAINS (rear)	75'	

FEET	0'	25'	50'	75'	100'	125'	150'

	Distance	
— REGULAR TIRES	60'	ON LOOSELY PACKED SNOW
13% BETTER SNOW TIRES (rear)	52'	
37% BETTER REINFORCED TIRE CHAINS (rear)	38'	

NOTE: 1. Studded tires refer to tungsten carbide studs.
2. Used tires had 2,500 miles of wear on clear pavement.

Cities Service Oil Co.

Keep tires inflated at the proper pressure.

150 studs. Since studs damage highways, they are banned in some states and can only be used during the winter period in others. If you are considering studded tires, be sure to check the regulations where you will be driving.

To make your tires last longer, keep them inflated at the recommended air pressure.

Rotate them at regular intervals, which is usually every 5,000 miles. If they seem to be wearing unevenly, see if the wheels need balancing or if there is a more serious problem.

Check regularly to see if the tires are getting worn. The tread should be at least as deep as one-half the width of a penny.

Correct and incorrect tire inflation.

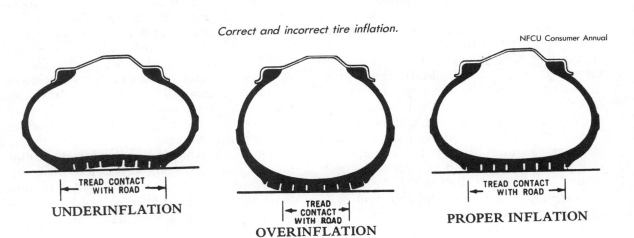

NFCU Consumer Annual

UNDERINFLATION

OVERINFLATION

PROPER INFLATION

YOUR RESPONSIBILITY AS A DRIVER

It's fun to step on the gas and go. In the excitement of being on their own many young drivers forget that they have a responsibility to others. A car is a vehicle that can be dangerous to you and others. Many people can be hurt if you are careless or reckless.

You have a responsibility to see that the vehicle is in good shape. It is poor economy to drive a car that is unsafe—one with poor steering, brakes that are not adequate, or bald tires. These can cause an accident.

Become a skillful driver. Learn to drive defensively. This means anticipating what other drivers will do. Avoid accidents when other people make mistakes.

The biggest single cause of accidents is drinking and driving. Neither the condition of the car nor your skill as a driver means much if you aren't in full control of yourself. Airline pilots are not permitted to have a drink within eight hours before flight time to prevent accidents in the air. Undoubtedly, we could prevent some automobile accidents with laws that impose stiffer penalties.

Many drugs also impair one's ability to drive and are surely a contributing factor in some accidents.

Seat belts can provide protection against death and serious injury in many types of accidents. Although seat belts have been required on all cars sold in the United States since 1968, many people do not use them. It's a little like having a vaccine for a serious illness and not using it.

A study of 28,780 accidents in Sweden showed no fatal injuries in crashes up to 60 miles an hour when lap and shoulder belts were used. Tests at the Cornell Aeronautical Laboratory also showed that seat belts can reduce injuries.

The proposal has been made to pass state laws that would make it illegal to ride without buckling up. Also, some cars have buzzers that remind the driver and passengers to fasten the seat belts.

A DRIVER'S LICENSE

The right to drive is a privilege. One must pass a series of tests—written, visual, and manual—to obtain a license. This right can be revoked as a penalty for a poor driving record. Some states have a point system. Acquiring too many points for accidents and violations results in loss of your license for a period of time.

If you move from one state to another, you are required to obtain a new license in that state. Usually you must take the visual, written, and manual tests over again.

RENTING A CAR

Renting a car is practical for the person who needs a car infrequently. Cars can be rented by the day, week, weekend, or month and often returned in another city. If you are going away to school with a lot of baggage, it might be practical to rent a car near your home and leave it in the town where the school is located as a way of moving. The rental rate is stated as a flat charge per period and varies according to the car which is rented. A luxury car will cost more than an economy model. Extras such as air conditioning or snow tires may cost more. Generally, there is an additional charge for each mile driven. Rates may include the cost of gas and oil. Be sure to check before you rent.

Some insurance is included in the rental charge, but most companies offer additional coverage at a small charge. Many people who rent cars buy extra collision insurance from the renting agency. This costs a modest amount a day more. You need a valid driver's license to rent a car, and usually you must be at least 18 years old. If you do not have a credit card that is accepted by the rental company, you may have to pre-pay some of the rental charges in cash.

LEASING A CAR

Leasing a car on an annual basis is becoming more and more common. Some people do it because they drive for business purposes, and this is a good way to keep a record of expenses, particularly those which are tax deductible. Generally, when you lease a car, you get a monthly bill for rental and maintenance charges. (Sometimes the rental fee includes maintenance; in other cases this is separate.) Other people feel that it is economical to lease because you don't have to make a large capital investment. Sometimes you have the option of buying the car at wholesale prices when the lease expires.

Many companies lease cars for their sales personnel. They feel that in this way they avoid the large capital outlay, have an outside organization that is responsible for service, and have clear records of costs for tax purposes. Also, in many leasing arrangements the leasing company will provide a car to use while the leased car is serviced.

FOR REVIEW

Points to Remember

- Decide what you need and can afford before buying a car.
- Visit several dealers and consider the following:
  a. What does the warranty or guarantee provide?
  b. Will the dealer service the car?
  c. Will the car pass a state inspection?
  d. What will its resale value be after it is paid for?
  e. Does everything work properly?
  f. Will repairs be made before you buy?
- Never be rushed or tricked into buying.
- Don't be afraid to make a lower offer.
- Shop for car financing; costs are not the same from all lenders.
- Never give a salesman a deposit until you have made a final decision.
- Buy from a reputable dealer or individual.
- Check out a used car before you buy.
- Don't sign a sales agreement until you understand the terms of the contract.
- Prudent drivers carry bodily injury and property damage liability insurance whether it is required or not.
- Automobile insurance rates are determined by a number of factors. Some of the most important are: the rating territory in which you live; how much coverage you want; your driver classification; and the age, make, and model of the car.
- Cars lose value with each year. The biggest loss occurs in the first year and decreases each year after that.
- Regular maintenance keeps a car running well and often reduces the need for bigger repairs.
- To get the most from your tires you need to match the tires to the car, the load, and the use, as well as your driving habits.
- Mixing tire types is dangerous and should not be done with either regular or snow tires.
- The driver of a car has a responsibility to self and others to maintain and operate a vehicle as safely as possible.

- The right to drive is a privilege which can be revoked for misuse.
- Transportation in urban areas has become a national problem. Imaginative solutions are needed to make it possible for people to get around in a way that is healthful, comfortable, and efficient.

Terms to Know

as is
assigned risks
automatic transmission
bodily injury liability
claim
collision insurance
comprehensive physical damage
coverage
deductible
demonstrator
depreciation
driver classification
executive or official car
factory air
factory rebuilt
financial responsibility laws
four-wheel drive
full power
insurance
manual transmission
medical payments insurance
mounted snow
no-fault insurance
overhauled engine
policy
power brakes
power steering
premium
property damage liability
protection against uninsured motorist
rating territory
rebuilt, remanufactured parts
reconditioned engine
under warranty

PROBLEM SOLVING: CHECK YOUR UNDERSTANDING

Who gets the benefits for each of these kinds of coverage?

- Bodily injury liability.
- Medical payments.
- Protection against uninsured motorists.
- Property damage liability.
- Comprehensive physical damage.
- Collision.

TO DO IN CLASS

Discussion

1. Ridgley Hunt, in "The American and His Automobile," wrote:

"For 70 years, the American male has carried on a love affair with his automobile, and like most lovers, he has usually acted less from wisdom than from passion. He has postponed marriage and plunged into debt to acquire his first car, then sold it when it was scarcely three years old and had only 30,000 miles on it—sold it for a newer and bigger and costlier model with a newer and bigger and costlier debt attached. In his zest for the open road, he has choked his streets with motor vehicles until the exhaust fumes sickened him and the traffic oozed to a stop."

Do you agree or disagree?

2. How does the automobile affect other aspects of the economy? What part does it play in the overall economy of the nation; the world?

3. Is the automobile a:
- Transportation device?
- Status symbol?
- Death-dealing weapon?
- Necessity or want?

4. What is an insurance agent referring to when he or she speaks of automobile

insurance as "Ten and twenty" and writes it as 10/20?

Activities

1. Visit a used car dealer. Have a salesman explain why he thinks two or three cars of different price levels are good buys. Take time to look at other cars while you are there.

2. Invite an automobile insurance agent to class to talk about insurance coverage. Ask about second car discounts, compact car discounts, driver education discounts, and safe driver discounts.

3. Ask a local police officer to talk to the class about your responsibilities if you have an accident.

4. Visit a local traffic court for one session.

5. Play the insurance baseball game. Divide the group into two teams; team leaders are the pitchers. One person on each team has to serve as umpire for the opposing team. (Designate bases around your meeting room.)

a. The pitcher throws a question to the batter. If the batter answers correctly, he or she goes to first base. The umpire decides if the answer is correct. If the umpire says the batter is right and he is wrong, he still goes to first base, but his answer should be corrected. If the umpire says the batter's answer is wrong and the umpire on the batter's team thinks it is right, he can say so. If the answer is right, the batter can take two bases.

b. Three wrong answers retires the side.

c. Set an inning limit for your game.

CHAPTER 7

Having Fun

Most people feel that it is important to have fun—to do things that they enjoy. Your parents may like to visit with friends on Saturday night, watch TV, go out to dinner occasionally, bowl, collect stamps, golf, or go camping in the summer. Perhaps you like to play tennis after school, watch a football game, or have a snack with some friends. Many people fish and hunt, ride motorcycles, or bicycle in the country. Others ski, ride horses or snowmobiles, skate, build airplane models, tinker with cars, or do other active things. Listening to music and watching TV are national pastimes. Can you think of other ways people enjoy spare time?

THE GROWTH AND DISTRIBUTION OF LEISURE

Today the average American has more waking time off the job than on it. Industrialization, with its highly productive tools, has made it possible for a person to produce more with fewer hours of work. The productivity of each worker in the United States has increased about 3 percent a year for most of the last 100 years. A century ago the working week averaged 66 hours in length; in 1940 it was about 44 hours; and today it is about 38 hours. Paid holidays and vacations add more time off.

A full-time worker can probably look forward to future reductions in the work week as well as more paid holidays. However, the usual working lifetime might be increased by raising the retirement age in many occupations.

There is a growing preference for blocks of time off, such as an extended vacation or a long weekend, rather than a shorter working day. A number of companies both here and abroad are experimenting with a four-day work week. In some cases weekly hours of work are reduced to fit into a four-day week; in others the same number of hours is condensed into four days. Some workers feel that a four-day work week results in an increase in useable leisure. For example, commuting time and costs are reduced. Some companies have also experimented with flexible hours, whereby workers have considerable choice in selecting their hours of work.

There are two opposite trends today. Some workers get a second job if their working hours are reduced; others prefer time off to more money. Generally, younger workers, older workers, and married women seem to prefer shorter hours to additional income.

Nonworking time is unevenly divided among the population. Generally, young people have considerable free time during the years before they start working full time. Most people enter the full-time work force at about age eighteen if they are not continuing their education. Many, however, have part-time jobs before that.

Proprietors, executives, and professionals generally have the longest working week, often as much as sixty hours a week. The homemaker with small children also works a long week, frequently fifteen hours a day, seven days a week. The working

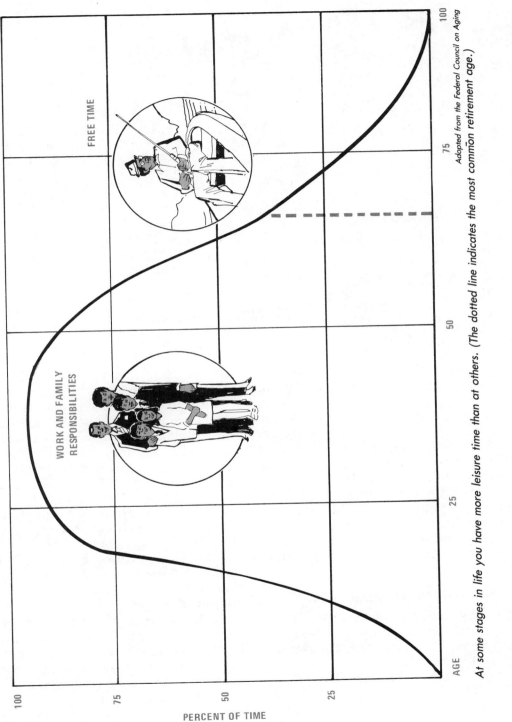

FREE TIME

WORK AND FAMILY
RESPONSIBILITIES

PERCENT OF TIME

100

75

50

25

AGE

25

50

75

100

Adopted from the Federal Council on Aging

At some stages in life you have more leisure time than at others. (The dotted line indicates the most common retirement age.)

159

Housing developments and motels often have swimming pools.

woman who combines a full-time job with family responsibilities puts in a long week too.

However, the homemaker with older children who does not have a paying job usually has daytime hours to use in leisure activities. Retired people may have much of the day for leisure pursuits.

One study shows that about 14 percent of the money spent for personal consumption is used for leisure-time goods and services. Projections are that this spending will grow with rising incomes and more time off from work.

THE USE OF LEISURE TIME

A growing number of Americans are enjoying recreational activities. Many feel that leisure activities are very important in giving meaning to life.

People use their leisure time in a variety of ways. How do your parents use their leisure time? What are some of your favorite activities? What are some of the things your friends do?

With the increase in available leisure time, deciding what to do with that time can become a problem. Educational activities, like reading, adult education programs, and classes in special interest areas offered by the YMCA, YWCA, or other organizations, are one possibility. Community service is another. Young people can volunteer to help with ecology projects, hospital work, tutoring, and fund raising, to name a few. Clubs and organizations are eager to have new members. Included are hobby clubs, scouts, FFA, FHA, junior achievement programs, and theater groups.

Hobbies provide still another avenue for leisure-time fun. Here are some hobbies that many young people enjoy: home sewing, model airplane making, crocheting, knitting, candle making, macrame, painting, playing an instrument, electronics, fixing cars, mineralogy, photography, and lis-

Many people feel that shopping can be a leisure activity.

tening to music. Perhaps you can name others.

Among young people sports and outdoor activities are particularly popular. Picnicking, swimming, and hiking are free or inexpensive in most areas, which makes them easily affordable for young people. Fishing has always ranked high in popularity. Recently bicycling, playing tennis, camping, riding a motorcycle or snowmobile, and skiing have grown in popularity.

It would be difficult to discuss in detail every kind of leisure-time activity in this chapter. Certainly not all of them are related to young people as consumers. Therefore only a few of the most popular hobbies, sports, and outdoor activities will be presented here.

Listening to Music

Young people make up a major portion of the market for records, tapes, and some concerts. Often they determine whether a recording is a marketing success by whether they buy the records or tapes. Clearly, many young people feel that it is important to have music wherever they go.

Older people often enjoy some of the same activities that young people like. Sometimes a hobby is pursued for a lifetime. Dancing for example, offers pleasure for people of all ages.

Eastman Kodak Co.

Many people like to take pictures.

If music is important to you, perhaps you own or want to buy a stereo system, phonograph, or components, such as an automatic record changer and speakers. These, plus tapes or records, can run into substantial costs, so plan before you buy. Consider carefully how much you will use the equipment and how. Don't pay extra for a portable model if it will only be used in your room.

Many young people cut the cost of musical equipment in a number of ways. First, there is a big market in used equipment. An expensive new outfit could sell for half price or less just a year later. Look in the classified ads of the newspaper. If you are going away to school, consider deferring your purchase until then. Most campuses have an informal but active exchange of used musical equipment. Second, if you are handy with tools, you might consider buying a unit that you assemble yourself or components that you hook up. Third, watch for sales. Often when a new model or feature comes out, the older ones drop in price.

For information on specific makes or models look in stores, read specialized magazines such as *Hi Fidelity* or *Stereo Review* and look for occasional ratings in *Consumer Reports* and *Consumers Research Magazine.*

Sometimes you can buy records or tapes at greatly reduced prices at sales, through the purchase of several at a time, or from a club. However, before you buy this way be sure that you are getting the ones you want and that the price is really a bargain.

Taking Pictures

People of all ages enjoy photography. For some this is a serious hobby; for others it is only a casual activity. If you are one of the casual picture takers—all you do is snap family and friends occasionally—you probably don't want a very expensive camera. Many people find that they get adequate pictures with a fairly simple, inexpensive camera.

Cartridge-loading cameras are simple to handle, and many are fairly inexpensive. Putting film in and taking it out is quick and easy, but you will probably pay a little more for the film. However, many people seem willing to do so if one can judge by growing sales of these cameras.

Learning to use a fine camera takes skill, which comes with practice and serious study. The most important feature of a fine camera is the lens, which must be precisely ground of a good quality glass. Many of the better cameras have interchangeable lenses. You can buy additional wide-angle or telephoto lenses. Also, a fast shutter speed is important in helping you get action pictures without blurring. If you plan to take many pictures, you might want a camera that uses 35-mm film, which is easier to enlarge than a smaller film type. Also, in 35-mm you can buy black and white film in bulk and cut your own roll to reduce cost. This is what professional photographers do.

Camera features, such as automatic exposure and rotating flash cubes, are convenient but more costly. Film for cameras that process pictures a few seconds after they are taken also costs more. In addition, these instant pictures are difficult to duplicate or enlarge.

If you want a fine camera at a budget price, consider buying one used. Many camera stores, particularly in large cities, take cameras as trade-ins on newer ones. Therefore they may have a number of good used cameras to sell. Also read the newspaper advertisements. Sometimes people sell cameras for one reason or another. If you are buying a used camera, deal with a reputable store or arrange to have a knowing friend or camera shop check your proposed purchase unless you are very knowledgeable.

To get the best results from your picture-taking, you may want to have your film processed someplace other than a drugstore or other store with a developing service. They usually send film to large commercial labs, which often do not have the time or skilled personnel to do the very best job. Many young people develop their own film. Another solution is to join a photo club and use their lab facilities to develop, print, and possibly enlarge your pictures. Or you might find a local photographer who is willing to do it for you at a nominal cost.

Bicycling

Bicycling has become a favorite activity for many. Some people claim it is America's fastest growing sport. Do you think of a bike as something for kids or only for use until you are old enough to drive a car? Well, that's no longer so. More adults in the United States are riding bikes than ever. Even in busy cities like New York people can be seen pedaling along the streets.

There are several reasons why bicycling has become so popular. First is the desire of many people to get in good physical condition. Another is an interest in reducing environmental pollution by using a bike instead of a car. Economy is important to some people. Lastly, the development of bikes that are easier to pedal on hills has helped stimulate the boom in biking among adults.

Bicycle buying is not a simple task. There are many places to shop and many makes, models, and styles from which to choose.

WHERE SHOULD YOU BUY?

You will probably find a variation of $10 or more between the large retail outlets, such as department stores, discount stores, catalog sales, and small specialized bike shops. However, don't be guided only by price. Some outlets sell bikes in crates, and you must assemble them yourself. Others assemble them but don't adjust handlebars or seats. If you want to buy a bike with a gear shift, it may take some time and a little know-how to get it set up.

A specialized bike shop may service the bike free for a month or two after the purchase. Usually they stock replacement parts for the bikes they sell and can also service them if problems arise.

Before you buy, think about whether you will need service or are willing to do the assembling, adjusting, and repairing yourself.

WHAT TYPE SHOULD YOU SELECT?

This depends largely on how you plan to use a bicycle. Most youngsters have ridden balloon-tire, single-speed bikes that weigh 55 to 60 pounds. These are fine for short distances or on hard, wet sand, such as the beach at low tide. However, if you plan to use a bike for transportation, longer trips, or where the terrain is hilly, you may want a bike with gears. These are much easier to pedal up hills. There are three main groups of gear shift bikes: three-speed, five-speed, and ten-speed.

Three-Speed Bikes

The three-speed bike has been the most widely used of the gear shift bikes. It is the least expensive of the three groups. The three ranges—low, normal, and high—are more versatile than a single-speed bike. They are fine for gentle, rolling hills, going to and from school, or riding around town. Young people with strong legs can often manage bigger hills by exerting a little more effort.

A three-speed bike generally weighs about 45 pounds. It has narrow tires that take 50 to 60 pounds of air pressure and 26-inch wheels. The gears are hidden within the hub of the rear wheel. Also, there are caliper rim brakes, rubber pedals, and a wide saddle on which you sit upright. The handlebars are the conventional upturned type. The gear shift is operated with a thumb-lever or a twist mechanism.

There is relatively little difference in construction between the various makes of three-speed bikes. Generally, the most im-portant considerations in selecting one are size, price, and service.

Five-Speed Bikes

For some reason the five-speed bike hasn't caught the public fancy as has the ten-speed. Yet it offers many advantages over a three-speed bike for a person who is going to be pedaling over hills or wants to take longer trips. A five-speed bike costs only a little more than most three-speed bikes, and it will give you much more power going up hills.

Unlike a three-speed bicycle, on which you change gears standing still, a five-speed bike can be shifted in motion, which makes for much greater flexibility. Gear shift changes are made externally, by means of a *derailleur,* which is attached to the rear wheel, and a shift lever on the handlebar. In the event of problems the derailleur can be fixed by a handy person, whereas repairs to the internal rear hub gears of a three-speed bike are complicated and generally require the aid of a mechanic. A five-speed bike is also lighter in weight than a three-speed, which makes it easier to pedal.

Ten-Speed Bikes

As more and more Americans have taken to the road on bicycles, the ten-speeds have boomed in popularity. These are luxury bikes. Generally, prices start at close to $200. In a way they compare to three-speed and five-speed bikes the way a fancy sports car compares to a medium-priced car. They are usually lighter in weight, better made, and have a number of extra features.

The first five speeds on a ten-speed bike are the same as on a five-speed bike. The extra five gears reduce the need for constant braking on the downhills, and also make for easier pedaling on level roads. However, they do not help uphill climbing.

Ten-speed bicycles generally come with dropped racing-style handlebars. The dropped bar may feel awkward at first, but it is better for long distances because it increases your pedaling leverage, distributes your weight better, and eases the vibration of the road surface.

The narrow racing saddle is usually also found on ten-speed bikes. At first, it will probably seem very hard and uncomfortable. However, most men feel more comfortable using it for long distances. Some women do too. Often a dealer will exchange a racing saddle for a touring model if you don't like it. (The racing saddles are more expensive.)

WHAT SIZE SHOULD YOU GET?

Size is one of the most important factors in selecting a bike. With a bike that is too small you don't get full power from your leg muscles. A bike that is too large is hard to handle and dangerous.

Bike frames for adults range in size from 19 to 26 inches. This is the distance from the bolt holding the seat post to the axle of the pedal.

Generally, when people talk about bike sizes, such as 26 inches or 27 inches, they are referring to the wheel size. Either of these sizes is used for adults. Generally, three-speed bicycles use 26-inch wheels. Most five- or ten-speed bikes use wheels with the narrower, high-pressure, 27-inch tires.

Try different bike sizes in the store. With the correct bike size your leg will be straight when your foot is on the pedal in the down position. It is possible to make small adjustments in the height of the seat to raise or lower your body. However, if the seat post is raised more than three inches above the bolt connecting it to the frame, you will be in an unbalanced position for pedaling and steering. It's best to buy a frame and wheels that fit your size, rather than try to make major adjustments in the height of the seat.

CHOOSING TIRES

Two types of bicycle tires are available, with tubes or without them. Each requires its own style of wheel rim. You cannot change from one type to another without also changing the wheel rim.

Generally, the tires with tubes are most practical. Sometimes they are called *clinchers* or *wire-ons*. These cost less than tubular tires, will take harder use, and are easier to repair.

Tubular tires, or those without tubes, are also called *sew-ups*. They are preferred by racers because they are lightweight and easy to change.

SAFETY STANDARDS

The Bicycle Manufacturers Association of America has adopted safety standards for bicycles. Their red, white, blue, and gold BMA/6 Seal of Certification tells you that a bicycle has met their standards for performance concerning the brakes, tires, the strength of the frame, and the steering mechanism, and has state-approved reflectors, reflectorized pedals, and reflective material on both sides of the bike. Look for this seal on the frame of the bicycle just below the seat post.

BASIC RULES FOR SAFE BICYCLING

- First, keep your bicycle in good condition. Check and clean it regularly. Make sure all parts are working well.
- Ride *with* the traffic except in those

TAKE GOOD CARE OF YOUR BIKE

SADDLE: Adjust height so leg bends slightly with ball of foot on pedal at bottom of stroke. Tighten securely.

COASTER BRAKE, HAND BRAKES: Must brake evenly every time. No slippage.

SPOKES: Replace broken ones promptly. Keep them tight.

REFLECTOR: Should be visible for 600 feet and be state-approved.

TIRE VALVE: Inspect for leaks and straightness.

CHAIN: Check for damaged links and a snug (but not too tight) fit. Clean frequently and lubricate with light oil.

HANDLE GRIPS: Replace worn grips. Make sure they fit snugly.

BELL OR HORN: Be sure it works.

HANDLEBARS: Keep stem well down in fork. Tighten securely.

LIGHT: Must be visible for 500 feet.

TIRES: Inflate to correct pressure. Check tires frequently. Remove imbedded glass, cinders, etc. Don't ride on worn-out tires.

WHEELS: Tighten wheel nuts.

PEDALS: Tighten spindles. Replace worn-out ones with reflectorized pedals.

Information supplied by the Bicycle Institute of America

Reprinted by permission from Changing Times: The Kiplinger Magazine (June 1974 issue) Copyright 1974 by the Kiplinger Washington Editors, Inc., 1729 H Street, N. W., Washington, D. C. 20006

states where you are required to ride against traffic.

• Keep to the right and ride in a straight line. Don't weave in and out of traffic.

• Check traffic carefully and signal before you make a turn. Remember that you must watch out for motorists. They may not always watch out for you.

• If you ride at night, be sure that you have a headlight that is visible 500 feet away. A rear light is also advisable, so that others can see you. If you don't have a rear light, be sure to use a rear reflector. Light-colored clothing is also helpful.

• When you ride, look out for cars which are turning or backing out of driveways and parked cars that may be starting.

• Watch for manholes and sewers that can catch your wheels and flip you off your bike.

• Be careful of wet pavement, slippery patches, sand, snow, and ice.

Camping and Backpacking

Camping is one of the most popular vacation pastimes for millions of Americans. Some people travel by car and camp out. Others hike the countryside, backpacking their food and equipment. Still others canoe or boat but pitch camp each night. Camping out doesn't cut transportation costs, but food costs are low, and shelter is inexpensive or free. Camping out can mean roughing it, but with modern equipment one can enjoy living outdoors in relative comfort.

Many people get great pleasure from hiking and camping out. There is a special joy in being out in the air, free from the schedules and demands of the industrialized world, and on your own. You can stop when you want, eat when you are

U. S. Forest Service

Dehydrated foods are popular with campers.

U. S. Army Photo

hungry, and enjoy the special beauty and music of the woods, fields, or mountains.

A large network of trails is available in many parts of the country as a result of the foresight and planning of a number of individuals and groups. The first one developed was the Long Trail through the Green Mountains of Vermont. Then the Appalachian Trail from Maine to Georgia, 2000 miles long, was built by volunteers. This is the longest marked trail in the world.

The National Trail System Act of 1968 planned a network of sixteen trails to be protected and held in trust by the Departments of Agriculture and Interior. Some of the trails are ones which the early settlers of the West used, the Lewis and Clark, the Sante Fe, the Old Cattee, and others. Under consideration is an Atlantic-to-Pacific trail which would make it possible to walk from ocean to ocean.

The same act also encouraged the development of trails by individual states. State and national park campgrounds were becoming very overcrowded, and people had begun to look for other alternatives. In many areas there are trails near heavily populated urban areas. Probably the best known of these is the Potomac Heritage Trail on the outskirts of Washington, D. C.

Backpacking is nothing more than hiking and carrying your own supplies and equipment. Almost any waterproof knapsack can be used with a blanket wrapped in a waterproof sheet or a bedroll with a waterproof cover. Perhaps you have been on camping trips with a school or a scouting group and have assembled some equipment.

If you are starting out from scratch, you might try borrowing equipment from a friend or renting the bigger items from an outing club or sporting goods store. Many will rent tents, packs, and sleeping bags.

If you are buying some things, you will probably want to get a modern backpack that weighs two pounds or less. These are framed of aluminum or magnesium and covered in nylon. This type of pack enables you to walk upright without strain. It's development is one of the things that has given added impetus to backpacking.

In addition to a pack and sleeping bag, a tent is handy if it rains. However, many people manage without one. You will also need some good walking shoes or sneakers, a map, a compass, and food.

You may be able to get free trail maps from the recreation or conservation departments of your local or state government. You can purchase topographical maps from the U. S. Geological Survey, Washington, D. C. 20244. (Ask for a free index of your state. They will send you instructions for ordering the maps and a booklet on how to read them.) In addition many hiking and outing clubs have maps and planned backpacking trips.

For cooking out you will need a small stove or a grill that you can stand over a fire. Although you may plan to catch fish in many areas, you will still need to carry some provisions. Freeze-dried foods are a boon. They are light in weight, and most are easy to cook in boiling water.

You will also need a cooking pot and some eating utensils. Experienced hikers often add a flashlight, sunburn cream, bandages, matches, soap, moleskin for blisters, and a canteen for water to their list of essentials, as well as a towel and personal clothing.

DRIVING AND CAMPING

Case Study. Barbara Melmud and her family want to take a two-week trip out West. There are four people in the family—her parents, Barbara, and her

National parks have been popular ever since 1872 when Yellowstone was first opened.

brother, Joe. They figure that if they stay in motels and eat in restaurants, the two-week trip will cost them over $1,400. However, by camping out and cooking their own meals, they can manage for about $700. These costs are based on daily costs of $60 a night for lodging (two rooms), $40-45 for restaurant meals, and the balance for gas, oil, and other expenses. It also assumes that they own camping equipment. To rent camping equipment they would need to spend an additional $200 for the trip. Buying it would cost several hundred more.

Camping out is not like living in a motel or hotel. You have to spend time and effort setting up your camping site and breaking it up when you leave. Shopping, cooking,

and preparing meals is also a job. If it rains, you may be cold and uncomfortable. However, as the increasing number of hikers and campers indicates, more people are enjoying spending time close to nature.

INFORMATION ABOUT CAMPSITES

There are many public and private campsites. However, with the growing popularity of camping it is often wise to plan ahead and reserve a campsite in the more popular locations. For information about federal campsites three government publications are available: *Camping in the National Park System, National Forest Vacations,* and *Vacationing with the Indians.* Your local public library may have them. If

USDA Photo

This youngster, who usually wears a brace on his leg, enjoys a stay at a special camp. People with handicaps can still enjoy many outdoor activities.

not, you can purchase them for a small charge from the Consumer Information Center, Pueblo, Colorado 81009. In addition, most states have a tourist office. This office can give you information about the many state-owned campsites. Some auto clubs will give you information about campsites. (The American Automobile Association, for example, has booklets that discuss campsites in the various regions of the United States.)

Skiing

Cross-country, downhill (alpine), and water skiing have become much more popular in the last few years.

CROSS-COUNTRY SKIING

In just a few years the number of cross-country skiers has doubled. One reason is that many people are developing a greater interest in outdoor winter activities. Also, cross-country skiing does not require great skill. Most energetic people can learn to get around quite easily. Another is that cross-country skiing is easily available in many places. You do not need expensive uphill lifts or tall mountains. All that is necessary is an open area or trails with a light snow cover. In addition, cross-country ski equipment is much less expensive than that for downhill skiing.

In selecting ski equipment of any type—cross-country, downhill, or water—the size of the ski and proper bindings are important. For snow skiing, boots are needed. The fit is particularly important for downhill skiing. What is right for a young girl will not fit a taller, heavier person. You may need help in selecting the right size if you are just starting out.

For a long time cross-country skies were made of sturdy wood. However, now lighter, narrower skis made of fiberglass are more popular. Also in great demand are skis with no-wax bottoms and "fish scale" or other finishes that reduce waxing. Plastic and metal skis do not seem to perform as well and are also more expensive. Many of the better skis have plastic bottoms. These aid in climbing and reduce maintenance.

Low-cut, lightweight, flexible boots, similar to low leather sneakers, are most popular. The best boots have leather tops which are silicone-treated to make them water-resistant.

The boots are fastened to the skis with bindings. Three-pin binding (boots are fastened in three places), particularly the step-in models, are most popular. Today boot widths and bindings are quite standard so that most adults' boots will fit a standard three-pin binding.

Aluminum poles are replacing bamboo as the best sellers.

Proper waxing can help you climb uphill and slide downhill. Waxing has always been one of the trickiest parts of cross-country skiing. There is a trend towards simplification, with several companies producing a two-wax kit, one wax for above freezing temperatures and another for below freezing.

Two magazines offer guidance on new models of equipment for both cross-country and downhill skiing—*Skiing* and *Ski*. A look at some sporting goods stores or departments will also give you an idea of what is new. However, many young people buy used equipment at ski swap sales to get started.

DOWNHILL SKIING

This is a much more expensive sport than cross-country skiing. Most people have to travel farther to find suitable skiing. Moreover, the areas with lifts usually charge high daily fees. Skis and boots are more expensive, and one needs greater skill to navigate down steep hills and mountainsides. However, many people find downhill skiing exciting. If you want to learn, you might start by renting equipment, rather than making a big investment.

Most ski areas offer packaged "ski weeks." These usually include 5 or 7 days of class lessons, graded according to your ability. Generally, you can arrange to rent skis, boots, and poles, and some packages include lodging. One of the most promising programs for beginners is the GLM technique, by which one starts off on short skis and gradually works up to longer ones. It is easier to turn on short skis, but longer skis give greater stability under most conditions.

The trend is for stiff boots and step-in bindings. Stiff boots give better edge control and step-in bindings are easier to get in and out of.

Most important of all, be sure to get safety release bindings and have them properly adjusted for your weight and ability to avoid unnecessary injuries. If you do not have access to a good release check, have the bindings set by someone who does—a friend or a reputable ski shop or department store.

WATER SKIING

This is a sport for good swimmers. Still, everyone should wear a flotation device for protection, a ski vest or belt. Some states require this by law.

Water skis are generally five to six feet long, although smaller sizes are available for children.

Most skis are made of wood, glass, or plastic. They are sold with bindings that are adjustable to allow for growing feet or use by several different people.

In addition, one needs a boat and driver for towing. The boat should have enough power to be able to pull a skier out of the water easily. It should be equipped with a good marine speedometer as well as a fire extinguisher, life preservers, and if the sides are high, a boarding ladder. A good rearview mirror will help the driver see what the skier is doing at all times.

Camping has grown in popularity as a form of recreation for the entire family.

The driver should be competent both in handling the boat and in towing a skier.

Specialized magazines, such as the *Water Skier,* are helpful in learning about the sport and equipment.

Fishing

About sixty million Americans will drop a fishing line this year—double the number of only twenty years ago. A young person often starts out casting a line and ends up with a lifelong interest in fishing.

Even though some people have expensive fishing gear, many people have fun without elaborate equipment. Some people make their own fishing rods or put together components—a rod, reel, and lures. Tying flies is an art, and many people make their own and are proud of their skill. Fishing equipment can be bought at moderate prices through mail-order catalogs and stores. A visit to a large sporting goods store can give you an idea of the price range for various types of equipment. Information on equipment is available in sports magazines as well as those that rate products.

Good fishing spots are easily available in much of the United States. Fish abound in brooks, ponds, lakes, rivers, coastal waterways, and marshes. In the last few years environmental management by the fisheries managers of the federal and state governments has resulted in even better fishing in many places.

Case Study. Bob Mackenzie lives on the shore of Lake Michigan about 100 miles north of Chicago. His parents moved there when they were first married, late in the 1950's, because they wanted to live near the water. At that time the beaches were clean and the lake abounded in trout. However, in 1959 the St. Lawrence Seaway opened a direct passage to Lake Michigan from the Atlantic Ocean. Along with large ocean liners came the parasitic lamprey eel which killed off the trout. The eel was followed by a small undesirable herring, the alewives, which multiplied rapidly. By 1964 fishing on Lake Michigan had almost disappeared, and many beaches were covered with the carcasses of the dead alewives.

Michigan remedied this situation by introducing Coho salmon. The Coho had several important qualities. It was popular with fishermen. Also it was a large eater that would feed on the alewives. Lastly, it could live in the polluted waters of Lake Michigan. Although the Coho was a salt-water fish abundant in the Northwest, biologists believed it would live in fresh water because some had survived in an Alaskan lake. The results were dramatic. The Coho salmon have thrived and multiplied so that once again Lake Michigan has good fishing for Bob's family and other fishing enthusiasts.

Programs are underway to transplant fish in many parts of the country. Striped bass, an Atlantic Ocean fish, have been introduced into the tremendous freshwater reservoirs of the South and Midwest. Species that have been driven out by man-made changes have been replenished. The original settlers of Maine caught Atlantic Ocean salmon in the Penobscot River where they spawned. However, beginning about 1870 dams were built on the Penob-

Eye Gate House

Fishing equipment need not be expensive.

scot which kept the salmon out. Recently Maine, in cooperation with the federal government, introduced a program to bring them back. An antipollution drive cleaned the river far enough for the salmon to spawn. Fish ladders—water-filled concrete steps—were constructed over the dams. Then the river was stocked with salmon, and once again salmon can be caught on the river.

Eutrophication—the overgrowth of the plant population—has clogged some lakes and ponds. Scientists are trying different ways to treat this. One of the most promising methods has been to use aluminum sulphate, a chemical employed to purify drinking water.

Tennis

In the early 1970's tennis became much more popular than ever before. It always

Riding in the daytime with the headlights on makes a motorcyclist more visible to drivers of other vehicles.

had its enthusiasts, but suddenly it took a great leap forward. More communities started building tennis courts, including indoor facilities for use in the winter or in bad weather, and many more people started playing. A number of communities initiated programs to teach people how to play.

If community courts are available, tennis costs involve a charge for the use of the courts (if there is a charge) and the purchase of a racquet, balls, sneakers, and tennis clothes (if desired).

Tennis racquets come in a range of prices. The least expensive are often wooden racquets. Metal ones can be considerably more, although some are available at lower prices. For the average player the difference in play between a medium-priced

wooden racquet and a metal one often is not tremendous.

Although some racquets are already strung, a medium- or high-priced racquet is often strung to order. Two general types of stringing are available, nylon and gut. Nylon is much more durable, will not be greatly affected by moisture, and is less expensive. Gut is preferred by competitors because a good grade gives a little extra zing to the ball. However, gut breaks much more easily and needs to be protected from moisture. (Competitive tennis players usually keep at least two racquets on hand in case a string breaks in competition.)

If you are interested in learning to play tennis, ask about teaching programs in your area. Group lessons are often available through schools, local adult education programs, the Y's, and recreation departments.

Motorcycling

There are close to 20 million motorcyclists in the United States. This is far less than the number of automobile drivers but a big group, nevertheless. The average motorcyclist is between the ages of 21 and 35.

Motorcycling is hazardous, far more hazardous than driving a car. The biggest hazards are cars and trucks. Motorcycles are hard to see from an automobile or truck driver's seat. Also, a motorcycle can get caught and be knocked down in the wind vacuum at the rear of a large, fast-moving truck. In addition, road hazards—wet pavement, mud, loose gravel, and even the smooth paint or plastic strips used to mark driving lanes can cause a motorcycle to skid and turn over.

The motorcyclist has none of the protection that the driver of a car has. No frame of metal surrounds the driver. There are no seat belts to keep one in place. A motorcy-

Conventional road tires such as the one on the left give far better traction on paved roads than do knobby or off-road tires (right).

Fuel tank lids that flip forward and protruding steering damper controls are notorious for causing groin injuries in crashes.

clist's vision can be hindered by heavy rain, snow, mud splashing up from the road, or a speck of dust in an eye.

Still, many people choose to take to the road or field on a two-wheeled vehicle. They can protect themselves a little by the use of a safety helmet (which is required by some states), goggles or a face shield, a leather jacket, sturdy trousers, and boots and leather gloves. In addition, accidents are less likely if the motorcycle is in good condition and equipped with a windshield and a rearview mirror. Most important of all, one needs to drive sensibly.

SHOPPING FOR A MOTORCYCLE

To begin with, you should consider that a motorcycle may not cost any less than a used car. If you are just looking for transportation, the used car may be a better buy. After all, a motorcycle is mighty cold on a winter night, wet when it rains, and not very convenient for carrying things.

However, a motorcycle will go four or five times as far as a medium-sized car on a gallon of gas and will probably cost only half as much to insure.

The very lightest motorcycles are generally the cheapest. However, many of these cannot keep up with traffic moving at 40 miles per hour, which makes them even more dangerous. A medium-weight machine will better enable one to keep up with traffic. A high-powered model gives more power than needed for ordinary riding, and it costs more.

There are two basic types of motorcycle engines—a two-stroke engine and a four-stroke engine. With some of the two-stroke engines you will need to add oil to the gasoline every time you fill the tank, as is necessary for some lawnmowers.

A wide array of accessories is available for motorcycles—which can run up the cost considerably. A windshield and rear-view mirror will improve the operator's visibility. Crash bars can provide some protection, and a luggage rack is useful. An electric starter is convenient, but it is not really necessary. Most other accessories are just decorative.

A secondhand motorcycle can be a bargain or a disaster. If you can find a used machine in good condition, that's great, but many first-time buyers don't know what to look for. Generally, it is wiser to buy a used motorcycle from a dealer who will guarantee it or with the help of someone who can check it out for you. You may be able to arrange to have a reputable dealer check out the machine you are considering.

If you are buying a new or used motorcycle from a dealer, check out shops within a reasonable radius. Prices vary. Also, machines are usually reduced in price at the beginning of winter and tend to rise with the approach of spring.

Be sure to select one that can be serviced in your area. Like foreign cars, some motorcycles may be hard to service in parts of the country.

Snowmobiling

Snowmobiling has become very popular all over the country. Although the snowmobile is used for essential winter travel by some people, it is a recreational vehicle for most. For many it is a way of getting out and having fun during the winter months.

However, accidents are common and the snowmobiler is in much the same position as the motorcyclist, with little to protect him or her in the event of an accident. According to *Consumers Research Magazine,* some of the most common causes of accidents are:

- Inexperienced, reckless, or careless operators.
- Traveling too fast for conditions.
- Operating in an unfamiliar or dangerous area without reasonable caution, as on ice-covered rivers, lakes or ponds, or in woods.
- Mechanical failure.
- Operating on a public road or highway.
- Inattention.
- Striking an unseen object (a boulder or a barbed wire fence, for example).
- Dangerous turns.
- Intoxicated drivers.

Manufacturers of snowmobiles and suppliers of auxiliary equipment have tried to improve the safety of these vehicles by better designs and equipment. Also, some states now license the snowmobile operator. However, in many places a snowmobile can be operated by anyone, including young children.

For your own protection use marked snowmobile trails where they are available. Learn about the area in which you will be riding. Don't assume that a layer of ice will hold the weight of the snowmobile. (Drowning is a major cause of snowmobile deaths.) If you are traveling in an area far from help, be sure to be accompanied by a buddy in another machine. Don't go so far that you cannot walk back in case you are caught in a storm or have a machine failure. Remember, a snowmobile is a motorized vehicle which can have mechanical problems.

CUTTING COSTS FOR RECREATION

One of the most obvious ways to cut expenditures is to reduce what you spend on recreation. A day spent hiking can cost less than an evening at the movies with a snack afterwards. Swimming at a public lake or pool is usually less expensive than several rounds of bowling. Many communities offer free or low-cost sports facilities, concerts, art exhibits, and dances. Taking advantage of some of these activities may help your budget.

Before you invest in recreational equipment, be sure you really will use and enjoy it. Rent if you can, borrow a friend's equipment for a day, or buy used equipment.

Often you and a friend can exchange items in order to help each other. Perhaps you can swap cassette tapes for several weeks. That way you both will have more to listen to without buying as much. A number of communities have regular swaps of sporting equipment. In some cases people offer used equipment for sale; in others it is really a trading arrangement—you give me roller skates, and I'll give you a hockey stick.

FOR REVIEW

Points to Remember

- Industrialization has resulted in most people working fewer hours per week.
- Leisure time is unevenly divided among the population. Young people, homemakers with school-age children who do not hold an outside job, and retired persons generally have the most time for recreational activities.
- A growing number of Americans are spending money on recreational activities.
- Among young people listening to music and some outdoor activities are particularly popular.

Mercury Marine

There are many inexpensive ways to have fun.

- You can often save money on sports equipment by renting, buying at sales, buying used equipment, swapping, and getting as much information as possible about the features before you make a decision.
- Many recreational activities are available free or at low cost in most communities.

Terms to Know	
alpine skiing	downhill skiing
backpacking	flexible hours
blocks of leisure	4-day week
clinchers	GLM technique
cross-country	sew-ups
skiing	tubular tires
derailleur	wire-ons

PROBLEM SOLVING:
CHECK YOUR UNDERSTANDING

1. What are some of the reasons for the trend toward a shorter working week?

2. In what ways is leisure distributed unevenly among the population?

3. What are some leisure activities that are particularly popular among young people?

4. What are the advantages and disadvantages of buying a bicycle from a specialty bike shop?

5. Why do most bicycle riders prefer tires with tubes?

6. Where can you get information about trails for hiking in your area?

7. What are some of the advantages and disadvantages of nylon stringing in a tennis racquet?

8. Why are motorcycles more dangerous to ride than cars?

9. What are some of the common causes of accidents on snowmobiles?

10. Why has cross-country skiing become more popular?

11. What are some of the ways in which people can cut recreational expenses?

TO DO IN CLASS
Discussion

1. How would you like to see the working week changed?

2. What do you consider leisure time activities? Is a do-it-yourself project such as building a fence or planting a garden a leisure activity? If so, why? If not, why not?

3. In what ways does your use of leisure differ from that of your parents?

4. What types of facilities does your community provide for bicycle riders? What additional facilities would be desirable?

5. What are some of the things that your community might provide to improve the recreational opportunities for young people?

6. If you were picking an ideal place to live, what would you want in the community? Consider both work and leisure activities.

7. What might you and your friends do to provide yourselves with better recreational opportunities?

Activities

1. Divide the class into teams to shop for various items: a three-speed bicycle, a ten-speed bicycle, a backpack, a sewing machine, a fishing rod, a camera, a stereo set, and others. Use as many sources of information and shopping resources as possible. Have the teams report their findings to the class.

2. Invite a representative of a local recreation or conservation group to class to discuss the availability of and plans for development of outdoor facilities in your area.

3. Make a map on a bulletin board of nearby hiking trails and campsites.

4. Have a committee assemble an exhibit of minimum supplies for an overnight camping or canoeing trip. Explain why each item was selected and why others were omitted.

5. Compile a list of free and inexpensive recreational activities that are available to young people in your community.

6. Invite a person from a senior citizen's group to talk to the class about the recreational needs of older people.

7. Find out how your community helps people with low incomes take advantage of recreational opportunities. Talk with the director of athletics at school and people in church and community agencies.

SECTION 3

Protecting Yourself

CHAPTER 8

Protecting Your Health

Ponce de León once searched for the *fountain of youth,* looking for magic water that would enable him to stay eternally young. Good food, improved sanitation, and the advances of modern medicine have given us some of what he sought. Today people in the industrialized nations not only live longer but also maintain their health and vigor for many more years than earlier generations. Just think about the growing number of retirement communities which include provisions for active sports such as swimming and golf.

The life expectancy of an American at birth is more than 71.2 years. By contrast, life expectancy in 1900 was about 49.6 years for most people.

THE MIRACLES OF MEDICINE

Great steps have been taken in the prevention, cure, and control of many diseases in the last fifty years. Potent new drugs have been developed. A greater understanding of the relationship between good nutrition and health has come about. Vitamins, both natural and synthetic, are available. There are vaccines for many diseases.

Between science and technology we have conquered diseases that have ravaged mankind for centuries, such as smallpox and typhus. We can now control and limit others, such as tuberculosis and dysentery. It is possible to imagine that cancer, heart disease, muscular dystrophy, and other deadly diseases might eventually be curable.

YOUR RESPONSIBILITY FOR GOOD HEALTH

Given a good body and a fairly healthy environment, each of us can improve or injure our state of well-being. Although good medical care is important, even the best medical care cannot give a person good health. We also need wholesome food, healthful living habits, and freedom from emotional disturbances beginning at an early age.

Healthful Eating

Many people are poorly fed either because they are ignorant of the rules of good

It is important to start good health habits early.

nutrition or they satisfy their food urges without regard to the relationship between good eating habits and health. Children under age twelve are our best fed group. Studies have shown that starting with the teenage period many people have poorer eating habits.

A well-balanced diet includes the following foods: leafy, green and yellow vegetables; other vegetables and fresh fruits; proteins in the form of meat, poultry, fish, or cheese; whole grain breads and cereals; milk and milk products; and butter or fortified margarine. Adequate amounts of these important food groups furnish us with the protein, energy, vitamins, and minerals necessary for growth and vigor.

Snacks

Nibbling foods has become part of our cultural pattern—a bag of popcorn at the movies, ice cream between meals, a hamburger or a hot dog at a drive-in restaurant, cold soda on a hot day, or potato chips to munch while watching TV. Our highways are lined with quick service food vendors, and our supermarkets have long aisles of snack foods.

Cultural patterns reinforce the need for between-meal eating. Young people often gather together after school at some local snack spot. Your parents may visit with friends and have food and beverages after dinner. If you want to be part of the gang, it may be hard to turn down an invitation to share a pizza at Sloppy Joe's. So pervasive have the new snacking habits become that many adults, who in their younger days never had access to snacks, now eat them regularly.

Trimming Down or Trying to Gain

Most people will not gain weight on three moderate-sized, well-balanced meals

a day. However, after the age of twelve, many people develop other eating habits. Breakfast may be eaten on the run, if at all. Lunch is apt to be eaten away from home. In addition, many people have a mid-morning or mid-afternoon snack. Many of the foods eaten as snacks or away from home are high in calories.

As a result, a growing number of people are fighting the battle of the bulge. In fact, obesity has become an important health concern. Statistics show that people who are overweight (more than ten percent above the normal range) have a shorter life expectancy and are more readily prone to such diseases as diabetes, heart disease, and arteriosclerosis. Of even greater concern to many people is the fact that being slim is more socially acceptable.

Dieting has become widespread. Best selling books and magazines tell of ways to lose weight. Periodically, a new diet fad takes hold as millions try it. Unfortunately, many of these diets are not well balanced

Lunch is often eaten away from home.

USDA

A steady program of exercise, such as bicycling, can help you stay in good physical shape.

USDA

RECOMMENDED DAILY DIETARY ALLOWANCES[1]

	(years)	Weight		Height		Energy
	From Up to	(kg)	(lbs)	(cm)	(in)	(calories)
Infants	0.0–0.5	6	14	60	24	kg[2] x 117
	0.5–1.0	9	20	71	28	kg x 108
Children	1–3	13	28	86	34	1300
	4–6	20	44	110	44	1800
	7–10	30	66	135	54	2400
Males	11–14	44	97	158	63	2800
	15–18	61	134	172	69	3000
	19–22	67	147	172	69	3000
	23–50	70	154	172	69	2700
	51 +	70	154	172	69	2400
Females	11–14	44	97	155	62	2400
	15–18	54	119	162	65	2100
	19–22	58	128	162	65	2100
	23–50	58	128	162	65	2000
	51 +	58	128	162	65	1800
Pregnant						+300
Lactating						+500

[1]The allowances are intended to provide for individual variations among most normal persons as they live in the United States under usual environmental stresses. Diets should be based on a variety of common foods in order to provide other nutrients for which human requirements have been less well defined.
[2]1 kg = 2.2 lbs.

Food and Nutrition Board, National Academy of Sciences— National Research Council

nutritionally, and some may be injurious to your health.

Do you dream of a slim, trim figure for summer fun by the pool, but right now you are a little bulgy in the wrong places, or are you so thin that clothes just hang on you? Whether you want to gain or lose weight, the first step is convincing yourself that you should and can do it.

Rate your figure or build; look at weight charts as well as the mirror. If more than a few pounds are involved, consult a doctor. Get a professional opinion on how much you should lose or gain. Find out whether or not you have any health problems that might influence what you do.

For almost all people, what is eaten controls weight. When you regularly eat more than your body needs, you are bound to become overweight. To lose weight your daily food intake must be cut to supply fewer calories than you need. Then your body will use up the reserve energy you have in those extra pounds.

Of course, if you are underweight, it probably means that you have been eating less than your body needs. Therefore you will have to increase your daily food intake.

It's amazing but true that if you change your weight slowly you will be more likely to maintain it. If you want to lose weight and keep it off, plan on a gradual change. A crash diet is all right for losing a pound or two, but if you want to take off ten pounds, plan on losing about a pound a week. Eat less and exercise regularly to burn up that extra fat. A sensible diet will keep you feeling well as you lose—no hunger pangs, dizziness, or other discouraging symptoms.

You shouldn't need pills unless you have an unusual medical problem, so never take them without medical supervision. Build your will power. Set yourself reasonable goals and stick to your plan. The most dependable way to lose weight is to use self-control and eat less.

How many calories do you need each day? It depends on your size, build, amount of activity, and metabolism. A tall person has a bigger body to fill up than a short one and generally needs more food. Two people of the same apparent size may have quite different builds. One is small and has narrow bones, and the other is broad shouldered. Their needs may be different. Generally, to lose one pound a week, you should eat five hundred calories less than your body needs each day.

People who are very active burn up more food. Boys on a football team may be able to eat three servings of a hearty dinner without gaining weight.

Here's how some activities burn up calories:

Running—19.4 calories per minute
Swimming—11.2 calories per minute
Bicycle riding—8.2 calories per minute
Lying down and reading—1.3 calories per minute

Metabolism is also important. This is the basic rate at which your body burns up food. Some people have a higher metabolic rate than others. This may explain why every crumb you swallow seems to show up as more pounds even though your best friend may not gain on spaghetti and ice

If you are very active, you will burn up energy more quickly.

cream sodas. Although many people blame their metabolism for extra pounds, the fact is that most people have a normal metabolism. However, metabolic rate does change at various ages. Babies need more energy per pound than you do because they grow so fast. Teenagers need more calories than their parents because they are still growing. Your mother may find it very hard to lose weight because her body burns food more slowly than yours.

Gaining weight can be just as hard as losing it, particularly if you are growing fast. Some very thin people are just too active. Slow down a little. You will burn calories more slowly. Don't get too tired. Often a short rest before a meal will make you more interested in eating. Avoid snacks that kill your appetite just before a meal. Instead, try to eat a little extra halfway between meals. Follow a sensible, balanced diet; don't eat just the so-called fattening foods.

Age as well as activity influences how many calories your body needs.

CALORIES NEEDED FOR VARIOUS ACTIVITIES

Type of activity:	Calories per hour
Sedentary activities, such as: reading; writing; eating; watching television or movies; listening to the radio; sewing; playing cards; and typing, officework, and other activities done while sitting that require little or no arm movement.	**80 to 100**
Light activities, such as: preparing and cooking food; doing dishes; dusting; handwashing small articles of clothing; ironing; walking slowly; personal care; officework and other activities done while standing that require some arm movement; and rapid typing and other activities done while sitting that are more strenuous.	**110 to 160**
Moderate activities, such as: making beds, mopping and scrubbing; sweeping; light polishing and waxing; laundering by machine; light gardening and carpentry work; walking moderately fast; other activities done while standing that require moderate arm movement; and activities done while sitting that require more vigorous arm movement.	**170 to 240**
Vigorous activities, such as: heavy scrubbing and waxing; handwashing large articles of clothing; hanging out clothes; stripping beds; walking fast; bowling; golfing; and gardening.	**250 to 350**
Strenuous activities, such as: swimming; playing tennis; running; bicycling; dancing; skiing; and playing football.	**350 or more**

Louise Page and Nancy Raper,
Food and Your Weight

Physical Fitness

If you are training for a team or competing in athletics, you know how important it is to keep in shape with regular exercise. However, many people forget that even if they are not competing in sports, keeping fit is important. Regular exercise helps one feel better and function well. The President's Council on Physical Fitness and Sports found that only a little over 55 percent of the adult population exercises regularly. (The council's definition of regular exercise is three weekly sessions of 25 minutes each.)

Here are some of the other things they found out:

• Of the 60 million exercisers, nearly 44 million concentrate on walking; 18 million

You can cut your caloric intake by substituting low-calorie foods for high-calorie ones—for example, tomatoes for buns and a salad instead of a potato with butter.

ride bicycles; 14 million swim; 14 million do calisthenics; and 6.5 million jog.

• More than half of the walkers get out for daily or almost daily sessions, and nearly three-fourths of these spend at least 20 minutes on each outing.

• Joggers, swimmers, and cyclists, however, tend to be less regular than walkers.

• Bowling scores as the nation's most popular competitive sport, with one person in ten signed up as an active member of a team or league.

Health Fallacies, Beliefs, and Practices

J. S. Buchan in *FDA Consumer* offers the following quiz:

Fact or Fiction: A Mini Quiz

1. Extra vitamins provide pep and energy.

2. You can reduce your weight substantially by a lot of sweating.

3. A bowel movement every day is necessary for health.

4. Wearing brass or copper jewelry can relieve the pains of arthritis or rheumatism.

5. Older people are more inclined to worry about their health than younger people.

Did you answer *yes* to any of these statements? Actually none of them is true. Generally, a balanced diet provides enough vitamins for health and energy. Sweating results in a temporary loss of water but not fat. The weight is quickly regained by drinking fluids. There is no medical evidence that a bowel movement every day is essential to health. Attractive as they may be, there is no indication that copper or brass jewelry has any medicinal effect. Also, young people are very much inclined to worry about their health and fitness.

Food Fads

At times among different groups of people some foods have been considered very desirable and others avoided. Some primitive people would not eat the meat of the timid deer. The Romans considered cabbage a miracle food. In the early 1800's settlers of the United States banned the sale of fruits because they felt that fruits were related to the spread of cholera.

Today *health foods* are popular. Generally, when people refer to *health foods,* they mean whole-grain products and vegetables raised without chemical fertilizers or pesticides.

This interest in whole-grain products is a rather interesting reversal of a trend. Until the age of industrialization white flour was very costly because it required much more refining. White bread was a delicacy for the rich; brown bread was for the less affluent. However, with mechanical methods of refining, white bread became a luxury everyone could afford. Now many people say that they prefer the taste of the darker breads made with flours that have been processed less.

Like many specialty foods, the so-called health foods often are expensive, particularly in specialty food stores or departments. The canny shopper often can find some of these foods at lower costs in supermarkets and grocery stores that specialize in ethnic foods.

Clearing Up Your Complexion

Acne is a real problem for teenagers. At some time or another most young people have some bumps or blotches. This is a medical problem. Generally, it's at least in part the result of imbalances in hormonal function.

Although doctors are not clear on all the causes, they do know that the sebaceous glands on the scalp, face, chest, and back become overactive and secrete fats and waxes to the surface of the skin. When a pore becomes blocked, this mixture combines with other oils and bacteria to form whiteheads and blackheads. A further excess results in an inflammation, such as pimples or pus-filled bumps.

What can you do about it? For mild or occasional cases you can help yourself by keeping your skin clean. Washing once or twice a day with soap (any ordinary soap will do) helps keep your skin free of excess oils, dead skin, and surface bacteria. Don't use hairdressings with a greasy or oily base. If you have oily hair, shampoo it at least once or twice a week, and keep it off your face.

Don't pick or squeeze the bumps. Touching them can increase the problem. A moderate amount of sunshine may help dry up some blemishes.

Should you use some of the preparations sold without a prescription for clearing up pimples? Some of these might help a mild case, but they could also be irritating. Others are ineffective. It's hard to choose wisely. If the condition persists or is severe, see a doctor. He or she can't cure acne but can help you keep it under control with medication and/or other treatment.

Smoking, Alcohol, and Other Drugs

For a long time the use of tobacco and alcohol has been part of the social pattern of many groups. More recently other drugs have been used, often by young people.

All the evidence clearly indicates that the regular use of tobacco, alcohol, and most other drugs is very harmful to health. Prolonged use of tobacco is clearly related to lung cancer and other disturbances.

According to the Federal Drug Commission, alcohol is the number one drug problem in the United States today. More people suffer from the harmful effects of its use than from any other drug. Surprisingly, even young people of elementary and junior high school age are becoming involved with alcohol. Alcohol is closely associated with violent crime, automobile accidents and deaths, suicide, broken marriages, and absenteeism from jobs. In addition, long-term use of large amounts results in debilitating diseases such as cirrhosis of the liver.

Heroin presents the next most serious problem. About 92 percent of the people dependent on hard drugs (drugs that cause addiction) are heroin users. This drug comes from the flower of the poppy plant. Its effect on the body is similar to other narcotics—a dulling of the senses including pain, depressing of the central nervous system, grogginess, and others. Too large a dose can result in a stupor or coma and death. In addition, injections from unsterilized needles often lead to serious infections.

Marijuana is the most controversial drug in use. It comes from the Indian hemp plant which grows easily in mild climates all over the world. Marijuana is commonly used in a form called *reefers, sticks,* or *joints.* These are made from the crushed dried flowers and leaves, which are rolled into cigarettes.

While hashish is a drug which also comes from the hemp plant, it should not be confused with marijuana. Hashish comes from the pure resin of the hemp plant.

The use of marijuana does not appear to be as dangerous as heroin. Studies are still underway to determine the long-term effects of marijuana on users as well as on the unborn children of pregnant mothers who use marijuana. Marijuana does have some physical effects that are already known, such as the reduction of body temperature and an altered sense of space (which is particularly dangerous when driving a car). To date, the medical evidence seems to indicate that it is not as harmful as tobacco and no worse for the user than alcohol. (As mentioned, however, the effects from use of alcohol can be very serious.) Unfortunately, many people who start on marijuana try other drugs that are more harmful.

The biggest public controversy about marijuana is largely over whether or not it should be illegal to use—with stiff penalties for selling and using it. At present there are clearly inconsistencies in the state and local laws regarding the use of alcohol and other drugs. In some states selling alcohol is legal and licensed, but selling marijuana is illegal. If one is caught selling marijuana in these states, there is a long jail sentence.

The experience of other nations has shown that it is possible to control drug usage more effectively than we are at present. Modern China has virtually wiped out opium addiction, which was widespread not long ago. Finland has imposed such stiff penalties for driving after drinking that accidents from drunken driving have been reduced sharply.

Often it is very hard for young people to resist the temptation to try something new or do what the group is doing. Unfortunately, this may lead to harmful experimenting. The best time to avoid the use of drugs is before you start.

If you have started using drugs, you can seek help. Many communities have clinics and counseling services for young people. In addition to the usual sources of information—doctors, school guidance departments, and the clergy—many communities have "hot line" telephone numbers which you can call for advice. There are a number of organizations that specialize in helping people with drug problems. The best known is Alcoholics Anonymous (AA).

DRUG ADDICTION

This case illustrates some of the ways in which drug addiction is spread:

The boy was seventeen years of age. He had a pleasant way of talking, punctuating his remarks with an occasional smile. His excellent grammar and quiet manners indicated a good home and background; the curly, light-brown hair and healthy complexion were well set off by neat sport clothes. He would be called a nice-looking boy. 'Likeable' is the word that might come into mind.

The illusion is spoiled by the fact that he is in police custody, the arrest report on the desk listing him as a dangerous repeater offender. The lettering on the door says, "Narcotics Division, Mercer County Sheriff's Department."

Is this a "dope fiend?" This is an inaccurate and seldom used term, but by all common standards and definitions the answer would be yes. Gene R____, the boy in custody, is a confirmed heroin addict, a "mainliner," injecting heroin directly into the main blood vessels of his arm. His body requires five to ten injections every day, costing him from $50 to $100 every twenty-four hours. He has managed to earn this amount by introducing other teenagers to amphetamines, barbiturates, marijuana, and eventually the use of heroin. The police report on the desk lists five separate cases where good-looking Gene R____ has inflicted the dope habit upon friends, all minors. Investigation indicates that four of these girls now pay for his, and their own, drug supply by means of prostitution.

Gene R____ is neither a usual nor an unusual case. Teenage narcotic addicts come from both sides of the tracks, from all races and religions, from all levels of intelligence.*

- Why do you think a boy like Gene turns to drugs?

- How do you think Gene feels about his situation?

- What do you think is his attitude toward his friends? What about theirs toward him?

- What can a community do to prevent addicts from needing to create new addicts to support their own drug use?

Over-the-Counter Medicines and Vitamins

A large number of people have become their own doctors, spending large sums of money for drug items they do not need. As a result, the sale of patent medicines and vitamin preparations has grown enormously. For most people this represents a waste of money. Of even greater concern is the fact that some people use self-prescribed medications and fail to consult a doctor about serious problems until too late. If you are concerned about a health problem, such as a very poor complexion, a lack of energy, regular headaches, or any others, see a doctor.

If you occasionally use over-the-counter drugs (nonprescription drugs), be sure to read the label. Federal law requires that all of these drugs must be labeled with directions for use by the average person. "This includes the conditions under which the drug should not be taken—for example, special instructions concerning its use (or nonuse) by infants, very young children, or the elderly."**

---

*The Mercer County Sheriff's Narcotic Education Department.

**"We Want You to Know What We Know about Medicines without Prescriptions," Food and Drug Administration.

Venereal Disease: A Growing Problem

Cokie and Steven V. Roberts report the following in the *New York Times Magazine:*

The Los Angeles Free Clinic is a small, rather shabby building wedged between a Chicken Delight ("We Deliver") and an appliance store ("Quality Merchandise—Best Service") across Fairfax Avenue from the West Coast headquarters of C.B.S. At about 5:30 the young people start crowding into a narrow alley alongside the clinic, waiting to sign in for treatment. They include well-scrubbed college students and scruffy street kids, both sexes, all colors, as young as 15 and as old as 35. Despite their diversity, they have two things in common. They need medical help, and they can't or won't get it elsewhere. Many just cannot afford a private doctor; others cannot afford to have their parents find out what's wrong with them. What's wrong with them could be almost anything—pregnancy, hepatitis, various infections and fears, tired blood and brains, maybe the flu or a bad cold—but more than 25 percent have V.D., venereal disease.

Shortly after World War II, many people believed that venereal disease was on the way out. Antibiotics and a widespread educational campaign had brought about a sharp decrease in its occurance. However, unfortunately, that trend has changed and venereal disease, according to the American Social Health Association, has now reached "pandemic proportions," meaning it is an epidemic which is unusually widespread and severe.

Contrary to popular mythology, people usually get venereal disease from sexual

Consumer Research Magazine
Many people use a wide variety of over-the-counter drugs. What problems might result from such use?

contact. The germs cannot live very long outside the human body. One estimate is that four million Americans contracted venereal disease in only one year. Moreover, young people have a particularly high rate. For instance, about half the cases of gonorrhea in the United States occur in people under 25.

Venereal disease can be treated very effectively with antibiotics. The earlier the treatment, the better chance of no serious damage to the body. However, untreated venereal disease will get worse.

TEENAGERS' RIGHTS AS PATIENTS

One morning a tired 16-year-old boy walked into the clinic of a large hospital and asked to see a doctor. He had been using drugs and wasn't feeling well. The lady at the admitting desk told him that they would have to notify his parents before he could be treated. Without a word he left.

In another city Susie, who was 17, sought contraceptives from her family doctor. The doctor insisted that he could not help her until her parents gave their approval.

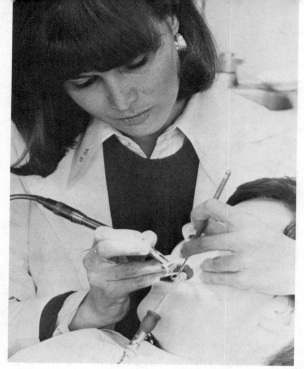

Modern medical and dental care is costly.

In the East a girl of 15 walked into a new hospital clinic program and said that she thought she was pregnant. First, they gave her a urine test to verify this. Then the people at the clinic talked with her about the various ways she could handle the situation.

There are a number of legal and ethical problems involved in whether young people can get medical care on their own. Should minors have the right to get medical and related services without the approval of their parents? Should a doctor hold in confidence a discussion with a teenage patient, or does the parent have the right to know? Should birth control information be available to unmarried people from community agencies? How do you feel about these complex questions?

Doctors and hospitals have been very reluctant to treat minors without parental consent for fear of law suits. A number of states have enacted laws clarifying what medical services minors are entitled to without parental consent, and there are a growing number of facilities where teenagers can go for medical advice and care on their own.

PREPAYING MEDICAL EXPENSES WITH HEALTH INSURANCE

About one out of every seven Americans is hospitalized each year. When this happens, the individual may be faced with a staggering economic burden. Modern medical techniques help save many lives, but they often require costly equipment, expensive medicine, and a highly specialized medical team.

Health insurance plans received a big boost in the late 1940's when the Supreme Court ruled that such plans could be a fringe benefit in wage negotiations. Today most health insurance coverage is through group plans provided where a member of the family works. People over age 65 are generally covered by federal programs—Medicare, which is administered by the federal Social Security Administration, and Medicaid, administered by the states.

Hospital Payments

This is the most common type of health insurance. It pays for hospital expenses for a limited period of time, generally from 21 to 120 days. The benefits include a semi-private room, meals, general nursing care, operating room charges, X-ray, many laboratory examinations, anesthesia, medicines, and surgical dressings.

Maternity benefits may be included. Generally, these cover the delivery of the baby and the hospitalization of the mother and baby for a few days after the birth.

However, most plans require that the insurance be in effect for ten months before the birth of the baby.

One of the most widely known plans for hospital payments is Blue Cross. Although the same name is used across the country, each state has its own plan and each is operated separately. The benefits and charges are based on the particular plan.

Hospital expenses have risen at a very rapid rate. In an effort to keep costs down, a variety of things have been tried: (a) reducing the hospital stay by having satellite nursing homes where patients who need less intensive care can be sent; (b) progressive patient care, where the patient does more for himself as convalescence progresses; and (c) the greater use of outpatient care. There is a trend for hospital payments insurance plans to cover some of these newer types of care.

Surgical Costs

This pays the doctor's fee for surgical procedures according to a schedule of fees which varies with different policies. It may not cover the entire fee. Emergency care given in a doctor's office and minor surgery may be covered.

Maternity benefits are available with some plans. Like the hospital payments insurance, these usually require that the mother be insured for ten months before the birth of the baby.

Although there are many reputable surgical expense insurance plans, one of the most widely known is Blue Shield, which is organized similarly to Blue Cross. Each state has its own plan. Blue Shield plans generally have an income qualification feature; that is, the participating doctors agree to accept fixed rates of payment as their full compensation if the patient's income is within certain ranges. However, a family with a larger income could be charged a higher rate. In this situation Blue Shield would pay an amount equal to what they paid for a patient in the fully covered income range. The additional charge would be paid by the person receiving the surgical care. If you choose a doctor who does not participate in the plan, you may be liable for additional expense even if your income qualifies. Blue Shield will pay a fixed amount, but the doctor may charge more.

Regular Medical Expenses

This type of insurance provides benefits that pay doctors' fees for nonsurgical care in a hospital, at home, or at the doctor's office. Some plans also pay for diagnostic X-rays and laboratory tests.

Most people with this type of insurance are covered with plans by Blue Cross, Blue Shield, or other medical-society-approved plans. Comprehensive prepaid plans, which are discussed later, also include regular medical expenses.

Major Medical Expenses

This covers prolonged and costly illnesses. Most major medical plans are designed to pick up medical expenses at the point where basic plans such as hospital payments and surgical costs stop. A common feature is for major medical insurance plans to have both *deductible* and *coinsurance* features.

Let's suppose that Jimmie Jones was hospitalized for a week following a serious automobile accident. His basic hospital payments policy covered the first $800 of expense, but the total bill was $2,100. The deductible amount on his major medical insurance was $800 for hospital payments,

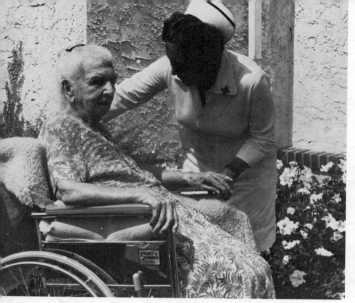

USDA Photo

Medicare provides health insurance for people over age 65.

so this policy paid nothing toward that first $800. However, on the balance of $1,300 the major medical policy paid 80 percent. The policy had a coinsurance clause which required that Jimmie Jones pay 20 percent of the amount covered by major medical benefits.

Jimmie's major medical insurance also paid a proportion of his doctor's bill above the amount paid by his surgical costs insurance policy.

Loss of Income

Loss of income (or disability income) insurance provides wage earners with regular payments when their income is cut off as a result of an illness or accident.

Short-term loss of income plans have a maximum benefit period of up to two years; long-term ones go beyond two years. Paid sick leave benefits and short-term disability benefits have increased much more rapidly than long-term benefits.

However, many wage earners are covered by longer term benefits under the social security disability plan and worker's compensation. (These are discussed more fully in the chapter, Social Insurance.)

Dental Insurance

Case Study. Bill Huber, a weather-beaten longshoreman on the Chicago waterfront, had a new bridge made and a number of large cavities filled. For a long time he had put this off. Initially, he hadn't thought about the need for dental care. Later, as it became obvious that his teeth needed attention, he was concerned about the high cost. Now, however, he is covered by dental insurance, a fringe benefit on his job. Most of the cost of his dental work was covered by his insurance.

Dental insurance is becoming more common as a fringe benefit, but as yet only a small number of people are covered. Dental insurance policies sometimes exclude work that is primarily cosmetic, such as orthodontics (braces), but cover most other kinds of care. It has been difficult to develop dental plans at a reasonable fee. Most people neglect their teeth. Once they are insured, the demands for service increase dramatically.

Evaluating Health Insurance Plans

Consider the following:

- What are the rates for specific kinds of coverage?
- What are the benefits for various kinds of services?
- What is the waiting period for benefits, if any?
- Is there a deductible clause? If so, what is the amount?
- Does the policy have a co-insurance provision? If so, what proportion of the expense will you have to pay?

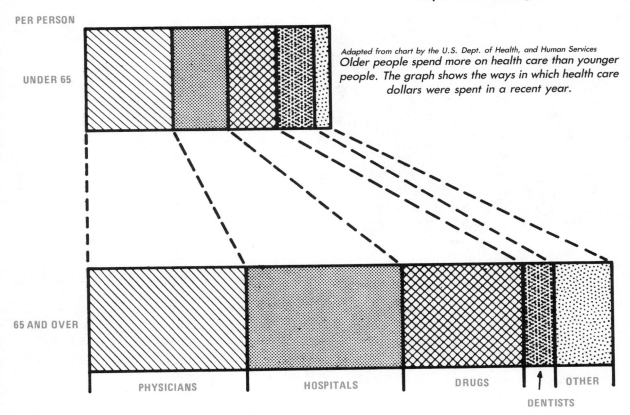

PER PERSON

UNDER 65

65 AND OVER

Adapted from chart by the U.S. Dept. of Health, and Human Services
Older people spend more on health care than younger people. The graph shows the ways in which health care dollars were spent in a recent year.

PHYSICIANS   HOSPITALS   DRUGS   ↑   OTHER

DENTISTS

Medicare

Medicare is a two-part program of health insurance for people 65 and over. It is part of the federal social security program.

Part A, the basic plan, provides hospital insurance, nursing home expenses, and some home nursing care. It is financed by payroll deductions and employer contributions made during one's working years.

Part B is voluntary and pays for doctors' bills. Starting at age 65 one can elect to pay a small monthly fee for this insurance. This fee is matched by a contribution from the federal government.

Who is eligible? Everyone age 65 or older who is eligible for social security benefits or railroad retirement benefits is automatically eligible for the basic plan without additional cost and the voluntary plan if they pay the monthly premium. In addition, some people who do not get either type of retirement benefit are eligible for one or both parts of Medicare. If you know someone who is over age 65 and doesn't get these benefits, check with your local social security office to find out if that person is eligible.

Medicaid

This is a joint federal and state program that pays medical expenses for needy people of all ages. The plans are drawn up by

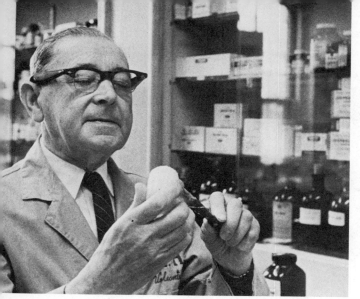

U.S. Dept. of Health, Education, and Welfare

A druggist must fill a prescription exactly as it is written.

the state and financed with state funds matched by federal funds. As a result, the various state plans differ as to who is covered and what they will get.

Prepaid Comprehensive Health Plans

Case Study. A young schoolteacher went to a seven-story hospital on one of San Francisco's windy hills to have her first baby. The healthy little boy and his mother had good medical care during the delivery and for the few days following delivery while they were in the hospital. Moreover, the whole hospital stay cost only $60. The rest of the bill was covered by her insurance because she belonged to a comprehensive prepaid medical plan.

About eight million Americans are now covered by comprehensive prepaid medical plans, such as the Kaiser-Permanente Medical Care Program, the Health Insurance Plan of Greater New York, and the Group Health Cooperative of Puget Sound. These plans provide very broad health care at moderate rates.

In the Kaiser plan, for example, subscribers' visits to doctors' offices are unlimited, with only a very small charge per visit. There is an additional charge for maternity care and delivery in a hospital but no additional charge for most other surgery or hospital care. Through the plan, medicines can be purchased at low cost.

At present, most of these prepaid plans do not include hospitalization for mental illness, treatment for alcoholism or drug abuse, cosmetic surgery, elective surgery such as sterilization, or dental care.

Lower costs for health care are made possible by a number of things: (a) Diagnostic services are available on an outpatient basis, whereas many other health insurance plans require that the patient be hospitalized to receive these services. (b) The greater use of preventive care. Since the cost is modest, more people seek early diagnosis and treatment. (c) The medical staff has an interest in seeing that the program operates efficiently. Generally, doctors receive a salary plus a bonus, or a percentage of the revenue.

Many people feel that comprehensive medical insurance plans are the coming thing, that this is the way to provide better medical care at a moderate cost.

CUTTING THE COST OF MEDICINE

The best way to save on medicine is to stay well. However, if you do need medication, you can sometimes cut costs with careful shopping. Buy medicines through reputable low-cost plans, if you can. As was mentioned earlier, some comprehensive health insurance plans make medicine available at lower cost. Some union groups and organizations for retired persons do the same.

Shop around. Prices are not the same at all drug stores.

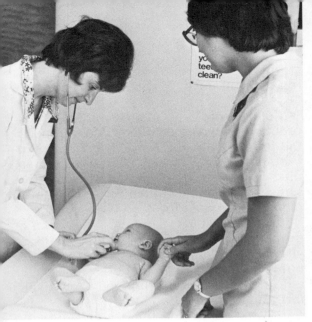

A prepaid comprehensive health plan can help reduce medical costs for you and your dependents.

Ask your doctor to prescribe the least expensive form of a medicine or to use the generic name of the product unless there is some special reason why one brand is preferable. (In prescribing medicine for a child, a doctor may want to have you get the one that tastes best so that the youngster will not balk at taking it. There may be other important reasons for preferring one brand over another.) At the present time a druggist must fill a prescription exactly as it is written. If your doctor prescribes a particular brand, the druggist must give you that brand. However, if the doctor prescribes a generic name (such as "peaches" rather than "XYZ Brand"), you can compare prices of the different brands as well as shop around in different stores. Often the only difference between drugs containing the same important ingredients may be the flavoring, coloring, the label, or something else that is not very important.

All prescription medications, both generic and name brand products, must com-

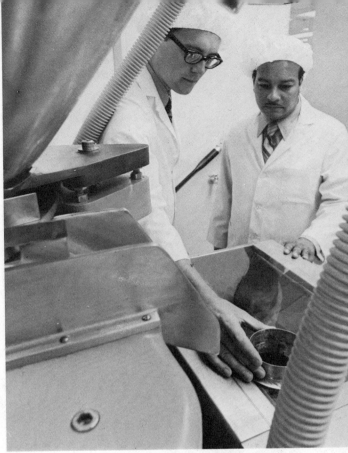

Two inspectors for the Food and Drug Administration examine a machine in a plant that makes drug capsules and tablets.

ply with the safety requirements of the Food and Drug Administration.

THE GOVERNMENT'S ROLE

The government performs many services to ensure the health of the public through federal, state, and local agencies. Inspection of our food, the development of safe and adequate water supplies, and control of waste products are government responsibilities. Often they test the swimming water at beaches and pools, drain and spray swamps to control the mosquitoes, and control landfill operations to prevent

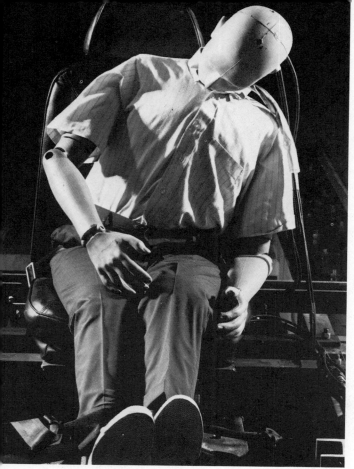

This dummy may save your life. It is used to test some mechanisms of a car.

the spread of disease. These are just a few public health activities. There are many more.

In addition, government agencies also provide some direct patient care. The Veterans Administration hospitals and armed forces hospitals are examples. Federal funds are used to provide needy people with food and health services, to assist in the health care of people over age 65, and for research.

Recently, the government has been taking a more important role in trying to prevent accidents. Accidents are the lead-ing cause of death for both sexes up to age 38.

Motor vehicle accidents are the worst problem. Howard A. Rusk, M.D., reports the following in the *New York Times:* "In Vietnam, a total of 39,979 American men died in nine years of the war. During the same period in the United States, the automobile accounted for 437,000 deaths."

Over the last 10 years, there has been a drop in accidents. Still, 50,000 deaths a year from automobile accidents is a large number. Injuries in automobile crashes are a leading cause of death among American teenagers.

Slower speeds and the use of seat belts can save lives. Help save your life. Buckle up and drive within the speed limit.

The federal government is now trying to make cars safer by requiring more stringent standards for such things as tires, many new types of safety devices, and other regulations. However, many people question whether enough effort is made to take the unsafe driver from behind the wheel. Are our laws for drinking and driving stringent enough? Why don't we have periodic checkups to be sure that every driver is able to see well?

Many home accidents are preventable. Greater care in the use of tools, stepladders, and other items around the home could reduce accidents. More stringent standards for household supplies, equipment, and materials would also help. It is possible to require, either through laws or regulations, that storm doors be made of unbreakable plastic instead of glass, that power lawnmowers come equipped with foot guards, that children's swing sets meet certain standards of stability, and other safety measures.

Some steps have been taken to reduce accidental poisonings. In 1971 the National Safety Council reported that more than 70,000 children under five years of age were accidentally poisoned. Aspirin was the leading cause. Since 1972 aspirin and some other drugs must be packaged with special child-resistant closures.

The 1970 Occupational Safety and Health Act was designed to "assure as far as possible every working man and woman in the nation safe and healthful working conditions." This has certainly not been achieved yet, although some steps forward have been taken.

Does the government have a responsibility to see that all people are provided with adequate health care? Although there is little question that the United States' productivity is higher than that of most other nations, statistics for life expectancy, infant mortality, and maternal health suggest that we lag behind many other industrialized nations in health care. This is particularly evident in the case of minority groups and people in rural areas.

DuPont

Careful testing of automobile parts and tires helps ensure quality.

FOR REVIEW

Points to Remember

- Given a good body and a fairly healthful environment, each of us can improve our health. We also need wholesome food, healthful living habits, and freedom from emotional disturbances.

- Obesity has become an important health concern. People who are more than 10 percent above the normal range have a shorter life expectancy and are more prone to certain diseases.

- If you want to lose more weight than a

USDA Photo

The Occupational Safety and Health Act sets standards for the protection of workers. In what ways is this worker protected?

pound or two, plan on a gradual change and a sensible diet. You will feel better while you lose and be more likely not to regain what you have lost.

- Regular exercise helps one feel better and function well.

- The regular use of tobacco, alcohol, and certain other drugs is harmful to health.

- Venereal disease is a growing health problem, particularly among people under age 25. Generally, it can be very effectively treated with antibiotics. However, untreated veneral disease will get worse.

- In the past it has been very difficult for teenagers to get medical care without parental approval. However, now a number of states have changed their laws to make some kinds of medical care available without parental consent. Also, there are a growing number of health facilities that will provide medical care to teenagers without parental consent.

- Many people prepay large medical expenses through the use of health insurance. Most health insurance coverage is through group plans provided where a member of the family works. People over age 65 are generally covered by a federal program, Medicare, or a federal-state program, Medicaid.

- Accidents, particularly car accidents, are the leading cause of death up to age 38.

- At present the government performs many services to ensure the health of the public. Many people, however, question whether the government is doing enough.

PROBLEM SOLVING:
CHECK YOUR UNDERSTANDING

1. What can you do to promote your own good health?
2. Why are some people who can afford

adequate food poorly fed?

3. Is a crash diet a good way to lose weight? Why or why not?

4. What is the number one drug problem today in the United States?

5. What is the leading cause of death for people under age 38?

6. Is it true that most people get venereal disease from dirty toilets?

7. How does a major medical insurance plan differ from a hospital payments plan?

8. What is a comprehensive health insurance plan?

9. What program pays medical expenses for needy people of all ages?

10. How are most people of 65 and over protected with health insurance?

Terms to Know

addiction	life expectancy
Blue Cross	Medicaid
Blue Shield	Medicare
calorie	metabolism
cultural patterns	nutrition
debilitating	obesity
free clinic	over-the-counter
generic name	drugs
health foods	potent
health insurance	sanitation

TO DO IN CLASS

Discussion

1. Why is food wasted in the school cafeteria? What could be done to enable more people to eat a better lunch?

2. What are some of the factors that have contributed to the growth of quick service restaurants along our highways?

3. Why do people get less exercise after high school?

4. Why are *health foods* so popular?

5. What can be done to decrease the use

of alcohol, tobacco, and other drugs, particularly among young people?

6. Should young people be able to get health services without their parents' consent?

7. In what ways might a comprehensive health insurance plan contribute to an improvement of the members' health?

8. How could the automobile accident rate among young people be cut?

9. Should the government provide health care for everyone?

10. Suppose someone in your family became seriously ill in the middle of the night and you could not get your regular family doctor. What would you do?

Activities

1. Invite someone from a local health agency to talk about health services in your community. Ask him or her to discuss these questions: Whom do they serve? How are charges set? What emergency facilities are available? Are there facilities for the treatment of alcoholics and drug addicts? What mental health facilities are available? Can teenagers get treatment without their parents' consent? If so, for what kinds of problems? What facilities are needed in the community?

2. Make a list of the prescription and over-the-counter drugs you find at home. Compile a class list. You will probably be amazed at the number.

3. With several other students shop for an over-the-counter medicine such as aspirin or a cough syrup. Read the label carefully. Then compare the price of this and similar products in a drug store, a discount store, and a supermarket.

4. Visit a nearby hospital and find out what kinds of clinics it runs.

5. Find out what kind of health insurance your family has. Make a brief outline of the benefits. Also, put down the cost of the policy. Ask your teacher to discuss health insurance available to teachers, if there is a plan in the community. Compare the various plans in class.

6. Invite some people from the community who are actively involved in working with young people to talk about health problems in the community. You might ask a guidance counselor, a doctor or health worker, a minister, a social worker, a police officer, or city councilmember.

CHAPTER 9
Social Insurance

Securing the necessities of life has always been one of man's basic problems. However, it was not until the dawn of the age of industrialization that governments instituted programs to protect people against life's hazards. The first national program of compulsory insurance against accidents, sickness, widowhood, and old age was instituted in Germany by Bismark in the 1880's. This was followed by Great Britain with a program for old-age pensions and unemployment insurance. Today most industrialized nations have some form of social insurance.

In the United States the first Social Security Act was passed in 1935 when the disastrous effect of the widespread depression was evident. Since then the feeling has prevailed that the government has a responsibility to prevent major depressions and to provide for at least a minimal level of financial security.

THE SOCIAL SECURITY PROGRAM

Every week millions of Americans have a deduction from their paychecks for "FICA." These are the initials for the Federal Insurance Contributions Act. This deduction is for a compulsory insurance plan administered by the federal government and referred to as *social security.*

There are two parts to this insurance program:

- *The Retirement, Survivors, and Disability Insurance Program.* Monthly cash benefits are paid to replace a portion of the earnings the family has lost when a worker's wages stop or are reduced because of retirement, disability, or death.

- *Medicare.* This provides hospital insurance for workers and their dependents beginning at age 65, which was discussed in the previous chapter.

Social security and other forms of social insurance are an attempt to provide some help against economic disaster. Generally, a family's economic security is threatened by these things:

- *Old age,* which decreases a wage earner's earning power;

- *Disability,* which cripples or incapacitates a wage earner;

- *Death,* which leaves dependents without support;

- *Unemployment or underemployment,* which leaves a wage earner without a job or with one that does not pay a living wage;

- *Special problems,* such as the breakup of a family or the prolonged and serious illness of a member.

Social security is only one of the social insurance programs established by the federal government. Some of the other major programs are: unemployment insurance, worker's compensation, and public assistance to the needy.

RETIREMENT, SURVIVORS, AND DISABILITY INSURANCE

Over ninety percent of the work force in the United States are buying protection for themselves and their families under this social security program. About five percent more are covered by federal, state, or local government retirement systems. Almost all self-employed people are covered by social security.

The basic idea is simple. During their working years, employees make payments to the social security fund. These payments are matched by their employers. Self-employed persons contribute at a higher rate because their contributions are not matched.

Becoming Eligible for Benefits

In order to be eligible for social security benefits for yourself and your dependents, generally you must have worked for a certain length of time at jobs covered by social security. (The Medicare program is an exception to this rule. Most people 65 and older are eligible.)

The working time needed to become eligible for benefits used to be counted in calender quarters of a year. Since 1978, quarters are based on the amount of annual earnings, rather than on actual calender quarters. Thus, an employee gets credit for a quarter of coverage if he or she earns a certain amount in a year—even if the job is part time.

Case Study. Suppose Susie Brown works during Christmas vacation as a salesclerk in a department store. She earns $85. Since this is a covered occupation, payments will be deducted for "FICA" and matched by the department store. Although Susie only works part of one month, she will receive credit for a quarter of covered employment on her social security earnings record.

Case Study. Her brother Tom worked during part of July and August on a nearby farm, cultivating and picking vegetables. Often, he worked overtime. FICA payments were deducted from his pay and matched by the farmer. However, Tom would get credit for four quarters of covered employ-

U.S. Department of Labor

The FICA contributions of working people like this man are used to pay benefits to those people who are retired or disabled.

ment because he receives credit for each quarter of a year of work, based on his earnings.

There are two categories of coverage: *currently insured* and *fully insured*. Benefits are greater for people who are fully insured in most cases.

Your status, fully insured or currently insured, depends on how many quarters of credit you have accumulated from working at jobs that are covered by social security.

If you stop working before you have enough credit to be insured under either category, you will not be eligible for any benefits. However, the payments that have been credited to you will stay on your social security record. If you take another job at a later time, credit for covered employment will be added to that already on your record.

Case Study. Let's think about Sarah Jacorski who worked for only a year after high school. She married right after high school, worked for a year as a secretary, then left to have a baby the next summer. Since Sarah had worked at covered employment from July through the following June, she earned credit for four quarters toward her social security benefits. She didn't return to paid employment for almost ten years. After Lisa, her first child, she had little Bobbie, and then Jackie. When she went back to work, she got a part-time job as a clerk. Again FICA payments were deducted from her salary and matched by her employer. Earnings for social security from her new job were added to what she had from her first job.

FULLY INSURED

To become fully insured, young people will need at least one-quarter of coverage for each year after 1950 up to the year of attaining age 62. Older people, who will reach age 62 (women) or 65 (men) before 1990, can become fully insured with less work credit.

Once you are fully insured, you retain that status for the rest of your life.

WHO IS ELIGIBLE FOR BENEFITS?

This table shows the principal types of benefit payments:

Retirement

Monthly payment to—

You as a retired worker and your spouse and child (and certain grandchildren).

Your dependent spouse 62 or over.

Divorced spouse 62 or over under certain conditions.

Survivors

Widow or widower 60 or over.

Widow, widower, or divorced wife (regardless of age) if caring for a child who is under 18 or disabled and is entitled to benefits.

Unmarried, dependent child (and certain grandchildren) usually to age 18 or until 22 if they are going to school full time.

Divorced spouse, 62 or over under certain conditions.

Dependent parent at 62.

Lump-sum death payment.

Disability

Monthly payment to—

You and your dependents if you are disabled.

Leisure Village

A small but growing number of retired people can maintain their lifestyles because they receive income from both a pension and social security.

WORK CREDITS NEEDED

Work Credit for retirement benefits

If you reach 62 in	Years you need
1975	6
1976	6¼
1977	6½
1978	6¾
1979	7
1981	7½
1983	8
1987	9
1991 or later	10

Work Credit for survivors and disability benefits

Born after 1929, die or become disabled at	Born before 1930, die or become disabled before 62 in	Years you need
28 or younger		1½
30		2
32		2½
34		3
36		3½
38		4
40		4½
42		5
44		5½
46	1975	6
48	1977	6½
50	1979	7
52	1981	7½
54	1983	8
56	1985	8½
58	1987	9
60	1989	9½
62 or older	1991 or later	10

Some people who do not have enough work credit to become fully insured may qualify as *currently insured*. You must have at least 1½ years of covered work and some work experience in the last 10 years to get benefits.

The Amount of the Payment

Being fully or currently insured does not establish how much you or your dependents will receive. It only means that you are eligible for certain kinds of benefits.

The amount of the benefit is determined by your average earnings under social security over a period of years. This is true both of benefits for you, such as retirement benefits, and benefits for your dependents.

The Social Security Administration will not figure the exact amount of a benefit until someone applies for it. The reason is that they will consider all of a wage earner's earnings up to that point.

However, you can estimate benefits by using the instructions and table in a current copy of *Your Social Security*. (This

Administration on Aging, Dept. of Health, Education, and Welfare
Retired workers and their dependents can get benefits.

also have received less if he had retired earlier.

If a widow elects to start receiving benefits between age 60 and 62, she will also receive permanently reduced monthly payments. The same is true of disabled widows and widowers who start receiving benefits early.

Sometimes a person is entitled to benefits based on the earnings records of more than one worker. For instance, a working wife might be eligible for retirement benefits both on her own individual account and also on that of her husband. The individual would receive the retired or disabled worker benefit plus the difference between that benefit and the amount of the wife's, widow's, or parent's benefit. One cannot receive both the retired or disabled worker benefit and the full dependent or survivor benefit.

Legislation was passed in 1973 so that in the future social security payments and pensions will be increased automatically to match increases in consumer prices.

Applying for Benefits

Social security benefits are not paid automatically. You *must* apply for them.

Here are some important times to check on eligibility for benefits:

- When there is a death in the family.
- If the wage earner becomes disabled.
- Before retirement.
- At age 70. (72 until 1982.)

If you know someone who might be eligible for social security benefits, have him or her check with the local social security office. It is listed in the telephone directory, sometimes under *United States Government Agencies.*

It is always wise to apply for benefits ahead of time, whenever possible. This reduces the possibility of a delay in receiv-

booklet is available without charge from your local social security office.) It is revised regularly as benefits change.

Case Study. Marshall Lincoln retired at the age of 65. He had worked at the maximum covered wage for enough years to be able to collect a monthly retirement benefit for himself and his dependent wife.

If he had elected to retire at age 62, or between 62 and 65, his monthly benefits would have been permanently reduced, depending on how many months before age 65 he retired. The benefits to his dependents and survivors are based on the amount he receives as a retirement or disability benefit. Therefore his wife would

ment is available to help pay funeral expenses.

Even if you do not retire, you may be eligible for Medicare benefits at age 65. Anyone who has been covered by social security is eligible, as well as most people who were not previously covered.

FURNISHING PROOF OF ELIGIBILITY

When you apply for benefits, you need to furnish evidence of eligibility. Your social security card or a record of your number is necessary. If you are applying for benefits based on another person's earnings, such as your father's or mother's, take that person's card or number.

Proof of your age is needed, so take your birth certificate or baptismal certificate. A husband, wife, widow, or widower applying for benefits on the spouse's earnings should take a marriage certificate. If children might be eligible for benefits, take their birth certificates.

Evidence of your earnings will be needed, so take your W-2 form for the last year or a copy of your last federal income tax form.

A parent who is applying for benefits on the earnings of a son or daughter must furnish proof that they were supported by that person.

Even if you do not have all these proofs, apply promptly for benefits. The people in the Social Security Administration office often can help you find the necessary proofs.

Benefits for Students

Although benefits for dependent children generally stop when they reach age 18, full-time students may qualify for benefits until age 22. A student can receive benefits while attending a public high school, a vocational school, a community

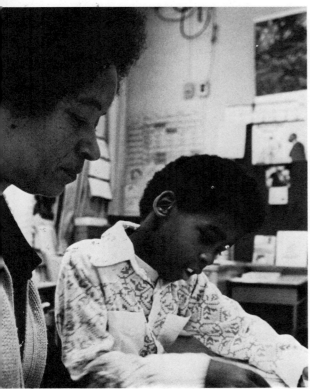

U. S. Department of Labor

A surviving unmarried dependent child may be eligible for benefits.

ing the first payment or losing some benefits altogether. If you cannot get to the social security office, telephone or write. For example, a man or woman who is approaching retirement might apply two or three months before he or she expects to start receiving benefits.

When a person who has been covered by social security dies, a member of the family should contact the Social Security Administration office regarding possible benefits. Many people forget that a lump sum pay-

A single working woman gets the same social security benefit payments as a man. However, a working wife may not.

certain level, some benefits will be withheld. Changes are made periodically in social security regulations and benefits, so check with the Social Security Administration about the limits if you plan to work part-time while receiving benefits. The following example is given by the Social Security Administration.

Case Study. One year, Bill Dailey worked for a construction company during his summer vacation. He earned $600 a month, or a total of $1,800 for the season. Since his earnings for the year were less than the limit, no benefits were withheld.

Case Study. Bill's friend, Jim Corkle, worked with him in the summer. He also earned $1,800. However, in addition, Jim worked during the school year as a part-time lab assistant. This part-time job paid a regular salary during the year. Jim's total earnings for the year were several hundred dollars over the limit. So, that year some money was withheld from Jim's benefits because he earned too much.

The Working Woman

A single working woman gets the same social security benefit payments as a man. For example, with the same earnings record both would receive the same amount per month at age 65.

This is different from the way an insurance company figures benefits. Insurance companies base their benefits on the life expectancy of the person. Since women generally live longer than men, a woman of age 65 would receive a smaller amount per month than a man who has the same size life insurance policy.

college, as well as an accredited college or university offering a program leading to the bachelor's degree. In addition, some unaccredited private schools, colleges, and schools outside the United States may meet the requirements. If you have any question about whether a school meets the eligibility requirements, contact your local social security office.

Benefit checks can continue during a vacation of not more than four months if you were a full-time student before the vacation and plan to return to school full-time after it.

You can work part-time or summers while you are a student receiving benefits. However, if your earnings reach above a

Everyone who works needs a social security card.

There are some advantages for a working wife in being covered on her own:

- She can receive benefits even if her husband is not getting any. For example, Barbara Sanchez decides to stop working at age 62. Her husband, who is the same age, wants to keep on working until 65. Barbara can begin collecting benefits at 62 when she retires although her husband is still working. (Benefits to a dependent wife are not payable until the husband starts getting benefits.) Even if Barbara starts getting benefits at age 62, she still has the right to switch to a wife's benefits, if they are larger, when her husband retires at age 65.
- If she has dependent children, they would be eligible for benefits if she dies, regardless of the father's earnings. (This is like having a life insurance policy made out for the benefit of her children.)
- If she is disabled, she and her dependent children may be eligible for benefits. (There are additional requirements for entitlement to disabilitybenefits.)

If You're Self-Employed

Almost all self-employment is covered by social security. If you have earned enough social security credit, monthly cash benefits can be paid to you and your family when you reach retirement age or become disabled. In addition, at 65, you have health insurance protection under Medicare, or, if you are disabled, after you have been entitled to social security disability checks for 2 consecutive years or more. Similarly, benefits can be paid to the survivors of a deceased worker.

Working after Payments Start

You can work and receive benefits.

- The amount will automatically increase in the future as the cost of living rises.
- If you earn more than the stated limit in one year, your benefits will be reduced, depending on how much you earn.
- You are eligible for benefits in any month in which you do not earn over a fixed amount or carry on substantial services in self-employment during the first year of benefits.
- Since 1982, for those over age 72, earnings have not affected benefits.
- If you are collecting retirement benefits, your earnings will affect your dependents' benefits as well as your own.
- If you are collecting benefits as a dependent or survivor on someone else's earnings credit, your earnings will only affect your own benefits.
- In computing total earnings, money from both employment and self-employment are counted. However, any income from savings, investments, pensions, or insurance does not count.

Your Earnings Record

You may already have a social security card. However, if you do not, you will need to apply for one at the social security office when you take your first regular job. (Almost all jobs are covered by social security today.) Your account number will be on this card.

Social Security Administration

Computers keep the earnings records current and supply the data for figuring the benefits payable when a worker retires, dies, or becomes disabled.

At least every three years you should check on the record of your account, just to be sure it is correct and you have all the credit you have earned. The Social Security Administration has a special card for this purpose, as you can see here, or you can write a letter asking for a copy of your record. Be sure to give your account number if you write a letter.

Disability Benefits

A person is considered disabled if he or she has a physical or mental condition which prevents carrying on substantial gainful work. The condition must have lasted, or be expected to last, for at least 12 months or be likely to result in death.

Benefits are available for:

• Disabled workers under age 65 and certain members of their family.

REQUEST FOR STATEMENT OF EARNINGS

SOCIAL SECURITY NUMBER →

DATE OF BIRTH →

MONTH	DAY	YEAR

Please send a statement of my Social Security earnings to:

NAME { MISS / MRS. / MR. } _____

STREET & NUMBER _____

CITY & STATE _____ ZIP CODE _____

Print Name and Address In Ink Or Use Typewriter

SIGN YOUR NAME HERE (DO NOT PRINT) _____

Sign your own name only. Under the law, information in your social security record is confidential and anyone who signs another person's name can be prosecuted.
If you have changed your name from that shown on your social security card, please copy your name below exactly as it appears on your card.

A form like this one can be obtained from your local social security office to check on your social security earnings record to date.

• People disabled before age 22. (Benefits can begin at 18 if a parent or grandparent is receiving retirement or disability benefits or if an insured parent dies.)

• Disabled widows and widowers and (under certain conditions) disabled surviving divorced wives of workers who were receiving benefits. This type of benefit can be paid as early as age 50.

The amount of work credit needed to be eligible for benefits depends on the age at which you become disabled:

• Before age 24, you need credit for 1½ years in the three-year period ending when your disability begins.

• From age 24 to 30 you need credit for one-half the time between age 21 and the onset of the disability.

• For age 31 or over, see the table on page 203.

There are special provisions for blind people. If you are disabled by blindness, you do not have to meet the requirement of recent work but do need credit for one-quarter year of work for each year since 1950 (or the year you reached 21, if later), up to the year you become blind. A minimum of 1½ years of credit is needed.

If a disabled worker returns to work, he can continue to receive benefits during a nine-month trial period. Vocational rehabilitation services, such as medical restoration, counseling, job training, training in the use of prostheses, and job placement available from state agencies do not reduce benefits.

Trends and Issues

Originally, social security was designed to provide minimal financial protection for retired workers who were largely male. However, the feeling has grown that benefits should support all people more adequately. As a result, payments have been increased greatly and more people are covered. As mentioned earlier, in the future benefit payments will increase automatically with rises in consumer prices.

The number of people receiving benefits has increased enormously as coverage has been extended to include almost all workers and self-employed persons. In 1940 only 222,000 people received benefits. By the 1970's about one out of every seven Americans was getting benefits.

There is pressure to increase benefits even more—to have retirement benefits that will enable retired workers and their families to keep up with the affluence of society in general, to allow retirement benefits at an earlier age, and to enact a national health insurance program that will cover people under age 65.

A growing concern has been the treatment of women. The Social Security Advisory Council made the following statement: "As more women work, as divorce becomes more common, and as the economic value of homemaking is increasingly recognized, concern about the way in which social secutity benefits are paid to women has grown." Changes in the system are likely to be made to address these concerns. There is a feeling that improvement is urgently needed.

The cost of these increased benefits is a growing concern to many people. One fear is that in an economic recession with many people out of work, the social security fund will not have enough money coming in to pay benefits. To solve this problem and also to decrease the burden of social security taxes for people earning low incomes, it has been suggested that parts of the social security program be paid out of general tax funds. Another question is how much the younger generation is going to be willing to pay in the future.

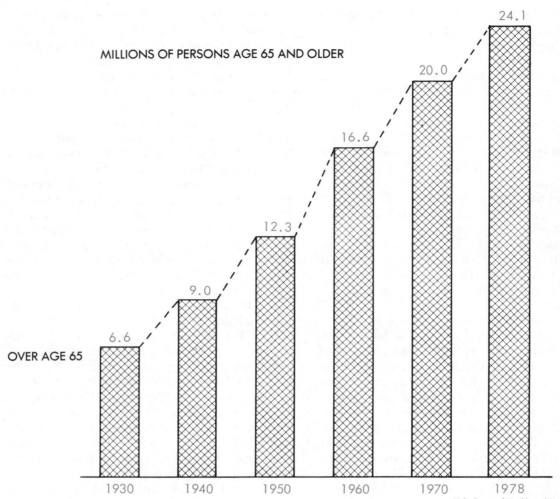

MILLIONS OF PERSONS AGE 65 AND OLDER

OVER AGE 65

6.6 — 1930
9.0 — 1940
12.3 — 1950
16.6 — 1960
20.0 — 1970
24.1 — 1978

U.S. Dept. of Health and Human Services

Part of the reason for the increase in the number of people receiving benefits is that there are more people over age 65.

Social security taxes, unlike a progressive income tax, place the heaviest burden on those earning the least amount of money, many of whom are young people.

UNEMPLOYMENT INSURANCE

A nationwide unemployment insurance program was established as part of the first Social Security Act in 1935. This is a joint federal-state program in which each state has its own plan. However, each plan must conform to certain general federal guidelines.

Most people who work for companies with four or more employees are covered under this program. However, certain occupational groups are excluded. Since the Constitution forbids the federal government from taxing state and local governments, employees of state and local governments are excluded. However, many state and local governments have similar unemployment insurance programs for their employees. Most states also exclude agricultural workers, domestic servants, people who work for nonprofit organizations, and self-employed people. Railroad workers are not covered but have a similar program administered by the federal Railroad Retirement Board. Civilian employees of the federal government and ex-servicemen are covered by a separate federal program administered by state unemployment insurance offices.

Who Pays for Benefits?

Benefits are financed by a federal and state tax on earnings, which is sometimes paid by the employer. In most states if an employer has a history of a low rate of unemployment, the tax is lower. The funds collected within a state are pooled, kept in a trust fund of the U.S. Treasury, and used to pay benefits to unemployed people from that state. If states run out of funds, they can borrow from the federal government to meet benefits.

Becoming Eligible for Benefits

Although the various state plans differ, they have certain common qualifications for benefits. The individual must:
- File a claim for benefits at the local unemployment insurance agency.
- Have worked at a job covered by unemployment insurance for a specified period of time.
- Have earned a certain minimum amount of money at jobs covered by unemployment insurance.
- Be able to work. Benefits are not usually paid to people who are unable to work.
- Be available and willing to work at a suitable job. Registration at a public employment office is usually required.
- Not be disqualified. The most common reasons for disqualification are: leaving a job voluntarily; being discharged for misconduct; refusing suitable work; and unemployment as a result of a labor dispute. Disqualification may result in postponement of benefits, cancellation of benefits, a reduction in benefits, or a combination of these.

Before a worker can begin to collect benefits, there is usually a waiting period of a week after becoming eligible for benefits.

Generally, seasonal workers are excluded from benefits because they cannot meet the wage and employment requirements.

A person has the right to appeal any decision on eligibility.

The Scope of Benefits

Weekly cash payments are available for workers who meet the eligibility requirements. In some states additional payments are made for dependents.

The size of the benefit depends on past earnings within limits set by each state. However, the amount of the benefit is usually much less than the worker previously earned.

Once benefit payments begin, they will continue for the number of weeks allowed by the state plan if the worker remains unemployed. Some states extend the duration of benefits in periods of high unemployment.

Partially unemployed workers may receive benefits in some states.

In many cases people can collect benefits even if they move outside the state where

Institute of Rehabilitation, NYU Medical Center
This young woman has a permanent partial disability as a result of a stroke.

they had been employed. The purpose is to help unemployed workers move to places where they can find jobs.

WORKER'S COMPENSATION

Every state has a worker's compensation law. Most states cover both public and private employment.

The purpose of these laws is to assure benefits to workers who are injured on the job, or if they are killed, to their dependents, regardless of who is at fault and with very little legal formality. It is really a kind of disability insurance.

At the present time most workers in the United States are protected by worker's compensation insurance. This replaces a system where the worker had to sue the

employer for benefits and prove that the employer had been negligent. According to the *Journal of American Insurance*, under the old system, "If a helper on a wagon was hurt in a runaway of horses, he might collect something from the employer if he could prove the horses were dangerous and the employer knew it but the driver did not. The helper's chance of collecting was slim indeed if the runaway was due to the driver's poor handling of the horses."

The *Journal* reports that "under a typical state workers compensation law, an employee who is totally disabled gets two-thirds of his average weekly wage up to a maximum amount. There are some limitations on this for temporary disability, but if a worker is permanently disabled he receives a given amount for life. Should an employee be killed on the job, similar benefits go to his dependents."

Benefits

Several kinds of benefits are available:

(A) *Medical care.* All states provide medical benefits, but the amount and duration of the benefits vary.

(B) *Disability benefits.* Payments may be made for three types of injuries:

1. *Temporary total disability*—the employee is unable to work while recovering from an injury but is expected to fully recover. This is the most common type of disability.

2. *Permanent total disability*—the worker is unable to work at all or unable to work regularly.

3. *Permanent partial disability*—the worker has a permanent injury but can work. If the worker cannot return to the old job, he or she may be able to be trained to do something else.

(C) *Death benefits.* Payments are made to the families and dependents of a deceased worker. There is a great deal of variation in the amount and duration of the benefits paid by the various state programs.

(D) *Rehabilitation services.* Although rehabilitation is considered an essential part of a complete worker's compensation program, only a few states have a program that includes counseling and guidance in selecting a new occupation, training, and job placement. (However, some of these services may be available under the Federal Vocational Rehabilitation Act from other agencies.)

PUBLIC ASSISTANCE TO THE NEEDY

The tradition of helping people in need has existed for thousands of years. Help for those who are less fortunate has been part of the activities of most religious groups through the ages. England adopted "Poor Laws" during the reign of Queen Elizabeth I in the late 1700's.

In the United States local and church responsibility for needy people started with the founding of the first colonies. As towns and counties grew, they assumed this responsibility. Then the states took on the job of assisting the local towns and counties. Finally, in 1935 the federal government began to help the state and local governments.

Today there are many different types of government programs designed to help people in need, both cash payments and other types of assistance. The following are some of the most important of these programs.

Aid to Dependent Children

This is the biggest program. Benefits and services are provided from a combination of federal and state funds. This program is designed to aid needy children when one or both parents are deceased, absent, or incapacitated, and the child is not getting help or only getting inadequate help from other sources. Benefits are also available for the parent or guardian who is caring for a needy child.

The Federal Supplemental Security Income Program (SSI)

This program helps people in many problem situations. It is administered and funded by the federal government. In an effort to increase the minimum amount that certain needy persons might receive, the federal government took over several of the programs that were formerly financed jointly by the states and the federal government.

USDA Photo
Aid to Dependent Children is the largest category of public assistance administered by the states.

Assistance in the form of cash payments is available to old people, blind adults and children, disabled adults and children, people who do not receive any help under other programs, and to those whose income, pensions, or benefits from other sources are not adequate.

Individuals can get help through the Supplemental Security Income Program (SSI) even if they are receiving benefits from another program, such as disability insurance or social security, if these other benefits are below a certain minimum amount.

In SSI the federal government makes monthly cash payments. Many states supplement these with additional benefits. If a state supplements the payment, it is combined with the federal funds, and the recipient automatically gets one check incorporating both benefits.

An applicant for financial assistance under this program must apply at the local social security office.

Additional services, such as homemaker service, for people in the Supplemental Security Income Program are provided by the individual states through their own offices. Application for an additional service must be made separately to the state welfare office.

All people eligible for the federal Supplemental Security Income Program or Aid to Dependent Children (ADC), Child Welfare, and the Cuban Refugee Program are also automatically eligible for Medicaid benefits. (See Chapter 8, "Protecting Your Health.")

Other Public Assistance Programs

The states administer a variety of programs involving both cash payments and services. Some states handle this directly; others do so through their county or local agencies.

GENERAL ASSISTANCE

This is paid from a combination of state and municipal funds to people who cannot get help under other public assistance programs. Funds can be used to supplement other income that is inadequate as well as for total support.

OTHER PROGRAMS

In addition, the states administer Child Welfare Service, which is funded jointly by the federal and state governments, and the Cuban Refugee Program, which is completely funded by the federal government.

Suggestions for Change

Many citizens are concerned about programs to aid the needy. Some people who really need help are not receiving adequate aid. Navigating the labyrinth to get help is confusing and exhausting, if not overwhelming. Often it is difficult to find out about all the benefits one might be eligible for, because they are administered by different agencies with varying criteria of eligibility. Also, at present there is little help available for families in need when both parents are present. (The little that is available is primarily from state funds, and many states do not have any such program.)

Some of these problems are administrative. A central clearing center within an area might help more people identify possible sources of help. Legislative action could simplify the administrative procedure and set up more coordinated facilities. Placing the federal Supplemental Security Income Program under the Social Security Administration, which took effect in 1974, was a step in this direction.

In addition, three other types of concerns about public assistance programs have been widely discussed:

- What is an adequate level of support?
- How can one aid people in need without discouraging those that might be able to work from doing so?
- Who should be eligible for assistance?

It is newsworthy when someone uncovers a glaring misabuse of a benefit by an individual. However, most of the people getting public assistance benefits are young children, old people, and people who are ill.

FOR REVIEW

Points to Remember

- Social security and other forms of social insurance aim to provide at least a minimal level of economic security for most Americans.
- Working people pay for social security benefits with payroll deductions listed as "FICA."
- In order to be eligible for social security benefits, either for yourself or your dependents, you must generally have worked a certain length of time at jobs covered by social security. (The Medicare program is an exception to this rule.)
- The major types of social security benefits are: retirement benefits for the worker and his or her dependents, death benefits for a worker's dependents, disability payments to a worker and his dependents, and health care for retired or disabled workers.

● The important times to check on eligibility for social security benefits are: when there is a death in the family, when the wage earner becomes disabled, before retirement, and at age 70.

● The amount of a social security benefit is determined by the worker's average earnings over a period of years.

● Social security benefits are not paid automatically. You must apply for them.

● Workmen's compensation is a disability insurance program for workers that is required by law.

● Public assistance programs are designed to provide people in need with some income and other important services.

Terms to Know

Aid to Dependent Children
calendar quarter
covered employment
currently insured
disqualification
earnings record
FICA
fully insured
permanent partial disability
permanent total disability
proof of eligibility
relief
Retirement, Survivors, and Disability
    Insurance Program
social insurance
social security
Supplemental Security Income
    Program
temporary total disability
unemployment insurance
Workmen's Compensation

PROBLEM SOLVING: CHECK YOUR UNDERSTANDING

1. In what ways does social security contribute to family protection?

2. Why is it better to be "fully insured" rather than "currently insured?"

3. How do you become eligible for social security benefits?

4. How is the amount of social security benefits determined?

5. What are some of the important times to check on whether you are eligible for social security benefits?

6. In what situations are benefits available to dependent children past age eighteen?

7. What are some of the advantages to a working wife in having her own social security earnings credit?

8. What two types of disability insurance are available to most working people?

9. What are some of the grounds for being disqualified for unemployment insurance?

10. Why do the unemployment insurance benefits of the states differ?

TO DO IN CLASS

Discussion

1. How is the need for social security related to the change of the nation from an agrarian society to an industrialized one?

2. What do you think might be an adequate social security benefit for a single woman, age sixty-five?

3. At the present time social security benefits for older people are paid by those who are still working. Do you think this is a good way to finance these benefits?

4. Should people be entitled to unemployment compensation payments if they leave a job without a good reason?

5. At what level should public assistance funds support a family?

6. At what level of assistance do you think people are discouraged from working?

7. What changes do you think should be made in the social security system?

8. If you can, tell the group about a family that has gotten into serious trouble through unemployment or illness. What were some of the problems they faced?

Activities

1. Invite a representative of your local Social Security Administration office to talk to the class about the program and how it operates.

2. Using the most recent table of social security benefits, compute the maximum that you could get in: (a) disability benefits at age 50; (b) retirement benefits at age 65.

3. Talk with a union representative about his or her view of the benefits available to workers under Workmen's Compensation.

4. Invite a worker from a local agency to talk about the needs of low-income individuals in your area.

5. Collect clippings from a newspaper on problems of people with low incomes. Post these on a bulletin board.

6. Visit a program designed to help low-income families at a housing project or other community agency. This might be on using credit, food buying, or any other topic.

7. Read the newspaper and magazines to find out which groups of people are currently unemployed. Why has this situation arisen? Have a panel present a report to the class on the groups which are currently unemployed and some of the causes.

CHAPTER 10
Your Legal Rights and Responsibilities

Laws are the rules by which a society is regulated. Among primitive societies the rules were based on superstition and witchcraft. As trade between groups expanded, the need arose for more formal rules. Almost 2,000 years before the birth of Christ, Hammurabi, the King of Babylon, set down the first written code of law. (His laws, which were carved on a slab of stone, are still preserved by the Louvre in Paris.)

Local communities usually regulate the disposal of home sewage. Here a septic tank failed to work, resulting in a health hazard and disagreeable odors.

USDA Photo

The ancient Greeks and Romans developed codes of law. When the Romans invaded Europe, they brought their system of law with them. This was revised about 600 A.D. by the Emperor, Justinian. Justinian's code is the basis for both the French and English systems of law, from which ours developed.

During the reign of the Emperor Napoleon, French law was codified. The Code Napoleon was brought to the United States when the French settled Louisiana. It is still the basis for state law in Louisiana. However, the rest of the states and the federal government have patterned their laws on the English Common Law.

At the time when England was united under one king, there was a hodgepodge of courts, each of which administered the law according to the customs of the area. Gradually, judges sifted out of these local laws broad principles which were applied everywhere. These principles were called *common law* because they applied all over the country.

When the thirteen American colonies declared their independence from England, they adopted the English Common Law as the basis for the government. However, in addition, the colonists wrote a federal Constitution and also one for each state. Each new state admitted to the union

USDA Photos

Local communities regulate whether power lines are underground. See how much more attractive the backyards are with underground wires. Also, with underground wires there is less chance of service interruptions due to storms. In addition, property values are enhanced.

wrote its own state constitution. Today we have federal laws which are binding on everyone and fifty sets of state laws which regulate the individual states. In addition, many cities and towns have lawmaking bodies.

Thus, there are three levels of government in the U.S., federal, state, and local. Federal courts enforce federal laws; state courts enforce state laws; and local communities enforce their own laws. These aren't the only sources of regulation in the United States. Courts interpret laws, usually based on established principles. A Supreme Court decision can change the conduct of activity. Certain things may be forbidden, such as segregated schools. Regulatory agencies may promulgate rules. For example, the Federal Trade Commission prohibits false and misleading advertising.

The field of law can be divided into two broad parts, *civil law* and *criminal law.* Civil law involves relationships between people. Criminal law is concerned with the relationship between individuals and the society.

CONTRACTS

Civil law deals largely with contracts. *A contract is an agreement between two or more people that is enforceable by law.* A legally binding contract has four parts:

● The parties involved must agree on all the terms.

Although a contract can be an agreement sealed with a handshake, most contracts are put in writing.

Milton Roy Co.

219

● There must be some consideration; that is, something of value must be exchanged.

● The parties making the agreement must be competent. For example, if a person is senile or a minor, he or she is not usually considered a responsible party in the eyes of the law.

● The purpose of the contract must be lawful. For example, illegal bets cannot be enforced through a court of law.

Generally, contracts are written in precise legal language which is difficult for the average person to understand. Before you sign any contract, read it carefully. *Be sure you know what you are agreeing to do.* If you don't understand it, take it to someone who can help you understand it before you sign it. When you are making a big purchase, such as a house, it is wise to have a lawyer to help you through the legal intricacies.

Some types of contracts which you will probably use are leases, retail credit agreements, a marriage contract, and mortgage

agreements. (Mortgages are discussed in Chapter 13.)

Signing a Lease

What is a lease? A lease is a legally binding agreement between you and the landlord. Except in very run-down areas landlords generally like written leases. These have fine print and spell out most of what the landlord expects of you as a tenant.

A lease generally states the name and address of both the landlord and the tenant, how much the rent is, when it is to be paid, the time period covered by the lease, and a description of the property. If the lease is for an apartment rental, it might say that it is for apartment 3E at an address which then follows. Other provisions of the lease vary greatly.

BE SURE YOU UNDERSTAND

You will need to understand the following when signing a lease:

● *What does the rent include?* Are heat and electricity provided? Will the landlord decorate? Is there a place to park a car? Is there a charge for this space? Are any other services included?

● *Who is responsible for repairs and maintenance?* If the pipe under the kitchen sink bursts, who will fix it? Generally, in apartments the landlord is responsible for building repairs. In a house the tenant usually has to make these repairs unless the lease says that the landlord will make them.

● *Is a security deposit required?* Most leases require that you make a payment, usually of one or two months extra rent, to be held by the landlord as a guarantee that you will leave the place clean and in good condition. If you leave the premises in good condition, all of the security deposit

Read contracts carefully before you sign them.

should be refunded to you. However, the landlord usually has the right to deduct charges for damages and cleaning if these are your fault. Disagreements often arise when the landlord and tenant disagree on what is ordinary wear and tear and what is "damage" to the dwelling.

• *Is there a late-payment charge?* Many leases require an extra payment when you are late with your rent.

• *How do you terminate the lease?* When must you notify the landlord of your intention to move? If you don't give the landlord sufficient notice of your intention to move, he may be entitled to deduct some of your security deposit. In other cases, the lease is automatically renewed if you do not give notice of your intention to move.

• *Can you sublet?* If you need to move before your lease is up, can you rent the place to someone else? There may be a charge for permitting you to sublet the dwelling.

• *When can the landlord or his employees enter your home?* A landlord has a right to inspect or may want to make repairs. You have the right to establish reasonable conditions.

• *What are the rules about what you can do to the apartment?* What are the limits on decorating, pets, installing appliances? Can you operate a business?

• *Is the landlord responsible for damage to your personal property?* If not, perhaps you should have insurance.

CAN YOU BE EVICTED?

You have responsibilities under the terms of your lease. If you don't meet them, the landlord can take legal action.

He can do two things:

• Get a court order directing you to meet your obligations under the lease, such as pay your rent, repair damage to the apartment, or stop making noise that disturbs others at 2 a.m.

• Get an eviction order from the court, which terminates the lease and orders you to move out right away.

Local laws prescribe just how an eviction must proceed. Usually the landlord must serve notice that he is taking legal action against you. Sometimes all he has to do is post a dispossess notice on your door. Then, after a fixed period of time—usually a few days—he can obtain an eviction order in court. This is when you can appear in court to argue your side. If you do not appear and the judge rules against you, the landlord can put you out. If you do not move voluntarily, he can get a sheriff to put you and your possessions on the street.

Fortunately, most landlord-tenant disputes can be settled without such drastic action.

Retail Credit Agreements

The Truth-in-Lending law helps consumers understand retail credit contracts. Here's how the law works.

When you decide to purchase something on credit, the creditor has three basic obligations to you.

First, he must tell you the dollars-and-cents cost of the credit, or *finance charge.* This is the sum total of all charges you will incur. Interest, loan and investigation fees, credit life insurance in some instances, insurance to protect the creditor against default—in fact, all charges involved in the credit transaction—are part of the finance charge.

Second, you must be told the *annual percentage rate.* Creditors cannot use misleading terms or percentages. Instead they must use a prescribed method that is the same throughout the nation. The annual percentage rate, which is the approximate true annual cost of borrowing, is given on tables which are available to creditors so that calculations can be made in a simple and uniform manner.

Third, you must be given a copy of the agreement you sign.

The following examples will show you how this applies when using credit.

Let's assume that after comparing several automobiles, your family decides to purchase one with a cash price of $3,600. This includes accessories, services, and taxes. The trade-in allowance on your family's old car is $970, and there will also be a down payment of $200 in cash. The unpaid balance of the cash price is $2,430, and your folks wish to pay it over a three-year period. Life insurance on the loan costs an additional $70. The total unpaid balance—the amount to be financed—would be $2,500, to be repaid over a 36-month period. The *finance charge* is $578. This, according to the approved table, is an *annual percentage rate* of 14 percent. The total cost is $3,078 or 36 monthly installments of $85.50. All of these facts must appear in the written contract before your parents sign. Once your parents have read the contract and are sure that all blanks are filled in with the correct facts, they may sign, taking a copy of the contract with them when they leave.

There may be two parts to the contract, the sales contract and the financing agreement. If you are financing the car where you buy it, these are usually combined in one contract. However, if you are financing the car with a loan from another source, such as a bank, you will have a separate contract, with the bank detailing the terms of the loan, as well as a sales contract with the car dealer.

In both cases the contracts will cover the terms of the sales and financing. Let's assume that you are financing a car through the dealer from whom you purchased it and see what is included.

The wording on sales agreements will vary from state to state, but what they cover is similar. The first portion gives the basics of the transaction: the name of the buyer and seller; the car model; the trade-in allowance, if any; discounts; taxes; fees; and how much cash is due on delivery of the car. This part is fairly straightforward and rarely causes problems.

It's the second part, usually on the reverse side and couched in legal jargon, that is often misunderstood. Here are some of the things to watch for:

The dealer doesn't have to give you a guarantee. He may, however, choose to provide one. Most used cars are not warrantied by the dealers, regardless of what a salesperson may say. If they promise you a warranty make them put the warranty in the contract. (New cars generally have some limited warranty from the manufacturer.)

The appraisal price of your trade-in car can be changed at the time of delivery of the newer one. The dealer has the right to reappraise it. If you have taken out the radio or stereo system or removed the spare tire or other accessories, the dealer can ask you for more money.

BE SURE YOU UNDERSTAND

You will need to understand the following when signing a retail credit agreement:

• *When is the contract binding?* Although an oral agreement is considered a contract, from a practical point of view a contract is usually enforceable only after you have signed and the salesman has accepted your deposit.

• *What happens if you miss a payment?* Check to see if penalty charges are mentioned in the contract.

• *Can you take the car wherever you want?* Some contracts say that you can't take the car out of the state until it is fully paid for.

You have the right to get your deposit back if for some reason the deal falls through, unless you have violated the terms of the agreement. A dealer may stall in giving your deposit back, hoping you will buy something more expensive. If you can't get anywhere by talking to the top person at the dealer's, try the small claims court or a local consumer protection agency. Small claims courts hear cases about small sums, and you don't need a lawyer. You can present your own case.

Small, as well as large, credit dealings are covered by the Truth-in-Lending law. If your family has a revolving charge account at a retail store, the law requires that you be provided with periodic statements, usually monthly, if a finance charge is made or if there is an unpaid balance of one dollar or more. These statements must inform you of the outstanding balance at the beginning of the billing period; the amount, date, and description of the merchandise purchased; and the total amount credited to the account during the period. The statement must indicate the amount of the finance charge in dollars, the *periodic rate* used to compute the finance charge, and the corresponding *annual percentage rate.* Also, it must state the *balance* on which the finance charge is computed, the *closing date of the billing* cycle, the amount of the *unpaid balance* on that date, and the *date by which payment must be made to avoid additional charges.*

To illustrate, suppose you receive a monthly statement from a department store. You had a previous unpaid balance of $40.00. During the month you purchased a skirt for $20.00 and a shirt for $10.00. The shirt, which was too small, was returned for credit, and you also made a payment of $10.00. Assuming the rate to be 1½ percent of the previous unpaid balance, your statement includes the following basic information: previous balance—$40.00; purchases—$30.00; *finance charge*—$.60; credits—$10.00; payments—$10.00; periodic rate—1½ percent of previous balance; *annual percentage rate*—18 percent; and the balance for computing *finance charge*—$40.00. You would also be informed of the date the billing cycle ends and advised when your new balance of $50.60 must be paid.

Other requirements of the law are concerned mainly with standardized language, timing of disclosure, rules for advertising, and the right to cancel certain transactions.*

IF YOU DON'T MEET THE PAYMENTS

Garnisheeing

The following explanation is offered in *It's Not Just Money* (editor, John R. Prindle, CUNA International, Inc.).

A wage garnishment is when an employer is directed by the court to take a regular amount of money from an employee's pay and give it to a creditor. This is done when an employee has not kept up credit payments. Only some states permit this.

Take the case of Tom Johnson. A piece of yellow paper was delivered to his boss one morning, and his life

---

Truth-in-Lending—What It Means for Consumer Credit, Series for Economic Education, Federal Reserve Bank of Philadelphia.

SAMPLE RETAIL INSTALLMENT CONTRACT AND SECURITY AGREEMENT

ACCOUNT NUMBER			

SEARS, ROEBUCK AND CO.

RETAIL INSTALLMENT CONTRACT AND SECURITY AGREEMENT

This agreement provides for a series of credit sales by Sears to me of merchandise and services for my personal, family or household use:

1) On my initial purchase and on any purchase made when I do not have a balance outstanding under this contract, I will receive a disclosure statement containing the credit terms applicable to such purchase. A subsequent purchase made under this contract may change the number and amount of my monthly payments, the amount of the Finance Charge and the Annual Percentage Rate as shown on such disclosure statement. Any such change will appear on my next monthly billing statement.

2) You may consolidate my subsequent purchases with my outstanding balance from previous purchases. On each such new purchase, I will pay a **FINANCE CHARGE** which will be the greater of a minimum Finance Charge in accordance with Sears established terms at the time of the subsequent purchase but not in excess of **$5.00** or: FOR EASY PAYMENT PURCHASES — an amount determined by applying an **ANNUAL PERCENTAGE RATE** of **20%** to the amount financed; FOR MODERNIZING CREDIT PLAN PURCHASES — an amount determined by applying an **ANNUAL PERCENTAGE RATE** of **14.75%** to the amount financed.

3) In accordance with Sears established terms:

   a) All purchases will be payable in installments.

   b) Finance Charge will begin to accrue on my next billing cycle closing date.

   c) Finance Charge will be computed only on each new purchase, and the amount financed and the Finance Charge of each new purchase will be added to my outstanding balance.

   d) Prior to the due date of the first monthly installment on each new purchase, Sears will furnish me in writing my new payment schedule which will include the number and amount of my monthly payments and my total of payments.

I agree to pay the amount of each monthly installment on or before the due date thereof until the amount financed and the Finance Charge for each purchase is fully paid. If I pay in full in advance, any unearned Finance Charge will be rebated under the Rule of 78. I will receive a sales slip identifying each item of merchandise subject to this security agreement. Sears shall retain ownership of each item purchased under this security agreement until paid for in full. My installment payments shall be applied as follows: in the case of items purchased on different dates, the first purchased shall be deemed first paid for; in the case of items purchased on the same date, the lowest priced shall be deemed first paid for.

Until each item is fully paid for, I agree that:

I have risk of loss or damage to merchandise; I will not sell, transfer possession of, remove or encumber the property without the written consent of Sears.

Upon one or more defaults in the terms of this security agreement, Sears may declare my existing outstanding balance due and payable and may repossess any merchandise for which Sears has not been paid in full. Upon my default, Sears may charge me reasonable attorneys' fees and collection costs.

Sears is authorized to investigate my credit record and report to proper persons and bureaus my performance of this security agreement.

The information furnished on the application on the reverse side is submitted to Sears for the purpose of obtaining credit, and I understand that Sears will rely upon this information in extending credit to me. I hereby certify that this information is true, correct and complete.

NOTICE TO BUYER:

A. DO NOT SIGN THIS CONTRACT BEFORE YOU READ IT OR IF IT CONTAINS ANY BLANK SPACES.

B. YOU ARE ENTITLED TO AN EXACT COPY OF THE CONTRACT YOU SIGN.

C. IF YOU PAY IN FULL IN ADVANCE, ANY UN-EARNED FINANCE CHARGE WILL BE REBATED UNDER THE RULE OF 78.

RECEIPT OF A COPY OF THIS SECURITY AGREEMENT IS ACKNOWLEDGED:

Signature_____

Print Address_____

City_____State_____Zip Code_____

SEARS, ROEBUCK AND CO.
("Sears") by_____

Date_____Store No._____

Can you find some important terms to recognize in this contract?

hasn't been the same since. The paper was a summons ordering Johnson's employer to begin withholding 15 percent of his weekly paycheck and to give it to a food freezer company.

Earlier, he had signed a sales contract he couldn't possibly afford. It included an $895 freezer, a $250 membership in something called a "food discount club," $168 in canned goods and meat, and $233 in "financial charges." He claimed he didn't know what the cost would be, but that doesn't matter. He signed the contract, and it was legal.

If Johnson's wages are *garnisheed,* he'll be fired (because this is the second time this has happened). The boss doesn't want to put up with the extra bookkeeping work, the time in court, and an employee with low morale.

Bankruptcy

Tom Johnson could escape garnishment by declaring *bankruptcy.* Personal bankruptcies have increased rapidly, particularly in states that permit garnisheeing. One U. S. District Court handles about 1,000 cases a month. Although bankruptcy absolves one from most debts, it is not without problems. First of all, not all debts are wiped out. Second, the person who goes bankrupt will have a major blot on his or her credit record, which will make it difficult to get credit from reputable sources in the future. Third, bankruptcy is a measure designed for extreme circumstances; the person who declares bankruptcy cannot use this method to get out of debt again for another six years.

RESPONSIBILITIES OF A CO-SIGNER

Let's assume that you are 17 and want to buy a car. You have saved enough money

for a down payment, and you have a steady job on weekends at a supermarket. The problem is that the auto agency where you found a car you think you can afford is asking that your parents *co-sign* the contract. The auto agency wants your parents to agree to meet the payments if you *default,* don't keep up the payments.

Anyone who co-signs a loan for someone else should be prepared to meet the payments in case the person who borrowed the money cannot.

Marriage and Family Relationships

Marriage is a type of contract. However, it differs from other types of contracts in which only two parties are involved. In marriage there are three parties involved, the man, the woman, and the state.

Usually in civil contracts the two parties can agree to terminate the contract. However, this is not the case with a marriage. Legal termination can only be done according to the laws of the state.

In small claims courts individuals can settle small suits without the expense of a lawyer.

JUSTICE

SMALL CLAIMS COURT

American Gas Assoc.

Marriage is a unique form of contract.

The legal requirements for marriage are determined by the laws of the state where the marriage takes place. All states require an application for a license, and some states require a waiting period of several days and a blood test.

If a marriage is valid where it takes place, the other states will recognize it as valid. However, each state has the right to govern its own citizens. Therefore if the resident of one state goes to another state to avoid certain restrictions in the home state, the home state may refuse to recognize the marriage as valid.

In many states a person under the legal age of majority can make a legal marriage contract. (Other contracts made by minors are not considered valid.) It may be neces-

sary for people under age to present evidence of their parents' consent.

Most states prohibit marriage between blood relatives closer than cousins. A person who still has a living husband or wife cannot enter into a legal marriage contract. Although customs and law are changing, some states still prohibit interracial marriages, as well as marriages of epileptics, alcoholics, and drug addicts.

COMMON-LAW MARRIAGE

A common-law marriage is one in which a man and woman marry without sanction of the state and without the presence of a minister, judge, or justice of the peace. If a man and woman live together and represent themselves as man and wife, they are considered married in those states that recognize common-law marriages. If the common-law marriage is legal in the state where it is made, it is recognized as legal by all other states.

THE RIGHTS AND RESPONSIBILITIES OF MARRIED PEOPLE

Currently, there is a great deal of controversy about the rights and responsibilities of a husband and wife. The wording of marriage ceremonies is often changed to reflect the fact that women feel much more independent than in the past.

For a long time a married woman had few legal rights. Any money that she might earn belonged to her husband. She couldn't sell real property—land or a house. She couldn't even give away her personal things without her husband's consent. Today a married woman enjoys almost all the legal rights that her husband does. In all states a woman may now enter into a contract in her own name. She can also buy and sell property independently.

In spite of these changes, the law in most states still outlines certain rights and responsibilities. Generally, the wife has the right to:

• Be supported by her husband. He must maintain a standard of living in the home in keeping with his means.

• The companionship of her husband, including cohabitation.

The husband has the right to:

• Determine where the family shall live.

• His wife's services. Many courts interpret this to mean the household activities involved in caring for the family.

• The companionship of his wife, including cohabitation.

The spouse's obligation to support the other spouse and the family may not end with the breakup of a marriage. One partner may be ordered by the court to pay the former spouse an amount of money regularly, (called *alimony*) and to support the children. However, this is changing. There is a growing feeling that each spouse should earn his or her own support if there are no small children and the spouse is able to earn a living.

Automobile Accidents

Lawsuits as a result of automobile accidents are very common. Here are some suggestions to follow if you are involved in an automobile accident:

• Exchange information with the driver of the other car, including the name and address of the driver, description of the car including the license plate number, driver's license number, and the name of the other person's automobile insurance company.

• Jot down a brief description of the accident and the name and address of any people who can serve as witnesses.

• Call the police if they are not there. If you are not at fault, their statement in court can be of help.

• If you think the other driver has been drinking or was under the influence of other drugs, make a note of this.

• Don't make statements indicating that you were at fault. Most important of all don't sign anything without first talking to your lawyer or insurance company.

Bailment Contracts

A bailment contract is made when one person delivers personal property to another for a particular purpose, with the stated or implied understanding that it will be returned after the purpose has been completed. The object of a bailment can be any kind of personal property, including money.

CLEANING AND REPAIR SERVICES

This is one type of bailment contract. The shoe repair shop that accepts your shoes for new heels is presumed to be able to exercise ordinary skill in repairing them. A cleaner should know that certain types of belts will not clean satisfactorily or that nylon zippers often are ruined by the heat of an iron.

Also, the service that accepts your shoes for repair or clothes for dry cleaning is responsible for exercising reasonable care to prevent their loss. It is often difficult to prove that a service did not exercise reasonable care, so it is always advisable to deal with reputable service organizations.

When service agencies accept personal property for repair or alteration, they have a lien on it for the cost of their services. Thus, a dry cleaner has the right to keep your jacket until you pay in full for the cost of cleaning it. Most service agencies insist

An agency that rents out a car has an obligation to see that the auto is in good condition.

Avis

that you pay before you remove the item, because their lien does not apply once the item is removed from their custody.

STORAGE AND CUSTODY SERVICES

Suppose you are moving and will have to store the furniture for a short time until you can get into your new home. The storage company has a responsibility to exercise reasonable care in taking care of your household things. If the living room couch is ruined because it was left out in the rain, rather than being brought inside as you had contracted, the storage company would probably be considered negligent.

The same principle applies if you park your car in an attended parking lot or garage. You have the right to expect them to exercise reasonable care. However, if you rent a parking space and park your own car, the contractual arrangement is somewhat different.

Suppose you check your coat at a restaurant. By mistake the checker gives someone else your coat, and you never get it back. The management would be liable for the loss up to the value stated on the check.

RENTAL SERVICES

Rental of a specific item for a specific purpose is another type of bailment con-

tract. The one who rents out the article has the responsibility to see that the property is suitable for the purpose. For example, if you rent a car for a day, the brakes should be in good condition. If you rent a power saw to cut up some logs, it should be in safe, usable condition.

On the other hand, the renter has an obligation to see that he or she takes reasonable care of the property and does not violate the contract.

For example, if you have an accident in a rented car because the brakes were faulty, it might be the fault of the leasing agency. On the other hand, if the car was in good condition and you were going 80 miles an hour, you clearly would be at fault.

Public Accommodations

The law states that people who provide transportation and hotel accommodations must meet certain requirements.

TRANSPORTATION

Public carriers, that is, those companies who are regularly in the business of providing service to the public, must take anyone who is willing and able to pay the fare. Also, the carrier must exercise reasonable care in transporting passengers and assume a limited amount of responsibility for the passenger's personal baggage, if it is checked with the carrier.

Private carriers, people who occasionally contract to carry passengers but are not regularly in the business of transporting the public, can refuse to take a passenger.

HOTELS AND MOTELS

Establishments that are in the business of offering accommodations to the public must accept any reputable traveler who is willing to pay for the accommodations, provided a room is available. Also the hostelry is responsible for exercising reasonable care in protecting the guests' safety and privacy.

The hotel's responsibility for personal belongings of the guests varies according to the laws of the state in which it is located.

A hotel or motel has a lien (a legal claim) on the guest's property and can retain it if the hotel bill is not paid.

CRIMINAL LAW

Criminal law is concerned with the relationship between people and society. Loosely defined, criminal law is anything that is forbidden by society. Unlike civil law, all criminal acts are written down as laws which clearly define the things for which one may be punished. The purpose of this is to protect the individual against dictatorship.

There are two classes of crimes: misdemeanors and felonies. Misdemeanors are the less serious crimes, such as drunkenness, disorderly conduct, assault and battery, and others. Guilty persons are usually confined to a local jail or fined.

Felonies are more serious, such as rape, robbery, arson, burglary, and murder. The punishments are more severe, and the guilty person is usually confined in a state prison.

In the United States there are certain broad principles that apply to criminal law:

• You are presumed innocent until you are proven guilty. This is quite different in much of Europe, where one is presumed guilty upon being accused of a crime and must prove innocence.

• In a criminal case an accused person must be proved guilty "beyond any reasonable doubt" before conviction. In most cases the accused is entitled to a jury, a panel of his peers to judge his guilt.

Hilton Hotel Corp.
A hotel or motel may keep your luggage until you pay the bill.

• Before an act can be called a felony the intent to commit a crime must be proved.

• No person can be tried for the same crime more than once.

When Do You Need a Lawyer?

You should have the advice of a lawyer when you are signing important contracts, such as for the purchase of a home. Sometimes you will need the help of a lawyer if you run into problems with contracts involving less money.

If you have to go to court as a defendant or the plaintiff (the person making the complaint), be sure you have a lawyer. Courtroom procedure is complex and unfamiliar to most people. You need a lawyer to see that you have a fair chance.

The only exception to this would be if you go to a small claims court. You don't need a lawyer to sue in a small claims court. In fact, some do not permit lawyers. These courts are designed so that people can sue for small amounts at low cost and quickly.

If you are arrested, get a lawyer. A lawyer can help see that your rights are protected.

If you are arrested, get a lawyer.

When someone is arrested, he or she has the right to make one telephone call. Most young people would call their family, and the family would then get a lawyer.

Cutting the Cost of Legal Aid

The following was cited by Byron E. Calame in *The Wall Street Journal:*

It was a dark and stormy night, and a lightning bolt sent a tree crashing down across the fence enclosing Clevon Cain's 3½-acre place near Shreveport, La. With the fence down, Mr. Cain's mule ambled out onto the road and into the path of a truck, which hit the animal. State police charged the mule's 60-year-old . . . owner with violating a law against letting livestock run free.

Faced with a $250 fine and a 30-day jail sentence if found guilty, Mr. Cain, a member of Laborers Union Local 229, remembered that his union and the city's bar association had just set up a prepaid legal insurance plan. Though he never had consulted a lawyer before, he decided to seek legal advice because there wouldn't be any charge.

The result: Shreveport lawyer Lewis Weinstein won a dismissal of the

charge . . . on the ground that the mule's escape was due to an "act of God" rather than negligence.

Group legal insurance is beginning to catch on. Some labor unions now have this benefit, and the service is actively used by these members.

People with low incomes can get free or low-cost help from the Legal Aid Society or a public defender in most urban areas. Unfortunately, both are often overwhelmed with cases and cannot give as much time and attention to each case as would be desirable.

PROTECTING THE CONSUMER

In a speech about consumers, President Kennedy stated certain important rights which every consumer should have:

- The right to be informed.
- The right to safety.
- The right to choose.
- The right to be heard.

This statement of rights has come to be accepted by many as a broad outline of what consumers should have in government protection.

Some steps have been taken to ensure these rights more effectively. For example, for a long time the federal government only required inspection of meat that was produced in one state and shipped to another. Now each state is required to inspect meat produced and sold within the state as well. The federal Food and Drug Administration has moved away from requiring that drugs must be proved unsafe before they can be removed from the market, to requiring that they must be proven both effective and safe before they can be placed on the market. A federal law now requires that if you are

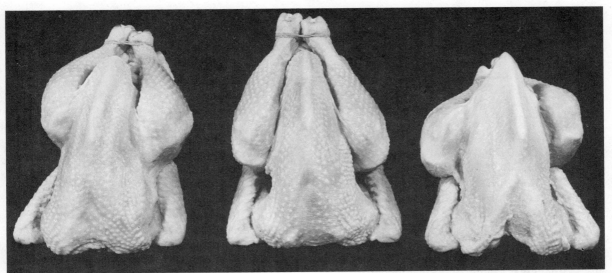

Federal inspection of meat and poultry takes place at the time the animal is slaughtered. Do you see differences in these chickens that might affect the grading?

turned down for credit, you have a right to know why. Prior to this, people often had difficulties in learning why they were refused credit. New cars must build in better safety protection. Fabrics in some public buildings must be flame resistant. Many other steps forward have been made.

However, much still remains to be done. Death on the highway is very high. Periodically, large packings of certain foodstuffs are found to be contaminated. Water supplies in many areas are poor and getting worse. The disposal of sewage and garbage has caused mounting crises in urban areas. Many natural resources, fossil fuels, lumber, and other resources are fast becoming in short supply. Often recreational areas are overcrowded and poorly cared for. Some beaches are shrinking due to erosion. Many public camping areas have long lines of people waiting to get in.

Federal Departments

In a broad sense almost every activity of government is concerned with consumers. A government report once listed 33 federal departments and agencies as having consumer protection activities. However, some are more directly involved than others with protecting the marketplace for consumer goods and services. The following are some of these consumer activities.

THE DEPARTMENT OF AGRICULTURE

The main function of the Department of Agriculture is to help farmers with problems of production, marketing, management, and land use. Although activities concerned with the improvement of the food supply are important to consumers, the more direct aids to consumers are the inspection and grading of meat and poultry in interstate commerce and some inspection within individual states. (These activities are discussed more fully in Chapter 4.)

Inspection only tells us that the meat or poultry was wholesome and safe for human consumption at the time it was slaughtered. It is not any assurance that meat has been shipped and stored well after slaughtering.

In addition, the Department of Agriculture publishes many booklets to help consumers. It is also involved with the extension services in each state which promote research and help consumers.

THE DEPARTMENT OF COMMERCE

The *National Bureau of Standards* is a division of this department. It maintains accurate standards of weights and measures, standard time, and even a musical note used by the manufacturers of musical instruments.

We rely on standard measurements. When your parents proudly announced your birth, they did so in standard measurements. Light bulbs can easily be replaced because they are made in standard sizes. You buy food by weights and measures which are standard.

Gradually international standards have been developed so that goods and services produced in one country can be used elsewhere. However, even today many industrial goods cannot be used in other countries because of differences in standards. For example, an American-made traveling iron may not fit the plugs and current in many European hotels.

THE DEPARTMENT OF HEALTH AND HUMAN SERVICES

There are a number of agencies within this department which are very important to consumers.

The *Public Health Service* has an important role in preventing the spread of disease and in administering an inspection program that promotes sanitation and public health.

The *Food and Drug Administration* shares with the Department of Agriculture responsibility for the safety, purity, and wholesomeness of our food. However, it has other functions too.

The FDA lists these laws as the basis for most of its activity:

• *The Food, Drug, and Cosmetic Act* is intended to assure the consumer that (a) foods are pure and wholesome, safe to eat, and produced under sanitary conditions; (b) drugs and medical devices are safe and effective for their intended uses, including drugs used in medicated feeds for animals; (c) cosmetics are safe and properly labeled; and (d) packaging and labeling of these products is truthful and informative.

The Food, Drug, and Cosmetic Act has been amended several times. The Food Additives Amendment of 1958 prohibits the introduction of new food additives until the manufacturer can prove their safety. The Color Additive Amendments of 1960 gave the FDA authority to control the conditions for safe use of a color additive, including the amount of color used in a product. The Drug Amendments of 1962 required, among other things, that all drugs be proven effective as well as safe. These amendments also gave the FDA authority to regulate prescription drug advertising. Responsibility for regulating the advertising of drugs sold over the counter is assigned to the Federal Trade Commission.

• *The Fair Packaging and Labeling Act* of 1966 requires that labels inform the consumer of the ingredients and weight of the package. FDA's authority is limited to foods, drugs, medical devices, and cosmetics. The Federal Trade Commission enforces this act for other consumer products.

• *The Radiation Control for Health and Safety Act* (1968) is designed to protect the public from unnecessary exposure to radiation from electronic products such as color television sets, microwave ovens, and x-ray machines. FDA sets performance standards for these and similar products.

• *The Public Health Service Act* (1944) is enforced in part by FDA. Two sections are enforced by FDA. One is the interstate sale of biological products such as vaccines, serums, and blood. FDA assures that these products are safe, pure, and potent. Under another section of this law, FDA assures the safety of pasteurized milk and shellfish. It also assures the sanitation of food services and the food, water, and sanitary facilities for travelers on trains, planes, and buses.

The Food and Drug Administration has neither the money nor the man-power to maintain continuous supervision in all food processing plants or even to check every food processor frequently. It generally has to rely on spot checks and the cooperation of manufacturers and producers.

Most food processors want to protect their reputation. Thus, they go to great lengths to ensure that processing standards are maintained. To assure safety, food products need to be carefully handled at all stages of food processing.

The *Social Security Administration* helps claimants and beneficiaries through local offices. It administers two types of programs, a pension for retired and disabled workers and their dependents and a health insurance program, Medicare. (The pension program was discussed more fully in Chapter 9, and health insurance was covered in Chapter 8.)

The *Department of Education* provides leadership in developing new directions in educational programs. Recently, there has been a great push to develop vocational programs that will enable young people to enter the market with salable skills.

THE DEPARTMENT OF HOUSING AND URBAN DEVELOPMENT

Although this department primarily administers federal housing programs, it also aids individual consumers directly primarily by guaranteeing home mortgage loans (FHA loans) and home improvement loans (FHA home improvement loans). Before these take effect, the department inspects the house or improvement. This procedure has helped to set some minimal standards for home construction.

THE DEPARTMENT OF THE INTERIOR

This department carries on many activities, including supervision of the development of mineral resources and administering the national park system. In recent years many people have been concerned about the use of public recreational areas and the growing demand for camping and hiking facilities.

The Department of Interior also has a voluntary inspection service (the producers must request it) for processed fish products.

THE DEPARTMENT OF LABOR

Activities of the Department of Labor are concerned with labor relations in many fields. As a result of a federal law designed to improve occupational safety and health in 1971, the department established the *Occupational Safety and Health Adminis-*

Many people are concerned about the future of our parks and recreational areas. Which setting has more appeal for you?

Yellowtail Dam, Montana. The reinforced concrete arch stretches 1,450 feet across the Bighorn Canyon. Nearly 500 feet below the crest is a power plant containing four generators, each producing 62,500 kw of electrical energy.

tration to develop and administer standards for industry in general and specific standards for some industries.

THE TREASURY DEPARTMENT

The *comptroller of the currency* has authority over the operation of nationally chartered banks.

The Treasury Department also regulates the labeling and advertising of alcoholic beverages.

THE POSTAL SERVICE

This semiautonomous agency administers the mail system and is charged with the responsibility to protect users from mail frauds.

Federal Regulatory Agencies

There are a number of agencies which regulate various areas of importance to consumers.

The *Federal Trade Commission* is pri-

Business Week

The CAB controls what airlines may fly a route.

marily responsible for maintaining a free and competitive market. For a long time the FTC concerned itself largely with the relationships between big businesses. However, more recently it has become involved with business and trade practices that apply directly to the individual consumer, particularly in the area of advertising and labeling.

The *Federal Reserve Board* is the managing group of the federal reserve banks. These are the bankers for other banks.

Federal reserve banks hold most of the cash reserves of the member banks, provide checking accounts for the U.S. Treasury, issue currency (federal reserve notes), collect checks, supervise member banks, and handle the issuance and redemption of government securities.

The federal reserve banks also exert an important role in the economy by increasing and decreasing the supply of money.

By making loans and investments, the federal reserve banks put more dollars in our banking system. When the federal reserve banks sell investments or have their loans repaid, they decrease the dollars in circulation. If they charge more on loans to member banks (raise the discount rate), the federal reserve banks make it more expensive for local banks to obtain extra dollars to lend. By lowering the discount rate the federal reserve banks reduce the cost of borrowing by local banks. Thus, they can lend more money. If the federal reserve banks increase the reserve requirements, it means that member banks must take additional money out of their lending fund and put in on reserve at the federal reserve banks. This means that less is available for them to lend.

The *Consumer Product Safety Commission* is one of the newest agencies. It sets and enforces safety standards for about 10,000 products, ranging from children's toys to mobile homes. It can also require that manufacturers attach safety warnings to products.

The *Atomic Energy Commission* controls the production and use of radioactive materials. It is also responsible for seeing that the public is protected from radiation hazards.

The *Civil Aeronautics Board* regulates airplane fares, controls how many planes and what lines may fly a given route, and grants subsidies to airlines.

The *Federal Aviation Agency* is responsible for aviation safety. It sets standards, controls navigational devices, approves the design of aircraft, and gives grants for the construction of airports.

The *Interstate Commerce Commission* regulates public carriers who operate across state lines. One of its functions is to set rates.

The *Federal Communications Commission* regulates telephone rates and services and also licenses radio and television stations.

The *Federal Power Commission* regulates wholesale rates for electricity and gas in interstate commerce and licenses hydroelectric power plants.

The *Securities and Exchange Commission* regulates the securities market—the exchanges, brokers, and investment companies. New issues of securities offered to the public must be registered by the commission and accompanied by a prospectus describing the issue.

The *Veterans Administration* insures home mortgage loans for veterans. Like the FHA guaranteed mortgages, the VA also inspects the homes to see that they meet certain minimum standards. The VA also provides medical services for disabled and needy veterans, as well as some other types of services.

Bureau of Mines, U. S. Dept. of the Interior

Navigational devices are needed to help planes when the visibility is poor.

The President's Committee on Consumer Interests

This committee is composed of two groups, the appointed members of the Consumer Advisory Council and representatives of the federal agencies most concerned with consumer affairs. It has no regulatory function but formulates suggestions for legislation and regulation. In addition, this group has helped focus attention on the needs of consumers in various areas.

State and Local Regulations

State agencies regulate enterprises that operate within the state. Although the laws in the different states are not the same, the following are some of the more important areas of state regulation:

* Water and sanitation—protection of the safety of the water supply and control of sewage disposal.
* Public education and, to a lesser extent, private education.
* Inspection of food produced and used within the state, public eating establishments, and food service in state institutions.
* Supervision of banking and credit transactions.
* Regulation of life insurance companies.
* Licensing of barber shops, beauty parlors, and alcoholic beverage stores.
* Standards—the testing of weights and measures used by stores, gas stations, oil delivery trucks, and others.

Some states have established consumer representation at the state level. Many people feel that this area should be strengthened because consumers can more easily make themselves heard at the state level than the federal.

Some cities and a few counties have instituted agencies to handle consumer problems. In addition, the local governments have many laws to aid and protect consumers.

FOR REVIEW

Points to Remember

- Laws are the rules by which a society is regulated.
- Never sign a contract unless you are sure you know to what you are agreeing.
- The law requires certain information on retail credit contracts to aid the consumer, and it also requires that you must receive a copy of the contract you sign.
- From a practical point of view, a contract is usually enforceable only after you have signed it and your deposit has been accepted.
- If you don't meet the terms of a credit contract, the seller or owner of the contract has legal rights and can use them to collect.
- Bankruptcy is a procedure designed for extreme circumstances and can only be used once every six years.
- Marriage is an unusual type of contract because three parties are involved, the man, the woman, and the state.
- Dry cleaning establishments or shoe repair stores have the right to keep your clothing or shoes until you pay completely for the work done.
- Public carriers such as trains and buses must take anyone who is willing to pay the fare.
- Hotels and motels must accept any reputable traveler.

Terms to Know

alimony
annulment
bailment contract
bankruptcy
civil law
common law
common-law marriage
contract
co-signer
criminal law
defendant
felony
Federal Reserve Board
Federal Trade Commission
Food and Drug Administration
garnishee
misdemeanor
National Bureau of Standards
plaintiff
small claims court

- A hotel or motel can retain a guest's property until the bill is paid.
- In the United States a person is presumed innocent until proven guilty.
- In a criminal case an accused person must be proven guilty before conviction.
- No person can be tried for the same crime more than once.
- A lawyer can be helpful when you are signing important contracts, such as for a home purchase and mortgage. Be sure to get a lawyer if you are arrested or have to appear in court as either a defendant or a plaintiff. (The one exception would be a small claims court. You don't need a lawyer there.)
- A number of government agencies are

responsible for regulating business and protecting consumers in various ways.

• The Federal Reserve System exerts an important influence on the economy by various means.

PROBLEM SOLVING: CHECK YOUR UNDERSTANDING

1. Steve left his shoes at a shop to get new heels. He was a little short of cash when he went to pick them up and asked if he could charge it. The shoe repair store refused to give him credit and would not return the shoes. Was the store within its rights?

2. Who owns the car while you are paying for it?

3. Linda, who is 17, wanted to buy a car. She made a down payment and signed a credit contract. When her parents saw the car, they felt that she had been gypped and insisted that the dealer give back the deposit and take back the car. Do they have a right to ask this?

4. Scott found just the motorcycle he wanted at a sport shop. His parents cosigned the note to pay for it, but they fully expected that Scott would take care of the payments. However, Scott lost his part-time job, and the cycle shop said that his parents would have to pay if he could not. Do his parents have to meet the payments if Scott does not?

5. Bob made a bet with his friend Joe on which team would win the World Series baseball games. Joe's team won, but Bob refused to pay. Can Joe take legal action?

6. Carey bought a refrigerator for her apartment from the outgoing tenants. It was purchased "as is." A week after she moved in it stopped working. Does she have any right to get her money back?

7. What are the legal rights of a husband in most states?

8. What are the legal rights of a wife in most states?

TO DO IN CLASS

Discussion

1. Should a wife be entitled to alimony?

2. Should teenagers be given credit by stores?

3. The service station that repairs your car has a lien on it until you pay your bill. How can you make sure that the bill will not be higher than you expect?

4. Barbara Grant was on her way home by train. She placed her suitcase in the rack over her seat and went to the end of the car to get a snack. While she was gone, her suitcase was stolen. Is the railroad company responsible? Why? What other alternatives were available to her?

5. Shortly before Christmas you receive a box of Christmas cards in the mail which you did not order. The enclosed letter says that you may keep them if you pay for them or that you should send them back. Do you have to pay the return postage? What is your obligation? (Check with your local post office if you need advice.)

6. What are some of the hazardous items now in your home? How might you be better protected by law or regulation against some of these?

7. Think of some recent advertisements that you saw on television. How might the advertising of products be improved to aid the consumer?

Activities

1. Divide into several committees. Each group investigate and report to the class on one of the following:

a. Where does your community get its electricity? Who sets the rates? If you build a house on an undeveloped piece of land, do you have the right to be hooked up to the electric line? Who pays for the hookup, and how is this determined? Are there any problems in the use of electricity?

b. Where does your household get its water? What regulations insure its safety? How do you dispose of waste water? Who regulates this? Are there problems in your area in the use and disposal of water?

c. What type of fire protection is available in your area? How is this maintained? Who pays for it? Is the equipment available adequate? How does fire protection relate to the cost of household insurance?

d. What type of consumer protection or complaint agencies are available in your community and state? Is there a small claims court or a consumer protection agency?

2. Invite speakers from some of the following groups to speak to the class about the activities of their agencies and problem areas:

a. A community health officer.

b. The district office of the Food and Drug Administration.

c. The district office of the Federal Trade Commission.

3. Often court cases involving problems about contracts are reported in the newspaper. Collect several of these case reports and discuss them in class. Consider:

a. What is the basis of the disagreement?

b. Why are the two parties arguing about it?

4. Collect samples of contracts—mortgages, leases, retail installment contracts, an application for a revolving charge account, an insurance policy, a warranty or guarantee. Study and discuss them. What are some of the things that are apt to cause problems?

Invite a lawyer to discuss some common types of contractual problems.

5. Visit a court in session.

6. Send for copies of a proposed state or local law pertaining to consumer rights. Study it carefully. Invite a member of a consumer group or the legislative committee of a group that is interested in the bill to speak to the class about:

a. The strengths and weaknesses of the proposed bill.

b. How you can make your voice heard.

SECTION 4

Looking Ahead

CHAPTER 11

Investing In Yourself

The best return you can get on your money usually comes when you invest in improving your earning power. Spending time and money wisely on education or training generally pays.

A HIGH SCHOOL DIPLOMA IMPROVES YOUR CHANCES FOR A JOB

A high school diploma is becoming the minimal requirement for most jobs. There has been a general upgrading of the educational level of workers in most occupations during the last thirty years. High school dropouts are in a very poor position in the labor market. They have to compete with people who have graduated from high school, those who have gone on to college, and people who have completed apprenticeship or technical training programs. Typically, the unemployment rate of high school dropouts is much higher than for high school graduates.

EDUCATION MAY HELP YOU EARN MORE MONEY

In the past the more education or training you had, the higher your income was apt to be. According to a recent survey by the Census Bureau, if the head of the household had finished four or more years of college, average family income was considerably higher than all households. However, if the head of the household had less than eight years of school, average family income was very much lower than all households.

Projections suggest that this may be changing somewhat. In the future, eighty percent of all jobs will not require four years of college. However, many of the highest paid jobs will require a college degree or more.

Will a college education really pay for me? Many young people are asking themselves this question. Beginning early in the 1970's college graduates were not in as great demand. Two factors contributed to this. First, there was a slump in the economy, so there were fewer job openings for everyone. Secondly, the number of young people entering the job market was at a record high.

The job market for new college graduates did not offer as many opportunities during the seventies as in the sixties. However, in the 1980's this should change. There will be fewer people in the college-age population and a growing number of jobs that require advanced education or training. Therefore, the people with the most education will have the best long-term job prospects.

CAREER PLANNING

Most young people in school find it difficult to see how they might fit into the job market. Often they are familiar with only a few of the many possible areas of work.

The first step in career planning is to make an inventory of your interests, abilities, and goals. Make a list of the school subjects, activities, and job experiences that you have enjoyed. One boy decided that music and art were his favorites. Another enjoyed industrial arts and his job in an auto repair shop. One girl liked science and working as a hospital volunteer. School guidance counselors can help you develop a personal inventory, possibly give you vocational interest tests, and point out work areas that are related to your interests.

In addition to your areas of interest and strength, you need to consider your own personality traits. Do you like to work alone, or do you prefer working with other people? Do you feel satisfied doing the same thing over and over again, or would you prefer something with more variety? Do you like to work with your hands? Would you prefer to be indoors or outdoors? Do you like to be an organizer or a follower?

Part-time and summer jobs often are a way of trying various kinds of work while earning money. Some programs combine job training and school. These can be helpful in finding out what you do and don't like.

There are books and government publications about occupations, such as the *Occupational Outlook Handbook* by the U.S. Department of Labor, which give detailed job descriptions.

When thinking about a career, you need to consider how much time and effort you are willing to invest in preparation. Remember that the educational level of workers will probably continue to rise and that if you want to increase your chances for a good job, you need to prepare for it.

Girls as well as boys should recognize the importance of post-high-school training or college—even graduate or profes-

USDA Photo

Most young people find it difficult to see how they might fit into the job market.

sional school. If you are not interested in going on for four years of college, it still pays to get some job training. There are more and better job opportunities for people with education and skills.

Look in your school or community library for information about occupations.

Institute of Life Insurance

For years, it was expected that when a young man left school he would support himself. Therefore, education and job training were very important. In fact, most men do work from their late teens or early twenties until they die or are retired or disabled—about 45 years.

Now, however, more people are recognizing the need for job training for women. Let's look at this situation cited by Gloria Stevenson in *Occupational Outlook Quarterly.*

"Why should I plan a career? I don't expect to work all my life. I'll probably work for a few years after I finish high school, get married, and then quit my job to raise a family. Besides, I'm so busy doing school work and going out with Tom and doing other things that it's hard to think about the future."

According to a number of individuals and groups which counsel women, many teenage girls share attitudes like these. As a report on a vocational counseling project run by the Los Angeles YWCA puts it, "All the current Women's Liberation movement publicity . . . to the contrary, the average girl still believes that she is not destined for paid employment except as a brief prelude to marriage and child bearing."

The record shows, however, that for many women, work is far more than a bridge between school and children. If present patterns continue, this is the role that employment is likely to play in the life of a typical young woman—let's call her Joanne—who is now in high school.

Joanne will probably graduate from high school but is unlikely to finish college. The Bureau of Census reports that only 16 percent of all women between the ages of 25 and 29 currently hold a college degree. However, the ranks of college-educated women have been growing and are expected to continue to expand.

Once out of school, Joanne, in line with her expectations, will probably get a job. Marriage is apt to follow quickly. Nine out of ten women marry at some time during their lives [many quite young]. Joanne is then likely to drop out of the work world to bear children. Eight out of ten women become mothers and half have their last child before age 30.

Then come the facts of life which many girls ignore. Joanne is apt to be about 36 when her last child goes off to school. With the busiest years of child-rearing over, she is likely to feel a need for new activities to fill her days and challenge her abilities. She may still have housework to do, of course, but work-saving appliances and convenient packaged food—possibly along with increased help from her husband—will enable her to take care of the home and family in far less time than it took her mother. Besides, Joanne, like many women, may well feel a need for more person-to-person contact and mental stimulation than generally is offered by unpaid work inside the home.

At this point in their lives, many women return to work. The Bureau of Labor Statistics reports that about half of all women aged 35 to 49 were working or looking for work in the seventies. Should Joanne return to the work force at about age 35 and have no more children, she can expect to average another 24 years of work. Thus, despite the popular notion that women work only a few years after leaving school and then devote their time to their families, many women actually combine marriage and a job for about a quarter of a century.

That is what lies ahead if Joanne's life follows the most common pattern. If she takes other paths, however, Joanne is apt to find work playing an even bigger role in her life. For example, Joanne may be the one woman out of ten who never marries. If so, she will probably work for about 45 years. On the other hand, she may be the one woman in ten who is widowed before age 50, or hers may be among the three out of every ten marriages which end in divorce. Joanne might then have to support herself, and possibly her children, alone.

There is also the chance that Joanne's husband will be unable to earn enough to support the family comfortably. In a recent year, nearly a fourth of all working women were married to men who earned less than it cost to support an urban family of four on an "intermediate" budget (as defined by the Bureau of Labor Statistics).

Young women as well as young men should recognize the need to plan for their earning years. If the present trend continues, women will be an increasing part of the work force. Paid employment no longer is something to fill the time between school and marriage. More women are working for a greater portion of their lives.

PREPARING FOR THE WORLD OF WORK

Two general kinds of preparation are needed for most occupations. One is a broad general education that enables you to read easily, handle numbers and measurements, communicate with others, and cope with change. The second is preparation for a specific job or job area.

General Education

One of the reasons why people with limited education are so often at a disadvantage is that they do not have good general skills, such as reading and communicating with others, which will enable them to work in better-paying jobs. In today's increasingly technical world it is important to be able to use written instructions, handle some numerical problems, and communicate with others in carrying on many job activities.

Generally, a high school education indicates that one has at least a certain minimal level of these skills. Post-high-school education, particularly a college diploma, usually indicates to a prospective employer that you can handle these areas more effectively.

Another reason why general education is considered so valuable is that it prepares you to cope with change. New machinery, new tools, new working organizations mean that people have to learn to manage in new ways. Someone with a broad general education is usually more adaptable.

Job Training

Job training can range all the way from acquiring minimal skills that will enable you to get a first job to training for highly skilled (and highly paid) occupations like accounting or medicine.

Job-training programs in high schools, both those offered in comprehensive high schools and vocational schools, generally offer courses to help you get a beginning job or become a semiskilled worker. Some

This young lady has learned to operate office machines.

IBM

U.S. Department of Labor

Air traffic controllers must be in excellent health. They must also have good vision and an excellent memory. They must be able to make decisions quickly.

of the most popular programs prepare typists, food service workers, auto repair workers, drafters, computer-related workers such as key punchers, and paramedical workers. A cooperative work-study program for a number of jobs is offered in many schools. Preparation for jobs in retail stores is often handled this way.

Training for a beginning job can be used in several ways. Some young people use it to help them get a job which they stay with for a long time. However, many see it just as a means of getting started. They may follow up later with additional training, either in more advanced programs or through their places of employment. (Some companies offer job training to help employees develop better skills. Still others may pay for or help pay for training elsewhere.) Some young people use their beginning jobs as a means of financing further education or training.

Although some high school programs, particularly those in vocational programs or schools, offer preparation for semi-skilled and skilled occupations, training for these is usually more available in post-high-school programs.

Typically, post-high-school programs prepare one to enter occupations at a more highly skilled level than high school programs, although there is considerable overlap. For example, a high school program may prepare nurses' aides, whereas a community college might offer a program leading to licensing as a practical nurse, and a four-year college may provide a program leading to licensing as a registered nurse.

A variety of post-high-school programs are available. A two-year community college might offer both vocational programs designed to help one enter the job market

U.S. Department of Labor
A secretary should have a sound knowledge of grammar and spelling. He or she should also have good typing and shorthand skills. Responsibility and alertness are also essential.

immediately and also a two-year program which is really the first two years of a four-year college program. In addition, many areas have post-high-school technical schools, both public and private, and private specialized schools.

Before you spend money for tuition at a vocational school, explore what is available in public institutions. There may be many programs that you are not aware of. Even if you are out of school, you can go back to your high school guidance office for information on post-high-school programs. This is usually a good source of information for programs in your area. You can also call or write to your county or state department of education to ask about programs in an area in which you are interested. Other sources of information are the library and the state employment office.

Some private vocational schools offer good job training programs. However, be wary of those that promise employment. Some exaggerate about employment opportunities. It is always a good idea to check with the state employment agency about job openings in a particular field before you sign up for an expensive training program. If you have any question about a particular school, check with the department of education in your state. Most states license private job-training schools, so they have some information about such schools.

For a long time training for skilled trades was done through an apprenticeship under the guidance of a skilled worker. This practice grew out of the European customs of the Middle Ages and still is carried on in many trades.

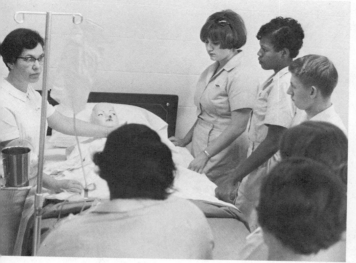

USDA Photo

A training program to become a practical nurse might be offered in a high school program, a community college, or by a hospital.

U.S. Department of Labor

Machine tool operation is offered in a number of programs.

Today, in addition to apprenticeship programs, there are other ways to obtain training for a skilled trade. Vocational schools may provide the preparation to become a licensed skilled worker. Many young people have learned skilled jobs in the armed services. Some opportunities for informal on-the-job training exist.

IF YOU ARE CONSIDERING MORE EDUCATION

Many young people are unsure about whether they want four years of college and whether they can afford it. Fortunately, there are many public institutions of higher education, which makes it possible to attend at moderate cost. There are many excellent private colleges and universities too, but the tuition charges are usually considerably higher than those of public institutions.

A two-year community college may offer some advantages to those who are undecided about their future plans. Often it is possible to take a program that will include job training as well as general education courses, enabling you to go on to a four-year program if you later decide to do so. Generally, it is possible to live at home and commute, which cuts costs.

Transfer from a two-year college to a four-year school is often made simpler when the student makes early contact with the second school. If you know what school you plan to transfer to and you also know your major subject of interest, contact may be helpful. Find out what is required for graduation in the subject area of your choice. Then at the two-year college take the courses that will help fill the requirements. Counseling may be needed. This procedure may save you time and confusion after transferring.

A growing number of states have established a network of four-year colleges. Often it is possible to commute to these if you live close enough and want to cut costs.

To encourage young people to go on for post-high-school education or training, many states offer financial aid for young people from families with small incomes. In addition, there are some other aid programs. If you think that you will need financial help for more education, ask your high school guidance office about financial aid programs and inquire at the schools that you would like to attend. Financial aid funds are usually very limited. An effort is generally made to stretch the funds so that as many people as possible can be helped. Most schools now offer a package of financial aid and part-time jobs to some of the people who qualify for help.

You might consider getting further training or schooling on a part-time basis. A growing number of schools are making it possible for people to attend evenings or Saturdays and complete the program over a long period of time. This may even have the advantage of helping you clarify your goals. Working often helps young people find out just what really interests them and what doesn't.

Perhaps you could get a job at a company that will help you get further training. Many large companies have educational programs for their employees. Often they will pay the tuition. Some will give you time off, such as leaving early to attend school, if they approve of the program or think it will help you on the job. Often a

job at an educational institution has as one of its benefits free tuition for a limited number of courses per semester. Many

Many students have to work to put themselves through college.

Savings Bank Assoc. of New York State

USDA Photo

There is a growing need for teachers of children with physical and mental handicaps. These boys are learning about nature with the help of braille.

companies prefer to hire people who show an interest in getting more education or training.

Educational loans generally do not have to be paid back until after you finish the program. Inquire at your bank and at the school you wish to attend for further information about educational loans.

JOB TRENDS

The Need for Workers

Demand for workers in a specific occupation depends on many factors. The birth-rate, technological advances, and economic forces all influence the growth and shrinkage of various occupations.

A declining birthrate has influenced the teaching field, which had a chronic labor shortage for years. A lower birthrate means fewer children in school; thus, fewer teachers are needed. Although the demand for teachers generally has been shrinking, there is still a growing need for teachers of the physically and mentally handicapped. The realization that many people can be helped with special education services has grown.

Technological advances, such as those in the field of engineering, have resulted in an increasing demand for engineers and a decreasing demand for beginning drafters. More of the simpler drafting work is now done by computers. At the same time skilled engineers are needed to keep complex machinery operating.

A generally rising level of prosperity in the United States has helped swell the demand for service industries and workers for these industries. We need people to fix our cars, as well as household and industrial tools, if they are to continue to be useful.

Longer paid vacations and more holidays, coupled with a shorter work week and prosperity, have swelled the demand for leisure activities. Recreation is a growing field.

White-Collar Versus Blue-Collar Jobs

White-collar jobs will continue to increase faster than blue-collar jobs in the years ahead. (Although fewer and fewer people are wearing white shirts these days, the term lingers on. White-collar jobs are generally those in which your hands stay clean and relatively little physical work is required. By contrast a blue-collar job is one in which your hands probably get dirty and physical work is often required. A factory job is considered a blue-collar job, whereas an office job is white-collar.)

Of the so-called white-collar jobs, professional and technical workers will be in the biggest demand. There will be a smaller but growing need for office workers. Opportunities for sales workers and managers will increase more slowly.

Of the blue-collar jobs skilled workers will be in the greatest demand followed by machine servicers. A slower rate of increase is projected for machine operators because many more jobs will become automated.

The Future of Farming

Jobs on farms will continue to decrease in number as machines replace manpower. Russell B. Flanders cites the following in the *Occupational Outlook Quarterly:*

> By 1980 it will take only about 3 percent of all the nation's civilian labor force to produce all the food and fiber needed in this country. What makes this so dramatic is that [as recently as 1920] approximately 30 percent of all employed persons worked on farms.

Beginning Jobs

Young people can be encouraged by the fact that in the 1980's there will be fewer entrants on the job market each year because of a reduced birthrate. Thus, if the economy is healthy, there should be less competition for beginning jobs.

Opportunities for Women and Minority Groups

For a long time women and members of ethnic minority groups have been restrict-

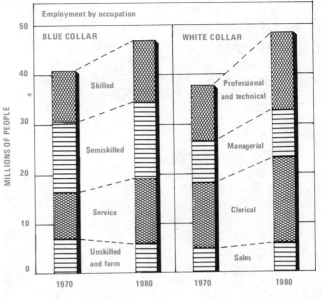

THE COLLARS ARE WHITER

FORTUNE MAGAZINE

National Canners Assoc.

Machines are replacing workers on farms.

ed in opportunities to get certain kinds of jobs and training. However, now the doors have begun to open, and many occupations and schools are actively recruiting members of these groups. Few people would claim that a woman or a black man has yet

This transcontinental airline pilot is making a preflight inspection of the landing gear.

an equal chance for a top-level position in most occupations, but at all levels opportunities now are far greater than in the past.

With this comes a growing need for women and members of minority groups to recognize that these opportunities now exist and to take advantage of them. Parents as well as young people need to develop an awareness about the possibilities available now. For example, girls need not be restricted to the traditional women's occupations, such as teaching, nursing, and clerical jobs.

Changing Opportunities for Men

Men are increasingly welcome in many occupations formerly staffed all or in part by women. Male nurses are in great demand, and many schools are looking for men to teach at the elementary school level. The distinction between men's work and women's work is beginning to blur in the working world as well as in the home. It is no longer accepted as necessary that certain jobs should be "male" or "female," which opens greater opportunities to all to choose what they want to do.

AN OVERVIEW OF SOME OCCUPATIONAL AREAS

Professional Occupations

Professional occupations often sound very tempting to young people. Usually there are opportunities for responsible, interesting work and often a high income. However, most professional jobs require a long, expensive period of preparation and training.

There are two major types of professional occupations. The biggest group includes engineers, physicians, dentists, specialists like economists, teachers, and others. Except for some beginning teachers these professions usually require a college degree plus an advanced degree. Increasingly, teachers at all levels need advanced education too.

The other major professional groups are performing artists and athletes. Here the emphasis is less on academic training and more on a high degree of skill. Performing artists usually need long years of training.

In a recent year two-thirds of all workers with a college degree were in professional occupations. Some administrative jobs previously held by employees with related experience are now being filled with college graduates.

Increasingly, new jobs in areas of management and supportive services require a college degree. For example, chemists are expected to be in demand as plastics, new fibers, and new fuels are developed. With rising standards of health care, professional health workers should continue to be in growing demand. College-trained management personnel, such as economists and accountants, will be needed to handle the growing complexities of business, finance, and public service industries.

Technical Workers

A growing demand for technicians and support personnel in various professional fields is expected. As a result of a shortage of professionals, technicians are being sought to relieve professional workers at many tasks.

You are probably aware of this in the health services area. Dental assistants, x-ray technicians, and other specialists have taken over jobs formerly held by professionals. This trend is expected to continue as the demand for health services increases, and government health programs expand.

Computer services is another area where the demand for technicians should continue to be strong. More companies are automating operations through the use of computers and will need people to help run the system.

Managerial Occupations

Whether a business enterprise succeeds or fails depends largely on how it is managed. There are both salaried business managers and people who manage their own businesses.

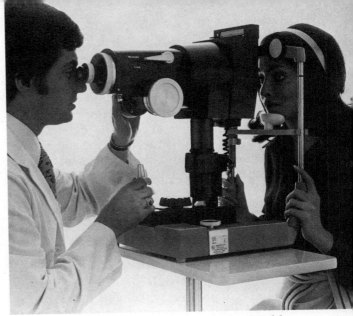

American Optical Corp.

It takes a trained person to measure someone's eyes for contact lenses.

Salaried managers make up a growing occupational group. With the increasing complexity of business, the demand for managers should continue to be strong. Employers are looking for managers with college degrees, particularly in business administration or accounting. Some want people with technical training in engineering, science, or mathematics. Others hire liberal arts graduates and give on-the-job training. However, few companies have management training programs. Often an individual progresses from a position as an accountant or salesman to management. Opportunities for a person without a college degree to progress through the ranks to a management position are becoming more limited.

The greatest number of salaried managers are employed in retail and wholesale trade. Others are employed by manufacturing firms, banks and financial companies, insurance, real estate, service industries,

253

transportation, and government. About one-third of all women managers are employed in retail trade, but opportunities in other areas are growing.

The responsibilities of a manager vary with one's level and employer. Most beginning management positions are supervisory or as a trainee. Going up the ladder, managers direct departments or segments of a business. The top-level managers make the major decisions of a company.

Sales Occupations

Sales work comes in great variety. There are jobs for people who have not completed high school as well as for people with a college degree. Some sales jobs require travel; others do not. One can be salaried or on commission. If you are very productive, you can earn a good income with a commission, which pays according to the quantity of sales you make. Some jobs combine salary and commission. There are also part-time sales jobs, particularly in retail stores. About one-fourth of all sales workers work part-time. Two out of five are women. Women tend to be employed largely in retail stores.

The training for sales work varies with the job. People who sell simple items, such as magazines, candy, or clothing, usually don't need any specialized training. The beginning salesperson usually works with more experienced salespeople initially. In a large store the employee may attend a short training course. A high school diploma is usually a help in getting this type of sales job, although it may not be required. High school courses in business subjects as well as courses in distributive education are also helpful.

The person who sells complex products or services usually needs much more training. Often college graduation is required.

Beginners may receive training which can last for three to six months. Technical knowledge may be acquired through courses offered by universities, manufacturers, or a combination of on-the-job experience and study.

The successful salesperson must be able to deal with strangers comfortably and understand the needs and attitudes of customers. Communication skills are important. The ability to do the arithmetic involved in handling money and making price computations is needed. Also, it takes energy and self-confidence to sell to others. Sales work outside retail stores often requires that the salesperson find potential customers and plan his or her own work schedule.

Job trends are somewhat mixed. Many retail stores are becoming self-service and using fewer salespeople. Many others, however, rely on part-time workers for busy hours and seasons so that opportunities for part-time employment should remain strong. Outside retail stores the demand for salespeople should grow with an increased population and the expansion of businesses.

Clerical Jobs

Clerical workers keep records and do the paperwork required in offices. Others operate office machines, handle phone calls, take care of the shipping and receiving of merchandise, and operate cash registers.

Currently, most clerical workers are women, about seven out of every ten. The largest group of clerical workers is secretaries and stenographers. Next are bookkeepers and accounting clerks.

Usually, the minimal educational requirement is high school graduation. Employers generally look for people with skills such as typing and shorthand. Graduates of high school and business school office education programs often have an advantage. Many large companies cooperate with these educational programs by providing part-time employment for students in office training programs. After employment, most companies give some on-the-job training in their own office practices.

In spite of the increasing mechanization of many offices, the outlook for employment in clerical occupations should continue strong. Although mechanical equipment will be used more for some jobs, such as keeping records and inventories and preparing payrolls, the growing complexity of business organizations will tend to generate more paperwork. At the same time, there should be a growing need for clerical workers who can use office machines.

Opportunities for advancement are particularly good in large companies. These tend to have several levels of responsibility. For example, a typist may be promoted to secretary and then on to an insurance claims adjuster (in an insurance office) or executive secretary or office manager. Many clerical workers are promoted to operating tabulating or keypunch machines, automatic typewriters, and other specialized equipment. Often an employer will train or send a worker to school to learn how to operate complex office equipment.

Large companies, where the advancement opportunities for clerical workers tend to be greatest, are concentrated primarily in urban areas. In these large companies office workers usually have many of the benefits of other large working groups, paid holidays and vacations, health benefits, as well as sick leave and retirement plans.

U.S. Department of Labor

A commercial artist must have excellent drawing skills.

Service Occupations

The training and level of skill required for service jobs varies with the occupation. Some service workers are highly trained college graduates. However, most have only a high school diploma plus some specialized training. The major groups of service workers are: (1) occupations related to food preparation and service; (2) building cleaning and servicing operations; (3) private household workers; and (4) protective service workers. Next are those who provide health care, grooming and personal services, and jobs related to entertainment and leisure activities.

Jobs in service areas are increasing faster than jobs in general. The areas where the greatest growth is expected are: medical services, recreation, protective services, and personal care. State and local governments are expected to grow and, to a lesser extent, finance, insurance, real estate, transportation, and public utilities.

Skilled and Other Manual Occupations

In the seventies blue-collar workers—skilled, semiskilled, and unskilled—were more than one-third of all workers. According to the *Occupational Outlook Handbook:*

> They work in hundreds of different occupations and perform many important functions in our economy. They transform the ideas of scientists and the plans of engineers into goods and services. They operate transportation and communication systems that tie the country together. They build homes, office buildings, and factories. They fabricate, install, control, maintain, and repair the complex equipment necessary for operation of our highly mechanized society. They repair automobiles, television sets, washing machines, and many other household appliances. They move raw materials, wrap and pack finished products, and load and unload supplies and equipment of all kinds.
>
> Young persons who have mechanical interests and abilities or who enjoy working with their hands, will find many employment opportunities among the hundreds of occupations in this group.

Employment openings for *skilled workers* of many kinds will continue. Some people move into the skilled trades after a period on a semi-skilled job. Often they have taken courses in a trade, vocational, or technical school to enable them to move

up. In the past very few women have been skilled workers, but the situation is changing.

A young person who does not plan to go to college might consider the advantages offered by the skilled trades over many other occupations that do not require higher education—higher earnings, greater job security, better chances for promotion, and frequently more opportunities to go into business on their own.

Semiskilled workers are the biggest single working group in the labor force, about one worker in every six. Truck drivers are the biggest group. Most others operate machines in manufacturing industries—food processing, textiles and clothing, automobiles, and industrial machinery. Some operate metal stamping machines or materials lifting equipment such as forklift trucks. Many are assemblers or inspectors in factories. Some are employed as assistants to skilled workers.

To date, women have made up a larger proportion of the semiskilled workers than skilled workers, about one-third. However, women have generally been concentrated largely in the apparel, textiles, and food industries, mostly as sewing machine operators, packers and wrappers, and assemblers. Relatively few were employed in factories that produced iron, steel, and petroleum products.

Most semiskilled workers receive only brief on-the-job training. Often they do the type of job in which the same operation is repeated over and over again, but they must learn to do it at a rapid and steady pace. Semiskilled workers are more likely to lose their jobs in periods of recession and stay unemployed longer than skilled or white collar workers.

Semiskilled work will not be one of the major areas of job growth. Job openings

American Telephone and Telegraph Co.
This young man helps route telephone calls.

will increase slowly. However, job turnover is very high in this area. Women workers often leave to marry, raise families, or to move to other areas when their husbands are transferred. Young workers, both male and female, often change jobs frequently in an effort to find something they really like and for better pay.

Semiskilled jobs will continue to be a major area of employment for young men and women with no training beyond high school. One area of growing opportunity will be as a driver of a commercial vehicle, a bus or truck driver. Another will be as an operator of power equipment, which is expected to replace some unskilled workers.

Most *unskilled workers* or laborers are those who do heavy manual work, such as digging, hauling, lifting, wrapping, and mixing. The majority are employed in manufacturing and construction. Others are employed by retail and wholesale industries, in transportation, public utilities, and some service industries.

Although jobs for unskilled workers in the construction industry pay fairly well, most earn less than semiskilled workers. Also, unskilled workers are more likely to lose their jobs than semiskilled workers in periods of recession.

There should be little or no change in the number of jobs for unskilled workers. However, with a growing job market this will be a smaller proportion of all jobs available.

LOOKING FOR A JOB

Many young people want and need to earn money while they are going to school. It is hard to get figures on just how many young people are working, because some

Gerber Products Co.
Many people work part time as baby-sitters.

jobs are irregular, such as shoveling snow. However, young people do work at a wide variety of things—pumping gas in service stations, cutting lawns, doing small painting jobs, clerking and stocking shelves in stores, driving delivery trucks, baby-sitting, and many others. In rural areas many young people work on farms and in orchards.

Frequently, there are fewer of these jobs available than the number of people who want them. As a result, many who want to work haven't always been able to find jobs.

Finding a job is hard work. With few exceptions it takes time and effort to find just the job for you—no matter what your age or education.

Let's assume that you have made an inventory of your strong points, special skills, experience, and interests, as was discussed earlier in this chapter. Also, you have an idea of some general occupational areas that sound interesting.

For a short-term or irregular-type job, such as baby-sitting, lawn mowing, pumping gas after school, or working in a library

A part-time job can often be found as a cashier or grocery store employee.

or supermarket, you may be able to land a job just by talking to your friends, relatives, neighbors, or the manager of a store, service station, or library. However, sometimes you may need to do more to land that job. Some young people advertise their availability in a newspaper or on a community bulletin board. "Responsible high school student available for baby-sitting evenings and weekends. $1.50 per hour. Can furnish references." "High school student looking for regular lawn-mowing jobs. Rate based on the size of the lawn."

Another possibility is to canvass the area. Ask at stores, factories, or service stations or call on the telephone. Inquire from friends who have jobs about whether there is likely to be an opening at the place where they work. Consult your high school placement or guidance office or a youth employment service, if your community has one.

The local state employment agency may be able to help you, particularly if you are looking for a full-time or summer job. Register at your local state employment service or a youth opportunity center. There is no charge for their service. Look in the telephone directory under *state government.* (The listing may be under the name of your state.) They can tell you where to get information about special summer work programs for young people as well as other employment opportunities. Visit or write your nearest Office of Personnel Management to inquire about the jobs they have available. This is listed under *U. S. government* in the telephone directory.

The federal government publishes a bulletin listing summer jobs in parks and federal agencies. Write to the Office of Personnel Management, Washington, D.C. 20415, for this free booklet. Generally, the jobs listed in it require at least a high school diploma.

It is important to apply early for summer jobs. Many are filled early, and there are usually more applicants than jobs. Some people look ahead and start applying for next summer's job at the end of the summer.

Here is just a partial list of summer jobs you may be able to fill. Some require experience; most do not.*

Summer Job Suggestions

Baby-sitter
Caddie
Camp Counselor
Cannery Worker
Car Washer
Cashier
Construction Helper
Delivery Person
Dining Room
    Attendant
Elevator Operator
Food Store Clerk
Farm Hand
Gas Station
    Attendant
Greenhouse Worker
Highway Helper
Hospital Worker
Houseworker

Laboratory Assistant
Library Aide
Lifeguard
Nurse's Aide
Office Clerk
Playground
    Attendant
Receptionist
Restaurant Worker
Sales Clerk
Telephone Operator
Ticket Taker
Tutor
Typist
Usher
Waiter
Waitress
Window Washer
Yard Worker

*U. S. Dept. of Labor

There are many reputable private employment agencies, but they charge a fee. Generally, private agencies cannot offer much help in finding part-time and summer employment while you are still in school.

A Resume: Selling Yourself on Paper

The U. S. Department of Labor says in its publication *Merchandising Your Job Talents* that "A written resume—really a summary of your background—can be very helpful. Many people enclose it with a letter to an employer asking about a job. Others leave a copy with each company that interviews them so that the company will be reminded of the applicant's qualifications for the job discussed or future openings."

The Department of Labor suggests this outline for your resume.

1. *Personal data*

Begin with your name, address, and telephone number. Other personal data, such as your date of birth (optional) and your marital status and dependents, may follow or appear at the end of your resume.

2. *Employment objective*

Indicate the kind of job you are seeking. If you are qualified for several jobs and are preparing one all-purpose resume, list them in order of your preference.

3. *Work history*

You can organize this information in two ways. Choose the one that presents your work experience better.

a. By job

List each job separately (even if the jobs were within the same firm), starting with the most recent one and working backward. For each job, list:
    Dates of employment
    Name and address of employer and
        nature of business

Position you held

Then describe your job, giving the following information:

Specific job duties—the tasks you performed, including any special assignments and use of special instruments or equipment

Scope of responsibility—your place in the organization, how many people you supervised, and in turn, the degree of supervision you received

Accomplishments—if possible, give concrete facts and figures.

b. By function

List the functions (fields of specialization or types of work, such as engineering, sales promotion, or personnel management) you performed that are related to your present job objectives. Then describe briefly the work you have done in each of these fields, without breaking it down by individual jobs.

4. *Education* (If this is your main selling point, put it before your work history.)

List your formal education, giving:

High school (can be omitted if you have a higher degree), college, graduate school, and other courses or training

Dates of graduation or leaving school

Degrees or certificates received

Major and minor subjects and other courses related to your job goal

Scholarships and honors

Extracurricular activities (if you are a recent graduate and your activities pertain to your job goal)

5. *Military experience*

List your military service if it is recent or pertinent to your job goal, indicating:

Branch and length of service

Major duties, including details of assignments related to the job you seek

(Indicate any pertinent military training here or under your education.)

6. *Miscellaneous*

If appropriate to your field of work, give such information as:

Knowledge of foreign languages

Volunteer or leisure-time activities

Special skills, such as typing, shorthand, or ability to operate special equipment

Membership in professional organizations

Articles published, inventions, or patents

7. *References*

Give the names, positions, and addresses of three persons who have direct knowledge of your work competence. If you are a recent graduate, you can list teachers who are familiar with your schoolwork. When possible, you should obtain the permission of the persons you use as references.

The Job Interview

This is the part of job hunting that frightens so many people. Remember that those interviewing you want to fill a job, they need someone, and they are interviewing you because they hope to be able to hire you.

Be prepared. If you have prepared a resume, take a copy with you. If not, take a copy of your school records, your social security card, and a list of your previous employers (if any) and the dates of employment. If you have any license that might apply to the job, take it. If you have served in the military, take a copy of your discharge.

Find out as much as you can about the company before you go to the interview—what they do, a little about the industry in general, and the jobs available. Many libraries can help you with the background

The Chase Manhattan Bank,
Photo by Jan Jachniewicz
Most jobs require an interview in order for a person to be considered for a position.

information. If you can, talk to people who work at the company or have worked there.

Find out the salary range of the job you are applying for, if possible. Look in publications of the United States Department of Labor, which are in most libraries. Check with the state employment office. Ask people who might know.

Make your first impression count. Appearance is important; it's what the interviewer sees first. Neatness and cleanliness are basic. Many companies are still conservative about extreme clothing and hair styles, so keep this in mind. (After you are hired, it is often easier to follow personal preferences in hairstyles and dress.)

There are three important points to make in selling yourself to a prospective employer at an interview:

- You can do the job; your training and experience have prepared you.
- You are able to work with others.
- You are anxious for the job and very willing to learn how to do it well.

At the conclusion of the interview thank the employer. If you have not been given a definite offer of employment, you can follow up a few days later with a note or phone call thanking the employer for spending his or her time with you and indicating that you are still interested in the position.

KEEPING UP-TO-DATE

If you work from age twenty to age sixty-five you will have a working lifetime of forty-five years. During this period you will probably change jobs a number of

USDA Photo by Roy Clark
Farmers benefit by studying new methods of farming.

times. Perhaps you will leave and reenter the work force one or more times.

Forty-five years is a long period of time in today's technological society. With the rapid changes taking place, many job skills that you learn in your teens or early twenties may become outmoded, perhaps in as little as ten years. Projections suggest that young workers of today may have to learn to update their job skills far more frequently than their parents or grandparents did.

Also, many people who are not interested in further education when they leave high school later change their minds and want to go back to school. As a result, adult education programs of all kinds are growing. These range from evening, weekend, and part-time programs for a college degree to daytime job-training programs, evening vocational courses, and courses for personal interest unrelated to a job. A study by the United States Department of Labor showed

that 1.5 million adults, one in fifty, 35 years of age and over were enrolled in or attending school in a recent year.

If at some future point, you become restless with your job, feel that it is going nowhere, or want to reenter the work force after being out, you may want to consider getting further education or training. A feeling of discontent can be constructive. It may encourage you to upgrade your job skills and get a better job. If the present trend continues, there will probably be a growing number of ways you can do this.

FOR REVIEW

Points to Remember

• The best return you can get on your money usually comes when you invest in improving your earning power.

• A high school diploma has become the minimal requirement for most jobs.

- The more education or training you have, the higher your income is apt to be.
- In planning a career consider your interests, abilities, and goals.
- Two general kinds of preparation are needed for most occupations, a good general education and more specific training for a job.
- The demand for workers in specific occupations depends on many factors, which change from time to time.
- Technological advances have increased the demand for workers with job skills and/or higher education and decreased the demand for unskilled workers.
- There are growing opportunities for women and minority group members in the working world.
- Finding a job usually takes considerable time and effort.
- In today's rapidly changing technological society most people will need to update their job skills during their working lifetime.

Terms to Know	
apprenticeship	resume
blue-collar job	semiskilled
community	workers
college	service industry
general	skilled workers
education	technician
job training	unskilled workers
reference	white-collar job

PROBLEM SOLVING: CHECK YOUR UNDERSTANDING

1. Why are high school dropouts at a disadvantage in the job market?

2. In what ways are education and income related?

3. What should you consider in planning a career?

4. Where can you get information about jobs, the skills they require, and the education needed?

5. Where can you get job training after high school?

6. What are some of the advantages of a community college?

7. In what ways has the declining birthrate influenced job opportunities?

8. Why is there a growing demand for technicians?

9. What are some of the skills that a successful salesperson needs to have?

10. In what ways is a job resume useful?

TO DO IN CLASS

Discussion

1. How can you increase your qualifications for a part-time job?

2. What are some of the advantages in getting some job training right after high school? What might be the disadvantages?

3. In what ways are the roles of women changing? How could the job market be changed in line with these changing roles?

4. What can you do to learn about part-time and summer jobs in your area?

5. Which is more important, job satisfaction or money?

6. What are some of the problems people you know have faced in the job market? Think of parents, friends, relatives, or neighbors.

Activities

1. Invite someone to talk to the group about opportunities for career training. Perhaps there is a person in your school guidance department; if not, ask an occupational counselor from an employment

agency or someone concerned with career education from a local, county, or state education department.

2. Make a survey of the juniors and seniors in your high school to find out the kinds of jobs they have held and who employed them. Summarize the findings in a class presentation or make up a bulletin board.

3. In a committee investigate and report to the class on the laws concerning teenagers working, the hours allowed, and limitations on types of work.

4. Invite a representative of a local company to talk to the group on what they look for when hiring a person.

5. Role-play some job interviews. Class members may make suggestions as to how the interviewees might have projected themselves more effectively.

6. Visit a community college. Find out as much as you can about its program offerings. Is it possible to work your way through? Are tuition scholarships available? If so, what are the qualifications?

7. Make some tentative career plans. What would you like to be doing one year from now, five years from now, and ten years from now? What do you need to do if you want to reach those goals? Find out as much as you can; then give a short report to the class.

8. Some people in the class probably have ideas about the work they would like to do. Have a series of short debates on several types of jobs: "Why I Want to Be a . . . . ," "Why I Don't Want to Be a . . . . . ."

9. Divide into a number of small groups. Each group learn about an occupational area—the type of jobs available, whether the field is expected to grow, what training or education is required, and what are current salary ranges. Report findings to the class and discuss the advantages and disadvantages of each area of work.

CHAPTER 12

Bank Services

Almost 1500 years before the birth of Christ, the Ming dynasty of China originated the use of paper money. The use of coins goes back almost 5,000 years. However, until the early 1800's much trade was done with barter, credit, and promissory notes. When money was scarce, the Roman soldiers were paid in salt—the origin of our word salary. Early American colonists were short of coins too, particularly in

Can you name some of the services provided by a bank facility like this one?

IBM

rural areas. Merchants often sold goods on credit, and settlers paid their debts with produce. Tobacco merchants would draw bills of exchange on English tobacco importers. The colonial governments paid soldiers and civil servants with commodities or land.

At the time of the American Revolution the Continental Congress issued paper money to finance the war. However, this was not very successful and *continentals* quickly went out of use.

Early in the 1800's the use of money began to replace barter for many transactions. Commerce and banks grew. However, it was not until 1863, under pressure to finance the Civil War, that the federal government began to issue paper money as we know it today. The development of industry brought banks into a more important role in the economy. In 1913 President Wilson signed the Federal Reserve Act, which marked a change from a local, decentralized banking system to a more centralized one.

The great depression of the 1930's brought about changes in the banking system of the United States. One was the prohibition of interest on checking accounts (demand deposits). Another placed a ceiling, set by the government, on the rates that could be paid on longer term savings accounts. Also, the Federal Reserve System was given the right to control bank credit. The Federal Deposit Insurance Corporation was established to insure deposits in banks.

More recently, the United States has moved to a system of using less cash. For example, checks and credit cards often substitute for coins and paper money. The growing use of electronic funds transfers (EFT) makes it possible to transfer funds quickly between accounts.

The services of banking institutions are not all the same. Certain differences are prescribed by law. Others have developed as a method of competing for your business.

TYPES OF BANKS

There are three general types of banks, commercial banks, savings banks, and industrial banks.

Commercial Banks

These are the department stores of finance, offering a wide range of services. The most widely used of these services are:

- Checking accounts.
- Savings accounts.
- Credit-card services.
- Savings certificates.
- Cashier's and traveler's checks.
- The sale and redemption of government savings bonds.
- Safe-deposit boxes.
- Loans and mortgages to businesses, farmers, and individuals.
- Trust services.

Commercial banks are owned by their stockholders as are other corporations. The bank may be chartered by the federal government or the state. If the bank is chartered by the federal government, it must have the word *national* in its name. A state bank may use the word *state* in its name.

Savings Banks

Most savings banks are owned by the depositors; others are owned by stockholders. They usually have fewer services than commercial banks. Savings banks developed originally to serve individuals and families rather than businesses.

Their most important services are:

- Savings accounts.
- Longer term savings deposits (two years or more).
- Mortgage loans. They are often a good source for individual home mortgages because most of their assets are invested in mortgage loans.

SOURCES OF MORTGAGES
Savings and loan associations
Savings banks
Commercial banks

- Loans to individuals—guaranteed student loans, passbook account loans, home remodeling loans, and in some states unsecured consumer loans.
- Safe-deposit boxes.
- Money orders and traveler's checks.
- Other services. In some states depositors can participate in a mutual fund. In a few states, low-cost life insurance is available to people who live or work there. Savings banks in some states also provide checking accounts.

Savings banks are chartered by a state and only operate in some states. These banks may pay higher rates of interest on savings accounts than commerical banks.

Industrial Banks

There are relatively few industrial banks. Generally, they are found in cities.

Industrial banks are stock companies that operate a little differently from other savings banks. They are only permitted to make certain kinds of loans, usually small loans. They have savings or thrift accounts which are similar to accounts in other savings banks. They may also sell savings or investment certificates. Loans are usually made for the same purposes as other banks.

OTHER FINANCIAL INSTITUTIONS

Two other types of institutions resemble banks in some of their services, savings and loan associations and credit unions.

Savings and Loan Associations

These may be called "building and loan associations" or "cooperative banks" in some states.

According to the United States Savings and Loan League, the first savings and loan association in the United States was organized in Frankford (a suburb of Philadelphia), Pennsylvania, in 1831. It was patterned after similar institutions which were already operating under the name of "building societies" in England. The American Association made its first loan on a house which is still standing at 4276 Orchard Street, Philadelphia. That first small association had only 37 people saving up their money out of weekly and monthly pay envelopes. Later, more associations were organized all over the United States.

Savings and loan associations are specialized financial institutions licensed by the federal government or the state. Their two most important services are:

- Savings accounts, technically the purchase of savings shares.
- Home mortgage loans.

Credit Unions

Each depositor is a shareholder in a credit union. Credit unions offer savings accounts and make low-cost personal loans to the members. Some will make mortgage loans, but they do not have many other services. (Credit unions were discussed in Chapter 3, *Using Credit.*)

Trust Companies

Certain banks are authorized by the state as trustees—to operate trust funds, manage real estate, or act as the administrator or executor of an estate. An institution may function only as a trust company. However, many banks also serve as trustees. The current trend is for banks to include trust services.

GETTING PAID BY CHECK

Are you looking for a part-time job? Do you expect to work next summer? There is a good chance that on the job you will be paid by check. Most companies handle their payrolls in this way. Suppose you get a job at a supermarket on Saturdays. The store probably pays its employees by check.

There are many reasons why companies pay by check. They don't have to have cash on hand to pay their employees. Checks provide an easy record of the fact that they have paid you.

What Is A Check?

It is a form furnished by the bank and directing the bank to pay a stated amount to a person or company from the funds of the depositor. Checks are often used in place of cash.

A Paycheck Voucher

Case Study. Mary Black worked during Christmas vacation as a salesclerk at Jones' department store. At the end of the week she was paid by check. Attached to her check was a *paycheck voucher*—a statement showing how much she had earned and what had been withheld for taxes and FICA (social security).

She saved these vouchers as a record of what she had earned and paid in taxes.

Endorsing A Check

When Mary wanted to use her paycheck, she had to *endorse* it, that is, sign her name on the back to show that she had received it.

There are several types of endorsement:

- *An endorsement in blank.* This is a check signed with only the name of the payee. Once a check is endorsed this way, it becomes payable to the holder. Anyone can endorse it again and cash it. Therefore a check should only be endorsed this way at the time that you are cashing it.

- *A Special Endorsement.* The check can be signed over to another person by writing "pay to the order of Sam Smith." This means that only Sam Smith can cash it.

- *A Restrictive Endorsement.* This is frequently used when a check is deposited by mail. The payee might endorse it with the instructions, "for deposit only," above the signature. This means that the check must be deposited to the payee's account. Sometimes people add their account number to the check. They may also name the bank—"for deposit only, Howard National Bank."

Cashing A Check

People who cash checks want to be able to collect. They don't want to cash bad checks. Therefore most places will ask for identification before they cash your check, especially if they do not know you well. Here are some of the things they might ask for:

- Your driver's license.
- Your employee's pass or badge.
- Major credit cards.

The verification of your identification, although annoying on occasion, is also a protection to you. Suppose some dishonest person finds your checkbook, writes a check for a large amount of money, and then signs your name on it. If the bank mistakenly pays the check, it could take a while to straighten out so you would have use of the money again. (Banks have an

Here are three ways to endorse a check.

ENDORSING A CHECK

Irene Oppenheim	Pay to the order of Jack Smith Irene Oppenheim	For deposit only Irene Oppenheim
ENDORSEMENT IN BLANK	A SPECIAL ENDORSEMENT	A RESTRICTIVE ENDORSEMENT

obligation not to honor checks with incorrect signatures.)

The easiest place for you to cash a check is at a bank or savings and loan association where you have an account. Some employers will arrange with a bank where they do business to cash their employees' paychecks.

Another place to cash checks is at a store where you are known. Supermarkets, stores, gas stations, and other places of business vary greatly in their willingness to cash checks. Some will cash paychecks from certain companies. Others will cash personal checks up to a limit of $25 or $50. Many will not cash checks at all.

In some communities check-cashing services will cash paychecks for a fee. Some will also cash personal checks.

What Happens to Checks?

After a check has been cashed, it is returned to the bank that issued it. This is usually done through a clearing house. Out-of-town checks, however, are sent by mail or cleared by the Federal Reserve System.

When the bank has paid the check, the check is stamped with the word *cancelled* or *paid.* This means that the check cannot be used again except as a receipt for a bill that has been paid.

Cancelled checks are periodically returned to the person who has written them, usually monthly. They are accompanied by a statement showing the deposits made to the account, the checks drawn, other charges, if any, and the balance remaining in the account.

A check eventually returns to the bank that issues it.

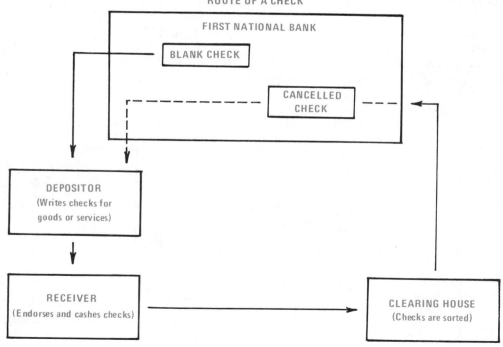

ROUTE OF A CHECK

FIRST NATIONAL BANK

BLANK CHECK

CANCELLED CHECK

DEPOSITOR
(Writes checks for goods or services)

RECEIVER
(Endorses and cashes checks)

CLEARING HOUSE
(Checks are sorted)

Deposit or Cash Checks Promptly

It is always wise to deposit or cash a check promptly. When a person issues a check to you, he or she generally does so with the understanding that sufficient money is in the account to cover the check. If the check is not cashed promptly, the issuer may forget it is outstanding and not keep sufficient funds to cover it. Moreover, the issuer may even close the account.

PAYING YOUR BILLS

A variety of tools are available for paying bills—probably more than you realize.

- Cash.
- Personal check.
- Bank check or money order.
- Postal money order.
- Traveler's checks.
- Payroll deductions.
- Barter—swapping goods and services.
- Credit cards.
- Electronic funds transfers (EFT).

Case Study. Nicole went shopping for a new pair of slacks. She found a pair that she liked for $18.95. She took them to the cashier and gave him a twenty dollar bill. In return she received slacks wrapped in a bag, a receipt, and her change.

This was a cash transaction. What is the advantage of using cash in this situation? What might be the disadvantage?

It's usually easy to dig into your pocket or purse and come up with twenty-five cents for a bar of candy, three dollars for a movie ticket, or lunch money. Generally, you are expected to pay for these purchases in cash.

Cash is an easy and convenient way to pay for many good and services. Also, some stores will not accept checks or credit card purchases from young people.

Burroughs Corp.

Checks are sorted rapidly by machine.

When you may need a receipt, methods of paying, other than cash, may be preferable. Suppose you are buying a uniform for your Saturday job. That could be a business expense that is deductible from your income tax. Maybe you use your car to make deliveries for a store. Some of your car expenses might also be deductible from your income tax. Will the Internal Revenue Service accept your statement that you spent a certain amount for new brakes or gas? Probably not, unless you can prove it. Receipts may supply the needed proof.

Personal Checks

If Nicole had paid for her slacks with a personal check payable to the store, she would have a receipt that would also serve as a legal record of payment. She could prove that she had paid the bill if a question ever arose. If it were an item she could use as a tax deduction, she would have a legal receipt. Also, if she had any problem with the item and needed to take it back to the store, she could show her cancelled check as proof that she had purchased it there, if she no longer had her store receipt.

There are many advantages to checks:

• They are safer than cash. If you lose a check, no one can legally use it. If you lose cash, however, anyone can use it.

• Personal checks are convenient for paying bills by mail. You can eliminate time-consuming trips to several offices by paying with checks.

• A personal check may be less expensive than other methods of paying bills. Going to several offices will probably cost you money in gas or carfare. The charge for a personal check may be less than bank checks, money orders, or postal money orders.

Certified Checks

There are some times when your personal check is not acceptable. For instance, when you buy a house, the seller may require a bank check or a certified check as payment.

For a small charge you can have your personal check certified by the bank. The bank will take the amount of the check out of your account and reserve it for payment of that check. Then they stamp the check, indicating that they guarantee that the money to pay the check is available.

Bank Checks or Money Orders

Banks will issue two types of checks which can be used to pay bills—a *cashier's check* and a *bank money order.* A cashier's check is simply the bank's check made out to you or whoever you designate. Suppose you make a large withdrawal from the bank to buy a car or for some other purpose. You may not want that much money in cash to carry around, so you ask that it be made out as a check, either to you or to the seller of the car. Also, if you bank by mail and send for a withdrawal, you will receive a cashier's check. Some banks have a small charge for a cashier's check when the funds are taken from your account; many do not.

To pay small bills many people use bank money orders. This is also a bank check, but the bank only fills in the amount of the check and signs it. You are given the check to fill in the name of the person or company to be paid and also a receipt to keep as your record of payment. There is a small charge for a bank money order, which varies with different banks. The person who receives a bank money order handles it like any other check. It can be deposited in a bank account (savings or checking), cashed, or endorsed to someone else as payment for something.

For people who only have a few bills to pay, bank money orders may be cheaper than having a personal checking account.

A traveler's check is a safe way to carry money.

American Express Co.

You still have the safety and convenience of paying bills by mail and having a receipt of payment. However, you have to go personally to the bank to get the money orders.

Postal Money Orders

These are very similar to bank money orders, except that you buy them at the post office. For a small fee you can purchase money orders up to $400. You get a receipt and a check on which you fill in the name of the person or company to receive the money.

The person who receives a postal money order can cash it at the post office or can deposit it like a check in a savings or checking account. If you have an account at a bank, they will usually cash a postal money order for you. Some stores and other places will also cash postal money orders.

Traveler's Checks

Traveler's checks are more like cash than a personal check but are much safer. A number of companies and banks now issue traveler's checks. The best known are probably the American Express traveler's checks.

These can be purchased in denominations of $10, $20, $50, and $100 for a small fee. Your signature is written on the top of each check at the time of purchase. When you are ready to cash the check, you write in the date, the town, the person or company to be paid, and your signature again on the bottom. The person receiving the check can compare your signature at the bottom with the one on the top to be sure that you are the person who purchased the checks.

American Express and some other issuers of traveler's checks will replace lost checks quickly. At the time of purchase

you receive a form on which you should list the serial number of each traveler's check. This should be carried separately from the traveler's checks. As you use each check, fill in the place and person paid on this list. Then if you lose your checks, you can report just which unused checks are lost. If you are away from home, you can report the loss to the nearest office of the issuer. They will stop payment on the missing checks and give you a replacement, often within a day.

Payroll Deductions

Another payment tool is to have money taken out of your paycheck before you receive it. This is called payroll deduction. Federal income taxes and social security are usually handled this way. Usually, pension contributions are deducted this way too. In many companies employees can request that savings bonds, union dues, United Fund contributions, mortgage payments, insurance, deposits to the credit union, and certain installment payments be deducted from their paychecks.

Many people find it easier to deduct payments before they get their paychecks rather than trying to pay these bills afterwards. In a way the government has built on the current trend of the widespread use of installment payments by collecting income taxes through payroll deductions from paychecks.

Barter—Goods and Services

Swapping goods and services directly is not as common as it once was. Still, there are many instances when people swap goods and services rather than exchange money. Friends often exchange goods and services. Among high school students girls often swap small clothing items. A neighbor might give a batch of cookies to the friend who helped her with shopping when she couldn't get out. Young families often swap baby-sitting services. A plumber and a painter might exchange services, each doing a job for the other. Johnnie might clean the neighbor's pool in exchange for the privilege of swimming in it. Postage stamps are often used to pay very small bills or as a mail refund for small overpayments.

Credit Cards

You really don't pay for anything with a credit card. A credit card only postpones payment to a later time, yet you can use it instead of money for buying. This opportunity to delay payment for purchases often is an advantage to many people, but it can also lead to overspending, with an overwhelming bill at the end of the billing period.

Choosing a Method of Payment

Which payment tool will you choose? Consider what will provide the features you need or want. These might be:

- Convenience—saves time and energy.
- A record of payment.
- Building a good credit rating.
- Postponing payment for something you urgently need.

CHECKING ACCOUNTS

Many banks will open a checking account for a high school student; others require that you be 18.

Opening an Account

The procedure for opening an account is quite simple. You will be asked to fill out a form with your name, address, telephone number, and your business address if you

work. You will also have to sign a signature card just as you will sign your checks.

How much money must you deposit to open a checking account? This varies with the type of checking account and the policy of the bank. Generally, you need to deposit at least $10.

It will probably take a few days to get your first checkbook because the bank will stamp a code of numbers and letters on each check to identify them as your checks. Each account holder has a different code number.

Some banks will also print your name and possibly your address on the checks. Printing your name and address may be a free service of the bank, or there may be an additional charge for this.

The Types of Checking Accounts

There are different types of checking accounts. Some require that you maintain a minimum or average balance of so many dollars. A minimum balance is the smallest amount in the account at any time during the month. Generally, computing charges on the basis of average balance costs less because it is larger than the minimum.

Others charge a specific amount for each check written. Some charge according to the total number of transactions—checks and deposits. An account may have no charge, or pay interest. (Analysis accounts, usually reserved for businesses, have a more complicated way of figuring charges.)

Which Bank Should You Use?

Banks are a business. Like many other businesses the charges vary somewhat from bank to bank, so compare costs before opening a checking account.

You may want to find out what the charge is if your account is overdrawn or if you have to stop a check—have the bank refuse payment after you have written it.

Convenience may also be a factor in your consideration. Do you want a bank that's nearby? On the other hand, many people handle most of their business by mail. Banks usually furnish their customers with postpaid envelopes for banking by mail.

Before you open a checking account consider these questions:

• Do you need it? If you will write only one or two checks a month, you might be better off paying your bills with a bank or postal money order.

• What will it cost? Could you earn more by keeping your money in a savings account and paying bills another way?

• Will you be tempted to overspend by carrying a checkbook?

• Would it be more convenient?

• Do you need receipts for tax purposes?

• Is it a safer way to handle money than your present method?

An Individual or Joint Account

Your first checking account will probably be an individual account. Only your signature will be valid on the checks.

Many husbands and wives have a joint account. Sometimes a parent and child will have a joint account. In these cases either signature is valid on checks.

If you have a joint account, you need to work out a plan with your partner in the account to keep a record of all deposits and checks written so that there will be enough money in the account to cover all the checks.

Joint accounts may have "rights of survivorship." This means that if either person dies, the money in the account will belong to the survivor.

Using a Checking Account

It doesn't take a financial genius to handle a checking account successfully, but you do need to be careful and systematic. You need to know how to write your checks correctly and how to keep a record of the ones you have written.

Write your checks so that they are clear and not easy for anyone else to change. Use ink or a typewriter.

WRITING A CHECK

There are several items which should be written on the face of each check. (See illustration on page 276.)

• *The check number.* Many people find it helpful to number their whole checkbook and the attached register (recording form) as soon as they get it if it is not already numbered. Number your checks consecutively, 1, 2, 3 . . . In subsequent checkbooks start the numbers where the preceding checkbook left off. If you don't number your checks in advance, be sure to number each one in order as you use it.

• *The date.* Use the date on which the check is written. Banks will accept checks dated on Sundays or holidays. It is not good practice to date checks ahead, planning to make a deposit before the check clears. This can result in an awkward or embarrassing situation. Perhaps you won't be able to deposit the money as you plan. Banks often won't honor a check which is dated ahead.

• *The payee's name.* Write the name of the person or firm to receive the payment right after the printed words, "Pay to the order of." If there is a space after the name of the payee, put in a dash to fill up the line.

If you want to withdraw money from your own account, write in your name or

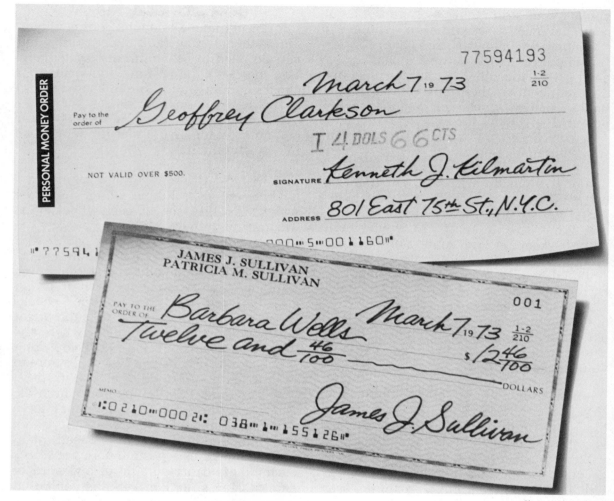

A bank money order and a personal check are two ways to pay bills.

Chase Manhattan Bank

cash or *bearer.* (Before you can cash a check made out to yourself or to *cash* or *bearer,* you must endorse it on the back.)

• *The amount in figures.* Close to the dollar sign write the amount of the check in numbers.

• *The amount in words.* This must be the same as the amount written in figures. If the two do not agree, the amount in words is generally considered correct by law. However, many banks won't cash a check with this type of error.

Write as far to the left as possible in the space given for the amount to be paid. Fill in any unused space with a line. In this way no one can add a word and thus raise the amount of the check.

• *Your signature.* Sign your name at the

bottom of the check in ink just as you did on the bank's signature card.

Write your signature only after the whole check has been filled in. *Never sign a blank check.* If you lose a signed blank check, someone else could fill it in and use it.

Don't cross out, erase, or change any part of a check. If you make a mistake, tear up the check and write another one.

• In addition, some checks have a space to indicate what the check is for. This can help you keep track of such information.

THE CHECK REGISTER

In your checkbook is a register for recording the checks you write and calculating what is in your checking account.

Before you use a check, be sure to record the number of the check, the date, the amount of the check, the payee, and if there is room, what the check is for.

Then subtract the amount of the check plus the charge for the check, if any and it is a regular amount, from the existing balance to see what is left in your account. This will help you avoid overdrafts.

Whenever you add money to the account, record this in the register. Add the deposit to the previous balance to get the amount that is in the account.

STOPPING PAYMENT

Once in a great while you may not want the bank to pay a check that you have already mailed or given to someone. If a check is lost or stolen, it is wise to place a stop payment order.

You do this by telephoning the bank, explaining the problem, and following up with a letter or filling in a bank form prepared for this purpose.

If the bank has not already cashed the check, it will put a signal on your account record and will not pay the check.

Usually there is a small charge for this service.

RECONCILING THE STATEMENT

The purpose of reconciling is twofold: (1) to find out what your bank balance is; (2) to be sure that there are no errors in the bank records.

Periodically (usually monthly), the bank will return your cancelled checks. These are the checks for which money has already been paid to someone.

With the checks is a statement of the amounts deposited, the checks drawn, any charges against the account, and the balance remaining in the account. If your check register is accurate and all the checks that you have written have been paid out, the register should agree with the bank's statement. However, often some checks or deposits have not reached the bank by the time the statement is prepared, so your checkbook register may not agree with the bank statement.

Here's how to reconcile a bank statement:

1. Sort the cancelled checks by number or date issued. Check them off in your register and on the bank statement.

2. Make a list of all checks that you have written but that were not paid by the time the statement was prepared, the amounts, and the check charges. Subtract this amount from the balance on the statement.

3. Add to this any deposits you have made which were not received by the time the statement was prepared. The result is your new balance.

Many banks now provide statements that are easily reconciled. (See page 278.)

SAVE CANCELLED CHECKS

Keep your cancelled checks in a safe place. They are legal proof of payment.

STATEMENT OF YOUR ACCOUNT WITH

URBAN NATIONAL BANK

ACCOUNT NUMBER
1234567

PERIOD ENDING

Mark L. Davis
1020 Holmes Avenue
Chicago, Illinois

CHECKS AND OTHER DEBITS				DEPOSITS AND OTHER CREDITS	DATE	BALANCE
				81.38	31	81.38
15.00	.10SC				3	66.28
25.00	.10SC				4	41.18
				81.38	8	122.56
5.05	.10SC	30.00	.10SC		12	87.31
2.00DM		15.00	.10SC	81.38	15	151.59
15.00	.10SC	30.00	.10SC		18	106.39
				81.38	22	187.77
15.00	.10SC	9.29	.10SC		24	163.28
.50SC					27	162.78

DATE LAST STATEMENT	BALANCE BROUGHT FORWARD	CHECKS AND OTHER DEBITS		SERVICE CHARGES	DEPOSITS AND OTHER CREDITS		BALANCE THIS STATEMENT
		TOTAL AMOUNT	NUMBER		TOTAL AMOUNT	NUMBER	
---	-----	161.34	10	1.40	325.52	4	162.78

SYMBOLS USED:	
CM-CREDIT MEMORANDUM	OD-OVERDRAWN
DM-DEBIT MEMORANDUM	PL-PACKAGE LIST
ER-ENTRY REVERSAL	RT-RETURNED CHECK
	SC-SERVICE CHARGE

UNLESS ALTERATIONS, FORGERIES, ERRORS OR OTHER DISCREPANCIES ARE REPORTED TO US WITHIN TEN DAYS FROM THE RECEIPT HEREOF, WE SHALL CONSIDER THAT YOU ACKNOWLEDGE THIS STATEMENT TO BE CORRECT. PLEASE EXAMINE CAREFULLY AND REPORT EXCEPTIONS AT ONCE TO OUR AUDITING DIVISION.

Wise Use of Buy Power (Chicago, Ill.: Continental Illinois National Bank and Trust Co. of Chicago)

A bank statement shows the amounts deposited, the checks drawn, any charges against the account, and the remaining balance in the account.

How long should you keep them? Certainly you should keep them for three years or until there seems to be no possible further need for them.

CUTTING THE COST OF A CHECKING ACCOUNT

Regardless of the type of checking account you use, you can cut the cost by careful planning of your transactions. Look at these two situations. In each example you start with a balance of $250 and write two checks, one for $100, and one for $50.

Example I

January 4, balance		$250
January 5, two checks		−150
	Balance	$100
January 7, deposit		+100
	Balance	$200

The minimum balance during this period was $100.

Example II

In this example the minimum balance during the period is $200.

January 4, balance		$250
January 7, deposit		+100
	Balance	$350
January 8, two checks		−150
	Balance	$200

Another way to cut checking account costs is to eliminate extra transactions.

• Find out if your bank will make regular payments, such as mortgage payments or taxes, directly from your account.

• When you deposit a check, keep out enough cash for regular weekly expenses.

• Pay some small bills in cash if it is convenient.

• If you are now paying some bills weekly by check, such as laundry or cleaning, see if you can pay them once a month.

Planning can be complicated by the fact that you are not supposed to draw on most deposits until your bank has actually collected them, although they may be listed as deposits on your account immediately. For example, it may take a week or more for the bank to collect on an out-of-town check written to you and deposited in your account. If you write a check against that money before it is collected, the bank may return it marked "insufficient funds" and charge you an extra fee.

The reverse is true if you write a check to a local store. It may take one to three days to be collected from your bank. If you send a check out-of-town, it can take longer than a week to be collected. If you are unsure of how long it will take a check to clear, ask the bank.

NEW TRENDS IN CHECKING ACCOUNTS

Did you ever wonder why checking accounts have not paid interest. In 1933, banks were prohibited by law from paying interest on demand deposits (checking accounts). However, recently there have been changes made to provide interest on checking accounts.

In 1972 two states, Massachusetts and New Hampshire, authorized an experimental program to permit commercial banks, savings and loan associations, and savings banks to offer negotiable orders of withdrawal—commonly called NOW. A NOW account is a savings account from which money can be withdrawn with a withdrawal order similar to a check.

At present, many checking accounts pay interest. However, some charge for checks and transactions. Compare interest rates and charges before opening an account.

SAVING MONEY

Why save? Most people save for something they want—new clothes, a car, an education, or just emergencies. Saving is easier when you have a goal.

Are you saying to yourself right now: "I can't save. I don't have enough money." Then maybe you need to consider savings as a fixed, regular expense, like lunches or carfare. Pay yourself first. Put aside a regular portion of your income as soon as you get it.

Many people who have steady jobs find it helps to use payroll savings plans, where an amount is taken out of their paychecks and deposited in the bank before they get the remaining money. Contractual savings is the easiest way for many people to save.

Interest Makes Money Grow

"Money makes money and the money that money makes makes more money," Benjamin Franklin wrote in *Poor Richard's Almanac.* Just look at these two examples and see how compound interest can make savings grow. A 5-percent interest rate is used only as an example.

Every payday, Jeff puts some of his earnings in the bank.

Institute of Life Insurance

A. A single $100 deposit, compounded and credited quarterly at 5%.

Year	Monetary Growth
1	$105.09
2	110.44
3	116.06
4	121.97
5	128.18
6	134.70
7	141.56
8	148.76
9	156.33
10	164.29

Total deposited	$100.00
Interest earned	$ 64.29

B. $100 deposited *monthly*, compounded and credited quarterly at 5%.

Year	Monetary Growth
1	$ 1,233.07
2	2,529.35
3	3,890.99
4	5,322.05
5	6,826.06
6	8,406.69
7	10,067.85
8	11,813.65
9	13,648.37
10	15,576.57

Total deposited	$12,000.00
Interest earned	3,576.57

Where Can You Save?

There are many different ways to save and invest money. Some people feel that paying off a home mortgage, for example, is one way of accumulating assets. However, to put aside some money for emergencies or a specific purchase like a car or a vacation, most people turn to savings accounts, credit union shares, and money funds. These offer both the convenience of getting your money when you want it and some security that it will be there. Although banks and savings and loan associations can require thirty days notice for withdrawals, they rarely do.

BANKS

A *savings account* can be opened with a small amount of money, usually $5 or $10, although some banks require more than that. You fill out a signature card, just as you would for a checking account. Generally, you receive a passbook with your account number, in which deposits and withdrawals are recorded. Recently some banks have initiated a no-passbook savings account. The depositor receives validated deposit and withdrawal receipts and may keep a record of his balance in a record book provided by the bank. Periodically, a statement is mailed to the customer, usually after interest has been credited to the account.

Savings account deposits and withdrawals may be made easily and conveniently

in person or by mail. To *deposit* money (in person or by mail), the saver makes out a savings account deposit ticket. He or she includes on the ticket the savings account number, name, correct address, a notation of the cash to be deposited, a listing of checks, and the total of the amount of money to be deposited. If depositing in person, the saver takes to the teller his passbook, the deposit ticket, and the checks and/or cash to be deposited. The teller records in the passbook the deposit made, any interest or dividends due, and the

Shown here is a completed signature card for a savings account.
Wise Use of Buy Power (Chicago, Ill.:'
Continental Illinois National Bank and Trust Co. of Chicago)

I HEREBY AGREE THAT THE BY-LAWS, RULES AND REGULATIONS OF URBAN NATIONAL BANK RELATING TO SAVINGS DEPOSITS SHALL GOVERN THIS ACCOUNT.	
SIGNATURE *Mark L. Davis*	
ADDRESS: 1020 HOLMES AVE. CHICAGO, ILL. 60600	TELEPHONE: 495-2901
WHERE BORN CHICAGO, ILL.	DATE OF BIRTH AUG. 12, 1957
OCCUPATION: MECHANIC'S HELPER	
EMPLOYER: FIX-RIGHT GARAGE, 1632 DUNDEE ST, CHICAGO	
DATE OPENED: JAN. 3, 82	INITIAL DEPOSIT: $5.00

IRS• 123-45-6789

A completed savings account deposit slip will look something like this.
Wise Use of Buy Power (Chicago, Ill.:
Continental Illinois National Bank and Trust Co. of Chicago)

PASS BOOK No. *123456*

URBAN NATIONAL BANK

UPON THE TERMS AND CONDITIONS CONTAINED IN THE PASS BOOK AND SUBJECT TO PROVISIONS OF THE UNIFORM COMMERCIAL CODE AND TO DETAILED VERIFICATION

CREDIT SAVINGS ACCOUNT OF

NAME *Mark L. Davis*

ADDRESS *1020 Holmes Ave, Chicago*
PLEASE NOTIFY US OF ANY CHANGE OF ADDRESS

DATE *Jan. 3* 19 *82*

LIST EACH ITEM SEPARATELY	DOLLARS	CENTS
CASH	5	00
CHECKS OR OTHER ITEMS		
TOTAL OF ITEMS LISTED	5	00
LESS AMOUNT RECEIVED FROM BANK	—	
SIGNATURE NET DEPOSIT	5	00

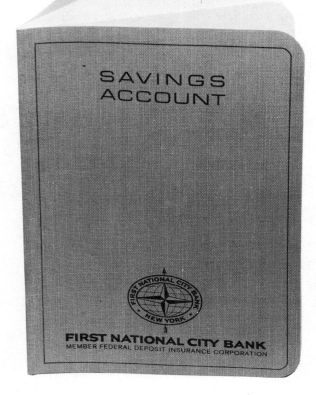

First National City Bank

Deposits and withdrawals are recorded in a savings account passbook.

	ACCOUNT OF	Mary Castro				
	DATE	WITHDRAWAL	DEPOSIT	INTEREST	BALANCE	TRANS.
1	1-03-82		5.00		5.00	24B*
2	1-10-82		5.00		10.00	24B*
3	1-17-82		5.00		15.00	24B*
4	1-24-82		5.00		20.00	24B*
5	1-31-82		5.00		25.00	24B*
6	2-04-82		30.00		55.00	24B*
7	2-07-82		5.00		60.00	24B*
8	2-14-82		7.00		67.00	24B*
9	2-21-82		5.00		72.00	24B*
10	2-28-82		5.00		77.00	24B*
11	3-07-82		5.00		82.00	24B*
12	3-14-82		6.00		88.00	24B*
13	3-21-82		5.00		93.00	24B*
14	3-28-82		10.00		103.00	24B*
15	4-01-82			.93	103.93	24B*
16	4-01-82	100.00			3.93	24B*
17						
18						
19						
20						
21						
22						
23						

MAIN STREET NATIONAL BANK

A savings account passbook page will resemble the one shown here.

new balance. If the saver deposits by mail, he or she sends the passbook, the checks and/or currency to be deposited, and the deposit ticket to the bank. The bank records the deposit and any earnings due, shows the new balance, and returns a receipt and the passbook. Registered mail is necessary only when depositing currency, provided checks are properly endorsed.

To make a *withdrawal,* the saver completes and signs a savings account withdrawal order. If he or she wants cash, that is all he needs to sign; if he wants a cashier's check, he completes and signs an additional form showing to whom the check should be made payable. (On withdrawals by mail, one form takes care of both, because the withdrawal is automatically made by cashier's check.) The saver then presents the withdrawal order and his passbook to the teller.

Savings certificates are also called certificates of deposit. They earn a higher rate of interest than regular savings accounts. However, one must usually put in larger sums of money than to open a savings account and leave it in the bank for a longer period of time to earn the higher rate of interest.

SAVINGS AND LOAN ASSOCIATIONS

When you open an account at a savings and loan association, you become a member of the association. The money you deposit earns dividends. The dividend rate is usually slightly higher than interest rates at nearby banks. Several types of accounts may be available, depending on the rules of the association.

Passbook accounts are similar to those in banks. Dividends are calculated periodically and recorded in the passbook (usually quarterly or semiannually).

Bonus accounts are similar to passbook accounts. However, bonus accounts earn higher rates of interest if a regular amount is deposited each month for a specific period of time.

Investment accounts pay interest periodically to the member by check. These are available in specific minimum amounts.

Certificate savings accounts are similar to savings certificates at a bank. They earn a higher dividend rate than other types of accounts. An account can be opened only with larger sums of money and must be left there for a longer period of time to earn the higher rate.

U. S. GOVERNMENT SAVINGS BONDS

There are two types, Series EE and Series HH. Series EE bonds pay interest on maturity. Series HH bonds pay interest twice a year.

Series EE bonds can be bought in amounts from $50 to $10,000. A bond which is worth $50 at maturity costs $25. HH bonds are sold in amounts of from $500 to $10,000.

Holders of the old Series E bonds and the current EE bonds may exchange them for HH bonds at current redemption values. (However, the bonds must have a current redemption value of $500 or more.) Some owners of Series E or EE bonds have deferred reporting the accrued interest on their bonds for federal income tax purposes. The interest, as it has accrued on those bonds which are exchanged, may continue to qualify for deferred reporting until the HH bonds received in exchange are redeemed, disposed of, or mature. Thus, a person who is approaching retirement might defer paying tax on income until after retirement by purchasing EE bonds and then exchanging them for HH bonds.

The Chase Manhattan Bank, Photo by Raymond Juschkus
A safe-deposit box can be used to protect valuable papers and jewelry.

Young people might choose government bonds for savings because often it is less tempting to cash a bond than to withdraw money from a savings account.

Government bonds can be purchased and redeemed at most banks and savings and loan associations as well as other sources.

CREDIT UNION SHARES

Savings are called "shares." Dividends are paid to the shareholders based on the earnings of the union. Generally, any profit, after expenses are paid and legal reserves set aside, is returned to members as dividends once a year. The rate paid may vary greatly.

How Safe Are Your Savings?

Will you get back the money you deposit plus the interest earned? In most cases insurance protects depositors if a savings institution fails. U.S. Government bonds are backed by the government.

The Federal Deposit Insurance Corporation insures depositors in member banks (checking accounts and savings accounts) to a maximum of $100,000. The same person can have insured accounts in more than one bank or two different types of accounts, such as a checking account and a savings account in the same bank. Look for the FDIC insignia to see if a bank is insured. Over 90 percent of all banks are insured by FDIC.

About 66 percent of the savings and loan associations are covered by insurance issued by the Federal Savings and Loan Insurance Corporation—FSLIC. Each account is covered up to $100,000 if deposited in a savings and loan association that is insured. To be sure you will be protected look for the FSLIC insignia.

Deposits in federally chartered credit unions are insured by the National Credit Union Administration. State-chartered credit unions may join this insurance plan if they meet the necessary qualifications. In addition, a few states have their own share insurance plans for state-chartered credit unions. Before you join a credit union find out if deposits are insured and for how much.

SAFEGUARDING VALUABLES IN A SAFE-DEPOSIT BOX

One of the ways in which people protect their valuable papers and jewelry is by placing them in a safe-deposit box. This is a metal box which can be rented at a bank or a savings and loan association. The box remains in their vault and will protect items from fire, theft, water damage, and loss. The charge is modest and depends on the size of the box that you rent.

The following are often kept in a safe-deposit box: deeds to property, wills, stocks and bonds, savings bonds, insurance policies, jewelry, and valuable coin collections. Many important papers can be replaced if lost, but the process is slow and cumbersome. Others are more difficult or impossible to replace.

A safe-deposit box can be rented by an individual, or it can be rented in conjunction with someone else. Many husbands and wives rent a box jointly. Sometimes a child and parent will rent a box together. Joint rental is convenient if one person will not be able to get to the bank easily. Under a joint rental agreement both people usually have the same right to open the box and withdraw any papers.

FOR REVIEW

• Commercial banks offer a wide range of services including checking accounts.

• Money deposited in a savings account earns interest, whereas deposits in checking accounts do not.

> (a) Savings banks may pay a higher rate of interest on savings accounts than commercial banks.
> (b) Savings and loan associations often pay more on savings accounts than either type of bank.

• A check is a form that directs the bank to pay a stated amount to a person or company from the funds of the depositor.

• It is wise to deposit or cash a check promptly.

• A check must be endorsed before you can cash it. There are several ways to endorse a check so that others cannot use it.

• It is important to keep a careful record of the checks you write and the balance remaining in a checking account if you do not wish to be overdrawn.

• A paycheck voucher gives a record of what you have earned and paid in taxes.

• In addition to cash and personal checks, one can use certified checks, bank checks or bank money orders, postal money orders, traveler's checks, and other methods to pay bills.

• Deposits in most savings institutions are insured. Check before you open an account.

Terms to Know

analysis accounts
bank money order
barter
bonus account
cancelled check
cashier's checks
certified checks
checking account
check register
commercial bank
demand deposits
discount rate
drawer (of a check)
endorse
endorsement in blank
federal reserve bank
FDIC insurance
FSLIC insurance
government savings bonds
investment account
joint account
mutual savings bank
NOW account
payee
payroll deduction
passbook account
postal money orders
reconciling a statement
restrictive endorsement
safe-deposit box
savings account
savings certificate
savings and loan association
savings shares
Series EE bonds
Series HH bonds
special endorsement
traveler's checks

PROBLEM SOLVING: CHECK YOUR UNDERSTANDING

1. How does a bank differ from a savings and loan association?
2. What organization insures the deposits of an individual in a bank?
3. How do Series HH government bonds differ from Series EE bonds?
4. List as many services as you can that a commercial bank may offer its customers.
5. How is a check collected after you cash it?
6. What is the maximum amount of insurance available on an individual savings account in a savings and loan association?
7. Name five different ways in which one could pay a bill.
8. How does the Federal Reserve System influence the amount of money available for loans by local banks?

TO DO IN CLASS

Discussion

1. How is saving different from being stingy?
2. What are the advantages and disadvantages of a checking account?
3. Name three situations for which you might need emergency funds.
4. Assume that you are working full time and living away from home. How much of an emergency fund do you think you should have?
5. Where would you keep your emergency money, and why?
6. How do the policies of the Federal Reserve System affect the individual consumer?

Activities

1. Divide into committees to find out about the rate of return of several savings

institutions in your community. Report back to the class.

2. Invite a banker to class to talk about bank services for individuals and small businesses.

3. Invite a credit union representative to talk to the class about the way a credit union operates.

4. Plan how you might use the services of some of the institutions in activities 1-3 when you start working.

5. Using a sample case, balance the monthly statement for a checking account.

6. Investigate community facilities to find the lowest priced method of paying five bills a month.

CHAPTER 13

A Roof Over Your Head

Where will you live after high school? Have you thought about it? Do you want a job right away? Will you go to school? Are you planning to be married soon after graduation?

Perhaps you are eager to get a job and an income of your own. The end of high school means that you will really be independent. You may have to move to a nearby city for employment. Perhaps you are hoping to get off on your own, not far from home.

If you continue your education, will you live at home and commute? Many students do this to cut costs. If you go away to school, will you live in a dormitory? Some students live off campus. Often they team up with other students and share an apartment or house. Living off campus is a fairly new trend in the United States, but it has been the pattern in many European universities for a long time.

Maybe you are planning to marry right away. Then you will need to think about the housing needs of two people. It used to be the dream of many young couples to have a little house surrounded by grass. However, today most jobs are located in urban areas where land is scarce and expensive, so many young people are solving their housing needs in other ways.

YOU HAVE SEVERAL CHOICES

Housing comes in several forms. For example, there are apartments to rent in tall or sprawling buildings, mobile homes, condominiums, and of course, the one-family house.

In urban areas apartments abound. As you move out from the central cities, you will probably find fewer high-rise buildings and more garden apartments. A wide variety of houses may be available for rent or sale. Mobile homes are generally found just outside the heavily built-up areas or in parks scattered in some suburban areas.

This wide selection is unique to the United States and parts of the western world. Mortgage credit for houses, apartments, and mobile homes makes it possible for many people of moderate incomes to have this choice. In many parts of the world young people must live with their families because there is no other place to go. Housing is so scarce and expensive that single adults and young families cannot live alone.

YOUR NEEDS WILL CHANGE

Your housing needs will be different at various stages of your life. The needs of a young man on his first job are quite different from those of a man in his thirties with several children. The young woman going to school will not need as much room as the mother of a growing family.

Starting Out

Case Study. Debbie Martin graduated from Jonesville High in June and had no trouble getting a job that she enjoyed. She had been trained as a beautician at the

Suburban-42.0 percent   Rural-26.5 percent   City-31.5 percent

Soil Conservation Service, USDA; Mobile Homes Manufacturers Assoc.; USDA Photo

The population of the United States is distributed among three major areas.

vocational high school. With her second paycheck Debbie made a small down payment on a used car. She also wanted an apartment of her own and new clothes. She soon found that she couldn't afford all of these. She knew two girls who were in similar situations. They were working too. In addition, one was going to school at night. The three girls found a garden apartment with two bedrooms and moved in together. Today many young people share apartments to cut costs. It can be expensive to maintain a place all by yourself, particularly when you are starting out.

The girls decided that since Nina was going to school she should have the smaller bedroom to herself. Debbie and Mary moved into the bigger one.

The girls brought some belongings from their parents' homes, but they didn't have all they needed. Each girl managed to get her own bed and chest of drawers. Debbie took the ones that she had in her room at home. Nina took her bed, but her sister needed the dresser. Therefore she bought an inexpensive one from the Salvation Army and painted it. Mary had a little money saved and wanted to get some nice things of her own, so she bought a new bed and chest. Also, they all were given a minimum of blankets, pillows, sheets, and towels from their families.

In addition, Debbie had most of a set of old dishes from her aunt. The three girls chipped in and bought an inexpensive set of stainless flatware as well as a card table and four chairs. Their families contributed glassware and a few pots and pans.

The living room was almost empty for a while. Then Mary's aunt moved and gave the girls a few more furnishings. There was an old folding cot and a chair. With a throw cover and some small cushions, the cot made a suitable couch. Gradually, they acquired what they needed, and the place became quite comfortable. However, they never did get a rug for the living room.

Case Study. Debbie's experience in setting up housekeeping was very similar to Juanita's. The only difference was that Juanita Perez was a university student. Juanita had decided that dorm living was too expensive and wanted a place where she could cook her own meals to cut costs. So Juanita and two other classmates rented an apartment in an old building near school. Although the apartment was rented to the students as unfurnished, the previous occupant, who was also a student, left a few items. This was very helpful.

Case Study. Pete Brown's situation was a little different. He moved to a nearby city for his first job. He didn't have any close friends there, and housing was very expensive. Just outside of town was a mobile home park. He rented a small mobile home for the first summer from some people who were coming back in the fall. It was completely furnished, so all he had to do was move in his clothes and personal things.

Case Study. Marilyn and Ken Ackerman married soon after graduation. They both had good jobs but not much money saved. After considering the alternatives, they decided on a studio apartment in a building with an outdoor swimming pool. The apartment was just one big room, with a kitchenette behind a sliding door. They felt that since they didn't have any furniture, a small apartment would be enough for a while. Besides, they lived in southern California where they could swim much of the year, and it would be fun to have a pool so handy.

What they lacked in worldly goods they made up for in enthusiasm. They planned to make or repair most of their furnishings. Their one big splurge was a nice sleeping couch which they bought on the installment plan. Ken planned to finish two unpainted chests, which would double as end tables, and to make a long modern coffee table. Marilyn was going to make the curtains and some large cushions for people to sit on. She would also paint an old dinette set that her parents gave them.

At the end of a year they had an attractive apartment, a great sense of pride and accomplishment, and a little money saved in the bank. What they hadn't counted on was how much they had learned about themselves. True, Marilyn could make drapes, but she didn't enjoy it a bit. In fact, she was relieved that they only had two windows. She much preferred making her own clothes.

Ken finished the unpainted chests, but he never got around to making the coffee table. Instead he took a night course on a subject related to his job that he hoped would help him get a promotion.

Having a year to discover how they wanted to live was a valuable, eye-opening experience for the Ackerman's—although they hadn't really planned it that way. They learned that they weren't the enthusiastic do-it-yourselfers that they thought they were.

The Growing Family

Case Study. Alan and Jennifer O'Shea bought a small, new house just a year after they were married. Timmy was one month old and they wanted to get out of the city into a house with grass and trees.

Both Alan and Jennifer had worked as keypunch operators for several years. Together they had saved enough for the small down payment. Jennifer took a leave of absence a few weeks before Timmy was born. Originally, she had planned to go back to work when he was about six months old. Now she was having a few second thoughts and wondering if she would find it easier to wait a little longer.

The house was in a new section of a development where they already had a few friends. Even if they hadn't known anyone, it would have been easy to get acquainted. Most of the families were young and had small children. As time went on, they became involved in a number of cooperative activities. The women baby-sat for each other during the day; the men formed car pools to the bus stop and cut expenses by exchanging tools and equipment. They all helped each other out in emergencies. As the children got older and more of the women went back to work, regular play groups, a nursery school, and a community center developed.

Moving in for Alan and Jennifer was fairly easy. The house was new and clean. It came equipped with a nice modern kitchen as well as a washer and dryer. Outside there was a rough lawn, a few shrubs, and a wonderful old shade tree. They had fairly new living room furniture from their apartment, the old bedroom set that had been Alan's before they married, and a dinette set, as well as a crib for Timmy. Jennifer's family gave them a chest for Timmy as a housewarming gift, but they didn't have anything to put in the dining room.

Dining room furniture would just have to wait. There were too many other expenses.

First they needed drapes for all the windows so that they would have some privacy. Then they needed storm windows and screens. These would cut heating costs in the winter and make them more comfortable all year long. They also needed some garden tools and a lawnmower. Timmy needed a playpen.

Timmy learned to walk when he was only eight months old, so they decided to fence in the back yard. To help him enjoy it Alan built a sandbox from four big boards. (Just lumber and paint cost almost $50.)

During the first few years in the house, Alan and Jennifer spent much time at home. It was easier with Timmy and Betsy, a new arrival. Also, it enabled them to do things around the house that they couldn't afford to hire others for. Many of their neighbors were in the same situation, so often on weekends a few families would gather for an outdoor supper or just to spend the evening together. Usually, each family brought some of the food and beverages.

Generally, the arrival of children means dramatic changes in the family's life style. Little children take time. Expenses increase. Often the family moves to a house or a bigger apartment. In addition to the obvious expenses, there is the cost of sitters.

As the children get older and the need for sitters decreases, other expenses go up. Clothing costs more. There are extra expenses when the children go to school—PTA dues, school lunches, more clothes, and school supplies. Social activities begin to cost more too. Many families move to bigger quarters as the youngsters approach the teenage years. The parents often want to be able to spread out, to have a quiet place away from the noise and activity of the older children. Other families fix up an

USDA Photos

Reasonably priced housing for the elderly is often difficult to find. This is publicly subsidized housing for the elderly at Villa Tranchese, San Antonio, Texas.

area for the young people, perhaps adding a room or finishing the basement.

The Later Years

Case Study. Retirement was a difficult time for John and Nora Campana. Both were in reasonably good health and interested in church and civic activities. They were not worried about getting bored, but they were worried about money. John had a small pension, they both had social secu-

rity, and there was a little money from John's life insurance policy that he had converted to an annuity. Still, this wasn't enough to go on living as they had.

The obvious solution was to sell their house and move to a small apartment. The Campanas had mixed feelings about selling their house. They had lived there a long time and were attached to it. However, it was getting to be a little too much for them to manage. John had always taken care of the big yard. Nowadays Nora didn't always feel up to climbing the stairs when her arthritis bothered her.

They expected to be able to get a reasonable price for their house. Although it was twenty years old, it had been well maintained, inside and out. Most important of all was the community. Their neighborhood was well kept with many one-family homes similar in value to theirs. The taxes were fairly high, but over the years the community had developed good schools and services. Families with school-age children were anxious to buy there. Also, there was good bus transportation to the center of the city, where many people in the community worked.

Finally, the Campanas put their house on the market. They listed it with a local real estate agent who was part of a multiple listing service. They felt that this would be better than trying to sell it themselves, because most people buy older houses through an agent. The agent would get a commission of about six percent of the sale price which they as the sellers would have to pay. Picking an agent who belonged to the multiple listing service meant that other agents could also show the house. If one of these other agents sold it, he or she would share the commission with the original agent.

Then Nora and John started to look for an apartment. They wanted one that they could afford. Also, they hoped to find one that would meet some of their special needs as older people.

They definitely didn't want stairs. This ruled out the new duplex apartments nearby, as well as apartments on the upper floors of buildings without elevators. Also, they wanted to stay in the same community if they could. They had lived there for

fifteen years. During that time they had made many friends and developed a feeling that they belonged.

The Campanas were lucky. They found a three-room apartment on the first floor of an older garden apartment house. It even had a small back yard behind the apartment where John could grow a few flowers. All the big outside maintenance—cutting the grass and shoveling snow—would be done by the management. They were pleased that there were young families in the building. Their grandchildren were so far away and they enjoyed seeing and hearing young children outside.

Many older people aren't as lucky as John and Nora. They had good health, a moderate income, and were able to find a nice place to live. In general, society has not provided adequately for the needs of older people. Housing is only one problem.

Often retired people want to stay in the same community. Still, they usually need less expensive housing that is easy to manage. In some ways their needs are similar to those of young people just starting out. However, the older person tends to be less mobile and is more dependent on other community services for transportation, health services, and recreation. Most important of all, older people find it harder to change neighborhoods and friends. Often they want to retain their old ties.

WHAT SHOULD YOU SPEND ON HOUSING?

There's no easy answer. Much depends on how important housing is to you. Some people spend as little as possible on housing because they want to use their money in other ways. Other people feel that a nice place to live is very important to them, so they are willing to skimp in other areas.

Budget for Housing ..

Sun	Mon	Tue	Wed	Thu	Fri	Sat
			1 335	2 336	3 337	4 338
5 339	6 340	7 341	8 342	9 343	10 344	11 345

ONE WEEK OUT OF THE MO.

19 353	20 354	21 355	22 356	23 357	24 358	25 359
26 360	27 361	28 362	29 363	30 364	31 365	

UNITED STATES GOVERNMENT

USDA Photo

Case Study. Your feelings about how much you should spend may change at various stages of your life. When Carol Lee was just out of school, she wanted to have fun. Housing was a necessity but something she didn't want to pay any more for than she absolutely had to. She decided to share an older apartment with three other girls, which was about the cheapest housing she could find. A few years later she married Bob Lyons and moved into the apartment he had shared with his brother who was now in the Navy. It was a little nicer than the one she had shared with the girls, but not much. The furniture was an assortment of odds and ends she and Bob had collected, mostly from friends and relatives who didn't want them. After they had been married for a few years, Carol and Bob bought a small new house. Then they were bitten with the desire to fix it up. They wanted everything new. No more old junk for them! Obviously, they had to spend more of their income on their home than when they lived in an apartment.

Are there some guidelines for how much to spend on housing? Yes. One is to spend no more than 20 to 25 percent of your income (after taxes) for housing. Another is to spend no more than one week's income each month.

Case Study. Sometimes people can't help spending more than the guidelines suggest. Sue and Ed Markham were stuck. Ed was transferred to an army base across the country. Housing for married couples was scarce and very expensive. If Sue wanted to be there with him, they just had to spend more than they wanted to on housing. Moreover, they would have to skimp on everything else.

Another popular guideline is that if you are buying a house, spend no more than two-and-a-half times your annual income. A family earning $15,000 a year could spend up to $38,000 for a house.

The catch is that there are variables in the cost of a house. In some parts of the country heating costs are very high. In others taxes are steep. It's sensible to aim for total housing costs that are about one week's income for a month's housing.

TO RENT OR BUY

Renting is popular among young people. You have very little responsibility. If a promising job or the social situation beckons somewhere else, it is fairly easy to pick up and move. Security deposits are small. Most important of all, you know what it will cost—a specific amount per month or week, if you have a lease. (Some leases have clauses permitting the landlord to raise the rent if costs, such as heating oil, go up.)

On the other hand, many people get a great deal of satisfaction from buying a house. They feel a sense of belonging. They like to be part of a community. Often they see it as a good investment in a period of rising prices, something they hope will be worth more in a few years.

Is a house a good investment? A lot depends on your judgment and luck. Some houses in some communities will be worth more when you want to sell. On the other hand, a house may be worth less than you paid for it, even if it is well kept.

Economic conditions influence the value of a house. People who bought houses in the 1920's and wanted to sell them in the middle of the depression of the 1930's were in trouble. The same thing happened again in the middle of the 1970's. Business conditions were so poor that many people didn't have enough money to buy houses. However, the history of this country has generally been one of rising prices. Since 1945 most people who have bought houses have found that the value has usually increased if the neighborhood has been maintained.

One can also rent a house or buy an apartment. Mobile homes are usually offered for sale, but sometimes one can be found that is available for rent.

RENTING A HOME

Apartments generally require the least amount of work. Hence, they are very popular with single people or couples without children. Young people starting out and older people without children often prefer the conveniences of an apartment. Also,

CHECKLIST FOR APARTMENTS

Building and Grounds		
☐ attractive, well-constructed building ☐ good maintenance and upkeep ☐ clean, well-lighted and uncluttered halls, entrances, stairs	☐ reliable building management and supervision ☐ attractive landscaping with adequate outdoor space for tenants	☐ locked entrances, protected from outsiders ☐ clean, attractive lobby

Services and Facilities		
☐ laundry equipment ☐ parking space (indoor or outdoor) ☐ receiving room for packages ☐ convenient trash collection and disposal	☐ adequate fire escapes ☐ storage lockers ☐ locked mail boxes ☐ elevators	☐ engineer on call for emergency repairs ☐ extras—window washing, decorating, maid service, shops, doorman

Living Space in the Apartment		
☐ adequate room sizes ☐ convenient floor plan ☐ suitable wall space for furniture ☐ soundproof. Listen for talking, footsteps, plumbing and equipment noise from other apartments or hallways. ☐ attractive decorating and fixtures ☐ pleasant views	☐ windows located to provide enough air, light and ventilation ☐ agreeable size, type and placement of windows ☐ windows with blinds, shades, screens and storm windows ☐ easy cleaning and maintenance ☐ attractive, easy-to-clean floors ☐ furnished appliances in good condition	☐ clean, effective heating, thermostatically controlled ☐ up-to-date wiring ☐ conveniently placed electric outlets ☐ well-fitted doors, casings, cabinets and built-ins ☐ extras—air conditioning, carpeting, dishwasher, disposer, fireplace, patio

This checklist reprinted from page 20 of the booklet titled YOUR HOUSING DOLLAR, copyrighted by the Money Management Institute of Household Finance Corp., Chicago, Ill.

some families with children do not want the work and expense of a house. Other families prefer the convenience of living near jobs rather than having the wage earners commute from a suburb.

In some areas older houses are available for rent at reasonable rates, whereas apartments are scarce or expensive. As a result, a growing number of young people are sharing the rent of a house. They may be a group of students at college or young people who are working.

A house usually has more living space and storage areas than an apartment. In addition, houses generally have a yard and a space to park a car without an additional charge.

Most landlords require that tenants, the people who rent a house or apartment, sign a lease. Generally, leases are written to protect the landlord. Therefore it is wise to read all the fine print carefully before you sign. (Leases were discussed more fully in Chapter 10.)

COOPERATIVES AND CONDOMINIUMS

Cooperatives and condominiums are apartments or townhouses (row houses attached to each other) with some of the rights of ownership that you have with individually owned houses. The purchaser of a *cooperative apartment* buys shares in a corporation which in turn owns the building. Ownership of these shares gives the purchaser the right to occupy one apartment. The purchaser of a *condominium* actually buys the apartment or townhouse directly, much like buying a house.

In addition, the purchaser of shares in a cooperative also pays a monthly maintenance fee for his or her share of the mort-

Westinghouse Electric Corp.

These townhouses near Baltimore are moderately priced. Each has three bedrooms, a family kitchen, oak parquet floors, private patios, a dishwasher, food waste disposer, and central air conditioning, as well as membership in the community swimming-tennis club.

Floor plans: some are so-so, some are better.

"The Smart Way to Pick an Apartment," reprinted by permission from Changing Times: The Kiplinger Magazine (copyright by the Kiplinger Washington Editors, Inc., 1729 H Street, N. W., Washington, D. C. 20006)

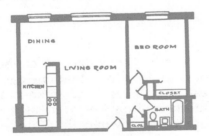

This is a very popular floor plan for one-bedroom apartments in elevator buildings.

The plan has its faults. Trace the path from entry to kitchen. That's the freeway, swooping straight through the living room. Result: Only two corners—up right, lower left—are available for furniture, however you shift it around. Furthermore, there's no way to arrange all living room furniture in one coherent grouping.

Guests in that lower left corner of the living room can peer directly into the bathroom. And if you're traveling bedroom to bath, better dress for the trip: you'll be on exhibit en route.

This is a better one-bedroom plan. Trace the entry-to-kitchen path here. See how relocating the kitchen eliminates the room-crossing freeway. Now the entire living room is one spatial unit. You can arrange furniture as you please, with no worry about cross traffic.

Note how the built-in screen at the door creates a small entry hall, also conceals the dining area from arriving guests. For the living room, the bath and bedroom are out of eyeshot.

A floor plan with these advantages is feasible and sometimes found in buildings that cost no more to build, cost no more to rent than those featuring the floor plan at the left with its shortcomings.

COMPARISON OF COOPERATIVES AND CONDOMINIUMS

Cooperatives	Condominiums
You buy a share in the corporation that owns the building and lease your individual unit.	You actually buy the unit you live in and get joint ownership of the building's common areas and facilities.
You pay a monthly assessment, depending on the size of your unit, for services, maintenance, taxes, and the mortgage for the whole building.	You pay your own mortgage and taxes directly to the lender plus a monthly charge to the group for maintenance.
You're financially responsible for your payments, plus extra assessments if a member defaults on his or her payments.	You have no financial responsibility for others who don't meet financial obligations.
You can't remodel, sell, or change your unit without approval of the corporation.	You can refinance or remodel your unit without approval of the other occupants of the building. Sometimes one must get approval of a prospective purchaser by an occupant group before the unit can be sold.

gage for the building and taxes and upkeep for common areas such as halls, lawns, laundry rooms, etc. The purchaser of a condominium must obtain an individual mortgage and pay taxes directly. However, a fee, usually monthly, is paid for the upkeep of common areas.

What are the advantages? Why would anyone buy an apartment or townhouse? Usually, cooperatives and condominiums are available at a lower monthly cost than similar apartments. This is particularly true if they are built by unions or other nonprofit groups for their members. By building a large number of units, financing part of the cost out of their own funds, and not making a profit, the cost of providing housing is less.

Another advantage of cooperatives and condominiums is that one can deduct real estate taxes and the interest charges on a mortgage from one's federal income tax, as other homeowners do. This becomes even more valuable as income increases. Therefore there is a market for expensive condominiums in many urban areas, as well as moderate-cost cooperatives and condominiums.

Some of the important differences between cooperatives and condominiums are summarized above.

SO YOU WANT TO BUY A HOUSE

How much should you spend? What kind of house do you want? Will it be new or old? Where will you look? Should you consider building a house? How will you finance it?

A house is the most expensive purchase most families make. A wise choice can contribute much to family happiness and financial security.

Don't Be in a Hurry

According to a study by the National Association of Home Builders, the usual decision to buy a house is made so quickly that it borders on impulse buying. People see something they just love and think they can't live anywhere else happily.

First, be sure about what you want. New houses and older homes in beautiful condition sell more quickly than shabby ones because most people want something that looks nice. Are you willing to work hard to fix a house up, or do you want something already spruced up? It's a little like choosing between a meal in a good restaurant and cooking a gourmet meal yourself. You might spend less if you are willing to do some of the work, but be prepared to spend time and effort, as well as money.

A House Is an Investment

In buying a house many people forget that they are investing dollars which can appreciate or depreciate. They can make money or lose it when it comes time to sell.

Most people buy their first house with the notion that they will be there for a long, long time. They may be, but one in every eight families moves each year. Jobs and changing needs often result in relocation. A careful investment can result in a profit when you sell, particularly in a period of prosperity and inflation.

The Location

Real estate agents have been quoted as saying that the value of a house depends on

Leisure Technology Northeast, Inc.
A house can eat up a lot of money.

location, location, and location. Still, most people buy the other way around. They find *the* house and give only casual consideration to its location. It's far smarter to pick an area and then look for houses.

Look at both the neighborhood and the town or city. When neighborhoods deteriorate, property values generally decline. On the other hand, property values tend to increase in a neighborhood that is well kept and attractively developed with good schools and services.

What are the zoning regulations? Can industry or a gas station move next door? Can a house be converted to a business use, such as a store, or divided into apartments?

USDA Photo

By using prefabricated panels, one builder cuts five to ten days from the construction of a house.

Sometimes zoning regulations are used wisely to build and stabilize communities. In other cases, zoning is used as a restrictive measure. Suburban communities often prevent people of moderate and low incomes from moving in by permitting only single-family homes and requiring very large lots.

Is highway construction planned very nearby? Check with the town or county engineer.

Finally, there is the hidden cost of the standard of living you buy with your house. The way your neighbors live, particularly if you have children, may exert some influence on how you spend.

What Community Facilities Are Available?

Are water and sewers provided by the community? Septic systems can be a problem. If you are considering buying a house with a septic system, check with the local health department. In areas where the soil is very heavy a percolation test may show that a septic system will be difficult to maintain.

What about recreation? For an active family community recreation facilities can be a bargain, even if they mean slightly higher taxes. They usually are far cheaper per family than private facilities for swimming, tennis, golf, and other activities.

Will you have to spend more for transportation? Higher commuting costs and parking fees may be an expensive extra. Many families find that they need a second car when they buy a house.

Will you have to pay for garbage collection or plowing snow in the winter? Who maintains the streets and roads?

Why Buy a New House?

The attractions of a new house are often the most visible ones—it's new and clean, and there's a modern kitchen and bathroom. It may even come with a dishwasher and laundry equipment. Usually, you can choose the paint colors. Sometimes wallpaper and carpeting are included as part of the price.

Financing a new house is generally easier than financing an older one. The amount required as a down payment usually is much smaller than for an older house. Often financing can be arranged through the builder.

Initially, inside maintenance is lower than with an older house because everything is new. Since new houses tend to be compact in plan and also have new heating systems, they may cost less to heat than an older house with about the same number of rooms. The floor plan and use of space is often better than in older homes.

On the other hand, landscaping is expensive, time-consuming, and takes a few years to look established. It takes tender loving care to establish a nice lawn, as well as dollars for seeds and fertilizers. Sod can be used, but this adds greatly to the cost.

Check carefully into what comes with the house and what you must provide. If some of the utilities and services are not yet installed, be sure to have a written statement saying the builder will provide them and when they will be completed. It is also wise to check on the reputation of the builder. You might look at other homes that he has built and find out if the buyers were satisfied. The Better Business Bureau in your area might be helpful. If there have been complaints about the builder, they might have a record of how they were handled.

CUTTING THE COST OF NEW HOUSING

Factory-produced houses and portions of houses have been proposed as a way of cutting the cost of new housing. However, although they are feasible from a construction point of view, many communities will not permit this type of building. Communi-

USDA Photo

Many communities will not permit the use of factory-made units like this bathroom, which cut costs.

301

This modular home was erected on the site in one day.

USDA Photo

CHECKLIST FOR HOUSES

Outside House and Yard

- ☐ attractive, well-designed house
- ☐ suited to natural surroundings
- ☐ lot of the right size and shape for house and garage
- ☐ suitable use of building materials
- ☐ compatible with houses in the area
- ☐ attractive landscaping and yard

- ☐ good drainage of rain and moisture
- ☐ dry, firm soil around the house
- ☐ mature, healthy trees—placed to give shade in summer
- ☐ convenient, well-kept driveway, walks patio, porch
- ☐ yard for children

- ☐ parking convenience—garage, carport or street
- ☐ distance between houses for privacy
- ☐ sheltered entry—well-lighted and large enough for several to enter the house together
- ☐ convenient service entrance

Outside Construction

- ☐ durable siding materials—in good condition
- ☐ solid brick and masonry—free of cracks
- ☐ solid foundation walls—six inches above ground level—eight inches thick

- ☐ weather stripped windows and doors
- ☐ noncorrosive gutters and down-spouts, connected to storm sewer or splash block to carry water away from house

- ☐ copper or aluminum flashing used over doors, windows and joints on the roof
- ☐ screens and storm windows

Inside Construction

- ☐ sound, smooth walls with invisible nails and taping on dry walls; without hollows or large cracks in plaster walls
- ☐ well-done carpentry work with properly fitted joints and moldings
- ☐ properly fitted, easy-to-operate windows

- ☐ level wood floors with smooth finish and no high edges, wide gaps or squeaks
- ☐ well-fitted tile floors—no cracked or damaged tiles—no visible adhesive
- ☐ good possibilities for improvements, remodeling, expanding
- ☐ properly fitted and easy-to-work doors and drawers in built-in cabinets

- ☐ dry basement floor with hard smooth surface
- ☐ adequate basement drain
- ☐ sturdy stairways with railings, adequate head room—not too steep
- ☐ leakproof roof—in good condition
- ☐ adequate insulation for warmth and soundproofing

Living Space

- ☐ convenient floor plan and paths from room to room
- ☐ convenient entry with foyer and closet
- ☐ convenient work areas (kitchen, laundry, workshop) with adequate drawers, cabinets, lighting, work space, electric power
- ☐ private areas (bedrooms and bathrooms) located far enough from other parts of the house for privacy and quiet

- ☐ social areas (living and dining rooms, play space, yard, porch or patio) convenient, comfortable, large enough for family and guests
- ☐ rooms conveniently related to each other—entry to living room, dining room to kitchen, bedrooms to baths
- ☐ adequate storage—closets, cabinets, shelves, attic, basement, garage
- ☐ suitable wall space and room size for your furnishings

- ☐ outdoor space convenient to indoor space
- ☐ windows located to provide enough air, light and ventilation
- ☐ agreeable type, size and placement of windows
- ☐ usable attic and/or basement space
- ☐ possibilities for expansion
- ☐ attractive decorating and fixtures
- ☐ extras—fireplace, air conditioning, porches, new kitchen and baths, built-in equipment, decorating you like

This checklist reprinted from page 21 of the booklet titled YOUR HOUSING DOLLAR, copyrighted by the Money Management Institute of Household Finance Corp., Chicago, Illinois

ties generally have building codes which require that most of the construction be done on the site. This means that much hand labor goes into constructing the typical house. However, if mass production of more houses and components were permitted, houses could cost less.

Why Buy an Older House?

Sometimes buying an older house in an established community with schools, transportation, and recreational facilities can be a bargain. You usually get more space for your money. You don't have to pay for landscaping and extras like storm windows and screens. Some people get a certain emotional satisfaction from the "lived in" quality of an older house.

However, there are some obvious hazards. Houses age. That means that their plumbing, wiring, roofs, and siding wear out. It also means that the house may have settled, the basement may leak, or the termites have been busy. The house may be a good buy, but it is always wise to have a contractor or independent appraiser look it over and estimate how much repairs will cost.

Financing an older home generally requires a larger down payment and/or a shorter repayment period.

Prices on new houses are set by the builder and are fairly firm. However, you can usually bargain with the seller of a used house.

WHAT TO LOOK FOR IN AN OLDER HOUSE

You can eliminate some older houses from consideration by a careful check, if you know what problems to look for.

• *The roof.* Roof repairs can be very costly. A roof of new asphalt shingles can cost $800 and up depending on the size.

Wood shingles will cost more, and ceramic tile, slate, and some metals are even higher.

Is the roof worn? Are the shingles broken or loose? What kind of roofing material was used? The most common type is asphalt shingles. Generally, an asphalt shingle roof of minimum grade (240 pounds per 100 square feet) will last about 10 to 15 years, depending on climate and location.

• *Gutters and down spouts.* Examine the gutters and down spouts. Are they smooth, well painted, and free of rust? They should be fastened securely to the house. Gutters should have enough slope so that water will drain through them into the down spouts. At the bottom of the down spouts there should be splash blocks so that the water will drain away from the house, or the down spouts should be connected by pipes under the ground to a dry well or sewer.

• *Exterior painting.* This can cost from $600 up depending on the size of the house, whether one or two coats are needed, and whether the surface needs scraping before painting.

Aluminum siding is a popular substitute for painting but initially much more costly. It can cost $5,000 or more for a house of about 1,800 square feet. However, aluminum siding only needs periodic cleaning and will last for many years.

Check the caulking and paint around doors and windows. These often need painting more frequently than the siding.

• *Termites.* Look at the outside foundation and other masonry for tunnels indicating termites. Are the wood members 6 to 8 inches off the ground? This will help prevent both termites and wood rot. Look inside the cellar for termite tunnels too. Repairing termite damage can be very expensive, depending on what needs to be done.

• *Grading and drainage.* Ideally, the ground should slope away from the house on all sides. If the house is nestled on the side of a hill, check for drainage to carry water away from the house. Visit after a heavy rainfall. Are there puddles around the house where the water stands?

Look at the cellar for evidence of water seepage in the corners and around the edge of the floor. Are there water marks on the wall or cabinets? Inquire from others, such as the town engineer, about the water table in the area. Some areas have persistent water problems.

• *Wiring.* Wiring in older houses is frequently inadequate. Today the recommendations for a new house are three wire, 240-volt, 100-ampere service. If there is an electric range, central air conditioning, or the house is very large, 150-amp to 200-amp is better. Before 1940 houses were generally built with 30-amp service; from 1940 to 1950, 60-amp service was usual.

The electrical capacity can be checked by looking at the size of the main breaker in the fuse box or circuit breaker box. If the amperage is too low for your expected use, it will probably cost several hundred dollars to increase it.

• *The kitchen.* Kitchens are often the selling point of new houses. In an older house they can add to or subtract from the value of the house. Consider the layout. Is it efficient? Are there adequate work areas, cabinets, electrical outlets, and light sources? Are the counter tops and floor easy to clean? Inquire whether the stove and refrigerator come with the house. Are they in good condition? Is there an exhaust fan? Remodeling a kitchen can easily cost from $4,000 to $5,000 or more.

• *The bathroom.* Next to the kitchen the bathrooms are considered selling features of a new house. In an older house look for signs of leaks in the plumbing. Be sure there is adequate ventilation—a window or exhaust fan. Remodeling a bathroom can cost from $500 to $1,000 or more.

• *Water and waste.* The first concern is whether the water supply is adequate. You can get some idea by turning on several cold water faucets at once. If the water pressure seems weak, there are several possible causes. The most common are an inadequate supply of water or corroded and clogged pipes. To check the adequacy of the water supply, look at the intake tank if there is a well. What does the pressure gauge show? Often the town or city health department can advise you about the adequacy of the water supply. Usually, they will also test the water for safety, if you request it. If you can't get the information you need either by checking the gauge or from the local health department, you may need an outside consultant.

Often there are some easy ways to see if the pipes are in good condition. Is the water rusty? Copper pipes are most desirable because they do not corrode. However, both copper and galvanized pipes can become clogged with minerals from the water in time. If there is pressure in the hot water tank before the water goes through the household pipes but only a feeble trickle of hot water, it may be that the pipes are clogged.

Is there enough hot water? Turn on some faucets and see if there is strong pressure. Hot water heaters are one of the first things to wear out in an older house. Usually, they come with a ten-year guarantee, which is about their life expectancy. A new hot water heater will cost several hundred dollars.

For a family of four or five people the heater's capacity should be between 40 and 50 gallons; for six people 50 to 65 gallons.

Check on the recovery rate of the heater, how fast it can provide hot water when you are using a great deal in a short time. A rate of 63 means that it will provide 63 gallons of hot water an hour if the water has to be heated 100 degrees.

How is waste water eliminated? City sewers tend to be the least troublesome. However, if the soil is porous and the houses are well spaced, septic systems will work. A septic tank should have a capacity of a thousand gallons for today's uses of water for a family of four or five. The local health department can probably tell you about septic systems in your area.

• *Heating and cooling.* These are usually the biggest household operating expenses.

If possible, check the heating system by turning the thermostat up high. Is there a prompt response of heat? Visit on a cold day, if possible, to find out if the heating system is adequate. This is particularly important in cold climates.

The two most widely used types of central heating are hot water and forced air. Either type can use coal, oil, or gas as a fuel.

In a hot water system the water is heated in a boiler and pumped around the house through pipes. The chief advantages of hot water heating are: (a) it gives a very even distribution of heat and (b) it can be adapted into a two-zone system where each area is controlled separately.

In forced air heating the air is heated in a furnace and blown through ducts to the various parts of the house. The advantages are: (a) it is easy to add central air conditioning because you can use the same ducts, (b) a humidifier can be added to moisturize the air before it is circulated, and (c) pipes will not freeze because there is no water in the system.

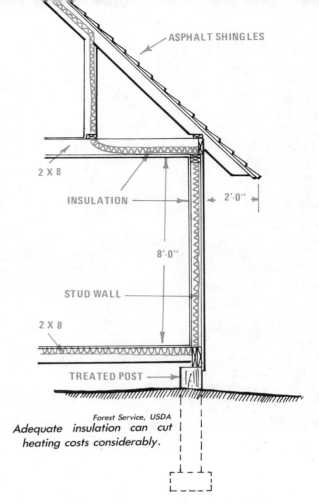

ASPHALT SHINGLES

2 X 8

INSULATION

2'-0"

8'-0"

STUD WALL

2 X 8

TREATED POST

Forest Service, USDA

Adequate insulation can cut heating costs considerably.

Some older houses and apartments have steam heat. This tends to be less even heating and is not readily adaptable to central air conditioning.

Electric heat is also used. Generally, baseboard units are placed around the house, usually on outside walls. However, there are also room units with blowers. The advantages of electric heat are: (a) it is very clean because there is no furnace and (b) there is no water in the system, hence, no danger of pipes freezing. However, electric heat is often more expensive than using other types of fuel.

Both heating and cooling costs are lower if there is sufficient insulation in the house.

305

Today mobile homes are a large portion of the new homes sold under $18,000.

Additional insulation can be added to an attic at moderate cost if the attic is unfloored. However, adding insulation to the walls is both more difficult and more expensive.

If you are considering an older house, you might ask to see the heating bills for the last year as an indication of the cost.

HAVE YOU CONSIDERED A MOBILE HOME?

Mobile homes are becoming increasingly popular, particulary for young people and the elderly. About 90 percent of the homes selling for less than $18,000 and almost half of all new one-family homes are mobile homes. This form of housing offers several advantages:

- The cost is moderate.
- In a single package, you can get a fully furnished home including carpeting and curtains.
- The total cost can be financed with a mortgage.
- Heating and maintenance costs are lower than on a standard house of the same size.
- If you move, it is possible to take a moderate sized mobile home with you. The very large and double wide mobile homes are harder to move and more expensive to haul. When you settle permanently, it can

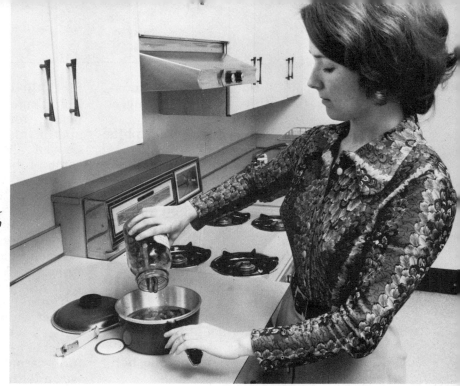

New mobile homes come equipped with modern kitchens.

Because they are relatively inexpensive compared to conventional housing, mobile homes are preferred by many for their first housing purchase.

be lived in, sold, used as a vacation home, or become the utility core for a bigger house.

Some of the disadvantages of a mobile home are:

• They tend to depreciate (be worth less) more quickly than a solidly built conventional house.

• They need to be well anchored to the ground so that they will not tip over in severe wind storms.

• Construction is lightweight for mobility, and they can be dented or damaged more easily than most conventionally built homes.

As the growing popularity of mobile homes attests, for many people the advantages outweigh the disadvantages. Here's the story of how one young couple happened to buy a mobile home.

Case Study. After graduation, Charlie Williams joined the Army. He wanted to get into the Army Engineers and learn to operate heavy construction equipment. He and Mary Ann had been going together since their junior year in high school and wanted to get married as soon as Charlie knew where he would be stationed. While he was in basic training, Mary Ann got jobs through an agency that specialized in temporary office help. She also went to one term of night school to pick up advanced courses that she hadn't taken in her high school business program.

The wedding was small. The couple's parents gave them the money that would have been spent on a fancy wedding. That, plus cash wedding gifts, came to about $2,000.

When they got to Charlie's base out West, they took a room in a boarding house. Mary Ann had no trouble finding a job, but finding an apartment was discouraging. Housing for enlisted men was bleak—it was drab and had no landscaping. There was a long waiting list. In a nearby town there were more attractive apartments, but they were very expensive. One of Charlie's buddies, faced with the same problem, had bought a mobile home. He invited Charlie and Mary Ann to come and have a look. They were impressed.

So the Willamses began to shop around. For a down payment of $1,700 and monthly payments of $160 they could have a new, completely furnished house. The sale price was $12,000 and was to be financed over nine years.

The mobile home was 60 feet long and 14 feet wide and even had a lovely modern kitchen with a dishwasher. Mary Ann was delighted—a new house with new furniture, carpeting, draperies, and appliances was a lot more than she had hoped for.

Also, the Williamses would be able to take their house with them if Charlie was transferred. Besides, he had just about decided that after he got out of the Army, he wanted to travel around working on big construction jobs. With a mobile home they could move fairly easily and still have a comfortable place to live.

They needed to rent a site for the mobile home, but that was fairly reasonable—about $80 a month. The fee for the site, which was located in a mobile home park, included gas service, as well as water and sewage hookups.

For Mary Ann and Charlie Williams, buying a mobile home was a good housing solution. If their plans change and they want to settle more permanently in a house or apartment, they can sell their mobile home. In general, mobile homes tend to depreciate in value as they get older, much as automobiles do. However, mobile homes generally depreciate more slowly than cars.

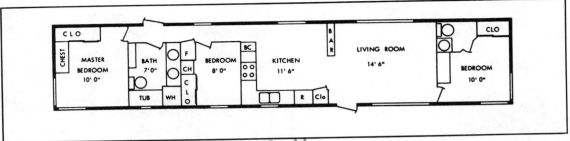

12-wide

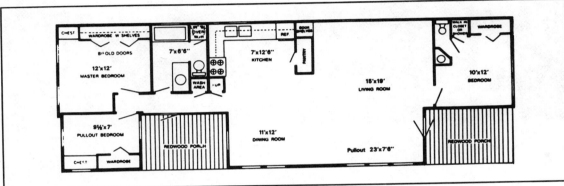

expandable

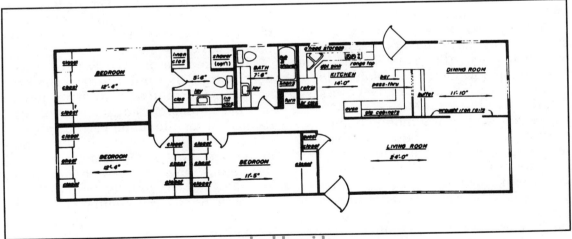

double wide

Council of Better Business Bureaus, Inc., and the Mobile Homes Manufacturers Assoc.

These floor plans show room arrangements for different types of mobile homes. Usually, only the more expensive models of twelve-foot-wide mobile homes have an extra half bathroom.

Some mobile home parks have recreational facilities.

In some parts of the country it is difficult to find a suitable site for a mobile home. Some are expensive. However, more and more facilities are being developed. Today there are many parks that are pleasant and moderate in price. Also, a mobile home can be used on an individual piece of land like any other house if you install the necessary utilities.

If you rent a site for a mobile home, get the regulations and restrictions in advance. You will probably sign a contract that is similar to an apartment lease. Be sure you know whether or not there are entrance or moving fees. The same kinds of problems can arise between the person who rents space in a mobile home park and the owner as with landlords and tenants in apartments.

Originally, mobile homes were used almost exclusively by people who moved frequently. However, today they are usually set up permanently. People buy mobile homes and plan to stay there for a number of years, either on a site in a mobile home park or on a private lot.

Today mobile home parks are available near many large universities. The homes are owned or rented by students and their families. Some retirement communities are located in mobile home parks.

The trend is to build the newer mobile home parks with more community facilities. Some have swimming pools, playgrounds, and community centers.*

Mobile homes can be financed similarly to houses, with conventional, FHA, and VA mortgages.

The following directory rates many of the mobile home parks in the United States annually: Woodall's Mobile Home and Park Directory, Woodall Publishing Co., 500 Hyacinth Place, Highland Park, Illinois 60035.

FINANCING YOUR HOME

Most people finance their home purchase with a mortgage. A *mortgage* is a loan with the house as security or collateral. If you don't keep up the payments, the lender has the right to *foreclose*—to take your house and sell it. In such cases you get back only what is left after the balance of the mortgage has been paid and the expenses of the sale have been taken out.

Shopping for a mortgage is as important as shopping for the house itself, because the two most important home costs are the purchase price and the financing charges. If you've bought a car, you may already know that there are a number of places to arrange financing and several types of loans. This is true of mortgages too.

Types of Mortgage Loans

Basically, there are three types of mortgages—conventional, FHA, and VA.

The *conventional mortgage* is an agreement between the lending agency and the borrower. Usually, the length of conventional loans is no more than 25 years, and the amount is not in excess of 70 percent of the appraised value of the property. Builders of new houses may offer better terms. The interest rates vary with the economy.

FHA mortgage loans are granted by independent institutions but insured by the FHA up to a certain amount. Interest rates are generally a little less than for conventional mortgages.

For the government insurance on the loan the borrower pays a premium to the government throughout the mortgage period. The FHA appraises the house and approves the loan before the lending institution grants it.

VA mortgage loans are available only to veterans. These loans are handled by lending institutions as are FHA mortgages. They are insured by the government up to a certain amount at no cost to the borrower. Rates are lower than for the other two types of mortgages.

Two Common Options

Two important options, which can be very useful, may be available with a home mortgage. They are the prepayment privilege and an open-end mortgage.

The *prepayment privilege* means that you can pay all or part of your mortgage before it is due. If you get a bonus at Christmas or inherit some money, you might want to pay off some of your mortgage. Interest rates could drop. You may want to take out a new mortgage at a lower rate and pay off the old one.

Some prepayment privileges have a charge; that is, you must pay a fee to the lending institution if you pay off all or part of the mortgage early. Others have no charge for prepayment privileges. VA loans permit prepayment without a penalty. FHA loans let you pay off a certain amount each year without a penalty.

An *open-end mortgage clause* operates similarly to a revolving charge account. Let's suppose that you were granted a mortgage loan for $25,000 at a rate of 7½ percent for 25 years. After ten years, you have paid off $8,000 of the loan. However, by this time your family has expanded and you need more room. You need money to finish the attic or convert the garage to a playroom. With an open-end clause in your mortgage, you could borrow up to $8,000 for this type of expansion or any improvement.

Tax Advantages of Mortgages

You can deduct interest and taxes from your federal income tax return. Thus, a person who is buying a home with a mortgage gets some help, in effect, from the government. The higher your income, the more this deduction is worth.

Sources for Home Mortgage Loans

Mortgage loans are available from several types of financial institutions in the United States. Shop around among the lenders. Interest rates and charges vary with the type of loan, how large a down payment you make, the length of the mortgage, and the availability of money. Sometimes one institution is in a better position to lend you money for a home mortgage than another.

Commercial banks give conventional, FHA, and VA loans. They are the most conservative of the lenders and usually require a 25 percent down payment.

How much house do you own?

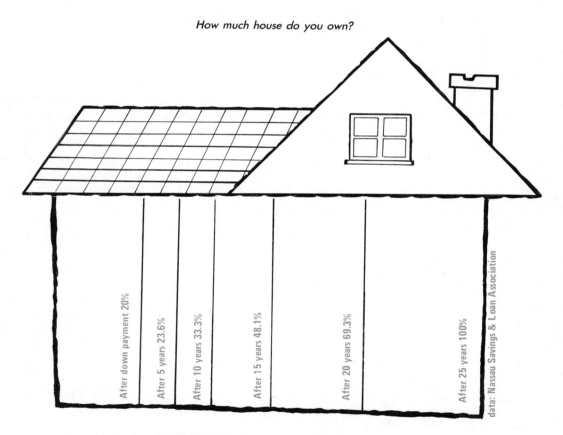

After down payment 20%

After 5 years 23.6%

After 10 years 33.3%

After 15 years 48.1%

After 20 years 69.3%

After 25 years 100%

data: Nassau Savings & Loan Association

INCREASE IN PERCENTAGE OF HOUSE OWNED

(25 Year Fixed Payment, 20% down payment)

Life insurance companies also make conventional, FHA, and VA loans. Generally, they require high down payments on conventional loans, but rates may be low, and they may give a long repayment period. In some areas loans may be handled by insurance agents or through an employer who has a group insurance policy with a company. However, these are generally arranged through mortgage companies or brokers.

Mutual savings banks are chartered in some states. They invest the largest part of their money in home mortgages. Their rates tend to be similar to those of commercial banks, but they may require a lower down payment and permit a longer repayment period.

Savings and loan associations were originally formed to help handle home financing. Rates are often similar to that of banks, but down payments are generally smaller. The repayment period is usually similar to that of a bank. They grant largely conventional mortgage loans but will also make FHA and VA loans.

Mortgage companies function in two ways. They may lend their own funds or arrange mortgages through other lenders. Conventional, FHA, and VA mortgages are available.

Other sources of mortgages which may be available are through the company where you work or a graduate student credit union.

A Second Mortgage

A second mortgage is an additional mortgage, usually on much higher terms, on the house. Often it is used to secure money to make the down payment.

The reason the rates are so high is that if you cannot meet the payments, the holder of the first mortgage will be the first one to get his money if the house has to be foreclosed and sold.

If you don't have enough cash to make the down payment, should you be making the purchase of a house? Maybe the house is more than you can afford. On the other hand, purchasing an older home requires a large down payment. Many people feel that they get such a good buy on an older home that it justifies taking a second mortgage.

Assuming an Existing Mortgage

Sometimes you can buy a house without taking a new mortgage. You can deal directly with the seller. Instead of a down payment you pay the seller the difference between the amount of the mortgage outstanding (the balance that is still left) and the sale price and assume the existing mortgage.

This can be a good deal for the buyer. Sometimes the existing mortgage was taken out when interest rates were lower. Also, you avoid some fees involved in taking out a mortgage.

However, assuming a mortgage may require a large cash payment.

A Binder or Preliminary Contract

Sometimes a home buyer will go through two contract stages in the purchase of a home. The first may be a *binder* or preliminary contract. Usually this is an agreement to purchase a home at a specific price. It generally states that the buyer must obtain a mortgage of a particular amount within so many days or the agreement is off. If you buy a home with a preliminary contract, be sure to see that it includes a provision stating that you can get out of the agreement if you cannot obtain the necessary financing.

Mortgage Points

This is a one-time charge that is assessed by a lending institution to increase the yield from a mortgage loan. When you apply for a mortgage, you may be asked to pay *points* in addition to the interest on the mortgage.

CLOSING COSTS

At the closing the home actually changes owners. It is often more expensive than the buyer expects. Although the costs vary from place to place, the charges generally include fees for: a title search and title insurance if you want it; a survey of the property; recording the deed; tax stamps which are levied on the transaction; and adjustments of the utilities. Suppose the seller has half a tank of fuel oil left or has paid the tax for the entire quarter of the year. You will have to pay for the remaining fuel oil and the taxes from the date that you take title. You might also have to pay for adjustments on household insurance and other utilities. Sometimes you have to pay for the lending institution's credit check on you and for the cost of preparing the legal papers involved in the transaction.

All this can add up to anywhere from $200 to $1,000 or more. When you are shopping for a mortgage, ask about closing costs. The charges will vary from lender to lender. At the time the mortgage loan is granted the prospective purchaser must be given a list of the closing costs. A certified check is often required for these.

In addition, you would be wise to spend some money to secure a lawyer, who will represent you. A house is a big purchase, and you should be sure that nothing in the legal fine print is wrong and that you have a clear title to the property. Some people cut costs by not having their own lawyer. The lending institution will have one, and the seller probably will. However, although it is possible to handle the paper work involved in the transaction through them, neither lawyer is really looking after your interests first.

INSURING YOUR HOME

Before you actually own the home, you will generally have to get insurance. If you are taking out a mortgage through a lending institution, they will probably require fire insurance to protect their loan. Fire insurance pays for the house, if it is destroyed by fire, or damages if it is partially destroyed.

Be sure you have enough insurance. If the house increases in value, adjust your insurance coverage. If you add a room or remodel, change your insurance coverage to reflect the value. If you fail to do this, there may be some problems if you ever need to collect from the insurance company.

Case Study. The Raymonds bought a house for $35,000 ten years ago. Over the years they added a porch. With the porch and inflation the house increased in value to $50,000, which is what their neighbors received for a similar house. Unfortunately, last winter the Raymonds' house caught fire and was totally destroyed. They had never increased their insurance coverage, so when it came time to collect, the insurance company claimed that they had been co-insurers. This means that the Raymonds had, in effect, been insuring the house for part of the value, as had the insurance company. As a result, the family only collected part of what the house was really worth.

In addition to fire insurance, it is pru-

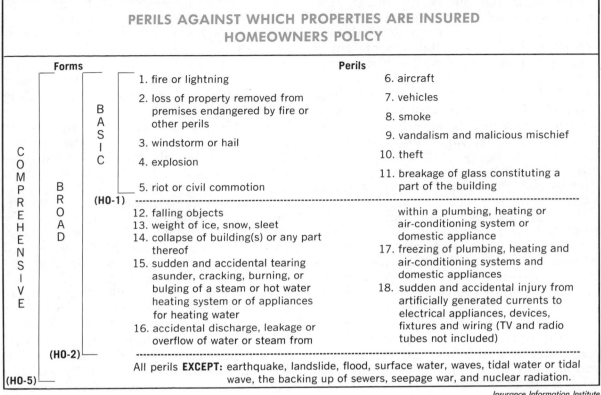

PERILS AGAINST WHICH PROPERTIES ARE INSURED
HOMEOWNERS POLICY

Forms / Perils

BASIC (HO-1)

1. fire or lightning
2. loss of property removed from premises endangered by fire or other perils
3. windstorm or hail
4. explosion
5. riot or civil commotion
6. aircraft
7. vehicles
8. smoke
9. vandalism and malicious mischief
10. theft
11. breakage of glass constituting a part of the building

BROAD (HO-2)

12. falling objects
13. weight of ice, snow, sleet
14. collapse of building(s) or any part thereof
15. sudden and accidental tearing asunder, cracking, burning, or bulging of a steam or hot water heating system or of appliances for heating water
16. accidental discharge, leakage or overflow of water or steam from within a plumbing, heating or air-conditioning system or domestic appliance
17. freezing of plumbing, heating and air-conditioning systems and domestic appliances
18. sudden and accidental injury from artificially generated currents to electrical appliances, devices, fixtures and wiring (TV and radio tubes not included)

COMPREHENSIVE (HO-5)

All perils **EXCEPT**: earthquake, landslide, flood, surface water, waves, tidal water or tidal wave, the backing up of sewers, seepage war, and nuclear radiation.

Insurance Information Institute

dent to have liability insurance. Suppose a neighbor slips on an icy front sidewalk, or your dog bites a child who comes in the yard. You could be sued.

A very common form of insurance today combines fire, natural disaster, theft, vandalism, liability, and perhaps other insurance in one homeowner's policy. Shop around for home insurance. Companies offer different combinations of protection, and rates are not all the same. Sometimes homeowners' insurance is available at low rates through a union or group where you work.

TAXES IN BRIEF

Taxes are one of the major expenses of home ownership. The amount that one will have to pay on a house is not the same everywhere. Rates are often stated as a percentage of an assessed value, which can be confusing. However, you can compare taxes on one house with those of another in dollars, how much is presently being paid.

Remember that the quality of services, facilities, and education offered by a community often depends on how much they are paying in taxes. Higher taxes could mean better schools and other community facilities. However, this is not always true. Many blighted urban areas have very high taxes and poor schools because services for low-income families eat up tax money quickly. In other communities a high proportion of industry to homes keeps tax rates low. The industry pays large taxes but uses very few of the expensive services such as schools.

Tax rolls are open to inspection. If you think you have been taxed too much, you can find out what is charged for similar houses. Also, you can appeal the evaluation or reevaluation of your property by appearing before a local board of review.

MOVING: THE BIG DAY

The difficulties of moving can be eased somewhat by a little planning and organization. For instance, if you can move during the fall or winter, it will be easier for movers to schedule you because they are not as busy as in June, July, and August.

If possible, time your move so that you won't be paying for two homes at once. Make arrangements for essential services like gas, electricity, the telephone, and heating fuel before you move. Take out or transfer your homeowner's insurance policy to insure immediate coverage on your new home and furnishings.

One of the best ways to cut moving costs is to get rid of everything you don't need. Sort out clothing, household effects, and furnishings. Make a plan of your new home and indicate where each item will go. In this way you can decide that some things are clearly extras. This plan will also help you direct the movers in placing things when you arrive at your new location.

If you pack yourself, you can save money. You can get cartons and wardrobes from most movers, but you will usually have to pay for them. By scouring the food markets you can probably get free packing boxes.

Shopping around for interstate moving rates doesn't save much because government regulations fix the rates for all companies. There may be slight differences in whether you will get a wardrobe for hanging clothes free or at lower cost. However, be wary of companies that give very low cost estimates. When you arrive, the charges will be based on the weight of the load and the distance traveled, not the estimate.

If you are moving within a state, shopping around can pay results. Local movers set their own charges. Moving insurance is a worthwhile investment. Things rattle around and can break in moving. Federal regulations state that interstate movers have a certain minimum liability, and the same is true within some states. However, these rates are very low. If you want insurance, be sure to say so before the move, and have it in writing on the contract, or better still take out a contract with an outside insurance agency. The replacement cost of one large item that is broken will probably be more than the cost of the insurance.

Be prepared to pay for moving costs on arrival in cash or with a certified check. Most movers require payment before they will unload the truck.

You can cut costs by doing some or all of the moving yourself. If you are moving locally, carrying the breakable items yourself can save costs and avoid damages. Rental trucks and trailers are far cheaper than moving companies. Many young people move this way. Generally, they don't have a great deal of heavy furniture, and they are willing to do the extra work of moving to save money.

- The difficulties of moving can be eased somewhat by planning.

FOR REVIEW

Points to Remember

- You have several choices concerning how you meet your housing needs.
- Your housing needs will change at different stages of your life.
- Some guidelines on how much to spend for housing suggest that you spend no more than 20 to 25 percent of your income, or one week's income each month.
- Renting an apartment has several advantages: (a) you can move more easily; (b) you generally know what it will cost; and (c) there is less work to maintain it.
- Owning a house has advantages too. Many people enjoy the stability and feeling of belonging by buying a house. In periods of rising values a wisely chosen house can be a good investment.
- Location is very important in determining the value of a house.
- An older house in a well-established neighborhood can be a good buy. However, houses age. Be sure it is in good condition.
- A lease is a legally binding agreement between the landlord and the tenant.
- Mobile homes are becoming increasingly popular because of their low cost and versatility.
- Financing costs are a very big part of housing expenses.
- Financing costs are not the same from all lenders.
- Taxes are another big housing expense.
- Tax charges are not the same in all communities.

Terms to Know

amount outstanding
closing costs
co-insurers
community facilities
condominium
conventional mortgage
cooperative
discount points
evicted
existing mortgage
FHA mortgage
foreclose
investment
lease
mobile home
mortgage
multiple listing
open-end mortgage
prepayment privilege
renew
second mortgage
security deposit
terminate
VA mortgage

PROBLEM SOLVING:
CHECK YOUR UNDERSTANDING

1. What are some of the housing choices available to a student who goes away to school?

2. What are some of the choices available to a person who is moving to another area?

3. What are some of the special housing needs of the elderly person?

4. How much should you spend on housing?

5. What are some of the advantages of renting?

6. What are some of the advantages of buying?

7. What is a lease?

8. How does a cooperative differ from a condominium?

9. What is the most important factor in determining the value of a house?

10. Why have mobile homes become so popular?

TO DO IN CLASS

Discussion

1. Assume that you have graduated from school, are married, and holding down a good job. Form teams to debate the advantages of home ownership versus apartment renting.

2. If money were no object, where would you want to live and why?

3. Selecting a place to live often means selecting a way of life. What are some of the important things to consider before you buy.

4. What are some ways to cut housing costs?

5. Debate the advantages of a new house versus a used one.

6. Many communities restrict the location of mobile homes. Zoning often prohibits them except in outlying areas or special parks. Discuss why this is a good or poor policy.

7. Many people find that they have to sell their house. Sometimes they outgrow the house or a job transfer requires moving.

In buying a house what are some of the considerations to keep in mind that will influence its future sale value?

8. When is a house a good investment?

9. What would your dream house have?

Activities

1. Visit a mobile home park and sales center. Ask a salesperson to discuss financing arrangements for the mobile home and its furnishings.

2. Invite a real estate broker to come to class. Ask the broker to show you a map of the zoning in the community and to discuss what is available at various price ranges in the community.

3. If there are new apartments under construction in the area, visit these and look at the floor plans and setting of the building. Ask what kinds of leases and security are required.

4. Invite a banker to discuss financing a house and closing costs. You might also ask about the type of title insurance that is used in the area.

5. Cut out the floor plan of an apartment from a newspaper or magazine. Redraw it large enough so that you can cut miniature furniture to scale. Try arranging it on the plan or use the floor plans in this chapter. This is an easy way to plan the basic furniture for a home.

6. Visit some furniture stores and study mail order catalogs to price furniture that you like for the floor plan you are working with in activity 5. What might it cost to furnish the apartment with new furniture?

7. Explore the sources for used furniture in your community—parent's and friend's attics, secondhand stores such as the Salvation Army, and newspaper advertisements. Plan how you might furnish the

same apartment in activity 5 at minimal cost.

8. Bring something to class that you would like to fix up for your family's home, your room, or a future use. If time and space permit, you might be able to use the resources of the industrial education department to help.

CHAPTER 14
Buying Life Insurance

Although the need for auto insurance seems real enough at this point in your life, the need for life insurance may seem remote. However, during the next few years you will be assuming more responsibilities. Life insurance can help protect you and your family against some of life's economic hazards.

HOW DOES IT WORK?

Through life insurance a large group of people get together and form a fund that provides money for some of these people under certain conditions. It is really a way of sharing risks with a group. Paying taxes to a local government to share the cost of police and fire protection is another example of sharing risks with a group.

All insurance is based on the principle that although one can't predict what will happen to a certain individual at a particular time, one can predict what will happen to a large group of people. A statistician cannot forecast how long you will live, but he or she knows that in a large group of people of your age and state of health, a certain number will become disabled or die each year. For example, insurance companies know that although most 40-year-old men will live to be 74, 3 out of every 1,000 will die before they are 41.

THE BASIC TYPES OF LIFE INSURANCE

There are three basic types of life insurance policies—term, whole life, and endowment insurance.

Term Insurance

This is like insurance on a car—pure insurance protection. At the end of the period covered by the policy, the policy has no further value. There are no savings features.

Since it has no savings features, term insurance costs less than other forms of life insurance that incorporate a savings plan.

Term insurance is particularly useful for the young person who wants maximum protection for dependents but cannot afford high premiums. Term insurance rates are lowest in the early years, when a young peron's income is likely to be low. Rates increase until age 45 to 50 when they are about equal to rates for whole life insurance.

Term policies may be *renewable* or *nonrenewable*. With a renewable policy the company agrees to reinsure the same individual for the face value of the policy without a new medical examination when the policy expires. Usually, there is an age limit of 55 to 65 for renewable policies.

Term policies are generally written for five-year periods. A five-year renewable policy is one that can be renewed at the end of five years without a new medical examination. However, the renewed policy will be at a higher rate.

A term policy may also be *convertible*. This means that it can be exchanged for a type that incorporates savings features without a new medical examination. However, the premium (or cost) will be deter-

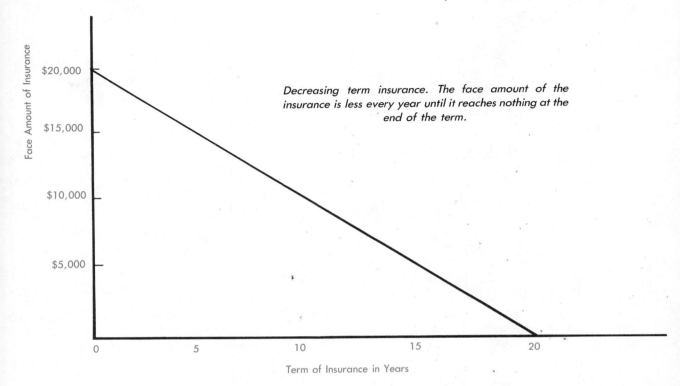

Decreasing term insurance. The face amount of the insurance is less every year until it reaches nothing at the end of the term.

Term of Insurance in Years

mined by the age of the insured person when the policy is converted.

There are two types of term insurance, *level term* policies and *decreasing term* policies.

A level term policy maintains the same face amount of coverage for the duration of the policy. A five-year, $10,000, level term policy remains as a $10,000 policy for the whole five years.

However, a decreasing term policy is lowered each year according to a fixed schedule. Suppose your parents took out a $20,000, 20-year, decreasing term policy to cover the remaining mortgage on the house. The face value might decrease as shown.

DECREASING TERM INSURANCE

Year	Face Amount in Force At Start of Year
1	$20,000
2	$19,000
3	$18,000
4	$17,000
5	$16,000

As you pay off the mortgage, the amount of insurance in effect decreases. If your parents keep up the payments on the mortgage and the insurance, the mortgage will be paid off and the insurance will decrease to no face value.

USDA

Whole life insurance policies have savings features as well as life insurance protection.

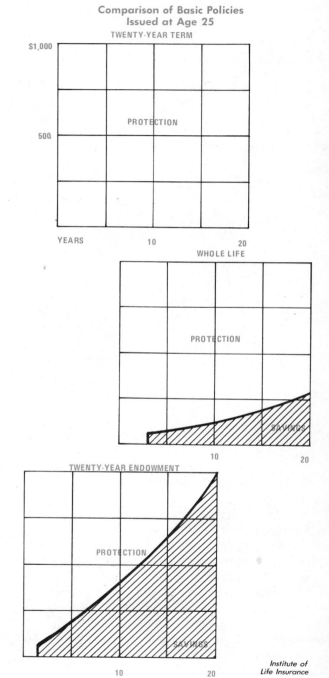

Comparison of Basic Policies
Issued at Age 25

TWENTY-YEAR TERM

$1,000

PROTECTION

500

YEARS   10   20

WHOLE LIFE

PROTECTION

SAVINGS

10   20

TWENTY-YEAR ENDOWMENT

PROTECTION

SAVINGS

10   20

Institute of Life Insurance

Whole or Ordinary Life Insurance

This type of policy provides insurance protection and accumulates savings in the form of a cash value. Many people want both insurance protection for their dependents and also a regular method of accumulating savings.

There are two types of plans for whole life insurance. With the *straight life* plan, the amount of the premium you pay stays the same as long as the insurance is in effect. However, today *limited payment* plans are becoming more popular. These concentrate the payments in a fixed period of time, usually 20 to 30 years. Generally, limited payment plans are arranged to end when the insured person reaches retirement. The annual premiums for limited payment plans are higher because the insurance is paid for in less time.

Endowment Insurance

These are insurance policies for fixed periods of time with very large savings features. Endowment policies are expensive because they build up savings quickly. They are often used to save for a child's education or for retirement income.

Until the policy is paid up, life insurance is in effect. Thus, if the policy holder dies before the payments are completed, his or her beneficiary will get the amount of the face value of the policy.

In summary:

• *Term insurance* is pure insurance. There are no savings features.

• *Whole life insurance* is insurance with a savings feature.

• *Endowment insurance* is really a savings plan with life insurance features.

Some Variations

The basic policies can be combined to meet various needs. One of the most common forms is a *combination policy*. For a family this might include:

• $20,000 of whole life insurance on the spouse earning the highest annual income.

• $5,000 of term insurance on the other spouse, if he or she is the same age as the partner. An older spouse might require less insurance; a younger one, more.

• $3,000 of term insurance on each child, even those born after the policy is taken out. This coverage will continue until the child is between 18 and 25. Then the child can convert to a plan that incorporates savings features up to $10,000 without a medical examination.

Premiums for combination policies generally are based on the father's age. For a small additional premium you get insurance on the other family members. Often there is a clause stating that if the father

Rutgers University

Endowment policies are often used to build an educational fund.

dies, the policies for the other family members will be considered paid up without further premiums.

Annuity Policies

An annuity is really a pension plan. The purpose is to provide retirement income.

Longer life is one of the blessings of modern medicine. However, it also means that most people have more years beyond retirement. Social security and company

323

Dept. of Health, Education, and Welfare
Annuities can help provide for the retirement years.

Many large companies like this oil refinery offer group insurance to their employees.

USDA Photo

plans often do not provide enough money for financial security and comfort. Often people purchase annuities to supplement these funds. Many people buy whole life insurance policies with the thought that upon retirement they will convert them to annuities.

For a long time annuities provided only a fixed income, a certain number of dollars for each hundred dollars of face value. However, a long-term trend towards inflation has convinced many people of the need to protect their retirement income against inflation. Therefore variable annuities were developed, which are available in many states. Generally, insurance companies invest variable annuities in common stocks. The value of these stocks fluctuates with the economy.

The purchaser of a variable annuity buys a number of units. The value of each unit is a share of the total variable annuity portfolio of the insurance company.

FORMS OF LIFE INSURANCE CONTRACTS

Life insurance is available in several forms, individual policies, group insurance, industrial insurance, and savings bank life insurance.

Individual Policies

Generally, these require a medical examination of the person who wishes to be insured. Rates are based on age and health. Some people are refused insurance or charged very high rates because of some health problem.

Group Insurance

Group insurance is generally term insurance issued to a group of people under a single master policy. Rates are low and medical examinations are not required.

Each member of the group receives a certificate indicating that he or she is covered.

Many large companies have group insurance. So do some professional and fraternal organizations. Sometimes the employer shares in the cost of the insurance for the employees.

Typically, group insurance ends when you leave the group, but some plans offer the opportunity to convert to an individual policy. Conversion generally is to a plan incorporating savings features and at a considerably higher rate.

Industrial Insurance

Industrial insurance is sold in small amounts with weekly payments. It was designed to provide insurance for workers in industry. However, today many large companies provide or make available low-cost group insurance, and industrial insurance has been discontinued by many insurance companies.

Savings Bank Insurance

A few states in the Northeast have savings bank life insurance. Under this plan savings banks accept payment for insurance policies similarly to the way they accept deposits for savings accounts. Generally, these are low-cost policies, and one can buy only a limited amount of insurance.

SHOPPING FOR INSURANCE

The first question is: Do you need life insurance at all? If so, how much do you need? What type would be best? Where should it be purchased?

If you aren't supporting anyone else, you only need to consider your own future. If you are supporting someone else, insurance is a way of providing additional income for them in case you become disabled

SUMMARY OF LIFE INSURANCE CONTRACTS

Kinds	Amount	Payment	Type of Payments	Physical Exam Required	Cost
Individual	$1,000 up	Monthly, quarterly, semiannually, annually	Mail	Yes	Moderate to high
Group	$1,000 up	Salary deduction	Employer collects	No	Low
Industrial	$ 100 up	Weekly	Agent collects	No	High
Savings Bank	$ 250 up	Monthly, quarterly, annually	Mail or bank deposit	Yes	Low to moderate

or die. Is anyone dependent on you? Are you planning on a family soon?

Since most people are covered by social security—either their own or that of a relative—the purpose of life insurance is generally to supplement social security benefits. Consider first what social security would provide.

Purchasing life insurance is a way that many people use to accumulate some assets. Except for term insurance, life insurance policies accumulate a cash value. This can be withdrawn or borrowed against in times of need. The average family's most valuable assets are their home and their life insurance. Many people feel that making regular payments for life insurance policies forces them to save. However, studies have shown that it is possible to earn more money through other types of investments. There is much the same attitude toward a Christmas club account. People feel they have to make the payments and do. Often they could make more money by depositing regularly in a savings account.

Here are some of the most common reasons for buying life insurance. To provide for:

- Family income if a wage earner dies.
- A regular way of saving.
- Retirement income.
- Funeral expenses.
- An education fund for children.
- For special purposes. A business firm might insure each of its partners so that if one becomes disabled or dies, the others would be able to buy his or her share.

Insurance Language

Many people are confused by the terms used to discuss life insurance. Here are a few of the most important ones.

- *Policy.* When you purchase life insurance, you are really making a contract with a life insurance company. That contract is called a policy.
- *Premium.* This is the charge you must pay for the policy—or the protection the policy gives.
- *Beneficiary.* This is the person (or persons) who would receive the money

from the insurance policy if the insured person dies. When you purchase a policy, you specify whom you want to receive the money. You can change the beneficiary as your situation changes.

• *Face value.* This is the amount of money that would be paid to the beneficiary. On a $10,000 policy $10,000 is the face value.

• *Cash value.* Policies other than term insurance policies have built-in savings features. The savings that accumulate form a cash value. You can borrow against this money or withdraw it. (If you withdraw it, the face value of the policy is reduced by the amount of the unpaid loan.) You can also choose to cancel the policy and take out the accumulated cash value, buy a smaller amount of paid-up insurance, or, in many policies, have it paid as an annuity when you retire.

• *Riders.* A rider is an addition to a life insurance policy. It can be added or removed without affecting the basic insurance policy. However, there is an additional charge for each rider.

When Should You Buy Life Insurance?

There is no right answer. A lot depends on your purpose—how you plan to use life insurance—and your financial situation. Some parents buy insurance policies for their youngsters to start them on a savings program at an age when premiums are low.

Many young people without family responsibilities buy life insurance because rates are low. It is a way of saving, and they are usually in good health and thus easily insurable. With each passing year a small proportion of the population develops ailments that prevent them from getting insurance or make it available only at high rates.

U.S. Department of Labor

One of the chief uses for life insurance is to replace a wage earner's income. This can be quite important to the surviving family.

If you are supporting someone, insurance is a way of building an instant estate. With the first premium you get the assurance that someone else would get some money if you die.

Let's look at Mike Ferguson's situation and see how his needs changed over the years.

MIKE FERGUSON, A YOUNG SINGLE MAN

Case Study. When Mike finished high school, he thought he was lucky. He had earned enough money during the summers and after school to buy a used car. Also, he had been hired by Joe Bigelow, a building contractor who was impressed with Mike when he worked for Bigelow as part of a work-study program at the high school. When Mike graduated, Joe offered him a regular job.

Mike liked the idea of making money and the security of a job—especially when

Insurance may be used to replace a wife's earning capacity.

Bureau of Indian Affairs

he was so young, the premiums were quite low.

For a young, single person like Mike the term policy is inexpensive but still provides protection for his parents. It is also flexible and as his situation changes, it can be renewed or converted to a different type of coverage. In many ways his term policy is like his auto insurance. He is insured only for the period covered by the premium. There are no savings features in this plan.

THE NEWLYWEDS

Most young people first think about life insurance after they get married. It is a stage of life which is changing dramatically. Five or ten years ago you could assume that the vast majority of people would marry in their early or mid-twenties. The new wife would work for a year or two until the first baby arrived. Then she would stop working and stay home to care for the new offspring and the one or two more that were likely to follow. If the wife returned to work, it was usually when the children were teenagers. Although her wages added to the family income, she was not the major wage earner. While the children were growing up, the family's standard of living and financial security usually depended on the husband's income.

However, family life-styles are changing. There is more variety in the way young people choose to share responsibilities and opportunities in the family. Newlyweds may wait longer before starting their families. Statistics indicate that families are having fewer children.

The role of the wife, particularly, is being redefined. Career alternatives for her no longer make it possible to assume that when children are born she will stop working for many years. She might want to

so many of his friends were sweating out job interviews or trying to get enough money to go to college or technical school. In addition, he felt that he should help his parents by paying board. His father was approaching retirement with only a social security pension. Therefore, Mike accepted Joe Bigelow's job offer.

After a few months, Mike decided to buy a new car. When he transferred his auto insurance to the new car, the agent suggested that he think about life insurance too. There was an element of risk on construction jobs and his parents were dependent upon him for part of their income. Mike decided to buy a $10,000, five-year, term policy that was renewable and convertible at the end of the five-year period. Because

continue working after children arrive or stop for just a short while on a maternity leave.

Frequently, the wife contributes as much to the family's income as the husband does. Sometimes she is the major wage earner. The husband may be in school or a training program. Perhaps he is ill. The couple may be separated, with the wife assuming a great responsibility for the family. Sometimes the family is as dependent on the woman's income as on the man's. If she were to become disabled or die, the family's financial well-being would be threatened.

All these factors should be considered by the newly married couple when they consider what insurance they need. Let's return to Mike Ferguson's situation.

After working for four years, Mike turned 23 and had finished paying for his car. Because he had been living at home, he managed to save about a thousand dollars. Most important, though, he met Linda and they decided to get married. At 21 she had been working in an office for three years. By taking night courses at a nearby community college, she hoped to become eligible for promotion. She hadn't saved much money, but she didn't have any debts either. They planned to furnish their new apartment by using credit for big items of furniture.

After they had been married six months, Mike was laid off from his job because of a slump in the construction business. While he was looking around for a new job, Linda continued to work and finished her night school courses. They learned that it can be difficult managing on one salary, but it's not impossible. Also, after job hunting, Mike realized that more opportunities would be open to him if he had more training. Therefore, with Linda's encouragement Mike went into a job-training program to become a skilled mason.

After six months of training, Mike landed a job with a large construction company. At this point Mike and Linda began to think seriously about their financial future.

Mike wanted to continue helping his parents, if possible, so he and Linda decided to renew the $10,000 term insurance policy he took out when he first started working. The rates would be a little higher than five years ago because of his age.

At about this time Linda's employer started a group insurance plan in the company. Linda could buy $10,000 worth of insurance for very little. Also, since it was group insurance, she didn't need to have a medical examination. She decided to take it and name Mike as the beneficiary.

Mike and Linda bought the most insurance protection for their money—term insurance. This is a particularly good buy for young people who need insurance protection, because it costs less than policies that include a savings plan.

If Linda leaves her job, she has the option of converting her group term insurance to a whole life policy without a medical examination. This plan would incorporate savings features and cost considerably more.

THE GROWING FAMILY

Four years passed. Mike became 27. With raises his income grew to $15,000 a year. At this time Linda stopped working in order to have their first child. During the time that they were both working, Mike and Linda had saved enough for the down payment on a small house which they bought shortly after the baby was born.

After the death of his parents, Mike changed his life insurance beneficiary so that if anything happened to him, the money would go to Linda.

Mike and Linda were elated by the arrival of their son, Jeff. Mike was also taken by a sense of responsibility. He was the sole wage earner and there were three people to support.

Linda dropped her insurance when she left work. It would have been too expensive for them to convert it to an individual policy. Mike, however, increased his insurance because others had become dependent on his income. His employer had a group plan for term insurance, so he decided to join. He took out $20,000 worth of insurance.

At this point many people buy whole or ordinary life insurance, which includes savings features. However, it is much more expensive. Mike felt that his family's more important need was for insurance protection. He hoped to start building a savings plan in the near future. There are many ways to do this. Life insurance with savings features is only one. The chief advantage of saving through a life insurance plan is that one must make the payments regularly. Also, most people aren't as tempted to spend the savings in an insurance policy as in a bank account. However, life insurance savings often earn less than other types of investments.

Should You Invest in Education Instead?

Instead of life insurance another possibility is to invest in career training for the wife as a kind of insurance, if the husband is the principal wage earner. A woman who can get a job if something happens to her husband will probably make more than she would get from the amount of insurance most families can afford.

Case Study. Tony and Betty Gardner decided to buy a small, low-cost, term insurance policy instead of whole life insurance. They used the additional money that they might have spent on premiums for a whole life policy on an educational program for Betty to become a practical nurse. This kind of protection is useful for all sorts of emergencies. If Tony can't work for any reason—illness, accident, or job layoff, Betty will be able to, and they will still have some insurance protection with their term insurance policy.

Other Uses for Life Insurance

The examples you have read show some of the ways that an individual and family can use life insurance. There are many more.

The Fergusons could build a fund for little Jeff's college education through an *endowment* policy. As you have read, this is an insurance policy that has very large savings features. Endowment policies build up cash values very quickly because the premiums include a large amount for the savings feature. If they had bought the insurance policy on Mike's life on an eighteen-year endowment plan when Jeff was born, there would be a fund for Jeff's education by the time he is nineteen. If Mike dies before Jeff turns nineteen, the face value of the policy would be payable to Jeff as the beneficiary. If Mike lives, then Jeff would get the face amount when he reaches nineteen.

Case Study. Other people use insurance as a way of providing extra retirement income. Tara Lewis, a friend of Linda and Mike Ferguson, never married. She took out a life insurance policy that would be paid to her mother if Tara dies before 65. However, if she lives, the money accumulated in the savings portion of the policy would be paid to Tara in monthly install-

Du Pont

People in hazardous occupations usually pay higher insurance premiums.

ments starting at age 65. This is an example of an *annuity* policy. The most common annuity covers only one person. However, Linda and Mike could take out a policy covering both husband and wife. This would provide income for the lifetime of the one who lives longer and insurance until they begin collecting the annuity.

Does It Pay to Shop for Insurance?

It certainly does pay to shop for insurance. Insurance rates vary among reputable companies. Costs are also influenced by your age and health. Insurance may cost more for people in poorer health. Information about insurance is available from many sources, such as *Changing Times* and *Consumer Reports*. It is also available in *Life Insurance and Annuities from the Buyer's Point of View* (revised regularly by the American Institute for Economic Research, Great Barrington, Massachusetts).

What Type of Insurance Would Be Best

This depends on whether you want to incorporate savings with your insurance protection. The table, *What Various Policies Cost,* gives rates for different types of

WHAT VARIOUS POLICIES COST (1981)

Approximate Annual Premiums per $1,000 (for $25,000 policy)			
Insured at Age	Ten-Year Term (Renewable and Convertible)	Straight Life (Ordinary Life)	Limited Payment Life (paid up at age 65)
18	$3.60	$ 9.00	$10.20
20	3.65	9.55	10.80
25	3.75	11.25	12.75
30	4.10	13.50	15.30
40	6.90	20.50	24.50

life insurance policies for men. Rates for women are a little lower because women have a longer life expectancy.

How Much Insurance Do You Need?

It's hard to say exactly how much insurance you need. Ideally, life insurance and other assets should support the family at the standard of living that they are used to, but most people can't afford that much insurance. The table *Average Size Life Insurance Policy in the United States* shows the increase in policy size.

To maintain a family's standard of living, it is estimated that social security benefits plus income from other sources should equal between 65 and 75 percent of their after-tax income. (This does not allow for inflation.)

In the final analysis how much life insurance you need depends on you. Who is dependent on you? Can they earn their own living? How much are you willing to set aside for future needs? Do you want a forced savings program or pure insurance protection?

LIFE INSURANCE FEATURES

The laws in many states, as well as the practices of many large companies, have resulted in the use of clauses that are common in almost all life insurance policies.

Contestability

When you apply for a life insurance policy, the company will ask for information from you and, if it is an individual policy, a medical examination. The insurance company uses this information to decide whether it will insure you at standard rates, at higher rates, or not at all.

If you make a mistake in giving this information or don't tell the truth, the company may be assuming a greater risk than they had contracted for. Therefore most policies provide that the company can *contest* the policy during the first year or two. This means that if the insurance company finds out that it has been deceived, it can cancel the policy. However, if the company does not contest the policy during this period, the policy becomes *incontestable*. This means that the company cannot cancel it.

If you incorrectly state your age, either by mistake or intentionally, the rate that you are charged for insurance will be wrong. Insurance companies base their rates, in large part, on your age. Therefore

AVERAGE SIZE OF LIFE INSURANCE POLICY IN THE UNITED STATES

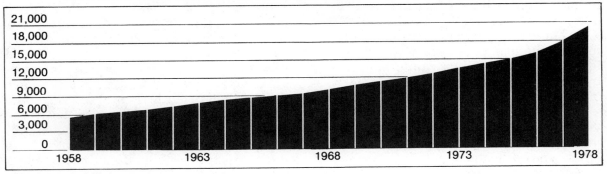

American Council of Life Insurance

the company has the right to change the amount of insurance to what the same premium would have bought if the age had been given correctly.

Grace Period

Policies generally provide for a grace period of a month or 31 days after the date the premium is due. During this time you can pay the premium without having the policy lapse. This protects the insured person in case he or she forgets to pay the premium before it is due.

Automatic Premium Loan

Policies that accumulate a cash value usually pay your premium when due if you fail to do so. The company will pay it for you with a loan from the policy, provided the policy has accumulated sufficient cash value. Sometimes this provision does not take effect unless you request the company to do this.

This loan provision can remain in effect until you have used up the cash value. At this point the policy is canceled.

At any time before the cash value is used up, you can resume paying the premiums.

If you die while the company is paying the premiums out of the cash value, the beneficiary would receive the face value of the policy minus the amount you owe, as with any other life insurance policy loan.

Cash Surrender Value

Life insurance policies, except for term policies, increase in cash value most years. There is little or no cash value for the first or second year, but after that there is a regular increment in cash values. The policy will contain a table showing this. At any point you have the right to terminate the policy and take the cash.

Provisions for Loans

Once a policy has accumulated a cash value, loans may be made against this money. Since the cash value increases from year to year (after the initial one or two years), the loan value increases too. The policy will contain a table showing the loan value and how it increases.

Insurance policy loans have some unique and useful features:

• The company cannot refuse to make the loan. (They do have the right to postpone giving the loan for from three to six months, depending on the state law. However, this right is rarely exercised.)

• The company cannot demand repayment of the loan at any time. However, the face value of the policy would be reduced by the amount of the loan in the event of a claim.

• The interest rate is fixed and stated in your policy. Generally, this interest rate has remained below the current rate for other types of loans.

Because of these features many people find that life insurance loans are very useful in an emergency.

Naming a Beneficiary

When you take out a life insurance policy, you have the right to name a beneficiary (or more than one beneficiary) and *alternate* or *contingent beneficiaries.* For example, the father of two children might name his wife as the beneficiary and the children as alternate beneficiaries. Thus, if both the father and mother died together, the money would go to the children.

You can change the beneficiary if you want to. A young man who takes out a policy when he is single might name his parents as the beneficiaries. Later, if he marries, he may change the beneficiary to his wife.

Settlement Options

Many people have the idea that all life insurance policies pay the beneficiary a lump sum. This is only one alternative, or *settlement option.*

When you take out a policy, you can name the settlement option you prefer, or you can leave the choice to the beneficiary.

Here are the options that are usually available:

• *Lump sum settlement.* There are advantages and disadvantages to this type of settlement. It's very useful for the beneficiary to have some cash for such expenses as: a last illness, the funeral, estate taxes, and outstanding debts. However, very few people hang onto cash very long. Studies have shown that regardless of the size of the estate, very few people can make it last beyond seven years. Most beneficiaries have little experience in managing large sums of money. Therefore they are not prepared to handle money in a way that will benefit them over a long period of time. A lump sum payment that covers final expenses is useful. However, if the face amount of the insurance is larger than this, other options, or a combination of options, might be more useful to the beneficiaries.

• *Installments for a fixed period.* This is particularly useful when the amount of insurance is more than needed for final expenses but not enough to provide a meaningful long-term income. For example, a husband might wish to see that his wife has an income until the children are of school age, when she could more easily return to work. If the couple is older, the husband might wish to provide an income until his widow can collect social security. Perhaps a parent might want to insure that a youngster has money for college.

• *Lifetime income.* This is a very useful settlement option for large amounts of insurance or when insurance income is designed to supplement other income such as social security payments or a pension. The amount that the beneficiary would receive under this option is based on the total amount of the insurance, the age of the beneficiary when payments begin, and whether the beneficiary is a man or woman. (As noted earlier, women have a slightly longer life expectancy than men. Therefore benefits to women tend to be slightly lower than those for men because women will usually receive them for a longer period of time.)

- *Other options.* Two other options are also generally available, the *amount option* and the *interest option.* With the amount option the insurance company pays the beneficiaries a fixed amount each month as long as the money lasts. With the interest option the company pays only interest on the policy until a stated point. For example, a working wife might be the beneficiary of an insurance policy. However, suppose she doesn't really need the money while she is working. It can be kept by the insurance company until she retires. During her working years she would receive only the interest, after that a monthly income.

- *Joint and survivorship income provision.* This is a variation of the settlement options that is often used with annuity policies. The insured person elects to have a certain income guaranteed to two people for as long as either one lives. A husband or wife might elect to have income guaranteed for as long as one of the couple lives. Of course, the size of the payment under this option would be less than the benefit the policy would buy if only one person were guaranteed an income.

Reinstatement Provisions

Sometimes people wish to reinstate a policy that has lapsed. Suppose you lose your job and let your policy lapse. After finding another job, you wish to reinstate your policy.

Some policies permit you to do this within a fixed period of time. Others require you to prove that you are insurable all over again. This would probably include passing a medical examination again. In both cases you would have to pay the missed premiums and the interest due on them.

Premium Waiver for Total Disability

Many policies provide that for a small extra charge you can secure a premium waiver provision. This means that if you become totally disabled, the company will pay the premiums. In general, this provision is only available for disability up to age 60.

Double Indemnity

For a small additional premium, many companies will include a clause stating that they will pay double the face value of the policy for an accidental death. Generally, there are many exclusions—death from medical or surgical treatment, suicide, aviation (except as a paying passenger on a regular airline), service in the armed forces, participation in strikes or riots, and violation of the law.

Its chief value is to young people who are unable to afford sufficient insurance and have a slightly higher risk of dying from the covered types of accidents.

Nonforfeiture Values

Except for term insurance, all policies provide certain *nonforfeiture values.* This means that a policyholder who stops paying premiums has some choices as to how the accrued cash value will be used, which was described earlier. As was stated, the policyholder can request that it be:

- Returned in cash.
- Used to purchase extended term in-

surance. This option will continue the face value of the policy for as long as the cash value will pay the premium.

● Used to purchase a smaller amount of paid-up insurance.

The Use of Dividends

Life insurance is available in *participating* and *nonparticipating* policies. Participating policies pay dividends.

With participating policies the insurance company returns to the policyholder part of the money that is left after the operating expenses of the company are met. These dividends really reflect the fact that the premiums are higher than necessary to meet expenses. The amount of the dividend will fluctuate from year to year, depending on expenses. Since dividends really reduce the cost of a particular policy, compare the dividend history of various companies when you shop for insurance. The net cost may be lower than with a nonparticipating policy.

Dividends can be used in the following ways:

● You can elect to receive them in cash.
● They can be used to reduce the next premium payment.
● They can be used to purchase additional insurance.
● They can be left with the insurance company to earn interest at a rate set by the company.

TYPES OF INSURANCE COMPANIES

There are two general types of insurance companies—stock companies and mutual companies.

A *stock company* is a corporation. It is owned by the shareholders who elect directors to set policy and hire executives to run the company, as do other large corporations. A stock company pays dividends

to its shareholders just as large corporations do.

A stock company can issue both participating and nonparticipating policies. The holders of participating policies will receive dividends.

A *mutual company* is owned by the policyholders. There are no stockholders. In effect, each policyholder is a member of the company.

Mutual companies sell only participating policies. If their expenses are not as high as anticipated, the excess is returned to the policyholders as dividends.

Both types of companies are licensed under state laws and regulated by state agencies to protect buyers from fraud. The state regulations limit the kind and proportion of investments insurance companies can make and control insurance rates to some extent.

UNITED STATES GOVERNMENT INSURANCE

Since 1970, all members of the armed forces have been automatically provided with Servicemen's Group Life Insurance of a fixed amount unless the member elects, in writing, less insurance or no coverage. Payment for the insurance is deducted from the pay. Upon leaving service the veteran is insured for 120 days without payment. During this period he or she may convert the insurance to an individual policy with one of the participating companies licensed in his or her state. The Veterans Administration will furnish the names of the participating companies. These companies have agreed to issue insurance to veterans at standard rates regardless of their physical condition.

Additional benefits are available to veterans with service connected disabilities.

Millions of veterans of World War I,

World War II, Korean conflict, and service-disabled veterans presently hold VA life insurance policies, which are no longer being issued.

For further information about insurance benefits consult your nearest Veterans Administration office. In some cases the widow and dependents of a serviceman are eligible for a pension. Also, the Veterans Administration will pay an amount not to exceed $250 toward the burial expenses of a deceased veteran.

TAX ADVANTAGES OF LIFE INSURANCE

Federal laws increase the value of life insurance through tax protection. Here are two of the ways in which this works:

• You don't pay tax on most life insurance benefits. Suppose Luisa Ramirez purchased a term life insurance policy and paid two premiums totaling $200. Shortly after paying the second premium, she was killed in an automobile accident, and her husband received a lump sum payment of $10,000. He would not have to pay tax on this money, except in an unusual situation.

On the other hand, if Luisa had bought a winning lottery ticket for her husband, the appreciation would be taxable. Thus, if she paid $1.00 for a ticket that won $10,000, the difference between the cost of the ticket and the $10,000 would be taxable. If she made a profit on a stock or land investment, it would also be subject to tax.

• Insurance contracts can be exchanged without tax. For example, a life insurance policy that has accumulated cash values can be exchanged for paid-up term insurance or an annuity without paying any tax.

WOMEN AND LIFE INSURANCE

Women buy life insurance for the same reasons that men do. They may have dependents for whom they want to provide protection, and they want to provide retirement income for their later years.

As women have taken a more active part in the business and professional world, their incomes have become a more important part of family incomes. In some families, women are the principal or sole supporters.

In addition, there has been a growing awareness of the economic contribution made by the wife and mother who does not hold a paid job. Life insurance on the wife is often used to protect the family against the loss of the mother.

SWITCHING POLICIES

Rarely is there any advantage in switching an old life insurance policy for a new one. Often there are many disadvantages. For this reason many states forbid life insurance agents to promote switching.

Some of the disadvantages of switching are:

• You will pay the initial cost for a new policy again. This includes a high portion of the first year's premium, which usually goes to pay the agent's commission. During this period you will not build up cash values as quickly.

• You will have a one- or two-year period during which the policy is contestable.

• If your policy is a few years old, the premium rates will probably be lower than you can obtain by switching.

• The interest rates for loans on an older policy may be at a more favorable rate than in a new one.

If your old policy no longer meets your needs, consider changing it, perhaps to an annuity or paid-up term policy with the same insurance company, rather than switching.

METHOD OF PAYMENT

Pay premiums annually, if you can. It usually costs less if you pay once a year rather than quarterly, semiannually, or monthly. Some people make a point of adding life insurance policies at different points during the year to spread the premiums, but they pay annually for each policy.

FOR REVIEW

- Insurance is based on the principle that although one can't predict what will happen to a certain individual at a particular time, one can predict what will happen to a large group of people.
- Life insurance can be used to provide money for your dependents if you die.
- Term life insurance is pure insurance. There are no savings features. This is less costly than whole life insurance.
- Whole or ordinary life insurance has built-in savings features and costs more.
- Endowment life insurance policies are really savings plans with some life insurance features.
- Many people feel that life insurance policies with savings features force them to save when they might not otherwise.
- Life insurance has some tax advantages.

PROBLEM SOLVING: CHECK YOUR UNDERSTANDING

1. What are some important reasons to carry life insurance?

2. How does whole life insurance differ from term insurance?

3. What is decreasing term insurance, and how is it used?

4. What type of life insurance provides the maximum protection for the least expenditure?

5. What is a limited-payment life policy?

6. What are nonforfeitable values?

7. What is the purpose of an endowment policy?

8. What is meant by an incontestable policy?

Terms to Know

annuity
automatic premium loan
cash value
combination policy
contestability
convertible policy
decreasing term insurance
double indemnity
endowment insurance
face value
grace period
group insurance
individual insurance
level term policy
life insurance
nonforfeiture values
nonrenewable policy
ordinary life insurance
policy
premium
premium waiver
renewable policy
riders
settlement options
term insurance
whole life insurance

TO DO IN CLASS

Discussion

1. What are some of the ways that a young family could have maximum protection for minimum cost?

2. Debate this topic: Life insurance is a good way to save money.

3. Suppose a widow of 45 is left $40,000 in insurance. What settlement options might she consider?

4. Automobile insurance rates are higher for young people, but life insurance rates are lower. Why does this difference exist?

5. Who *needs* life insurance?

6. Do you know any people who have been the beneficiaries of life insurance? If so, have you any idea how they used the money?

7. How might the loan provisions of life insurance be useful?

8. What are some of the sources of funds, other than life insurance, that a family left without a wage earner might have?

Activities

1. Invite a life insurance agent to class to discuss why people need life insurance.

2. Ask an insurance agent for a copy of a whole life insurance policy or get one elsewhere. Project the policy on a screen and discuss the features. Try to clarify the ones that are confusing.

3. Look at the cash value table in the sample contract in activity 2.

a. What is the cash value of the policy after ten years?

b. How much would term insurance for the same period have cost? (Use the booklet on comparative life insurance costs listed in the chapter or one available in your local library.)

c. What would you have saved by buying term insurance?

d. What would you have been able to earn on this difference in cost if you had invested it in:

- A savings bank. (Check the interest rates for the last ten years at your local bank, and compute what the savings could have earned.)

- A high-grade corporate stock. (Look up back issues of newspapers to find out the purchase price and dividends over the last ten years.)

4. Compare the costs of:

a. Term policies from a number of companies. Consider policies that pay dividends as well as those that don't.

b. Whole life policies.

5. Many companies have life insurance as a fringe benefit. In some companies it is provided free to employees; in others the employees can purchase low-cost group insurance under a company contract.

a. Ask the members of the class to gather information about the fringe benefits available to members of their families.

b. Ask your teacher to tell you about the insurance benefits available to teachers in your community.

c. Invite the personnel representative of a large company or a union to come to class to talk about fringe benefits.

CHAPTER 15

Other Investments

Are you hoping to buy a house? Did a relative give you a U. S. savings bond? Do you collect stamps or coins? Perhaps your parents own some stock. Then you may know a little about investments already.

Many people use extra money in ways they hope will earn more. That is the principle of investing.

As was mentioned earlier, the purchase of a home is often regarded in part as an investment. Life insurance is another common investment for families. Some people buy antiques. Others collect coins. There are many types of investments available. This chapter will discuss briefly some which have not been covered in earlier chapters.

FIXED-DOLLAR INVESTMENTS

Some investments give a definite rate of return. These are called fixed-dollar investments. A savings account in a bank has a stated rate of interest. U. S. savings certificates have a specific rate of return. Life insurance policies guarantee a certain amount of money to a beneficiary. Many annuities and pension plans guarantee a specific income per month after retirement. Some other widely used fixed-dollar investments are bonds, commercial paper (loans to business companies), and government securities.

EQUITY INVESTMENTS

These are purchases that do not pay a fixed rate of return. People buy them in hopes that they will increase in value faster than fixed-dollar investments.

You may have heard some people say, "My house is my hedge against inflation." What they mean is that they hope their house will increase in value as fast or faster than the rate of inflation.

Suppose the rate of inflation is 11 percent a year. If you put $100 in a savings account in a bank that earns 5 percent, you will have about $105 (depending on how the bank compounds the interest) at the end of a year. However, you will need over $111 to buy what your $100 bought when you deposited it. Thus, your investment did not keep up with the rate of inflation.

On the other hand, you feel reasonably secure knowing that your money is in a bank and it is also insured by the Federal Deposit Insurance Corporation. Equity investing generally involves more risk than fixed-dollar investing but promises the possibility of a higher rate of return.

Assume that a family invested $40,000 in a new house ten years ago. If they picked a neighborhood that has developed attractively in a desirable community and the house has been well maintained, they may be able to sell it for twice as much today. They will earn more than most fixed-dollar investments pay. However, they did take a chance that the value could go down.

COLLECTIONS

Many people enjoy collecting. Stamp collecting is a popular hobby. Some people

Many people regard a home as an investment that will grow in value.

collect old bottles or china. Others look for coins, old books, barbed wire, and street car transfers. Insulators formerly used on telephone wires and old milk bottles are collected too.

Most people build collections for the sheer pleasure of doing so. If they are interested in something, they may decide to collect it. However, this type of collecting is largely for personal entertainment. Although some of the things collected may appreciate in value, this approach to collecting is not the same as collecting primarily for investment purposes.

People who collect for investment purposes generally concentrate on fields with a well-defined market. This means that there is a fairly steady demand and easily available information on values. Stamps, coins, rare books, autographs, art, and antiques are widely used for investments. Remember, however, that a collection earns no interest. Only when you sell it at a profit do you gain.

The serious investor wants items that will probably appreciate in time. Generally, this means that they must be somewhat scarce, of excellent quality, and in demand. For instance, there are only a limited number of Rembrandt's oil paintings, his work is widely recognized as excellent, and many museums and individuals want to collect his paintings. As a result, his paintings sell for huge sums of money.

One doesn't have to collect expensive oil paintings to be a serious collector. There are many modest opportunities. First, one must really know what he or she is buying.

Stamp and coin collections can be interesting hobbies and valuable investments.

This means knowing the market for the item, what is available, how to judge quality, and what is likely to appreciate in value. To make a good investment requires knowledge. Helpful literature is available in the form of books, magazines, newsletters, and catalogs. The potential collector will find these in each area of investment collecting.

Stamps

Collecting stamps is one thing; buying for investment is quite another. Not all old stamps are valuable. General collections and stamps of many countries are not greatly in demand.

Contrary to popular belief, U. S. commemorative stamps may have little investment value. Since 1940 they have been printed in enormous quantities—140 million per issue or more. Therefore they are unlikely to be scarce in the foreseeable future.

Stamps that were printed in small quantities may become valuable, partly because they are scarce. For example, in 1965 the Republic of Korea issued a souvenir set of five sheets which showed the flags of several countries and General Douglas MacArthur. (Souvenir sheets can be used for postage but are mainly issued for collectors.) At the time of issue the sheets cost just 12¢. Only 100,000 sheets were printed, and these caught the fancy of the public. In four years these sets were worth ten times their original price.

What stamps should you collect that may grow in value? First, the trend today is toward specific topics—sports, space exploration, UNICEF, President Kennedy, and other such issues. Also, collections of stamps from a single country are in demand.

Some stamp dealers recommend buying issues that are already several years old and becoming scarce if you are looking for an investment. Buying new issues is more risky because it is hard to be sure which ones will be printed in small amounts and what will catch the public fancy.

Sometimes stamp albums help to forecast where the demand will be increasing. As new specialized albums are published, the stamps of that country tend to increase in value.

In addition to scarcity and topical interest, the condition of a stamp is important if you are buying for investment purposes. There are a number of classifications of stamp condition, but those in mint condition (like new and well printed) are apt to be in greatest demand.

Where should you buy? There is an advantage in dealing with a local dealer whom you can see face to face. There is no standard price for stamps, so you should get acquainted with several dealers. Some department stores also have stamp departments. Check their prices too.

If you want to trade by mail, select a dealer who is a member of the American Stamp Dealers Association. Some dealers will sell on approval. They will send you stamps by mail which you can either keep and pay for or return within a certain number of days. However, because this procedure increases the dealer's cost, prices are apt to be high.

Information on stamps is available from many sources. Stamp catalogs give prices. Listed prices are often general estimates rather than exact values. Two of the leading catalog publishers in the United States are Scott and Minkus. The U. S. Post Office publishes the *United States Stamp Catalog,* which lists U. S. stamps issued for over 100 years. There are also a number of philatelic (stamp) periodicals, which are helpful in keeping up with the market. Probably the most widely used one is *Linn's Stamp News* (Box 29, Sidney, Ohio 45365). *Minkus Stamp Journal* (116 West 32 St., New York, N. Y. 10001) is also very popular. There are a number of others. Perhaps your local library has some.

Coins

Coins are popular with both collectors and investors. Many a youngster has filled a coin card with pennies. Many adults carefully examine their change in hopes of finding a valuable coin.

Coin values depend on the condition of the coin, how large a supply there is, and the denomination. *Uncirculated* refers to a perfect coin that has never been in circulation. This is the finest quality and preferred by most investors.

There are two useful books for those who are interested in finding out about the values of U. S. coins, the *Handbook of United States Coins* and the *Guide Book to United States Coins.* (Both are published by the Western Publishing Co., Inc., Racine, Wisconsin, and revised annually. Many libraries have them available.) The first book gives an approximate price that a dealer will pay for a coin (the wholesale price) and how many were minted each year. The second lists the retail selling price of coins, what you would have to pay to buy a specific coin.

Generally, investors in U. S. coins trade in uncirculated rolls. If you look in coin magazines or newspapers (such as *Numismatic News, Coin World,* or *COINage Magazine*), you will find advertisements to buy or sell uncirculated rolls.

If you are buying or selling coins, look for a reputable dealer. Members of a local coin club probably are acquainted with dealers in your area. For buying or selling by mail look for members of one of the coin dealers organizations, the Professional Numismatic Guild or the Retail Coin Dealers Association. Also look for dealers who are affliated with coin clubs, such as the American Numismatic Society or the American Numismatic Association.

What is likely to increase in value? Generally, coins of *low mintage* (fewer have been made) increase the fastest. Some experts suggest that certain series of U. S. coins will probably appreciate in value faster because of the small numbers produced—Lincoln pennies, Jefferson nickels, Roosevelt dimes, and the Franklin half dollars.

If you want to invest in coins, check the reference books and find out which years and mintages were produced in the smallest quantities. Remember that pennies and nickels are generally in greater demand than larger coins because many collectors are young and have limited funds.

Bernard & S. Dean Levy, Inc.

Fine antiques are another type of equity investment.

Autographs

Autographs are another type of collection with an established market. Although many people enjoy collecting them, autographs and signed photographs of movie, stage, and sports stars have little value as an investment. The signatures of former U. S. Presidents, statesmen, famous authors, composers, and scientists are of value.

Generally, a signature alone has little value. Signed material is what dealers look for—books, letters, maps, original manuscripts, drawings, and similar items.

Supply influences value too. Some famous people wrote many letters, whereas others wrote few. William Shakespeare wrote considerable literature but rarely signed things. Only six items with his signature are known, and each is very valuable. However, there are many items signed by Samuel Morse, the inventor of the telegraph, and each is worth relatively little.

Demand also depends on current interest, which changes. Interestingly, a handwritten letter signed by John Kennedy is worth more than one by George Washington. Generally, values are influenced by the quality of the material. An important letter or document is generally worth more than one dealing with a less significant topic.

Autographs are one area in which a clever collector can obtain material for little cost. Some living notables are quite willing to autograph material. Some collectors ask a famous person to autograph a copy of a document associated with them, thus increasing the autograph's investment value. Others speculate by getting autographed copies of new books of famous authors. Often these are easily available when the book is first published.

You can get an idea of autograph values by studying the catalogs of various dealers.

Books, Art, and Antiques

These are other areas in which people buy for investment purposes. They are complex markets, and study of each area is required to recognize quality and good buys.

Rare books are not the same as old books. Old books are bought and sold by the pound. According to the Antiquarian Booksellers' Association of America, "The books most sought after are the first editions of great books in literature, art, and science." A first edition is the first printing of a book. The highest value is paid for books in perfect condition. Books that are acknowledged as important literature are in greatest demand. Today modern poetry is highly regarded, and some people are putting away first editions of some contemporary poets in hopes of appreciation. Others are buying first editions of noted authors.

Old books, not necessarily first editions, dealing with aspects of American history are also sought after. Many books of this sort are buried in attics and trunks. Sometimes one can find them in yard and auction sales.

Art is a booming field. There are a growing number of people collecting. Exhibitions of fine work can be seen at museums and galleries around the country.

Learning to judge quality takes time, study, and skill. There are many books on the subject. Your local library and museums probably have a selection. Art auction catalogs are another source of information. *Time* and *Newsweek* magazines discuss art regularly. The Sunday edition of the *New York Times* has well-recognized art critics. Visiting museums and galleries can be both fun and a way of learning more about art.

For people with limited means, fine prints—lithographs, etchings, engravings, and woodcuts—are a good investment. Often they are available at modest cost. This type of work usually has long-term value as opposed to mass-produced art or mediocre work available in many places.

A number of museums and galleries sell fine prints. Associated American Artists in New York City was one of the first to offer a program for purchasing prints from recognized artists at moderate costs. They commission limited editions which are sold reasonably.

If you know what you are buying, bargains in old prints can sometimes be found at yard sales and auctions. However, this is not a good way for most people to invest a substantial amount of money.

Antiques are old, man-made things of value. Generally, an object must be 75 to 100 years old to be considered an antique. There are well-defined markets for different types of antiques, primarily American, English, and French furniture, china, and glass. The most stable market is in fine quality antiques, which are very expensive.

Some people, however, collect antique country furniture, which is much lower in price. They buy carefully at auctions and house sales, knowing that the resale value will be better than that of commercially made furniture if they ever want to sell.

If you are interested in antiques, learn all you can about them. Specialize in a limited area, so you really know it well. There are many books on the subject and a number of magazines (*Antiques, Antique Trade, Antique Monthly,* and others), as well as museum displays, antique exhibitions, and auction catalogs.

REAL ESTATE

Many people regard real estate as a good equity investment, particularly in periods of inflation. Real estate is something concrete; it can be seen and examined. As was mentioned earlier, the purchase of a house or mobile home is often considered partly an investment.

In addition to a single-family dwelling, some people invest in unused land, farms,

Some people invest in farmland near urban areas.

USDA Photo

multifamily houses, and commercial property.

In metropolitan areas the demand for land has grown with the population. Today people are pushing out even further from the cities to buy land at moderate cost. Investing in land has its pros and cons. On the plus side, good land is fairly scarce. There is a limited amount of good building sites or property on existing lakes, hills, and high-quality farmland.

Many people are attracted to land as an investment because it can often be pur-

chased with only a small down payment. On the other hand, land costs money to maintain. If it is bought with a mortgage, there are regular payments to be made. Also, taxes must be paid. These can be very steep if the area is under development. Some investors meet this problem by buying only land that produces an income while they hold it—farmland under cultivation, a lot used for parking, and so forth.

Investing in land has caught the public fancy, and quite a number of companies are engaged in selling land, particularly retirement and vacation property to people many miles away. It is unwise to buy property that you have not examined. Many people have been fooled into buying land that is under water, a desert, or otherwise undesirable.

Another way to invest in land is in a group. Large parcels of land are often available more cheaply per acre than small ones. Investment groups and syndicates commonly buy this way. Some of these have been very successful in making money; others have not. One of the problems with investing this way is that it is often difficult for an individual investor to sell out if the need arises.

Land investment can be a long-term proposition. Not every parcel will appreciate in a short time. It may take ten, twenty, or more years to be able to sell at a profit.

Many people with moderate funds to invest buy multi-family houses. A two-, three-, and four-family house which is bought at a good price will often make it possible for the owner to live rent free and possibly come out ahead. However, there is a management and maintenance problem involved. Rental property needs care and attention. Generally, apartments with moderate rentals are easiest for the owner to rent, because many people want to live in the moderate-rent apartments.

Commercial and industrial property usually requires a large investment which most small investors cannot manage.

The legal process of buying real estate can be quite tricky. It is wise to get the help of an attorney before you sign anything, whether you are buying or selling.

STOCKS

These are a widely used type of equity investment. A *share of stock* represents ownership of a portion of a company.

Suppose you invent a new typewriter stand. It is sturdier than most of the ones on the market but also folds up easily. You think it might be very useful for students who go away to school and thus it would sell well. Consequently, you decide to go into business making and selling it.

After investigating, you find that you can rent a vacant gasoline station as a factory and get some used machinery largely on credit. You will need at least $25,000 in cash for a deposit on the building and machinery, materials from which to make the typewriter stands, and salaries for your two workers and yourself. You can't get a loan of this size at the bank because you haven't yet established your ability to repay it, and no one else will lend you that much money. However, you think you might be able to get some friends and relatives to lend you smaller amounts. Some local business groups might also be willing to encourage new business in town by lending smaller sums. At this point you decide to incorporate (form a corporation) and sell shares of stock in the Sturdi-Typewriter Stand Company. You issue 30 shares of common stock and set a *par value* (initial price) of $1,000 each. (Each share represents ownership of $1/30$ of the company.) Luckily, you are able to sell 25 shares fairly quickly. You keep five. Then you are ready to get started in business.

All the owners of stock shares meet to discuss operational problems. First, they decide that it is very difficult to run a business and have to consult all the shareholders on each decision. Therefore they elect you as president and someone else as treasurer-secretary. You will be responsible for running the company after consultation with the treasurer-secretary. If this were a big company, a board of directors might be elected to set policy. They, in

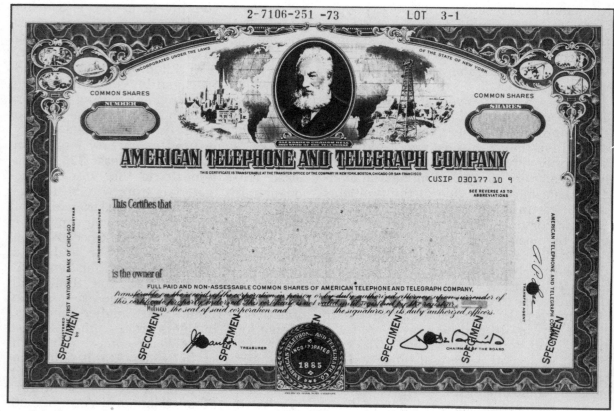

A stock certificate.

American Telephone and Telegraph Co.

turn, would select the operating officers, such as president, treasurer, and secretary. Each year the operating officers prepare an *annual report* and have an *annual meeting* with the stockholders to tell them about the company's operation.

During the first year the Sturdi-Typewriter Stand Company makes a small profit and distributes part of it to the stockholders as *dividends*. The total profit of the company is $9,000, but they decide to use $6,000 for reserves and distribute $3,000.

Thus, each share earns $100, or 10 percent, on the initial investment of $1,000.

The following year business is also good, and the officers decide they ought to expand the factory. Upon securing the stockholders approval, they decide to go ahead.

To provide money for the expansion, they will need to use their reserve of $6,000 plus the $9,000 profit for the current year, and they must borrow an additional $5,000. They could borrow from a bank now that they have established a credit rating in the community, but interest rates are very high.

Instead they decide to sell *preferred stock.* Preferred stock is much like a bond in that it pays a fixed rate of interest. Also, in the event that the company hits hard times and has to be liquidated, preferred stockholders are paid before common stockholders. Ten shares of preferred stock are issued at $500 each. They are sold to people in the community who by now regard the Sturdi-Typewriter Stand Company as a good business.

The preferred stock has a *cumulative dividend* of 10 percent. This means that each year a preferred stockholder should receive $50 per share. However, suppose one year the company is unable to pay the dividend. With a cumulative dividend, they must pay both the skipped dividend and the regular dividend the next year. Any time they have to skip dividends they must pay all the missed dividends as well as the current one before common stockholders can get any dividends.

When a company grows very big, it may have its stock traded on an exchange. These are markets where people buy and sell the stocks of large companies. There are a number of exchanges in various regions of the country. The biggest is the New York Stock Exchange. Next is the American Stock Exchange.

BONDS

A bond is really a corporation's I.O.U., or promise to repay a loan. Another name is *promissory note.* Specifically, a bond is a document which tells that the company has borrowed money from you and will pay a certain rate of interest on the loan until it is repaid. This is stated in financial language by saying that bonds are *floated*

New York Stock Exchange
Trading on the New York Stock Exchange.

(issued) at a specific rate of interest. The bonds will be *redeemed* (the loan repaid) on a specific date, which is called the date of *maturity.*

Bonds of reputable companies are considered a conservative investment. In the event that the company which issued the bonds has to liquidate, bondholders must be paid before holders of either common or preferred stock. Thus, a bondholder is protected more than a stockholder.

349

Eastman Kodak

American Telephone and Telegraph Co.

The stocks of many companies are traded on exchanges. What companies and products do you see represented in these photos?

U.S. Department of Labor

U.S. Department of Labor

In periods of recession bonds are generally desirable because of their security feature. However, in periods of inflation stocks generally increase in value faster, which protects one's investment better.

There are a number of types of bonds. These are the most common. A *debenture* is a bond that is backed by the general credit of the company. Many large companies float debentures. A company may issue *mortgage bonds,* take a mortgage on their real estate property or equipment.

Some bonds are *convertible;* each bondholder has the right to buy a specific number of shares of stock at a given price. These combine both the income feature of bonds and the equity investment of stocks. (There are also *convertible preferred* stocks on the market.)

Interest rates on bonds depend both on the quality of the bond and general business conditions at the time of issue. Two organizations rate new issues of bonds, Moody's Investors Service and Standard and Poor's Corporation. Moody's grades bonds from Aaa down to Aa, A, Baa, etc. Standard and Poor's uses capital letters, AAA, AA, etc.

Often the interest rate on a bond is referred to as the *coupon rate.* For many years bonds had coupons attached. Every six months the bondholder would clip a coupon and present it for payment. Originally, bonds were not registered in the owner's name, as are stocks, and were called *bearer bonds.* Therefore instead of having the interest mailed, the owner had to present a coupon for payment. However, in the last few years many bonds have been *registered,* so the owner's name is on them. Some still have coupons to clip, but in many cases the company issuing them sends the interest check automatically every six months.

SELECTING STOCKS AND BONDS

Some people buy stocks with the hope of making money fast. However, the more prudent investor generally looks either for well-managed companies to produce regular income or for *growth stocks*—shares of industries that are likely to grow in value with the passing of time.

Looking ahead, there are a number of broad trends which should influence stock growth. Health services are expected to continue to increase, and the use of computers should continue to grow. Pollution, particularly water and air pollution, is probably going to be a major concern. Developing domestic sources of fuel and scarce minerals is likely to be another. Housing has been regarded for some time as an industry which should boom because there is a shortage of good housing. The housing trend will probably be away from single-family homes and toward multi-unit projects and greater factory construction of sections, as is done in many European countries now. With the trend toward more time off from work, leisure industries should continue to develop too.

Once you have decided to invest in a certain industry, look carefully at the companies. Not all companies in growth industries will prosper. Some are better managed and more efficient.

Before you invest, get as much information about the companies as you can. Read their annual reports. Consult reference sources such as Standard and Poor's publications or Moody's. Look at financial newspapers such as *Barron's National Business and Financial Weekly* or *The Wall Street Journal.*

Two things that conservative investors look for in stocks are a long period of growth and a consistent increase in *net earnings* (earnings after expenses are paid).

Bureau of Indian Affairs

USDA—Soil Conservation Service

There is a continued shortage of adequate housing. Do these photos reflect a possible trend of the future in housing?

Utility stocks are generally regarded as a conservative investment.

American Telephone and Telegraph Co.

As mentioned earlier, bonds are another type of conservative investment. There are three methods of measuring the value of a bond:

• First is the *interest rate* stated on the bond. A 5 percent bond with a face value of $1,000 earns $50 a year (5 percent of $1,000).

• Next is *current yield* (current income). Suppose a bond has a face value of $1,000 but is currently selling for $750. On the basis of a purchase price of $750, the same bond has a current yield of 6.66 percent. In other words, you pay $750 for a $1,000 bond and earn $50 a year, which is 6.66 percent of $750.

● Finally, there is the *yield to maturity.* This includes both the current yield and the profits or losses on maturity. Suppose you bought a $1,000 bond at a *discount price* of $750 and held it for 10 years until maturity. You would get $1,000 for it as well as the yearly interest on the bond. In this example, the yield to maturity would be 9.99 percent; $50 a year in interest plus $25 a year in appreciation on $750.

The Financial Page

The financial section of many large newspapers has a great deal of information about stocks, bonds, and economic trends. Many people just skip the stock market reports, which appear in many daily papers. They may have no interest in stock and bond prices, or they don't understand how to read price reports. Given below is the report for the common stock of AQZ Corporation (a fictitious company) as it appeared on the financial page.

Let's examine these numbers. Under *High* and *Low* are the highest and lowest selling prices for the stock since January 1. Next is *AQZ,* the abbreviation for AQZ Corporation.

Under *Div.* is listed the dividend, $2.90. The letter *e* indicates that this amount was declared or paid during the preceding 12 months. (If a stock dividend includes a letter in it, check the explanatory notes on the financial page to see what it means.)

P-E refers to the price-earning ratio, that is, how the selling price of a share compares with the annual *earnings* per share. AQZ stock sold at ten times the company's earnings per share on the day referred to earlier. Earnings are not the same as dividends. For example, a company may earn $10 per share, but only declare $4 as dividends. The difference might be retained by the company as reserves to build a new factory, buy more materials for production, or for other reasons.

Sales in 100's tells how many shares of stock were sold on a day.

The *High* and *Low* columns indicate the high and low prices paid for AQZ Corporation's common stock on that day. The stock market is really an auction market. People bid for stock at certain prices, while other people offer it for sale. The *close* column is the final price paid for the stock that day. The last column, *Net Chg.,* indicates how the closing stock price has changed from the closing price on the preceding business day. A plus sign indicates that it has gone up, whereas a minus means it has gone down.

Now can you understand the figures in today's newspaper for the common stock of AQZ?

Bond prices are quoted differently. Bonds are generally issued in multiples of $1,000. After issue, the bonds are traded publicly, and their prices change. In reporting the current price, ten percent of the full price would be listed. For example, suppose a bond is selling at $870. The price would be listed as 87.

LISTING FOR AQZ COMMON STOCK

High	Low	Stock	Div.	P-E Ratio	Sales in 100s	High	Low	Close	Net Chg.
$72^3/_4$	$57^3/_4$	AQZ	2.90e	10	2373	$71^3/_8$	70	70	$-1^1/_8$

LISTING FOR AQZ BONDS

	Bonds	Cur. Yld.	Vol.	High	Low	Close	Net Chg.
AQZ	9s95	9.3	35	96½	95½	96½	−½

Above is a sample of how AQZ bonds were listed one day.

These AQZ bonds are 9 percent bonds which mature in 1995. This is what *9s95* means. Their current yield is 9.3 percent. The number (Vol) traded on the day shown was 35. The highest price paid for them was $965 (96½ × 10), the lowest $955 (95½ × 10). The closing or final price was $965 (96½ × 10) which was a decrease of $50 from the previous day's closing of $970.

You have probably seen reports on TV and in the newspaper of stock market trends. The *Dow Jones composite average* of stock prices is an important indicator often mentioned. These are the 65 stocks whose prices are averaged into the one figure reported each trading day.

Thirty Dow Jones Industrial Average Stocks:

Allied Chemical	Inter Harvester
Aluminum Co	Inter Paper
Amer Brands	Johns-Manville
Amer Can	Merck
Amer Tel & Tel	Minnesota M&M
Bethlehem Steel	Owens-Illinois
Du Pont	Procter & Gamb
Eastman Kodak	Sears Roebuck
Exxon	Std Oil of Calif
General Electric	Texaco
General Foods	Union Carbide
General Motors	United Technologies
Goodyear	US Steel
Inco	Westinghouse El
IBM	Woolworth

Twenty Transportation Stocks:

American Air	Pan Am World Air
Burlington North	St. Louis-San Fran
Canadian Pacific	Santa Fe Indust
Chessie System	Seaboard Coast
Consolid Freight	Southern Pacific
Eastern Air Lines	Southern Railway
McLean Trucking	Transway Int'l
MoPac	Trans World
Norfolk & West'n	UAL Inc
Northwest Air	Union Pac Corp

Fifteen Utility Stocks:

Am Elec Power	Niag Mohawk P
Cleveland E Ill	Pacific Gas & El
Colum-Gas Sys	Panhandle EPL
Comwlth Edison	Peoples Energy
Consol Edison	Phila Elec
Consol Nat Gas	Pub Serv E&G
Detroit Edison	Sou Cal Edison
Houston Indust.	

Buying Stocks and Bonds

Most people who buy and sell stock deal with a stockbroker. A stockbroker is a member of a firm which is able to deal on various financial exchanges. However, it is possible for an individual to trade directly. For example, your father might sell you some stock, or a large institution might buy directly.

When you tell your broker to buy or sell, you are placing an *order*. There are several types of orders:

• You may specify a price at which you wish to buy or sell. For example, "Buy 100 shares of General Motors at 69." The broker can't buy the stock unless someone is willing to sell at that price.

● You may say, "Sell *at market.*" This means that you want the broker to sell at the best price available.

● Most orders are *day orders,* that is, good for only the day that the order is given.

● You can also place a *GTC order* (good till canceled).

Stock market transactions must usually be settled on the fifth business day after execution. If you buy stocks or bonds, you must pay for them within five business days. If you sell them, you must deliver the stock certificates by then, if you have not left them in the care of the broker.

Stockbrokers charge a *commission,* which is a fee for their services. This varies with the size of the order and differs with different brokers. It pays to compare rates.

Stock purchases are usually made in *round lots*—units of 100 shares. If you buy or sell an *odd lot* (1-99 shares), you will pay an additional fee called the *odd-lot differential.* This is because odd-lot transactions are handled by a special odd-lot dealer who also gets a commission.

Bonds can also be purchased through a stockbroker. However, you will pay an extra commission charge. There is no commission charge if you buy them through a *bond house,* a broker who specializes in buying and selling bonds. (A few large stock brokerage concerns also act as bond brokers, but most do not.) A bond house gets its profit through the *spread,* the difference between the wholesale cost and retail selling price of the bonds.

Stocks and bonds can be bought on credit. If you have established a credit rating, you can buy on *margin.* This means you pay a portion of the cost and borrow the rest from a brokerage firm. The amount that

you may borrow (margin requirement) is set by the Federal Reserve Board and varies from time to time. The cost for this credit depends on prevailing interest rates. If you buy on margin and the price of the stock goes down, you may be asked to put up more money.

Managing Stocks and Bonds

Once you have bought a stock or other investment, keep track of it carefully. You will need records for tax purposes.

Note the purchase price and commissions paid in a record book.

File the brokers statement that comes with stock certificates.

When you sell, put down the sale price and commission.

Keep a record of dividends, both cash and stock ones, as well as any *warrants* on stock that you may receive. Warrants are an option to buy a security above the market price and are usually issued for a period of time. You may hold them, hoping the price of the stock will rise, or sell them.

Keep the stock certificates in a safe-deposit box or allow your broker to keep them. Although they are registered in your name, it is slow and sometimes expensive to replace them.

Study the progress of the stock at regular intervals. Read all the reports sent to you by the company.

Most bonds and preferred stocks have *call provisions.* This means that if the company has enough money, it may pay the stocks and bonds off before maturity. If you purchase bonds, particularly bearer bonds, it is important to keep abreast of call (redemption) notices. These are usually placed on the financial page of leading newspapers. Suppose a corporation decides to call your $950 bond for $1,000. You could make a profit by redeeming the bond. However, the selling price may be higher than the call price. Then you either have to redeem (cash in) the bond or sell it before the final call date.

INVESTMENT FUNDS

Many people prefer to buy shares of an investment fund rather than shares of company stock. There are two main reasons for this.

First, with a small amount of money to invest you can buy into a fund that owns stocks of many companies. That is, the fund may own shares of automobile, chemical, utility, and many other kinds of stock. This variety offers protection because one industry or company may be in a slump when others are not.

Another reason is that these funds have professional managers, trained people who devote full time to managing them. Often they can keep abreast of changing conditions in a company or industry more effectively than someone who can only devote part time to it.

Types of Funds

There are several types of funds. An *open-end* or *mutual fund* has no limit on the number of certificates it will sell. As purchases are made, new certificates are issued. When you invest in a mutual fund, you get a certificate telling how many shares of the fund you own. Then, on a quarterly basis you are sent a report and a check for your share of the fund's earnings. Generally these are *redeemable.* Upon demand the purchaser can usually get the value of the shares at that time. This doesn't mean that the purchaser will get back what they invested, rather what the share is worth when it is sold. This may be more or less.

Mutual funds are sold by salesmen and stockbrokers who receive a commission on each sale. In the case of small investments the fee is usually a percentage of the purchase. In addition, they generally charge a small management fee.

Many funds have *front-end loads.* This means that you pay all or most of the commission when you buy into the fund. Some funds are of the *no-load* type. These funds do not charge commissions. All of the money one invests goes for the purchase of fund shares. This may be an advantage, but even more important is the performance of the fund.

A *closed end* fund is one in which a limited number of shares are issued. The shares are bought and sold on a securities exchange like the stock of other companies. Closed-end funds have not caught the public fancy. However, during periods of inflation closed-end funds are often a conservative investment because they tend to sell at a discount from net asset value. For example, a company may have a stock portfolio that is worth $35 per share but sells at only $30 per share. So if you invest $30 per share, you are really buying a portfolio worth more.

Selecting a Fund

Most investors want a fund that will produce growth but which will also keep their investment reasonably secure. Although no equity investment can be completely secure, some funds are more speculative than others. To find out about a fund read the *prospectus,* the official company circular that describes it.

Also look at the fund's performance over a period of five or ten years. There are a number of sources for this information. Standard and Poor Corporation's *Stock Re-*

ports rates the performance of funds periodically. *Forbes* magazine publishes an annual survey of funds and their performance. Arthur Wiesenberger's *Investment Companies* (New York: Nuveen Corporation, latest edition) is also a well-regarded reference.

Look for answers to the following questions. Has the fund performed better or poorer than changes in the stock market? How does its performance compare with other funds? Also consider what fees the fund charges. When are they assessed? What is the size of the fund? How diversified is the portfolio of stocks?

GOVERNMENT SECURITIES

Government agencies as well as private companies issue bonds when they want to borrow money. You are probably familiar with U. S. Savings Bonds (Series EE and HH). These are sold by most banks without a commission charge.

There are many other government securities. Local, state, and federal governments issue notes and bonds.

Municipal bonds have been attractive to some investors because the interest on them is tax exempt. These bonds are issued by states, cities, counties, toll roads, school districts, and other local authorities to finance various public facilities.

Municipal bonds are bought and sold much like other bonds, through bond dealers.

These are the basic types of municipal bonds:

• *General obligation bonds* are backed by the full faith and credit of the authority issuing them. Many large cities use this type of bond for much of their financing. The rate paid by such bonds depends on the economic condition of the city issuing them. Even in the depths of the depression of the 1930's almost all general obligation bonds paid interest.

• *Limited tax bonds* are backed by a segment of the taxes of the issuing authority. For example, some are backed by gasoline taxes, others by property taxes.

• *Revenue bonds* are backed by the income of an issuing authority. It may be a water department, toll road, or other agency.

• *Housing authority bonds* are backed by the rents from the low-income housing projects they finance and also the fact that they are government agency bonds. As a result, often they have been highly rated, although some of the local housing authorities do not seem to be on a very sound financial basis.

• *Industrial revenue bonds* are backed by the rental payments of tenants who use facilities financed by the bonds.

• *Notes* are loans to a governmental agency, not necessarily backed by any specific source of income. In times of difficulty these are paid after general obligation bonds, and often after other bonds with specific revenue assignments.

Treasury bills are short-term loans—3, 6, 9, or 12 months—made to the U. S. Treasury. New issues are sold in denominations of $10,000, although earlier issues of smaller sizes can still be purchased through a broker or commercial bank.

The federal government also issues *Treasury notes* with a maturity of from one to seven years. There are also federal agency securities which are used to finance the activities of these agencies. Treasury notes start with the minimum denomination of $1,000 and most federal agency securities at $5,000. The chief attractions of these government securities are that they often

HOW MUCH DO THEY PAY?

Amount Paid Out for Each Dollar Bet	
97.3¢	Most Gambling Casinos
95.5¢	Bookmaker Bets on Sports Events
75¢–95¢	Las Vegas Slot Machines
82¢–83¢	Horseracing Bets (at the track, at a N. Y. legal off-track betting parlor, or with a bookmaker)
40¢–45¢	State Lotteries

Consumer Reports

earn more than a savings account, and funds are quite secure. Small investors can buy government securities indirectly by investing in a fund for this purpose.

INVESTMENT CLUBS

The growth of investment clubs has been very rapid. Many small investors start as members of an investment club. Typically, a club is composed of a dozen or more members who are neighbors, friends, or co-workers. Each person generally invests $10 or $20 a month. The funds are pooled so that the group can buy various securities. Decisions to buy or sell are usually made after considerable discussion among the group and a vote among the members.

LOTTERIES AND GAMBLING

Much of the lure of lotteries, bingo games, and other forms of gambling is that some people do make money. Many people are tempted by the notion of a really big payoff for a small investment. However, people often spend much more than they make. Most forms of gambling are set up to yield a profit to someone other than the bettor. Obviously most people would do far better investing their money than risking it on games of chance.

FOR REVIEW

Points to Remember

- Investments that give a definite rate of return are called fixed-dollar investments.
- An equity investment is a purchase that does not guarantee a rate of return.
- Some things that people collect, such as stamps, coins, autographs, art, and antiques, may be used for investment purposes.
- Real estate and stocks are equity investments.
- Many large companies are publicly owned. Shares in these companies can be purchased on a stock exchange.
- A bond is really a corporation's or government's I.O.U., or promise to repay a loan.
- Notes are loans, usually to governmental agencies, that are not backed by specific revenues.
- The financial section of many large newspapers has a great deal of information about stocks, bonds, and economic trends.
- Most stocks and bonds are sold with the help of a stockbroker.
- The income on most bonds of local and state agencies is exempt from federal income tax.

● Treasury bills are short-term loans made to the U. S. Treasury.

● Once you have bought a stock or other investment, keep track of it carefully. You will need records for tax purposes.

● Most people cannot make money on gambling and lotteries.

Terms to Know (Continued)
redeemable shares
round lot
share of stock
spread (as regards bonds)
Treasury bills
yield

Terms to Know

antique
bearer bond
bond
closed-end fund
closing price
commemorative issue
convertible bond
coupon rate
cumulative dividend
day order
discount price
dividends
equity investment
float a bond
fixed-dollar investments
front-end load
general obligation bonds
growth stock
investing
low mintage
maturity of a bond
mint condition
net earnings
no-load fund
odd lot
open-end fund
par value
promissory note
prospectus
rare books
redeem a note

**PROBLEM SOLVING:
CHECK YOUR UNDERSTANDING**

1. Why are equity investments usually more desirable than fixed-dollar investments in periods of inflation?

2. How does a collection assembled as a hobby differ from one planned as an investment?

3. What are some of the important things to consider if you are collecting stamps for investment purposes?

4. What type of material should one look for if collecting autographs as an investment?

5. What is the difference between stocks and bonds?

6. What is the big advantage of municipal bonds?

7. What are some of the reasons why small investors buy into a stock fund rather than invest in individual stocks?

8. Where can you learn about daily stock and bond prices?

TO DO IN CLASS

Discussion

1. What are some of the factors that encourage people to look for investments other than a bank savings account?

2. Suppose that your parents have $5,000 in savings. What are some of the ways in which they might invest it to

produce the greatest return? What are some of the reasons against these investments?

3. How would the investment needs of a young person differ from those of his or her parents?

4. Think about a house that you are familiar with. (It could be your family's home.) Would it be a good investment to buy now? If so, why? If not, why not? What might be a better buy?

5. Pick out twenty stocks on the New York Stock Exchange. Discuss which of these is likely to undergo the greatest fluctuation and why.

6. What are some of the important trends in real estate values in your community?

7. Why isn't it a good idea to put all your money in equity investments?

8. Why isn't it a good idea to put all your funds in fixed-dollar investments?

9. Who are some famous living people whose signed papers will probably be of value in years to come?

Activities

1. Invite someone from a stamp club to talk to the class about trends in stamp values.

2. Ask a member of a coin club to bring his or her collection to class and discuss collecting U. S. coins.

3. Get a map of your school district and have a group of students explore which areas are under development. Show the areas on the map. Report to the class on any trends that will influence whether new homes will be a good investment.

4. Take a trip to a local stockbrokerage office or a securities exchange, if you are near one.

5. Pick out ten companies which are listed on the New York Stock Exchange. Pretend that the class invested in ten shares of each of these companies. Chart your progress for the rest of the term.

6. Invite a member of a consumer protection agency, chamber of commerce, or local consumer organization to discuss the problems consumers face when they invest in land or new businesses.

7. Invite a panel of parents or community members to class to talk about "The Best Investment I Ever Made."

8. Divide the class into four teams. Have each team look up price trends for the following over the last thirty years:
   a. Stocks.
   b. Houses.
   c. Bonds.
   d. The cost of a college education.

SECTION 5

The Environment and the Economy

CHAPTER 16

Protecting the Environment

It was a hot and muggy day in New York City. The heat was stifling and the air was heavy with the ingredients of pollution—carbon monoxide, sulphur dioxide, and others. Commuter traffic was snarled as one car after another overheated and stalled. A sea of hot, sticky people crowded into the subways, which were slowed down by a lack of sufficient power.

Across the country a rock concert left a Denver stadium ankle deep in debris—largely food and candy wrappers, bottles, and cans. This was the normal aftermath of such an event.

Open spaces are being destroyed. Oil and gas are being used up. Many rivers and streams are polluted. Logging operations are tearing down forests faster than they can be replanted. Strip mining is turning large areas into slag heaps. Many highways have an unattractive and confusing array of shops and signs. The ecology of the Moja-

ve Desert in Southern California faces ruin from motorcycles and dune buggies that rip up delicate plants and compact the soil.

Few would deny the many comforts and conveniences that modern technology has made possible, but many people now realize that we have ignored the related deterioration of our environment.

As recently as a hundred years ago, people were largely scattered across the United States. Towns were fairly small, factories few and far between. Most people lived on family farms, and the wastes produced there were easily disposed of in the air and streams. Only in the relatively few cities and towns were waste and sanitation a problem.

Today, however, one can fly across the country and see great towers of sooty smoke spewing forth from factories. Whole areas are covered with smog—a haze of smoke, dust, and fog. Parts of every state

Many highways and streets are cluttered with an array of shops and signs. Are there scenes like this in your community?

USDA Photo

Is there a pollution threat in this photo?

Here is an example of what happens to land used for strip mining.   **363**

U.S. Bureau of Outdoor Recreation

Recreational vehicles like this dune buggy may be fun but are often hazardous to the environment. What signs of plant life do you see in this photo?

have been denuded by vast strip mining machines. Miles of open land are interlaced with tremendous urban corridors where most people now live.

People are now concerned about the pollution of our environment. A report of the Environmental Pollution Panel, President's Advisory Committee, says, "Environmental pollution is the unfavorable alteration of our surroundings, wholly or largely as a by-product of man's actions, through direct or indirect effects of changes in energy patterns, radiation levels, chemical and physical constitution and abundances of organisms. These changes may affect man directly, or through his supplies of water and of agricultural and other biological products, his objects or possessions, or his opportunities for recreation and appreciation of nature."

Some major areas of concern are: population pressure, land use, water and air pollution, the use of energy, rising noise levels, and the use of public resources.

POPULATION PRESSURE

There are two major aspects to the present concern about population and the environment: (1) the rapid increase in the population of the world and, to a lesser degree, of the United States and (2) the growing trend for most people in industrialized nations to live in urban areas.

The Growth of Population

For centuries population growth was held in check by a limited food supply, the ravages of disease, poor sanitation, and other hazards of life. However, today good food, modern medicine, and improved sanitation have cut down the death rate of industrialized nations dramatically. This is also true to some extent in less industrialized nations. Although there has been some slowing down of the birthrate in industrialized nations, the world population is growing very rapidly.

It took ten years to construct the Aswan Dam in Egypt. This dam increased the arable land in the country by one-third. However, at the same time the population of Egypt increased by almost one-half. Obviously, more land for growing food was made available, yet there was less land for feeding each person than before the dam's construction began.

A noted biologist, Dr. Paul Ehrlich, projected that Egypt would need four more Aswan Dams in the following 24 years in order to maintain the same amount of arable land for each person in the country at that rate of population growth.

Many people feel that this rapid growth is a real peril to the future well-being of the people of the world. They are concerned that population growth is outrunning resources. The World Health Organization estimates that at present 10,000 people starve to death every day, and about one-third to one-half of the people of the world are undernourished.

In the United States projections are for a population increase of fifty percent in 30 years.

THE USE OF LAND

Eighty percent of the population of the United States is crowded into cities and suburbs on less than ten percent of the land. Forty-nine percent of the nation's land is classified as farm but has only five percent of the population. As former Secretary of the Interior, Walter Hickel once remarked, "We don't have too many people. The trouble is that they're concentrated in the wrong places."

Jobs have brought people to urban areas. With each new technological development in agriculture fewer people were needed on farms. At the same time factories and service occupations in urban areas offered employment opportunities.

As a result, in industrialized nations people have become concentrated in urban areas. In the United States the rural population has been fairly stable since 1920, but the urban population has almost tripled. Moreover, the urban areas have grown even bigger. About 35 percent of the U. S. population now live in areas that have over one million people.

How is the quality of life affected by this trend? It's difficult to assess. Quality of life cannot be measured by easy indicators. Generally, people in urban areas have better incomes, more women can find employment outside the home above the subsistence level, a lower proportion live in substandard housing, and there is better access to medical facilities and college education.

However, people in urban areas are less likely to own their own homes, they are exposed to a much higher level of air pollution and noise levels, and they are more apt to be victims of crime.

The concentration of people in limited geographic areas also aggravates environmental problems.

A variety of suggestions about land use have been made to relieve the problems of population density. Some industries have moved out of heavily populated areas. Many people think that more should do so. However, what would happen to the city dwellers who now depend on these industries for jobs?

Another proposal is to build new cities on open land with industries, shopping centers, and homes. To some extent this has happened in suburbia. One experiment of this sort was Reston, Virginia, a community that was built from scratch on farmland.

Another suggestion has been for a new type of Homestead Act to encourage people to settle on undeveloped federal lands. However, many people believe that government land—forests, beaches, and other undeveloped areas—should be kept as undeveloped as possible so that they will exist as a natural recreational resource for future generations. There is opposition to the use of government forests for logging, ski resorts, or other commercial purposes.

A related concern is the need to plan for the use of privately owned land. Should population density be concentrated by building multifamily dwellings and preserving large open spaces, or should people be spread out as thinly as possible on

Reston, Virginia, is a planned community with a variety of dwellings, a shopping area, and an industrial area.

individual plots? At the present time the suburbs are very much concerned with this issue.

WATER

Water is vital to man. An adequate supply is essential to survival; a safe one contributes to good health.

The Availability of Water

Like other resources fresh water is unevenly distributed around the world. Vast areas, such as the Sahara Desert, have little water, and few people live there. Some areas have a great abundance of water, such as the lush rain forests of Puerto Rico. Areas that ordinarily have enough water may experience periods of long drought. In the early 1970's the people of Africa who lived south of the Sahara Desert were devastated by several years of severe drought. Crops could not grow, herds were destroyed, and many people starved to death.

In the United States the eastern half of the country generally has enough rainfall to supply adequate water, but the western half is less abundantly supplied. In an effort to use available supplies more efficiently vast dams have been built, large scale irrigation projects undertaken, and water for household use is often piped great distances.

Water Safety

Much of the world still lacks a safe supply of water. Unsafe water is the leading cause of disabling sickness and infant deaths in many developing nations. Diseases such as cholera, typhoid, and other dysenteries are spread when sewage contaminates drinking water supplies. In Thailand where only ten percent of the people have piped water, water-borne dis-

eases cause forty percent of all deaths and sixty percent of all illness.

The United States and other industrialized nations have eliminated many of these diseases through improved sewage disposal and controlled water supplies. However, problems arise from time to time, and reports indicate that the quality of much of our water is not as good as it might be. For example, recently, Nassau County on Long Island had a problem of sewage seeping from septic tanks into water supplies. Largely rural Vermont has curbed some housing developments, particularly around ski areas, because in the spring when melted snow saturated the ground, septic tanks overflowed.

Many people now drink bottled water because they are concerned with the taste and purity of the water. Robert A. Wright in the *New York Times* reports the following:

When John Wedberg's mother-in-law came here from Nebraska recently to look over her new grandchild, she talked a lot about how good the water was back home.

So Mr. Wedberg, a stockbroker, ordered bottled water delivered to his Bel Air home for the duration of the grandmother's visit. Now the Wedbergs have joined a million southern Californians as confirmed bottled-water drinkers.

Southern California, basically a desert, has by far the largest number of bottled water drinkers in the nation; the market here has doubled in the past decade. . . . It is [also] growing throughout the country.

Bottlers report that sales have doubled in the last five years in Miami,

Boston, and Pittsburgh. Sales are up 75 to 100 percent in Chicago, 50 percent in Atlantic City, and 40 percent in Dallas.

Sources of Pollution

Today there is concern about what is going into the water supply—detergents from home laundering, excess fertilizer that runs off farmlands, wastes from various industries, and even heat when water has been used and returned to a stream.

DETERGENTS

Since World War II three developments have revolutionized how people wash clothing—automatic washing machines, phosphate detergents, and synthetic clothing. Phosphate detergents enabled people to wash these new fabrics in automatic machines very successfully, and the sales of washers, synthetic fabrics, and detergents soared. In a 25-year period, detergent sales rose from nothing to 27 pounds a year per person, while soap use declined from 27 pounds to 5.

After laundering, phosphate detergents are discharged as sewage into waterways. Phosphate is one of a number of nutrients that spur the growth of plant life, and in the past few years large masses of algae (seaweed) have been appearing in lakes and ponds. These algae absorb the oxygen from the water, which is needed by fish. As algae increase greatly, many types of fish die.

An increase in the algae of lakes and ponds will occur naturally but very slowly as nutrients are washed down from surrounding land. Old or eutrophic (rich in nutrients and often low in oxygen) ponds have been found in areas of Alaska that are still unsettled. Green Bay, Wisconsin, was

named by early settlers, who found it covered with large masses of algae.

Although there is still much to be learned about how much of each nutrient will stimulate the growth of algae in different bodies of water moving at different speeds, phosphate is recognized as one stimulant to algae growth. There seems to be agreement that rapid increase in the use of phosphate detergents and fertilizers containing phosphates which run off into streams and lakes, discharges from industries containing phosphates and other nutrients, and the increase in sewage discharged into streams have hastened the eutrophication (aging) of many bodies of water.

For a while detergents with phosphate were banned and discouraged. However, it was found that alternatives were very caustic and dangerous to little children who accidentally swallowed them. Also, phosphate detergents do not remove some fabric finishes as do some other products. Efforts are under way to develop new laundry products that will replace phosphates and will not be harmful in other ways.

SEWAGE AND INDUSTRIAL WASTES

Both sewage and industrial wastes are major causes of water pollution. Efforts at improvement were initially focused only on the building of treatment plants for waste water. Industries often shared in the cost of building these plants and were heavy users. However, many people now believe that a more efficient way to reduce some industrial pollution would be through recycling and product recovery. This is now widely used in the industrial Ruhr of West Germany. In the United States some large chemical companies

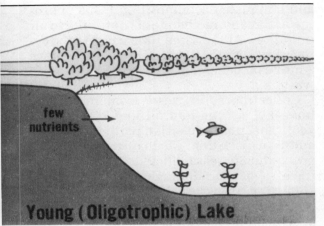

Young (Oligotrophic) Lake

few nutrients

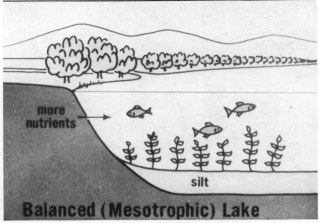

Balanced (Mesotrophic) Lake

more nutrients

silt

Photos on this page: The Soap and Detergent Assoc.
Fish cannot live in bodies of water that contain too many nutrients.

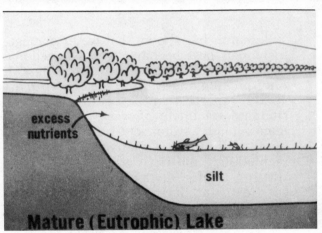

Mature (Eutrophic) Lake

excess nutrients

silt

have undertaken programs of recycling. *Business Week* reports the following: "In brief, because its effluents [wastes] are often valuable, the chemical industry is in a better position to offset environmental costs than, say, the smelting or electric utility industries, where typical pollution is relatively useless particulate matter or oxides of nitrogen and sulfur."

CONSERVING WATER

For a long time the United States was under no pressure to use water carefully. The supply seemed ample. However, it is now clear that the pressures of population and technology which require water for various processes have placed a strain on water supplies. Therefore we need to think about conserving water. In Europe, where supplies have never been as large as here, many kinds of household equipment, such as washing machines, use much less water.

Some Swedish washing machines are designed to use only five gallons per load. Also, waste products are washed away with much less water. Probably we need to reconsider the use of many appliances. For example, a food disposal uses both power and water in its operation and then discharges semi-solid material into the disposal system. Industrial processes also need to be improved.

Collecting trash is increasingly costly for communities.

Research has shown that water management can best be handled on a regional basis. Allen V. Kneese in *Protecting Our Environment and Natural Resources in the 1970's* reports that "in addition to the standard treatment of waste waters, such management systems could include a number of other alternatives . . . riverflow regulation, putting air directly into streams, brief periods of high level chemical treatment during adverse conditions, and others."

A GROWING MOUND OF HOUSEHOLD TRASH

About six to seven percent of our solid waste comes from homes, schools, office buildings, stores, hospitals, towns, and cities. Another three percent is from industry, and the rest—about ninety percent—is from agriculture and mining.

The disposal of solid waste from households is a growing problem. Cities are running out of space to dump trash and for landfill operations. (In a landfill operation dirt is placed over garbage to reduce odor and stimulate decomposition.) Open burning and many incinerators contribute to air pollution. At the same time we are producing more trash each year. The average American generates five pounds of solid waste a day.

Collecting solid waste from individual households runs into billions of dollars a year. The most expensive part is collection and transportation. Mechanization can cut costs and increase efficiency. Compacting trash saves by reducing the volume. Large collection trucks that pick up trash mechanically and compact it cut costs. Some apartment houses and office buildings now compact their trash. Some households have home compacters. An installation in Florida uses a pneumatic tube system to move refuse to a central collection terminal. This is being considered for large apartment and commercial buildings. Disposal costs can also be cut by having several small communities share disposal plants and facilities.

Recycling Trash

Different ways have been tried to use the millions of tons of refuse in constructive ways. Reuse could cut disposal costs and save natural resources which are rapidly being depleted. Some cities use powerful magnets to separate metals which can be reused from other solid wastes. Structural aluminum is now made from recycled cans. Cattle feed is produced from cannery wastes. An electric company in St. Louis uses solid waste as fuel to generate electricity. Solid waste—layers of it covered with layers of dirt—has been used to build Mt. Trashmore, a large hill for recreational activities. Experiments are going on to see if refuse can be reduced to basic chemicals which have commercial value.

Here you see an aerial view of Mt. Trashmore, a large hill built for recreational activities from layers of compacted garbage and dirt.

Mt. Trashmore has turned garbage into a place for fun.

FRUGALITY IS LAW

Norman Webster in the *New York Times* reports the following:

"Should a Chinese inventor come up with the throwaway bottle, it is unlikely the Orient would beat a path to his door. . . .

"This is a frugal society. . . . Old equipment here is repaired and used to set up new small-scale factories. Industrial wastes are reclaimed and made into something else. Clothes are patched and re-patched. Paper, boxes, and cans are saved.

"Chinese society has traditionally been thrifty and short of consumer goods."

Much trash can be returned to useful purposes, such as crushed glass from used bottles for paving materials. However, this will require new facilities and equipment as well as further technological development in some areas.

Reducing the amount of waste is another avenue. To reduce litter, Vermont has imposed a tax that makes it more expensive to sell soda in throw-a-way containers than in those that are reusable. People can learn to litter less, as is noticeable in parts of Europe.

Innovations in the production of materials and packaging could reduce the amount of waste material. For example, although it is not yet widely used, there is a new plastic material that is biodegradable; that is, it will decompose into simpler elements with weathering.

ENERGY

Prosperity and the efficiency of modern industry and technology have made it possible for 98 percent of American homes to have at least one television set. Now that window air conditioners sell for modest sums, almost half the homes in the country own at least one. In addition, many households have a wide range of other equipment—clothing washers and dryers, dishwashers, vacuum cleaners, toasters, electric frying pans, automatic coffee-makers, electric toothbrushes, and others. The result has been that each person uses much more electricity than 10 years ago.

One-third of the nation's electrical energy is consumed by residential and commercial users, schools, and government facilities. The balance, about two-thirds, is used by industry.

The Energy Crisis

(Condensed from a U. S. Department of the Interior publication)

In simple terms, an energy crisis is the insufficiency of energy sources, such as oil, natural gas, and coal, to provide power for America's homes, offices, factories, and schools. It is also the insufficiency of fuel for heating and for the more than 112 million motor vehicles on the road.

Of all the environmental problems we face, the energy problem—how to provide enough power to keep America running without further polluting it—is perhaps the greatest. Certainly, it is the most complicated. How the energy problem is resolved will affect each of us—how we live, work, travel, and play.

Projections are that by 1985, our annual requirement for energy will nearly double the 1971 rate of consumption. By the year 2000, it may triple.

Massive additional amounts of energy will be needed just to clean up the environment. Sewage treatment plants, recycling machinery, and air scrubbers on industrial smoke stacks all run on electricity. In order to produce no-lead gasolines, refineries will require 15 to 20 percent more oil.

Meanwhile, we are faced with a shortage of all kinds of energy. Oil provides 43 percent of our total energy, but except for Alaska, reserves in the United States are declining. Natural gas, which provides 33 percent of our energy needs, is in short supply. A number of cities are unable to take on new gas customers. Coal has supplied 18 percent of our energy needs, but this figure is shrinking because the burning of coal does not meet environmental standards. Hydroelectric power, the harnessing of rivers to create energy, supplies about four percent of our total needs, but few accessible undeveloped sites remain. Nuclear energy provides less than one percent of our energy.

How did we get into this predicament? One reason is the tremendous increase in our energy demands. Americans comprise only six percent of the world's population, but we consume one-third of the world's total energy production. Another reason is that the United States has done little exploration for new fossil fuels (coal, oil, and gas) until recently. Finally, rising energy demands collided several years ago with the new public concern for the environment. These concerns about the possible environmental consequences of energy development have, to a great extent, delayed efforts to expand the energy supply.

Providing for the Future

Government efforts to develop new energy sources are needed. There are a number of possibilities which could be explored—breeder reactors, gasification of coal, fusion research, and others. Also, the federal government needs to develop careful guidelines for environmental protection that could aid state utility commissions in planning and approving new facilities. Such guidelines could be used as a basis for settling controversies between environmental interests and those of the developers of power sources.

Industry is clearly going to be expected to play a big part in some immediate problems such as reducing air pollution through the installation of flue scrubbers. Also, they need to develop more practical ways of removing sulfur oxides from stack gases.

Also, the power industry needs to work on planning a nationwide, computer-controlled, power grid that will make it possible to transmit high voltages over longer distances. This would make it possible to reduce the chance of a blackout (loss of all power) anywhere. Also, it would aid environmental conditions by enabling local power plants to shut down when air pollution reaches dangerous levels.

Individuals can help by cutting their use of fuel and power wherever possible. Some suggestions that have been made for energy conservation are:

• Reduce your use of the automobile whenever possible. About half of America's oil consumption is for the production of gasoline.

• Use heating and cooling appliances with care. These appliances are the big energy users. Operate your home heating efficiently. Use air conditioning only when you really need it.

• Add weatherstripping and storm windows to reduce heat losses.

• Try not to wash small loads of clothing.

• Use the kitchen range carefully. Cook an entire meal in the oven or on the top burners.

• Evaluate your use of small appliances. Some are necessities—an electric can opener to a person with arthritic hands. Some can save energy—a small broiler for two hamburgers instead of the large broiler in the oven, or an electric coffeepot. Eliminate ones that only add a small amount of convenience and consume valuable energy.

When selecting new appliances, consider how much energy they use. Select those that are most efficient for your needs.

• Try to use electricity during off-hours—the early morning, late evenings, and weekends—to relieve pressure during peak times.

A voluntary labeling program for energy-consuming appliances has been introduced. The purpose is to provide information on the energy consumption and efficiency of appliances at the point of sale. Page 374 shows the energy guide label for an air conditioner.

EER (Efficiency Energy Ratio) is a single number that is the result of dividing Btu's used per hour by the watts needed to run the unit. The higher the EER number, the more cooling capacity the air conditioner has for each unit of power used. A unit with an EER rating of 9.3 would use less electricity to get a room cool than one rated 5.5.

AIR

In recent years pressures have grown to clean up polluted air in the United States. Simmering in the minds of many people is how this can be done most effectively.

It is not completely clear whether the chemicals that modern man now spews into the air can cause disease. However, there is little question that air pollution aggravates the condition of people with existing diseases of the lungs and heart, such as emphysema, bronchial conditions, and arteriosclerosis. Also, air pollution irritates the eyes and throats of people who are otherwise healthy. Controversy exists over whether the carbon monoxide from automobile exhaust or sulphur dioxide from the burning of coal and oil are the biggest causes of dangerous pollution.

Concern with the quality of the air is not new in the history of man. The physicians of ancient Greece were concerned with what the winds blew over their patients. In 1661 John Evelyn wrote about the effects of soft coal and peat on the London air. In this

---

ASDF Corp.   Model 5508A10

8,000 Btu per hour
(cooling capacity)

860 watts

115 volts   7.5 amperes

Data on this label
for this unit certified by

energy guide

EER=9.3
Energy Efficiency Ratio expressed in Btu per watt-hour

For available 7,500 to 8,500 Btu per hour 115 volt
window models the EER range is

EER 5.4 to EER 9.9

For information on cost of operation and selection of correct cooling capacity, ask your dealer for NBS Publication LC 1053 or write to National Bureau of Standards, 411.00, Washington, D.C. 20234

IMPORTANT...

for units with the same cooling capacity, higher EER means:
Lower energy consumption
Lower cost to use!

Tested in accordance with

U.S. DEPARTMENT OF COMMERCE ENERGY CONSERVATION LABELING PROGRAM

EER for this imaginary model is 9.3 (largest figure). This model has cooling capacity of 8,000 Btu's per hour (upper left). Since room air conditioners are classified by their Btu range, this model can be compared with other 115-volt models that offer 7,500 to 8,500 Btu's per hour (2 lines below EER). EERs for all 115-volt models in this class range from 5.4 to 9.9 (figures in box); thus, this model has high efficiency rating. The range for each class of air conditioner is different.

Sample of energy efficiency tag on air conditioner.

century three disasters have been identified with air pollution. During one of these, an air inversion held heavy smog over the affected area, and the death rate went up noticeably. Most of the victims had pre-existing heart and lung diseases which were aggravated by chemicals in the air.

Air pollutants are heavily concentrated in areas where there are many people and cars. As New York City's Environmental Protection Administration stated, "Each year approximately 1,000 pounds of pollutants are dumped into New York City's air for each man, woman, and child living here." Of the 2.5 million tons of carbon monoxide released annually 98 percent comes from automobiles.

Emission control devices have been required on new automobiles since 1968 to reduce air pollution. Other types of auto-

mobile engines, such as the gas turbine, electric, and steam engines, have also been suggested for use as a way of reducing pollution. Some critics of the automobile engine are convinced that Detroit needs a new type of engine to really reduce air pollution. Most of the auto industry claim that they do not have anything well enough developed with which to replace the present type of engine. The only major change in engines has been the rotary engine, which is supposed to pollute less.

In addition, the fuel and automotive industries have been testing unleaded gasolines and other fuel changes.

Airlines are also under pressure to reduce pollution. Anyone who has watched a big plane take off and climb into the sky will remember that it probably disgorged a smoky trail behind it. On newer planes

What will clean air cost?

375

Mercury Marine
Some activities that are fun are also noisy.

engine modifications allow for smoke-emission controls, and older aircraft are being retired early.

NOISE

Clang, bang, rattle, and roar—the noise level is getting louder, particularly in urban areas. A growing wave of noise is encroaching on our environment and possibly threatening our health, but so far very little has been done about it.

Urban noise levels are increasing rapidly. Factory machines drown out communications between workers. School lessons, church sermons, and even debates in Congress are hard to hear in the roar of jets landing and taking off. Construction crews

drill and bang to build and rebuild. Apartment dwellers can often listen to the arguments and TV sets of their neighbors. The quiet of the rural open spaces is broken by the roar of boats, trucks, trail bikes, and snowmobiles.

The biggest noise producers are motor vehicles, contributing 75 percent of the noise in large cities. Buses and trucks are noisier than cars. The bigger the truck, the noisier it is. Garbage trucks, particularly those that compact trash, are noisiest of all.

Building and construction are next. Air compressors and jackhammers make a terrific racket as housing is built, offices erected, highways and streets paved, or telephones and sewers repaired.

Inside the house we generate noise too with an orchestra of unmuffled appliances. The dishwasher, the blender, the window air conditioner, and the TV set all contribute to the noise level. How many noisy appliances do you have on at one time?

This annoying din of sounds is not necessary. Automobile engines have been muffled for years, particularly in big cars, because customers wanted an engine that purred instead of roared. Heavy trucks and small cars could have quieter performance built in. Recently, citizen pressure got New York City to buy garbage trucks that didn't wake people up at dawn.

With the clatter growing louder, we need to work actively to reduce the noise level. Local ordinances or building codes could require sound deadening materials in new construction, as has been done in parts of Europe for some years. The noise level needs to be reduced in many factories. In part, this is good economics because a quieter work atmosphere often results in less absenteeism and fewer accidents. Some corporations provide the manufacturers who use their products with help in noise control. Consumers can demand products that are quieter. One manufacturer found that his super quiet vacuum was rejected by consumers because they didn't believe that anything so quiet could also clean.

Hints for a Quiet Home

(From a U. S. Environmental Protection Agency Publication)

• Use noise-absorbing materials on floors, especially in areas where there is a lot of traffic.

• Hang heavy drapes over the windows closest to outside noise sources.

• Put rubber or plastic treads on uncarpeted stairs. (They're safer, too.)

• Use upholstered rather than hard-surfaced furniture to deaden noise.

• Install sound-absorbing ceiling tile in the kitchen. Wooden cabinets will vibrate less than metal ones.

• Use a foam pad under blenders and mixers.

• Use insulation and vibration mounts when installing dishwashers.

• Install washing machines in the same room with heating and cooling equipment, preferably in an enclosed space.

• Remember that a hand-powered lawnmower does the job and gives you exercise too. If you use a power mower, operate it at reasonable hours so you don't disturb others.

• Use a headset when you are the only one interested in listening to the stereo. Also, keep the volume down.

• Place window air conditioners where their hum can help mask objectionable noises. However, try to avoid locating them facing your neighbor's bedrooms.

• Be aware that children's toys need not make intensive or explosive sounds. (Some

can cause permanent ear injury in addition to getting on your nerves.)

• Compare the noise outputs of different makes of an appliance before making your selection.

• Stay away from major noise sources such as airport flight paths, heavy truck routes, high-speed freeways. When buying a home, check the area zoning master plan for projected changes. (In some places, you can't get FHA loans for housing in noisy locations.)

• Look for wall-to-wall carpeting, especially in the apartment above you and in the corridors.

• Find out about the wall construction (staggered-stud interior walls are among the quietest.) Can you hear a portable radio at normal volume in the adjoining apartment?

• Check the electrical outlet boxes. If they are back-to-back, they will act as noise transmitters.

• Ask about the door construction. Solid or core-filled doors with gaskets or weather stripping are quieter.

• Make sure sleeping areas are well away from rooms with noise-making equipment.

• Check the heating and air conditioning ducts. Inside insulation makes them quieter.

THE ECONOMICS OF IMPROVING THE ENVIRONMENT

Individual Americans and industry have been accustomed to handling the use of resources in a way that has the least direct cost. This has long been considered the most efficient. However, we now need to reevaluate our ideas. To many people it no longer seems efficient to produce coal by large scale strip mining if this means destroying millions of acres of land. Howev-

USDA—Soil Conservation Service

*These cattle are grazing on land that was used for strip
mining of coal but which was reclaimed.*

er, it is possible to strip mine and rehabilitate the land. Disposal of a home's sewage in an individual septic tank may spoil the water supply for many other people. Dumping trash in an old gravel pit may seem cheap and economical for many communities. However, this may waste valuable materials which could be recovered and reused. In addition, the dumped trash may spoil the appearance and smell of the nearby area.

Only recently have we recognized the perils of a policy that saved immediate costs at the expense of the environment. It may be possible to make some improvements at little or no long-term cost. The chemical industry might be able to recover enough from its waste products to offset the cost of salvage, as one chemical compa-

ny now suggests. Recycling materials and using garbage for fuel might offset some of the cost of mechanizing and setting up recovery plants. However, many other changes that are needed do not seem to offer this possibility. Barry Commoner reports in *The Closing Circle* that . . .

"nitrogen fertilizer provides an . . . informative example of the link between pollution and profits. On a typical United States Corn Belt farm, a yield that is more than from 25 to 30 bushels per acre below present averages may mean no profit for the farmer. . . . Present corn yields depend on a high rate of nitrogen application. Under these conditions, the uptake of nitrogen by the crop is approaching saturation, so that an appreciable fraction of the fertilizer drains from the land and pollutes surface waters. In other words, under present conditions, it appears that the farmer *must* use sufficient fertilizer to pollute the water if he is to make a profit."

Unpopular as it may be, each of us will have to pay for a cleaner environment, either in higher prices, higher taxes, or both. The auto industry estimated that emission control devices to meet federal standards added about $350 to the cost of a new car and also cut gasoline mileage by 10 to 15 percent. The latter becomes particularly important when gas supplies are costly. Controversy arises over which gets priority—emission controls or conserving gas.

UNRESOLVED ISSUES

Some environmental issues cause little controversy—the need to conserve resources that are becoming scarce and also the need to improve the disposal of trash. Other aspects of improving the environment are more controversial. For example, which resources would be given priority. Should we recycle more paper to conserve the dwindling forests from which paper is made? Unfortunately, the present processes used to recycle paper require a great deal of water, which is also becoming scarce. As the oil shortage in 1973-74 showed, strict standards for the burning of high grade oil, which pollutes less, tend to be relaxed if there is not enough heating oil to keep people warm in the winter. There are many other situations in which decisions about improving the environment are not easily made.

Hopefully, new technological developments will help us solve some of these problems. Perhaps a new type of automobile engine will be developed that uses fuel from energy sources that are not in scarce supply and will burn without emitting unpleasant pollutants. New processes for the development of industrial products might also help eliminate some present problems. However, until this happens we will need to weigh our priorities and consider what is most important to the majority of people.

THE NEED FOR COOPERATIVE EFFORTS

More effective management of our resources will require both the push of legislation and the cooperative efforts of many groups. As was mentioned earlier, water management is best handled on a regional basis. It may be more economical to handle other things that way too. One of the more imaginative solutions to the problem of solid waste was a joint effort of two communities. Mt. Trashmore was built by Virginia Beach and the city of Norfolk.

This need for cooperation does not end with national boundaries. Mexico is very concerned with how the United States uses the waters of the Colorado River since it flows south from the U. S. to Mexico. The addition of too much salt to the river's waters in the United States can ruin crops in Mexico.

In the fall of 1972 a big step forward was taken when the Stockholm Conference established an International Earthwatch Program to monitor and evaluate environmental trends in the atmosphere, oceans, land, and human health.

FOR REVIEW

Points to Remember

- There is widespread concern about the pollution of our environment.
- There are two major aspects to the concern about population: (1) the rapid increase in the population of the world and (2) the growing trend for most people in industrialized nations to live in urban areas.
- Much of the world lacks a safe and adequate supply of water. Also, water reserves are being depleted. Many nations are using up water faster than it is replaced. Pollution is ruining some supplies of water.
- The disposal of solid waste is a growing problem.
- The United States uses a tremendous amount of the world's energy. Supplies of existing sources of some fossil fuels are decreasing. How the energy problem is resolved will affect each of us—how we live, work, travel, and play.
- The noise level is getting louder, particularly in urban areas.
- It may be possible to make some changes that will clean up the environment

at little or no long-term cost. However, many needed changes will mean spending money, either as higher costs for goods and services or through taxes.

Terms to Know

algae	landfill
effluents	pollution
energy	recycling
eutrophic	smog
fossil fuels	

PROBLEM SOLVING: CHECK YOUR UNDERSTANDING

1. Assume that you live in a town with one major factory where most residents work. At present this factory discharges wastes into the river which runs through town. The town wants the factory to stop polluting the stream. The factory management says that it will cost them so much to reprocess their wastes that they will have to close down. What can and should be done?

2. Your community is running out of space for landfill operations. What might be done to reduce the amount of waste that needs to be buried?

3. How can you cut the use of energy in your own home?

4. Why would some environmental problems be reduced if people were not concentrated together in cities?

5. What can each individual do to reduce the amount of litter?

6. Assume that you are starting out on your first job and will be living away from home. What environmental conditions would be important in choosing a place to live?

TO DO IN CLASS

Discussion

1. What are some of the advantages and disadvantages of the location of your community? Was the community originally founded for some particular reason, such as the water supply, a junction of two roads, as a gateway for recreational activities, or others?

2. How might a long-range plan influence the development of your community?

3. How do you use electrical energy in your day-to-day life? List the household appliances that you think are essential to your family.

4. What are some of the ways in which noise could be cut in your home and in the community?

5. Should an area of spectacular beauty be destroyed for recreational or commercial purposes? Should scenic areas have dams or power stations built on them? Should highways be permitted through national parks? Should ski resorts be built in national forests?

6. What is meant by air pollution? What does it do to living things? Where is it most common? What can be done to relieve the problem?

Activities

1. Where does your community get its water? Have a committee from the class report on the following: (a) How much water does your town use on an average day in the summer and in the winter; (b) Are there any problems with the water supply; (c) Is the water of a satisfactory quality; (d) Is a shortage of water expected in the future?

2. Another group can investigate the town's source of electrical energy. How is

it produced? How much is consumed on an average day? The members of this group could keep a record of the times that each one used electricity for one day and for what purposes.

3. Find out the cost of garbage collection in the community. Is it private or public? Are people satisfied? A committee might visit the disposal area and see how it is handled. Can the community continue to handle garbage in this manner?

4. Take a walk around the school neighborhood. Look for smoke coming from chimneys, open burning, and other evidence of air pollution.

5. Place a clean piece of paper on a windowsill in the classroom. See how quickly it gets dirty. How do you think dirty air affects your life?

6. Have several class members keep a log of gasoline use in their families for one week. Combine these logs and report to the class on how much gasoline was used and for what purposes.

CHAPTER 17

You and the Economy

Our lives are greatly affected by the economic conditions under which we live. Are you free to decide what type of work you will do? Are jobs plentiful? Are the prices of goods and services rising faster than your income? These are controlled or influenced by the economy.

YOUR ROLE IN THE ECONOMY

We each have three important roles in the economic system. As *workers* we earn money for ourselves and our families. Thus, we are interested in such things as educational opportunities, attractive jobs near where we want to live, and wages, salaries, or commissions that are adequate to support us comfortably.

As *consumers* we buy the goods and services we need and want. In this role we are concerned with having a broad range of goods and services available to us. We want prices and terms we can afford to pay. Also, we have a stake in the services provided by government, such as education, recreation, and water.

As *citizens* we support government activities that serve us with our taxes. Also, we elect representatives who decide upon laws and important economic policies. These laws, regulations, and policies affect many aspects of our lives.

TYPES OF ECONOMIC SYSTEMS

In a *traditional or agrarian economy* you would probably have a limited choice of jobs. One hundred and fifty years ago most people in the United States worked at farming because raising food was the main occupation. Today we are industrialized and a wide range of choices exist. In some parts of the world tradition or religious custom still govern what type of job you can get. Religion plays an important part in India. In many of the developing nations tradition is important.

In a *directed or controlled economy* the basic economic decisions are made by a central authority who decides what will be produced, how much, and by whom. The Soviet Union and China are examples of a directed or controlled economy. Central government groups plan production and assign people to work at jobs that are needed.

In a *market economy or capitalistic society* production is controlled by what people are willing to buy. No government or agency determines what is to be produced. Producers provide the goods and services which they believe consumers want and on which the producers can make a profit. The business person, the consumer, and the worker all have a choice. A manufacturer can choose not to make a product because it won't yield a profit. Individuals can choose not to buy some products. Workers are free to choose their line of work.

Today there probably are few pure economic systems. Although a society may be labeled as capitalistic, agrarian, or controlled according to its main characteristics, most countries have mixed economies. Over a period of time economic systems tend to add modifications from other types of economies. Although labeled as capitalistic, the United States, for example, has many social, insurance, and welfare programs once thought of as belonging to other types of economic systems.

THE U. S. ECONOMY

A market economy, such as the United States has, is sometimes referred to as *self-regulated* or *self-controlled*. Competition among producers tends to keep prices for similar things in proportion to each other. Suppose you are in the market for a TV set. A number of companies produce TV sets. When you are shopping around, you will probably find that all the small black and white sets are in a certain price range and the large color ones are in a higher price range.

However, government does regulate some aspects of the economy. Some of this is direct regulation. For example, the government is concerned about the radiation hazard from television tubes, so minimum standards have been set for this. Also, the government wants to maintain competition between producers; thus, there are regulations about trade practices too.

Many people believe that the government should take a more active part in regulating additional things such as what is shown on the television screen. In some other countries the government runs the broadcasting stations, and some people feel that the programs are better.

On the other hand many people feel that the government is regulating too many things. The great increase in government regulations has increased the cost of many products, and saddled both individuals and businesses with extra paperwork.

Business Cycles

Using the television set as an example, let's consider how business conditions and government policies might affect your ability to buy a new set.

A *business cycle* is a series of alternating periods of business expansion and contraction. In a period of prosperity things are booming. There are plenty of jobs, and people have money to spend. Conversely, during a *depression* many people are unemployed and have little money to spend. A *recession* is the downswing before a depression or a mild depression. *Inflation*

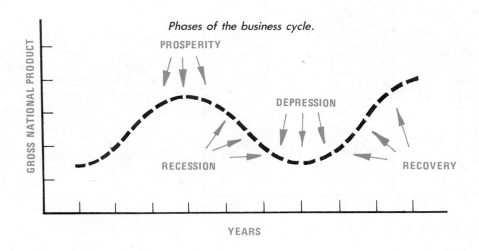

Phases of the business cycle.

is when most prices are rising and money is worth less.

Suppose it is a recession period and you are unemployed. You probably won't feel that you should spend money on a new TV set. It may be a while before you get another job, and you might need whatever money you have for more important things. However, if you have a good job and the times are prosperous, you are much more likely to buy that new TV set. In fact, you might even feel like splurging and getting a higher priced set than you had originally planned to buy.

The history of the United States shows recurring cycles of prosperity alternating with recession. Over the years tools have been developed to measure these changes.

Economists talk about such things as the *national income,* the total amount received by all people who in some way contributed to the production of goods and services. The incomes of the owner or manager of a company, the workers, the landlord, and bank are all included.

Another widely used measure is the *gross national product* (GNP). This is the market value of all the goods and services produced in the U. S. during a year—consumer expenditures plus business investments, government expenditures, and net foreign exports. By comparing the GNP or national income with an earlier period, economists try to predict whether or not the economy is growing and prosperity is likely to prevail.

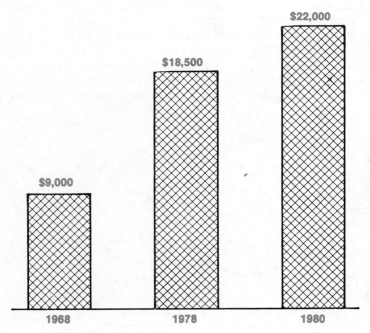

Inflation (higher prices) reduces purchasing power. This chart shows that inflation reduced purchasing power between 1968 and 1980. In 1980, it took $22,000 to buy what $9,000 would have purchased in 1968.

Income Needed to Equal 1968 Purchasing Power.

Fiscal or Economic Policy

Although there is a good deal of disagreement on all the causes of business cycles, we do know that the government's fiscal policies have an important influence on these cycles.

MONEY AND CREDIT

The availability of money and credit influences business conditions. If the government follows a policy of making large amounts of credit available, credit rates tend to drop. Individuals and businesses can borrow more easily and cheaply. As a result, businesses find it easier to expand, and more jobs are created. Also, people can get lower rate mortgages, and more houses will be started. In addition, that TV set you were hoping to buy may be available at a lower price if the merchant pays a lower credit cost for carrying inventory. You will probably get better credit terms if you want to finance it.

GOVERNMENT SPENDING

The government is both a big consumer and a big employer. If government operations expand, more money is pumped into the economy. More people may be employed, or more money spent on social security, welfare, and other benefits. In reverse, if the government closes down installations or reduces the size of some of its agencies, people will be out of work and, thus, will have less money to spend. Another possibility is that the government may reduce cash benefits for health, welfare, or other programs.

THE FEDERAL BUDGET

Another influence on the economy is whether or not the federal budget is balanced; that is, spending equals income. Like individuals, governments can spend more than they receive in a particular year through the use of credit. Government credit is obtained by selling U. S. bonds or Treasury notes. Have you ever bought a U. S. savings bond? This is one way the federal government borrows money. In recessionary periods the government often tries to stimulate business activity by spending more than it receives. During inflationary periods governments may try to have a budget surplus (more income than is spent) to reduce total spending and to slow down business activity and price rises.

CHANGES IN TAXES

By reducing or increasing taxes the government also exerts an important influence on the economy. Higher taxes mean that people and businesses will have less to spend. New jobs will be created more slowly, if at all, and consumers will have to cut down on their spending. By decreasing taxes people and businesses have more money to spend, thus creating a demand for more goods and services. Sometimes there is a question about whether to cut the taxes on businesses or the taxes that consumers pay in order to stimulate the economy. The big argument in favor of cutting taxes on businesses is that then businesses will have more money to put into expanding, thus creating more jobs. The main argument for cutting consumer taxes is that people will have more money to spend and will create a greater demand for goods and services.

Since the devastating depression of the 1930's, people in the United States have come to rely on government policy to offset the extremes of the business cycle. The government, in turn, may employ one or more of the tools available to it. For example, to cut down an inflationary spiral, the government may raise taxes and tighten credit. To stimulate the economy, a greater budget deficit may be maintained.

INTERNATIONAL TRADE

The United States buys many raw materials and finished goods from other countries. In turn, we sell many of our products abroad. About five percent of all U. S. trade is in international commerce. For example, we export wheat but import some of the rice used in this country. We export many highly technical machines but import considerable clothing from places where the labor costs are less. There are many other examples.

If we sell more abroad than we import, other countries end up owing us money. This is called a positive *balance of trade.* If we buy more than we sell, we end up owing other countries money. This is a negative balance of trade. Although international trade and exchange is a highly complex business, basically, it boils down to the fact that if we don't sell as much as we buy, we must pay other countries the difference, usually in dollars or gold. If they buy more than they sell us, they must pay us the difference.

The federal government tries to offset the extremes of the business cycle.

No country likes to have a large outflow of its currency. It tends to weaken the value of the currency. It's much like a person who overbuys; others may lose faith in his or her ability to pay. Therefore most countries try to keep their balance of payments about equal.

There are a number of ways to do this. Let's suppose that we have sold more to Canada than we have bought. We can even up the difference in several ways. First, the U. S. could buy more from Canada. Another way would be to encourage Americans to visit Canada more and spend American money there. The U. S. could also sell less to Canada. Lastly, the United States could *devalue* its dollar so that it would be cheaper for Canada to buy American goods. At the same time, it would become more expensive for the U. S. to buy from Canada, and we would probably buy less. Governments use all of these methods from time to time, depending on the situation.

Suppose the situation were reversed, and we owed Canada money. We might try to buy less and sell them more. The government might discourage people from spending money in Canada by limiting the amount of money one could take out of the country, by import quotas on businesses, or by imposing a stiff *tariff* (a tax paid when goods are brought into the country).

A tariff may be used for other reasons as well. If workers in less developed countries have much lower wages, it may be cheaper for Hong Kong, Taiwan, or other countries to manufacture clothing than it is for the United States. Under a totally free market economy people will tend to buy the same product where it is cheapest, and the U. S. clothing industry could be forced out of business or badly hurt. To prevent this, government may protect domestic industry and impose a high tariff, thus bringing the cost of imported items closer to the price of those produced ·in the United States.

This is an oversimplified explanation of international trade relations. In the United States buying and selling with other countries is carried on largely by individual companies. Often it is difficult for the government to plan long in advance for the various buying and selling activities of so many diverse groups. World conditions change. One year it may be cheaper to buy foreign oil from the Middle East. A large find elsewhere in the world may make another source cheaper. Perhaps the development of new sources of energy will mean that these are cheaper and more efficient. Labor conditions, the rate of exchange, shipping costs, taxes, the development of substitute or improved products, the cordiality of relationships between countries, changing consumer tastes, and many other factors all play an important part in international trade.

Consumer Attitudes

Consumer optimism and pessimism are important influences on the economy. If a large proportion of the nation is optimistic about their personal economic futures, the demand for goods and services will be high. Business activity will be better than if many people feel pessimistic about their future earnings. If your Dad expects to get a good raise and his job is secure, he is much more likely to buy a new car or TV set than if he thinks he might lose his job. How people feel about their personal economic futures can affect the national economy. By taking surveys of *consumer purchasing expectations,* forecasts are made of what the demand for products will be. Perhaps you

have seen a report in the newspaper on a recent survey of consumer buying intentions.

Taxes

Federal, state, and local governments provide services for the common welfare of individuals and businesses. The cost of these services is paid for with taxes.

Excluding social security taxes, most of the federal government's money comes from individual and corporate income taxes, with the bigger part from individuals. (You read about social security taxes in an earlier chapter.) State governments get their income primarily from sales and income taxes. Local communities rely largely on property taxes.

Over the years government services at all levels have increased tremendously. As a result, taxes at all levels have grown too. Today, property taxes, sales (or excise) taxes, income taxes, and social security taxes are the most widely used types of taxes in the United States.

PROPERTY TAXES

These are levied on real property, such as a house and land, or personal property, such as a car, household furnishings, and other goods. Basically, a property tax can be imposed on any individually owned property that can be bought and sold.

A property tax is the total amount imposed by the units of government. For instance, homeowner Joan Peterson gets a single property tax bill from her local township. However, this bill combines the state, city, county, and school district taxes on her house.

The property tax is based on value. For real estate local assessors make an estimate of value, which is the basis for the tax.

Property taxes are levied on personal property such as homes.

Often the *assessed value* is a percentage of the probable sale price.

INCOME TAXES

Most working people must pay a federal income tax. Generally, this is deducted from your wages by the employer before you get paid. However, in some situations deductions are not made or are insufficient and you must pay additional tax when you file your income tax return. Self-employed people pay their tax directly to the Internal Revenue Service, usually on a quarterly basis.

Who must file a return? If you earn more than certain minimum amounts, you *must* file an income tax return even if you don't owe any tax. The minimum amounts are different for dependent children, single adults, married people with dependents, self-employed people, and adults over age 65. Moreover, these amounts are changed from time to time as the tax structure is modified. If you have a question about whether you must file, check with the nearest Internal Revenue Service office. A telephone call will do.

If you have had federal income tax withheld but have not earned enough to have to pay any income tax, you must file an income tax return to get your refund.

At the end of each year an employer must send each employee two copies of a *W-2* form, stating how much you earned during the year. One copy must be filed with your income tax return; the other is for your file. Another copy must be sent by your employer to the Internal Revenue Service. Even if you only worked for the summer, you should receive W-2 forms. If for any reason you do not, ask your employer for them.

The Internal Revenue Service has Form 1040 for filing individual income tax returns. Many people can use the simpler short form. However, in a year of heavy medical expenses or other substantial deductible expenses you may be able to reduce your tax by completing the longer form.

With a little patience most people can fill out the short form themselves. The government publishes a guide, which is revised annually, to help you fill this out. if

Sales taxes are levied on purchases.

you have any questions, you can call or visit the local IRS office for help.

State and local income taxes are usually a percentage of your federal income tax. However, be sure to get instructions for filling out state and local tax forms. There may be some additional deductions to which you are entitled or other differences. Also, some state income taxes are not a percentage of the federal income tax.

SALES OR EXCISE TAXES

This is a tax on purchases. It may be levied at several levels, on retail sales, on wholesale sales, on raw commodities sold, gross sales, or gross profits.

A sales tax may be *general* or *selective*. Many states have a tax on all purchases. This is a general sales tax. Taxes on individual items—cigarettes, liquor, gasoline, and your telephone bill—are selective sales taxes.

BUSINESS TAXES

Business is taxed as well as individuals. In addition to federal and/or local income taxes businesses may be required to pay fees or taxes to the government (local,

state, or federal) for licenses, permits, franchises, the use of natural resources, or other aspects of their operations. Trucking companies pay taxes to maintain the roads. Medical groups pay for licenses. Companies may need permits to connect water. Many states levy payroll and sales taxes. These are just a few examples.

GIFT AND ESTATE TAXES

A gift tax may be levied when one person gives another something of substantial value. This is a way of ensuring that people do not give away a large part of their estate before death without paying any taxes.

Inheritance or death taxes are levied by both the federal government and states. The federal government relies largely on the estate tax, which is calculated on the entire net estate before it passes to the heirs. States generally use an inheritance tax or share tax. This means that the tax may be taken out of each share if a will so states. Some states tax the portion of an estate that goes to a distant relative more heavily than that to a spouse or children or tax only the portion remaining after specific bequests have been distributed.

OTHER TAXES

There are many other special taxes levied by the levels of government. There is a tax on legal papers in the form of a stamp to be purchased and affixed to certain documents such as a real estate deed. States charge licensing fees for automobiles, hunting, and fishing. You may need a special permit for your dog. There are many others.

WHAT IS FAIR?

One of the factors leading to the American Revolution was a tax on tea imposed by the King of England on the American Colonies. "No taxation without representation" was the cry of the founders of this country. Today in the United States taxes can only be imposed by legislation. Each person through his or her elected representatives has some voice in the imposition of taxes, at least in theory.

How shall taxes be levied? There are two general approaches, levying taxes on people according to their ability to pay and levying taxes on the buyers of goods and services.

Income taxes are based on one's ability to pay. They are assessed at a progressively higher rate as income increases for the most part.

With a sales tax those people who spend more pay more. The chief argument against a general sales tax is that people with low incomes pay a disproportionately large amount.

States traditionally have relied heavily on sales taxes for revenue. Many attempt to meet the problem of the burden on people with low incomes by the use of a selective sales tax, often excluding such items as food or clothing. However, many states now also have an income tax.

Labor and the Economy

Labor is essential to the operation of a market economy. Without people to produce, deliver, and sell goods and services our economic system would not function.

In an economic sense the term *labor* is very broad. It means all forms of human effort, both physical and mental, that either provide a service or add value to goods or services. Thus, labor includes services performed by engineers as well as factory workers, truck drivers, bookkeepers, government employees, and many others. It also includes services that are not related to production, such as those of doctors, dentists, teachers, lawyers, and others.

More commonly, the term refers to workers who are employed by others. Originally, this narrower definition of labor included only people who did factory work. However, it has gradually been broadened to include people who work in a wide variety of occupations. Today office workers, teachers, and others are considered part of the labor force.

In general, workers do not own or control the businesses in which they work nor the goods they produce. However, some workers do have a share in the business they work for, either directly or indirectly. Many workers own stock in the company where they are employed. Some unions also own stock.

LABOR UNIONS

More than 300 years ago some journeymen in Europe formed guilds to bargain with their masters for better wages and working conditions. Early in American history (1794) the Federal Society of Journeymen Cordwainers was established in Philadelphia. However, the real growth of labor unions began with industrialization.

This sewage treatment plant is supported by both taxes and users' fees.

The development of factories and the decrease in individually owned family farms resulted in large numbers of people working for a single company. To bargain more effectively for wages and working conditions, the workers banded together and labor unions slowly developed. They have been important in improving the level of living for the working man and woman. Today more than 18 million Americans (out of about 75 million workers) carry union cards. Organized labor is a key influence on the economy. In addition, many people who are not members of a union may benefit because union wage scales tend to raise the wage level of all workers.

Although there are many different types of labor unions, there are some basic similarities:

• Labor unions are *associations of workers* whose purpose is to secure economic advantages for the members.

• Some of the *economic advantages* which unions press for are higher wages, better working conditions, job security, and fringe benefits such as pensions, disability benefits, medical care, paid vacations, and others.

• Labor unions work through *collective action* (a large number of workers acting together) for the economic advantages listed above.

First, elected labor union leaders negotiate a contract with management for large numbers of workers at one time. The contract is a binding agreement between the workers and a business firm or government employer for a specified period of time and spells out wages, working conditions, and other benefits.

On occasion other types of collective action are used. A *strike* is when the workers as a group stop working. In a *boycott* other people refuse to buy the products produced by the company or farm organization. A *slowdown* is when workers deliberately produce less than their usual amount.

SETTLING DISPUTES BETWEEN LABOR AND MANAGEMENT

Gradually, some methods of settling disputes between workers and employers have developed. A *grievance procedure* is often included in contracts between labor and management. A typical grievance procedure would include the following steps:

1. The employee complains to the *shop steward.* (The shop steward is the labor union representative for the organization.)

2. The steward talks to the *shop foreperson* (the management's supervisor) about the problem and they try to settle it.

3. Both the shop steward and the worker talk with the foreperson.

4. If the problem still isn't settled, the steward goes to the chief plant steward or a company grievance committee, depending on the organization.

5. The next step might be to go to someone in top management, such as the personnel director.

6. Next, a national union representative might negotiate with a higher company official.

7. Finally, a government mediator may try to get the two sides to agree on a settlement. Although the mediator has no legal power, the federal government can require a *cooling-off period* or delay before a strike. Often this is invoked when a mediator is unable to bring about a resolution of the problem.

THE GOVERNMENT'S ROLE

Government agencies play an important part in labor-management relations. As was mentioned above, the government may participate in the settling of disputes between workers and management.

Also, there are many laws at all levels of government concerned with employment practices. Some of the most important areas of legislation are the:

- Setting of health and safety standards for working conditions.
- Regulation of minimum wages and maximum working hours.
- Prevention of discrimination in employment based on race, nationality, or sex.

In addition, government agencies check on working conditions. While the functions may overlap, federal agencies are generally concerned with the hours of work and wage scales. State and local agencies check on the on-site conditions and the employment of women and young people.

CURRENT ISSUES

Labor unions are still concerned with their original issue, getting higher pay for their workers. The unions want the workers to get a bigger share of the income of the country.

Moreover, they are worried that *inflation* may wipe out pay raises. As you have read, inflation occurs when prices rise faster than wages increase. It does little good for a worker to get a ten percent raise if food and other needs and wants have increased more than that.

Today many union contracts have *escalator* clauses. This means that workers get automatic increases in wages when the *cost-of-living index* goes up a certain amount. This index is computed by the U. S. Department of Labor based on a sampling of prices for certain items in a number of cities around the United States.

Labor unions have sought an increasing number of *fringe benefits*—sick leave, pensions, insurance, medical and dental care, stock options, and others.

Management is concerned about the cost of paying for increases in wages and fringe benefits. Unless each worker produces more in the same length of time, management must either cut into profits to pay these additional costs or raise the price of the products. Some companies or producers have a large enough profit margin to raise wages without raising prices, but many do not. A raise in workers' wages is often accompanied by a rise in the price of the goods they produce.

To reduce inflation the government at times has tried *freezing wages and prices,* not permitting either one to be increased.

Automation, the mechanizing of an operation, is also of concern to workers who do not want to lose their jobs. The history of industrialization shows that machinery has taken over work formerly done by hand. On farm and in factory machines are now doing many operations formerly painstakingly done by individuals.

At each step of the way dislocations occurred. Families were forced off individual farms as large scale machinery made small farming operations unprofitable. The advent of automobiles meant that horses were displaced as the main means of transportation. As a result, many people, such as blacksmiths, were in less demand. As railroads reduced the services on trains, there was less demand for people to work on trains. However, at the same time, the airplane industry grew, and there was a demand for people to work on planes and provide support services for them.

Although the development of new industries creates new jobs, these are often not in the same area as they were originally. New England, once the home of the textile industry, has many old textile factories now used for other purposes or empty. The company that mechanizes may move to a new location. It may be cheaper to build a new, automated fertilizer plant at a location far from the original one than to rebuild the old factory. The cost of electricity for an automated plant is an important factor in selecting a new location.

Often the push to mechanize comes from the higher wage demands of the workers. Faced with the need to raise prices for its products, a company may decide to mechanize and keep the prices down. Perhaps they feel that at a higher price their product won't sell or will not sell as well. Labor unions are often faced with the difficult job of trying to get better wages, working conditions, and fringe benefits for their members without forcing the company to automate further and put workers out of jobs or price their products so high that they must close down or move.

Still another issue is the *organization of new groups* of workers. Only about one-fourth of all workers are union members. For a long time office workers, teachers, and social workers were not unionized. However, there is a growing trend for these and other white collar workers to belong to unions.

What should be done about the pressure from *lower priced foreign goods?* If it is cheaper to buy textiles made abroad, the domestic industries will probably sell less. Should the government protect industries with high tariffs?

Lastly, there is some question whether government employees or workers in essential services, such as firemen, teachers, or policemen, should have the right to

Gerber Products Co.
Will this young child grow up with the same opportunities that others have? In what ways should government try to equalize opportunities for all people?

strike. At present the law forbids many of these people from striking.

EQUALIZING OPPORTUNITIES: THE GOVERNMENT'S ROLE

Since its founding, the United States has often been referred to as the land of opportunity. For many people it is. However, there is a decided difference in what individuals and families earn. For the most part this difference is based on education and occupation, although race, sex, level of health, imagination, and other things may have an important influence.

Each year government programs to aid various groups are proposed. At issue is how far the government should go in trying to equalize income and opportunities for all people, and what means would be most effective. How do you make opportunities equal for everyone? Can government stimulate individual initiative or only stifle it?

Should free public education through college be available? How can health services be provided most effectively? What do you believe are the most important priorities with which the government should deal?

FOR REVIEW

Points to Remember

• Our lives are greatly affected by the economic conditions under which we live.

• We each have three important roles in the economic system, as a worker, as a consumer, and as a citizen.

• In a market economy, such as in the United States, production is controlled largely by what people are willing to buy.

• Business conditions may affect your ability to buy.

• Government policies exert an important influence on the economy.

• The balance of trade is important to the economic situation.

• Consumer attitudes about the economic situation influence whether people will buy and, in turn, economic conditions.

• Taxes are the government's chief source of income. If the government provides more services, then additional income is needed. Generally, this means raising taxes.

• Labor is essential to the operation of a market economy.

• Labor unions are associations of workers whose purpose is to secure economic advantages for the members.

• Each year a variety of government programs is proposed to aid various groups. At issue is how far the government should go in equalizing income and opportunities for all people, and what means would be most effective.

Terms to Know

agrarian economy
automation
balance of trade
boycott
business cycle
consumer expectations
controlled economy
cooling-off period
cost-of-living index
depression
escalator clause
excise tax
fiscal policy
freezing wages and prices
fringe benefits
grievance procedure
gross national product
income tax
inflation
labor
labor union
market economy
mediator
mixed economy
national income
property taxes
prosperity
recession
sales tax
shop foreman
shop steward
slowdown
stamp tax
strike
tariff

PROBLEM SOLVING: CHECK YOUR UNDERSTANDING

1. In what ways are our lives affected by economic conditions?

2. How does your role in the economy differ from that of a person in China or an undeveloped country?

3. What influence does the buying choice of many individuals have on production in the United States?

4. How might your ability to buy goods and services be affected by the business cycle?

5. What can the government do to ease the problem of a recession in the economy?

6. Why is trade with other countries important to the United States?

7. How can tourist travel affect the United States' balance of trade.

8. What are some of the arguments in favor of a sales tax as a method of producing revenue for the government? What are the arguments in favor of an income tax?

9. How do individuals pay for the cost of public schools?

10. Suppose you worked last summer and had federal income taxes withheld. What must you do to get a refund if you are eligible for one?

11. What is a labor union?

12. What are some current issues of concern to labor unions?

TO DO IN CLASS

Discussion

1. Why does full employment tend to create inflation? What measures could be used to counteract this? How would these affect the economy?

2. Should we have tariffs to protect American workers?

3. Some union contracts provide that all workers in each category be paid the same wage. However, people may differ in relation to their abilities and productivity. What do you think of this provision?

4. What are some of the services provided by government that private business probably would not supply?

5. Per capita income (income per person) varies widely from one part of the country to another. Why do you think this difference exists? How might it be changed?

6. Your community is widening the road from the middle of town to an outlying area. Part of the cost will be paid by state and federal funds. The rest is to be paid by the town, partly from general revenues and partly from an assessment (tax) on property owners along the road. Some people in town believe that all of the town's share should be paid out of general revenues; others think that all should be paid by the property owners along the road. What do you think would be fair?

7. Should a single person pay a higher income tax rate than a married person? Is this fair? Why or why not?

8. What are some of the imported products that you use? What would happen if these products were no longer available?

Activities

1. Read the business and financial section of a large Sunday newspaper. What are some of the measures of the economic situation that are discussed? How do these relate to the prediction of economic conditions?

2. Interview several people who belong to labor unions about what union membership does for them. Report to the class.

3. Assume that during the summer John Mercino earned $400 from which federal income tax was withheld. He also received $12 in annual interest on his savings account. Fill out a short federal income tax form 1040 to get his refund.

4. Invite a speaker from a local business or the Chamber of Commerce to talk about how business uses capital to create jobs.

5. Get a copy of the current year's budget for your local community. Make a chart for the bulletin board showing where funds come from and how they are used.

6. What general taxes other than federal income taxes are levied on people in your town? Find out what these would cost a family of four with a combined family income of $12,000 a year.

7. Attend a meeting of some government agency in your area—the recreation committee, town council, or any other. What are some of the problems that they have to handle? Discuss these in class.

Index

A

Accidents, 140, 147, 148, 154, 196, 197, 200, 227, 228, 231, *Also see* Safety and Insurance
Account, *Also see* Credit
bonus, 283
charge for teenagers, 46
checking, 272, 274–279
due, 52
individual, 275
joint, 275
overdrawn, 274, 275
savings, 280–283
Accountant, 253
Accused person, rights of an, 229–230
Acetate, 116
Acne, 186
Action line, 96
Activities
banking, 286, 287
car, 157
clothing, 129
credit, 62
economy, 396, 397
education, training, and jobs, 264, 265
environment, 381, 382
health, 199
housing, 318, 319
investments, 360
legal rights and responsibilities, 239, 240
life insurance, 339
money management, 42
recreation, 178
shopping, 102, 103
social insurance, 217
spending, 24, 25
Activity, caloric needs, 184
Addiction, 187, 188
Additives, 232
Administration, Veterans, 237
Administrator, estate, 268
Adult education, 160
Advertising, 18, 19, 23, 65, 67, 72, 91–93, 232, 235
Advisory Council, Consumer, 237
Age
car insurance, 145

earning, 200
majority, 226
Aged, *see* Senior Citizen
Agency
consumer, 96, 223
employment, 208, 247
federal, *see* Commission, Federal Agencies, Government, and United States
health, 96
regulatory, 96, 235–237, *Also see* specific name
Agrarian system, 382
Agreement, credit, 221–224
Agriculture, U.S. Department of, 195, 231, 232
Aid, *Also see* Income, and Public,
legal, 96, 230
needy, 213–215
Aid to Dependent Children, 213, 214
Air conditioner, 140, 305, 306, 371, 377
automobile, 140
noise, 377
Air pollution, 362, 363, 372–376
Airplane, 236, 374, 376, 377
route, 236
subsidy, 236
Alcohol, 154, 186, 187, 194, 235, 389
advertising, 235
automobile accidents, 154
labeling, 235
tax, 389
Alcoholics Anonymous, 187
Algae, 368
Alimony, 227
Allowance, 29, 33
Alternate beneficiary, 334
Aluminum siding, 303
American Automobile Association (AAA), 170
American Express, 50, 273
American Gas Association (AGA), 87, 89
American Institute for Economic Research, 331
American Standards Institute, 87
Americans, spending, 108

Ampere, 95, 304
Anniversary sale, 74
Annual percentage rate, 57
Annuity, 293, 323–325
Antibiotics, 189
Antifreeze, 138
Antipollution, 173
Antiques, 344, 345
Apartments, 288, 290, 295–297
Appearance, 123, 126, 127, 262
Appliance labels, 373, 374
Application
credit, 51, 58, 59
job, 258–261
Social Security, 205
Appraisal
car, 222
house, 53, 311
Apprenticeship, 247, 248
Approval seals, 86, 87, 89
Arson, 229
Art, 160, 344, 345
Arteriosclerosis, 373
Arthritis, 293
Artists, 252
Assemblers, 256
Assessment, 315, 387, 388
Assets, 58, 280
Assigned risks, 147
Assistance, 200–210, 213–215, *Also see* Aid, Income, and Public Assistance
Aid to Dependent Children, 213, 214
Child Welfare Services, 215
Cuban Refugee Program, 214, 215
Social Security, 200–210
Supplementary Security Income Program (SSI), 213–215
Associated American Artists, 345
Athletes, 252
Attitude, spending, 10–14, 18, 387
Attorney General, 96
Auction, 72
Auto Red Book of Used Car Prices, 141
Autographs, 344
Automatic premium loan, 333

Automation, 251, 255, 392
Automobile, *see* Car
Average balance of checking
    account, 274

B

Baby-sitter, 34, 258, 274, 291
Backpacking, 20, 166–170
Badge, employee, 269
Baggage, 228, 229
Bailment contract, 227, 228
Bait and switch, 91, 92
Balance
    credit, 49, 51
    diet, 181
    outstanding, 51, 223
    trade, 386, 387
    wheels, 137
Bank, 51–53, 253, 266–287, 312
    activities, 286, 287
    assets, 267
    borrowing, 51–53, 56, 57
    checks, 268–272, 274–279
    credit cards, 50, 274
    deposit insurance, 266, 284,
        285
    Federal Deposit Insurance
        Corporation (FDIC), 266,
        284
    Federal Reserve, 236, 266, 355
    Federal Savings and Loan
        Insurance Corporation
        (FSLIC), 285
    industrial, 267
    interest, 280, 284
    jobs, 253
    money order, 271–273
    problem solving, 286
    review, 285
    safe-deposit box, 284, 285
    savings account, 281–283
    savings and loan association,
        267, 268, 285
    supervision of, 237
    terms, 286
    types, 267
BankAmericard, *See* VISA
Bankruptcy, 61, 225
Barber shops, licensing, 237
Bargain, 72–76
Barron's National Business and
    Financial Weekly, 351
Barter, 266, 273
Base units, 95
Basement sale, 72
Bathroom, 304
Battery, car, 138

Beaches, 231
Bearings, wheel, 137
Beautician, 237, 288
Beneficiary, 326, 327, 334
Benefits
    education, 249, *Also see*
        Veterans
    fringe, 392
    government, 385
    job, 255
    retirement, 209, 210
    Social Security, 201–210
    Worker's Compensation, 212,
        213
Better Business Bureau, 93, 95,
    96
Bicycle, 163–166, 184, 185
Bicycle Manufacturers
    Association of America
    (BMA), 165
Billboards, 66
Billing cycle, 223
Billing date, 49
Bills, 49, 60, 223, 227–229, 271
    consolidation loans, 60
    hotel, 229
    paying, 271
    services, 227, 228
Binder, 313
Binding contract, 219, 222
Bingo, 76, 77
Biodegradable, 371
Birthrate, 250
Blank check, 277
Blank spaces in contract, 57
Blind people, benefits for, 208
Blood test, marriage, 226
Blue Book (car prices), 131
Blue-collar workers, 250, 251,
    256
Blue Cross, 191, 192
Blue Shield, 191
Board, Civil Aeronautics, 236
Bodily injury liability insurance,
    142, 143
Bonds, 237, 267, 349, 351, 354,
    355
    government, 267
    prospectus, 237
    Securities and Exchange
        Commission (SEC), 237
Bonus account, 283
Bookkeeper, 254
Books, collecting, 344, 345
Borrowing, 52–57, *Also see*
    Credit
Bottled water, 367, 368

Bowling, 185
Boycott, 65, 391, 392
Brakes, 138–140, 152
Brand name, 66, 82
Bronchitis, 373
Buddhism, 13
Budget, 48, 72, 108–110, 245,
    385, *Also see* Spending
    clothing, 108–110
    credit, 48
    federal, 385
    intermediate, 245
Building codes, 376
Building and loan association,
    268
Building maintenance, 255
Bureau, credit, 61
Bureau of Standards, 151, 232
Burglary, 229
Bus, 133, 135
Business, 47, 253, 255, 383–386,
    389
    administration, 253
    cycles, 383–386
    credit, 47
    managers, 253
    owners, 253
    school, 255
    tax, 389
Business Week, 369
Buying
    ahead of need, 74, 76
    bank services, 266–287
    clothing, 104–129
    credit, 44–62
    education, 242–265
    environmental improvements,
        362–381
    goods, 64–103
    health care, 180–199
    housing, 288–319
    investments, 340–359
    life insurance, 320–339
    parties, 71, 72
    problems, 87–95
    recreation, 158–177
    social insurance, 200–217
    stocks and bonds, 354, 355
    stores, 51, 52, 64, 66–73, 76,
        77, 90, 91, 163, 164

C

Cabinets, kitchen, 304
Calendar of sales, 75
Calendar quarter, Social
    Security, 201
Calisthenics, 185

Call provisions, bonds, 355
Calories, 181–184
Calvin, John, 13
Camera, 162, 163
Camping, 166–170, 172, 231, 233, 234
Cancel
  check, 270, 277–279
  contract, 223
Cancer, 180
Candela, 95, 97
Candle making, 160
Capitalistic economy, 65, 382
Car
  accidents, 196, 227, 228, 231
  activities, 157
  air conditioner, 140
  antifreeze, 138
  appraisal, 222
  as is, 136
  bargaining for, 140, 141
  battery, 138
  bodily injury liability
    insurance, 142, 143
  brakes, 138–140
  checking used car, 137–140
  collateral, 52
  collision insurance, 143
  compact, 131, 132
  convertible, 133, 134
  credit contract, 223
  deductible insurance, 142
  demonstrator, 136
  depreciation, 148, 149
  discussion, 156, 157
  drinking and driving, 196
  driver responsibility, 154
  driving habits, 150, 151
  executive car, 136
  factory rebuilt engine, 136
  financial responsibility, 145, 146
  four-wheel drive, 137
  full power, 137
  full size, 131, 132
  generator, 139, 140
  guarantee, 136, 137, 140, 222
  hobby, 160
  inspection, 137
  insurance, 142–148, 154, 155
  intermediate, 131, 132
  leasing, 154, 155
  maintenance, 148–153
  mileage, 138
  models, 133–135
  need, 131
  oil, 138–140
  operating cost, 148–153

overhauled engine, 136
  parking contract, 228
  paying for, 48, 52, 140–142
  pollution, 374, 376
  prices, 140–142
  problem solving, 156
  renting, 50, 154, 228
  repairs, 136–140, 147, 248, 250
  responsibility of driver, 154
  review, 155, 156
  road test, 138–140
  safety, 154, 196
  sedan, 133, 134
  shock absorbers, 137, 138
  shopping, 131–142
  specialty, 133, 135
  spending, 22, 133, 135, 148–153
  sports car, 133, 135
  state insurance requirements, 142
  station wagon, 133, 135
  steering, 138–140
  subcompact, 131, 132
  suspension, 137
  temperature, 139
  terms, 156
  tires, 137, 151–153
  trade-in, 222
  transmission, 136, 137, 140
  types, 133–135
  uninsured motorist, 144
  used, 133, 136–141
  van, 133, 135
  warranty, 136, 137, 140, 222
  wheels, 137
  wholesale prices, 131
Carbon monoxide, 373
Card
  credit, 50
  Social Security, 207
Care
  clothing, 113, 118–123
  fibers, 115–117
Career, 242, 328
Carpeting, 377
Carrier, public, 228, 236
Carte Blanche, 50
Carver, George Washington, 13
Case studies
  buying ahead of need, 74, 76
  camping, 168, 169
  cash buying, 271
  clothing, 109, 110
  couple, 39
  credit shopping, 56, 57
  credit usage, 45, 46

dental insurance, 192
drug addiction, 187, 188
education vs. insurance, 330
guarantee, 77
home parties, 70–72
house insurance, 314, 315
housing, 288–290, 294, 295
legal aid, 230
life insurance, 327, 328, 330, 331
mobile home, 308
money management, 34–36
needs and wants, 32
paycheck voucher, 268, 269
prepaid health insurance, 194
recreation, 173
sharing money management, 39
Social Security, 201–204, 206
spending, 13–15
student, 34, 35, 36–38
warranty, 77
working woman, 244
young couple, 38, 39
Cash
  benefits, 385
  buying, 271
  check, 269–271
  loans, 48, 52–54
  payments, 213–215
  value, 327, 333
Cashier's check, 267
Catalog, 67, 69, 172
Caulking, 303
Celsius (C), 95, 97, 98
Centimetre (cm), 98
Centigrade (C), 97
Certificate
  savings, 283
  stock, 348
Certified check, 272, 316
Chain store, 68
Chamber of Commerce, 95, 96
Changing social patterns, 17, 18
Changing Times, 79, 91
Charge, *Also see* Credit
  accounts, 23, 46, 47, 49, 60
    teenagers, 46, 47
  card, 72
    loss, 50
  credit, 50, 51, 221, 222
Charts
  accidents by age of driver, 147
  braking distance, 152
  calendar of sales, 75
  calories needed for activities, 184
  car

insurance rates, 144, 146
operating cost, 150
sizes, 132–135
types, 133–135
check route, 270
clothing
needs, 106
shirt buying, 114
useful life, 122
complaints, 96
credit
contract, 224
rating, 59
estimate of expenses, 37, 38
fiber care, 115–117
food grades, 84
gambling, 358
house
checklist
apartment, 296
house, 302
cooperative vs.
condominium, 298
insurance, 315
percent owned, 312
income, 35
leisure time, 159
life insurance costs, 332–333
middle income family
spending, 40
needs and wants, 32
operating costs, car, 150
recommended dietary
allowances, 182
retail outlets, 68–70
shopping facilities, 68–70
Social Security benefits, 202
spending plan, 35
spending records, 34–36
store types, 68–70
tire inflation, 153
values, 15, 16
weekly spending plan, 39
Chattel mortgage, 51
Checking
contract, 228
used car, 137–140
Checklist
apartment, 296
house, 302
Checks, 236, 267, 271–279
cashier's, 267
cashing, 47, 269–271
certified, 272
charges, 274
endorsing, 269
route, 270, 271
students, 47

travelers, 267, 271–273
Chemicals, 378
Chemist, 253
Children
care and cost, 291
Child Welfare Services, 214,
215
eating, 180
recreation, 310
Social Security benefits, 202,
207
Choice
consumer, 230
price, 65
Cholesterol, 83
Christmas Club, 76
Cigarettes, 389
Circulars, 66
Circulation, money, 236
Citizen, 382
Civil Aeronautics Board (CAB),
236
Civil law, 219
Civil Service Commission, 260
Claim, unemployment
insurance, 211, *Also see*
Social Security
Class activities, *See* Activities
Class discussion, *See* Discussion
Clause, escalator, 392
Cleaning
bailment contract, 227, 228
clothing, 120, 121
Cleanliness, food, 84
Clearing house, 270
Clerical jobs, 254, 255
Clinchers, 165
Clinics, 187
Closing Circle, The, 378
Closing costs, 314
Clothing, 67, 104–129, 368
activities, 129
budget, 108–110
buying a shirt, 114
care, 113, 118–123
case study, 109, 110
color, 112
construction, 114
costs, 291
discussion, 129
dry cleaning, 121, 122, 227,
228
fabrics, 113, 115–117
fashion, 67, 104, 105
fibers, 113–117, 253
fit, 112, 113
flame-resistant, 117, 118, 231
investment, 105

labels, 99, 113, 118–121
laundering, 120–122
lines, 111, 112
needs, 105–108, 113
packing, 123–125
problem solving, 128
quality, 113
recycling, 106, 107
repair, 122
review, 128
selection, 110–118
separates, 107
shoes, 107, 108
shopping, 104–129
sizes, 67, 88, 99, 113
slimming, 112
spending, 108–110
storage, 122, 123
synthetics, 368
terms, 128
travel, 123–125
useful life, 122
values, 108
Clubs, 160
Coal, 372
Code Napoleon, 218
Codes, (building), 376
Coed, 72
Coin World, 343
COINage Magazine, 343
Coins, 266, 285, 340, 342, 343
Coinsurance, 191, 192
Collateral, 52, 53, 56, 57
Collection
agency, 60
garnishee, 223, 225
high pressure, 54
Collections of things, 340–345
Collective action, 391
College, 242, 246–249
Collision insurance, 143
Color (clothing), 112
Color Additive Amendments,
232
Combination life insurance
policy, 323
Commerce, U.S. Department, 82,
232
Commercial banks, 267, 268
Commission
Civil Service, 260
Consumer Product Safety, 236
Federal Communications
(FCC), 237
Federal Power (FPC), 237
Federal Trade (FTC), 235, 236
Interstate Commerce (ICC),
236

sales, 65
Securities and Exchange
(SEC), 237
stockbrokers, 355
Common Law, 218
Common-law marriage, 226
Common name of food, 81
Commoner, Barry, 378
Community college, 246, 248
Community facilities, 30, 31,
160, 300, 310
Community service, 160
Commuting, 130, 131, 248, 288,
296
Compact car, 131, 132
Comparison shopping, 65, 66,
194, 195
Compensation, 148
Complaints, 52, 95, 96, 229
Complexion, 186
Comprehensive health
insurance, 191–194
Comptroller of currency, 235
Compulsory insurance, 200
Computers, 72, 250, 253
Condominium, 297, 298
Conservation of water, 369, 370
Constitution, U.S., 218, 219
Construction
clothing, 114
grants, 236
house, 302, 377
mobile home, 308
noise, 376
Consumer
agencies, 95, 223
complaints, 95, 96
credit, 44, *Also see* Credit
demand, 45
economy, 15, 18, 45, 65, 236,
382–397
finance companies, 53
needs, 237
organizations, 96
prices, 65
problems, 87–95, 238
protection, 223, 230
purchasing expectations, 387
representation, 237, 238
rights, 230
Consumer Advisory Council,
237
Consumer Information Center,
79, 170
Consumer Interests, President's
Committee, 237

Consumer Product Safety
Commission, 236
Consumer Protection Agency,
223
Consumer Reports, 79, 80, 137,
162
Consumers Research Magazine,
79, 80, 162
Consumption, *See* Spending
Container size, 83
Contaminated food, 231
Contestability, 332, 333
Contests, 92
Continentals, 266
Contingent beneficiary, 334
Contract
blank spaces, 57
cancel, 223
car rental, 228
co-signer, 225
credit, 44, 47, 51–53, 55, 57
default, 225
fraud, 94
lease, 220, 221
legal rights, 219–229
marriage, 225, 226
parking, 228
sample, 224
small claims court, 225
Contribution, Social Security,
201
Controlled economy, 382
Conversion
house, 299
metric, 95, 97–100
Convertible
bonds, 351
car, 133, 134
insurance, 320, 321
Conviction, 229
Cooling-off period, 223
Cooperation (resource
management), 379
Cooperative
banks, 268
health, 194
housing, 297, 298
retail, 68, 70
Cord, 115
Correspondence schools, 93, 94
Co-signer, 53, 225
Cosmetics, 22, 79, 80, 127, 128,
232
Cosmetology, 247
Cost
car operation, 150

checking account, 279
closing, house, 314
clothing, 118, 291
credit, 49, 54–57, 142
education, 248
energy, 74
goods, 387
health care, 193
heating, 295, 300
hidden, 300
house painting, 303
landscaping, 300–302
leisure activities, 177
living, 392
mobile home, 306
money, 74
moving, 316
opportunity, 33
recreation, 160, 177
Social Security benefits, 209,
210
time, 74
Cost-of-living index, 392
Costume details, 112
Cotton, 115
Counseling
credit, 61
education, 249
health, 187
job, 208, 213, 247
vocational, 208, 213, 247
Couple
housing, 290–292
spending, 38, 39
Coupon
food product, 76
rate, 351
Court, 60, 96, 219, 221, 223,
225, 229, 230
small claims, 96, 225, 229
Coverage (insurance), 142, 145
Covered employment (Social
Security), 201, 202, 211
Credentials, 242
Credit
abuse, 47
activities, 62
add-on rate, 221
annual percentage rate, 221,
222
application, 51, 58, 59
bankruptcy, 225
bureau, 58, 59, 61
business, 47
car, 141, 142
cards, 49–52, 60, 267, 271, 274

name lists, 50, 51
case study, 45, 46
charge account, 60
collection agency, 60
contract, 44, 51, 52, 55, 57, 221–224
co-signer, 225
costs, 49, 51, 54–57, 142
counseling, 61
court procedure, 60
default, 60, 61, 225
demand, 45
discount rate, 221
discussion, 62
durable goods, 48
economic changes, 54
family use, 48
finance charge, 221, 222
garnishee, 60, 223, 225
government policy, 45, 385
guidelines for use, 48
help, 60
history, 44–46
identification, 50
information, 52, 57
influence on spending, 18
interest rate, 54
legal
    age, 56
    obligations, 46, 47
    procedure, 60
    requirements for disclosure, 57
legislation, 44
limits, 48, 49
long time payments, 54
misleading information, 59
money supply, 54, 385
mortgage, 48, 49
needs, 47, 48, 54
overuse, 29
pawnbroker, 54
payments, 48, 223
points, 59
prepaying, 57, 142
problem solving, 61, 62
problems, 60, 61
rates, 57, 58
rating, 57–59
reasons for use, 46, 47
record, 49, 58–61
refused, 231
repayment, 54, 61
review, 61
risk, 53, 54, 57
service, 48

settlement, 60
shopping, 55–57
similarity to renting, 46
slip, 90
small loan company, 57
spending, 18, 47, 48
students, 47
supervision, 385
teenagers, 46, 47
terms, 54–57, 61
travel, 47
Truth-in-Lending law, 57, 60, 221
types, 48, 49
union, 53, 56, 223, 285, 268
use, 18, 46–48
work under Social Security, 208
Creditors, 60, 61, 221
Criminal law, 219, 229, 230
Crisis (energy), 372, 373
Crocheting, 160
Cuban Refugee Program, 214, 215
Cumulative dividend, 349
CUNA International, 223
Current, electric, 232
Current yield, bonds, 352
Currently insured, Social Security, 201, 203
Currency, 95, 235, 236, 386
Currency, Comptroller of, 235
Cycle billing, 223
Cycle News, 174
Cycles, business, 383–386

D
Daily needs (food), 182, 183
Damages
    car insurance, 148
    goods, 174
Dangerous products, 178
Date
    check, 275, 276
    food, 83
Day order, 355
Dealer, car, 52
Death
    benefits
        no-fault insurance, 148
        Social Security, 200, 202
        veterans, 237
        Worker's Compensation, 213
    tax, 389
Debenture, 351
Debt, 46–49, 60, 61, 225, 266

bankruptcy, 61
collection, 46, 47
default, 225
discharge, 61
fraudulent contracts, 94
government, 266
limits, 48
reinstate, 61
Decreasing term insurance, 321
Deductible insurance, 142, 191, 192
Deductions
    income tax, 271, 272
    medical, 191, 192
    payroll, 273
Deeds, 285, 314
Default, 60, 61, 225
Defendent, 229
Dehydrated food, 167
Demand deposits, 266
Demonstrator (car), 136
Density, population, 365–367
Dental
    assistant, 253
    insurance, 192, 194, 392
Dentist, 252
Department of, *Also see* Commission, Federal Agencies, Government, and United States
    Agriculture, 195, 231, 232
    Commerce, 82, 232
    Education, state level, 247
    Health, 96
    Health and Human Services, 232, 233
    Housing and Urban Development, 233
    Interior, 233
    Labor, 260, 262
Department store, 68, 69
Dependents, Social Security benefits, 204
Deposit
    box, 285
    contract, 222, 223
    Federal Reserve Banks, 236
    refund, 223
    rental, 220, 221
    slip, 281
Depository, 267, 268
Depreciation, 149, 308
Depression, 200, 383, 385
Derailleur, 164, 165
Detergents, 368
Devaluation (of currency), 386

Diagnostic health care, 191
Diet, 181, 182
Diminishing marginal utility, 32
Diners Club, 50
Directed economy, 382
Disability
    life insurance, 335
    recreation, 170
    Social Security, 200, 202, 203,
        208, 209
    Supplementary Security
        Income Program, 214
    teacher, 250
    veterans, 237
    Worker's Compensation, 192,
        212, 213
Disadvantages of shopping
    facilities, 69, 70
Discharge debt, 61
Discount
    rate, 221, 236
    store, 68, 69
Discrimination, 251, 252, 392,
    394, 395
Discussion
    banks, 286
    car, 156, 157
    clothing, 129
    credit, 62
    economy, 396
    education, training, and jobs,
        264
    environment, 380
    health, 198, 199
    housing, 318
    investments, 359, 360
    legal rights and
        responsibilities, 239
    life insurance, 338, 339
    money management, 42
    recreation, 178
    shopping, 101, 102
    spending, 24
    social insurance, 216, 217
    transportation, 156, 157
Disease, 180, 189, 196, 373
Display panel of package, 81
Disposal, sewage, 237, *Also see*
    Waste
Disputes, labor, 392
Disqualification, unemployment
    insurance, 211
Distribution of leisure, 158–160
Dividend
    cumulative, 349
    life insurance, 336

Divorced wife, Social Security
    benefits, 202
Doctor, 189–191, 193, 194, 252
Do-it-yourself projects, 21
Door-to-door sales, 68, 69, 92, 93
Double indemnity, 335
Dow Jones Industrial Average,
    354
Down payment, 51, 300, 312
Downspout, 303
Drafters, 246, 250
Drainage, 304
Drinking and driving, 196
Drive-in store, 72
Drivers
    habits, 150, 151
    insurance rates, 145, 146
    jobs, 257
    licensing, 154, 269
    responsibility, 154
Drugs
    alcohol, 186, 187
    addiction, 187, 188
    advertising, 232
    car accidents, 154
    inspection, 195
    over-the-counter, 79, 80,
        186–189
    prescription, 186, 194, 232
    safety, 154, 195, 232
    use, 180
Dry cleaning
    clothing, 121, 122
    contracts, 227, 228
Dryers, 371
Durable goods and credit, 48
Dysentery, 180

E

Earnings
    education, 242
    old age, 200
    Social Security benefits, 200,
        207, 208
Earthwatch Program, 379
Eating
    away from home, 181, 182
    children, 180
    establishments, 237
    food fads, 185, 186
    habits, 180, 181
    snacks, 181
    teenagers, 180
Ecology, *See* Environment
Economic
    systems, 382, 383

waste, 67
Economist, 252, 253
Economy, 15, 18, 45, 65, 236,
    382–397
    activities, 396, 397
    credit, 54, 236
    discussion, 396
    environment, 377, 378
    Federal Reserve Banks, 236
    prices, 65
    problem solving, 395, 396
    review, 395
    spending, 15, 18
    terms, 395
Education, 93, 94, 160, 205, 206,
    237, 242–265, 330
    activities, 264, 265
    correspondence schools, 93,
        94
    discussion, 264
    financial aid, 205, 206, 208,
        237, 249, 250
    investment, 330
    leisure activity, 160
    part-time, 249
    problem solving, 264
    public, 237
    review, 263, 264
    Social Security benefits, 205,
        206, 208
    terms, 264
    veterans, 237
Efficiency Energy Ratio (EER),
    373, 374
Eggs, 86, 87
Ehrlich, Dr. Paul, 364
Electric, 95, 235, 237, 304, 305,
    371, 373, 374, 377
    efficiency, 373, 374
    engine, 374
    heat, 305
    household use, 95, 304, 377
    power, 235
    rates, 237
Electronic funds transfers (EFT),
    267, 271
Electronics
    equipment, 72
    hobby, 160
Eligibility
    Social Security benefits,
        201–209
    unemployment insurance, 211
Emergencies, use of credit, 48
Emphysema, 373
Employee

appearance, 123
badge, 269
federal, 211
insurance, 210–212
Employment
    agencies, 208, 259, 260
    frauds, 94
    part-time, 255
    Social Security benefits, 201,
        202
Emotional
    handicap, 250
    illness, 180, 194
Endorse
    check, 269
    loan, 53
Endowment insurance, 320, 322,
    323, 330
Energy, 30, 74, 235, 371–374
    costs, 74
    personal, 30
    Efficiency Energy Rating
        (EER), 373, 374
    use, 235, 371–373
Engine, car, 374
Engineers, 250, 252, 253, 256
English Common Law, 218
Employment, *See* Jobs
Entertainment jobs, 255
Entrance fee, mobile home park,
    310
Envelope system, money
    management, 34, 35
Environment, 160, 172, 173,
    195, 196, 362–381
    activities, 380, 381
    discussion, 380
    problem solving, 380
    review, 379
    terms, 380
Equalizing opportunities, 251,
    252, 392, 394, 395
Equipment
    fishing, 172, 173
    household, 289–291, 294, 295,
        297, 371
    mobile home, 306
Equitable taxes, 390
Equity investments, 340
Escalator clause, in union
    contracts, 392
Estimate
    expenses, 37, 38
    repairs, 90
Eutrophication, 179, 369
Evaluating

bank services, 266–287
clothing needs and purchases,
    104–129
credit use, 44–62
economy, 382–397
education and job-training,
    242–265
environmental impact,
    362–381
health care and insurance,
    180–199
investments, 340–359
legal rights and
    responsibilities, 218–239
life insurance, 320–339
money management, 26–43
recreation, 158–177
shopping skills, 64–103
social insurance, 200–217
transportation, 130–157
Evelyn, John, 373
Eviction, 221
Exchange, stock, 349, 350
Executive car, 136
Executor, 268
Exercise, 184, 185
Expenses
    car, 271
    clothing care, 118
    health, 193–195
    housing, 293–295
    income tax, 271, 272
    prices, 64
    recreation, 177
    values, 293

F

Fabrics, 114–118, 231
Face value, 327, 330
Facilities
    community, 300
    recreation, 310
Factory
    air, 137
    housing, 301
    rebuilt, 136
Fads
    clothing, 74
    food, 185, 186
Fahrenheit, 99
Fair Credit Billing Act, 52
Fair Credit Reporting Act, 58–60
Fair Packaging and Labeling Act,
    81, 232
Fallacies, health, 185
Family

break-up, 200
camping, 172
credit, 48
general assistance, 215
income, 242
life style, 328
relationship, 225–227
spending, 15, 22, 40, 41
Farming, 251
Fashion, 67, 74, 104, 105
Fatality, 196
Fatty acids, 83
Federal agencies, 231–238, *Also
    see* Commission,
    Department, Government,
    and United States
    Aviation Agency (FAA), 236
    Civil Aeronautics Board
        (CAB), 236
    Communications Commission
        (FCC), 237
    Deposit Insurance Corporation
        (FDIC), 266, 284
    Food and Drug Administration
        (FDA), 80, 81, 96, 195, 230,
        232, 233
    Housing Administration
        (FHA), 233, 237, 310–313,
        377
    Insurance Contributions Act
        (FICA), *see* Social Security
    Power Commission (FPC), 237
    Reserve, 236, 266, 355
    Supplementary Security
        Income Program (SSI),
        213–215
    Trade Commission (FTC), 76,
        93, 96, 232, 233, 235–237
Federal courts, 219
Fees
    closing, 314
    mobile home park, 310
Felonies, 229
Fibers, 113–117, 253
Figure, 182
Film, 162
Finance
    car, 141, 142
    charge, 53, 55, 56, 221, 222
    home, 300, 310–313
Financial
    aid, 205, 206, 208, 237, 249,
        250
    jobs, 253, 256
    responsibility laws, 145, 146
Finish, fabric, 117

Fire insurance, 315
Fish inspection, 233
Fishing, 172, 173
Fit, clothing, 112, 113
Fitness, physical, 163, 184–186
Fixed-dollar investments, 340
Flame resistant fabric, 117, 118, 231
Flanders, Russell B., 251
Flannel, 115
Floor plans
  apartment, 297
  house, 300
  mobile home, 309
Flu, 189
Flyers, 67
Food
  additivies, 232
  brand name, 82
  calories, 181–184
  colors, 232
  dating, 83
  dehydrated, 167
  eating habits, 180, 181
  fads, 185, 186
  fortified, 83
  grades, 84
  health, 180–183
  ingredients, 81, 82
  inspection, 84, 186, 195, 237
  jobs, 255
  labels, 81–87
  lunch, 181
  needs, 182, 183
  obesity, 181–183
  packages, 81, 82
  quantity, 81, 82
  safety, 195, 232
  snacks, 181
  stamps, 196
  standard of identity, 81
  supply, 364
Food and Drug Administration, 80, 81, 96, 195, 230, 232, 233
Forbes, 357
Forecast, jobs, 251
Foreign goods, 393
Foreperson, shop, 392
Form 1040, 388
Fossil fuels, 231
Four-wheel drive, 137
Frame, bicycle, 165
Franchise, 389
Fraud, 91–95, 235
Free merchandise, 94
Freeway, 377
Fringe benefits, 249, 255, 392

Front-end load fund, 356
Fuel, 94, 231, 314, 370, 372, 379
Full power, car, 137, 140
Full warranty, 78, 79
Fully insured, 201, 203
Fund
  investment, 356
  unemployment, 211
Furniture, 289, 290, 294, 295, 306
Future Farmers of America (FFA), 160
Future Homemakers of America (FHA), 160

G

Gabardine, 115
Gambling, 358
Garage sale, 72
Garnishee, 60, 223, 225
Gas
  rates, 237
  turbine, 374
Gasoline, 372, 389
Gear
  fishing, 172, 173
  shift, 137, 140
General
  assistance, 215
  education, 245
  obligation bonds, 357
  tax, 389
Generator, 139, 140
Gift tax, 389
Giveaways, and consumer fraud, 94
Goals
  career, 242–265
  personal, 33
  spending, 33
Gonorrhea, 189
Good Housekeeping, 87, 89
Good till cancelled (GTC), 355
Goods, 50
Government, *Also see* Commission, Department, Federal, and United States
  booklets, 79, 96
  budget, 385
  construction grants, 236
  drug inspection, 195
  fishing, 172
  food inspection, 84, 86, 195
  food labels, 81–87
  health services, 84, 86, 187, 195–197, 218, 253
  jobs, 255, 256

labor relations, 392
levels of, 219
maps, 168
regulation, 383
retirement systems, 200, 201
savings bonds, 267, 284
securities, 236, 267, 284, 357, 358
spending, 385
spraying, 195
subsidy to airlines, 236
Grace period, 333
Grades of food, 82, 84, 85, 231, 304
Gram (g), 98
Grievance procedure, 392
Grooming, 79, 80, 123, 127, 128, 255
  jobs, 255
Gross national product, 383, 384
Group
  influence on spending, 16, 17
  insurance, 324, 325, 329
Group Health Cooperative of Puget Sound, 194
Guarantee, *See* Warranty
Guests, hotel, 228, 229
Guidance, 249, 259
Guide Book to United States Coins, 343
Guidelines for use of credit, 48
Guilds, 390
Gutters, 303
Gyps, *See* Fraud

H

Habits, eating, 180, 181
Hair, care of, 126, 127
Hammurabi, 218
Handbook, jobs, 243
Handbook of United States Coins, 343
Handicapped, *See* Disability
Hardtop, 133, 134
Hashish, 187
Health, 94, 163, 180–201, 214, 215, 226, 237, 253, 255, 362, 372, 373, 392
  acne, 186
  activities, 199
  air, 362, 372, 373
  alcohol, 186, 187
  cost, 194, 195
  counseling, 187
  dental, 192, 194
  discussion, 198, 199
  fallacies, 185

foods, 185, 186
fringe benefits, 392
government, 84, 86, 187, 195–197, 218, 253
habits, 180, 181
insurance, 190–194, 214, 215. *Also see* Social Security, Worker's Compensation, Life Insurance, Medicare, and Medicaid
jobs, 249, 253, 255, 392
landfill, 195, 196
marriage, 226
Medicaid, 214, 215
Medicare, 190, 193, 200, 201
medicine, 79, 80, 186, 188, 189, 193–195, 200, 201
physical fitness, 163, 184–186
preventive care, 180, 194
problem solving, 198
review, 197, 198
smoking, 186
spraying, 195
standards, 392
teenagers, 189, 190
terms, 198
veterans, 237
Worker's Compensation, 213
Health Insurance Plan of Greater New York, 194
Heart disease, 180
Heating, 295, 300, 304–306, 377
Hectare, 98
Hemp, 187
Hepatitis, 189
Heroin, 187
Hi-Fidelity, 162
High income, 252
High school, 93, 242, 245
diploma, 242
Hiking, 20, 161, 233, 234
History
car repairs, 137, 140
credit, 44–46
Hobbies, 160, 161
Holder-in-due course, 52
Holidays, 255
Home, *Also see* Apartments and Housing
accidents, 196
improvements, 93, 233, 310
mortgage, 48, 49, 51, 52, 233, 267, 268, 288, 312–314, 320
parties, 70–72
sewage, 218
sewing, 118, 160
Homemaker, 160, 337

Homeowners insurance, 315
Hospital payments, 190, 191
Hotels, 228, 229
Household
equipment, 371
workers, 255
Housing, 233, 288–319, *Also see* Apartments and Home
activities, 318
authority bonds, 357
discussion, 318
eviction, 221
inspection, 237
insurance, 314, 315
investment, 340, 341
mortgage, *See* Home, mortgage
problem solving, 317, 318
recreation, 160
review, 317
selling, 69
taxes, 387, 388
terms, 317
Housing authority bonds, 357
Hydroelectric power, 235

I

Identification
check cashing, 269
credit cards, 50
Impulse buying, 26–28
Income
credit use, 49
education 242, 252
insurance for loss, 192
irregular, 34
life insurance, 334, 335
public assistance, 213–215
qualification for health insurance, 191
retirement, 323, 324
Social Security, 200–210
tax, 49, 271–273, 298, 388, 389
Individual account, 275
Individual policy, 325
Independent store, 68
Index, cost-of-living, 392
Industrial
bank, 267, 268
insurance, 325
revenue bonds, 357
Industry
advertising, 66
energy, 372
safety, 233, 235
service, 250
society, 65

Inflation
economic, 299, 384–386, 392
tire, 153
Information, *Also see* specific topics advertising, *See* Advertising
government publications, 79, 96
library information, 96, 243, 247
maps, 168
misleading, 59
right to, 230
Ingredients, food, 81
Inheritance, 94, 389
Injury
car, 227
Worker's Compensation, 212, 213
Illness, *Also see* specific illnesses
alcoholism, 194
drug, 194
emotional, 180, 194
insurance, *See* Disability, Public Assistance, Social Security, and Worker's Compensation
Inspection
car, 137
drug, 195
food, 84, 86, 195, 230, 231, 233, 237
restaurant, 237
stamps, 84, 86, 87, 89, 165
Inspectors, 256
Installment
accounts, 47, 49, 51, 52
life insurance, 334, 335
Insulation, 305, 306
Insurance
car, 142–148, 154, 155
dental, 192, 194
disability, *See* Life Insurance, Social Security, Supplementary Security Income Program, Vocational Rehabilitation, Veterans Administration, and Worker's Compensation
health, 190, 193, 194, 214, 215
house, 314, 315
job, 200, 253, 256, *Also see* Worker's Compensation
legal, 230
life, *See* Life insurance

loss of income, 192
Medicaid, 193, 194, 214, 215
Medicare, 193, 200, 201
mortgage, 237, 321
motorcycle, 148
personal property, 221
Social Security, 190, 192–194, 200–210, 215, 233, 293
unemployment, 200, 210–212
veterans, 336, 337
Worker's Compensation, 192, 200, 212, 213
Insurance Information Institute, 142
Interbank credit cards, 50
Interest
inventory, 242, 243
option, life insurance, 335
rates, 51, 53, 54, 60, 267, 284, 349, 352
Interior, Department of, 233
Intermediate budget, 245
Internal Revenue Service (IRS), 47, 271, 388, 389
International
standards, 232
trade, 386, 387
Interstate commerce, 231, 236
Interview, job, 261, 262
I.O.U., 349, *Also see* Credit
Isaiah, 13
Insulation, 377
Inventory of interests, 242, 243
Investment
accounts, 283
activities, 360
car leasing, 155
clothing, 105
clubs, 358
discussion, 359, 360
Federal Reserve, 236
funds, 356
house, 299
in yourself, 242–265
problem solving, 359
review, 358, 359
terms, 359
Investment Companies, 357

J
Jesus, 13
Jewelry, 285
Jobs 242–247, 251, 252, 255, 256, 261, 262, 268, 392, *Also see* specific topics
automation, 251, 255, 392
beginning, 251
benefits, 255

information, 96, 243, 247, 260
interview, 261, 262
minorities, 251, 252, 392, 394, 395
part-time, 268
resume, 260, 261
summer, 259, 260
training, 208, 213, 243, 245, 254, 256, 262, 263
updating skills, 262, 263
women, 251, 252
young people, 242–247, 251, 258, 259, 268
Jacobson, Margaret, 15, 16
Jogging, 185
John the Baptist, 13
Joint account, 275
Joint and survivorship life insurance, 335
Journal of American Insurance, 212
Judeo-Christian ethic, 11, 12
Junior achievement, 160
Justinian's code, 218
Jury, 229

K
Kaiser-Permanente Medical Care Program, 194
Kelvin, 95, 97
Kennedy, John 230
Keypunch operator, 255, 291
Kickback, 94
Kilogram (kg), 95, 98
Kilometre (km), 98
Kilowatt, 235
Kitchen, 67, 304, 306
Kneese, Allen V., 370
Knitting, 160

L
Labels, 79–87, 89, 99, 113, 118–121, 236
alcoholic beverages, 235
appliances, 373, 374
clothing, 99, 113, 118–121
Fair Packaging and Labeling Act, 81, 232
food, 81–87
Food and Drug Administration, 80, 81, 96, 195, 230, 232, 233
home sewing, 118
metric, 97–100
personal products, 79–81
safety, 236
seals of approval, 86, 87, 89
Labor, 233, 235, 251, 390–392, *Also see* Jobs

Department of, 233, 235
economy, 390–392
force, 251
manual, 251
relations, 233, 235
Lakes, types of, 368–369
Land
out-of-state, 94
use of, 364–367
Landfill, 195, 196
Landscape, 300–302
Lapse of policy, 335
Laundering, 120–122
Lawnmower, 377
Laws, 145, 146, 218–239, *Also see* Federal, Government, Legal and United States
activities, 239, 240
civil, 219–229
Code Napoleon, 218
contracts, 219–229
criminal, 219, 229, 230
discussion, 239
English Common, 218
financial responsibility, 145, 146
Hammurabi, 218
Justinian's code, 218
local, 218, 237, 238
Louisiana, 218
problem solving, 239
review, 238, 239
small claims court, 225
state, 237, 238
terms, 238
Lawsuit, 148
Lawyer, 96, 229, 230
Leak, car, 138, 140
Lease
car, 155
home, 220, 221, 296
Legal, *Also see* Law
aid, 96, 230
age, 56
insurance, 230
responsibilities, 218–239
rights, 218–239
marriage, 225–229
Leisure, 72, 158–178, 255, 297, 300, *Also see* specific activities and Recreation
distribution of, 158–160
facilities, 297, 300
jobs, 255
spending, 160, 177
vacations, 250
Lenders, 44–61, *Also see* Credit
Length, 98

Lenses, camera, 162, 163
Level
  government, 219
  term insurance, 321
Liability
  car, 148
  credit card, 50
  insurance, 148, 315
  products, 78
Library, 96, 243, 247
Licensing
  business, 237
  drivers, 154, 269
  hydroelectric plants, 237
  job-training schools, 237
  nurse, 246
  radio and television stations, 237
Life
  expectancy, 180
  stages, 288
  styles, 291, 328
Life insurance, 53, 56, 237, 292, 320–339
  activities, 339
  annuity, 323, 324
  beneficiary, 334
  cash surrender value, 333
  contestability, 332, 333
  discussion, 338, 339
  dividends, 336
  double indemnity, 335
  features, 332–336
  government, 336–339
  grace period, 333
  group, 325
  individual, 325
  industrial, 325
  language, 326, 327
  loans, 333, 334
  method of payment, 338
  nonforfeiture values, 335, 336
  ordinary, 322–325
  premium waiver, 335
  problem solving, 338
  reinstatement, 335
  savings bank, 325
  settlement options, 334, 335
  shopping for, 325–332
  switching policies, 337
  tax advantages, 337
  term, 320, 321
  terms, 338
  types
    companies, 336
    policies, 320–325
    versus education, 330
    veterans, 336, 337

  whole, 322, 323
  women, 337
Lifetime income, 334
Light
  houses, 304
  metric, 95–97
  truck, 133, 135
  values, 112
Limited
  payment life insurance, 322
  tax bonds, 357
  warranty, 78, 79
Limits, debt, 48
Line, clothing, 110
Linen, 115
Linn's Stamp News, 343
Liquor, *See* Alcohol
List, credit card holders, 50, 51
Litre (l), 98
Loans, *Also see* Credit
  bank, 52–54, 267
  billpayer, 60
  education, 250
  Federal Reserve, 236
  life insurance, 333
  mortgage, 233, 311
  prime rate, 54
Local
  consumer representation, 237, 238
  government jobs, 255, 256
  ordinances, 237, 238, 376
  unions, 200, 201, 390–392
Longevity, 180
Loss
  credit card, 50
  income, 148, 192
Lotteries, 358
Low income
  family, 27, 245
  health care, 193, 194
  legal aid, 230
Low mintage, 343
Loyalty, shopper, 76
Luggage, 228, 229
Lumber, 231
Lump sum payment, 202, 334
Lunch, 181

M

Machine operator, 251
Macrame, 160
Magazine advertising, 65, 66
Mail
  postal service, 96, 235, 271–273
  shopping, 68–70, 172
Mailing lists, 50, 51

Maintenance
  car, 148–153
  home
    house, 300
    rental, 220
  tires, 151–153
Major medical health insurance, 191, 192
Majority, age of, 226
Management
  credit, 60
  environment, 172, 173
  jobs, 252, 253
  money, 9–62
Manufacturing
  jobs, 253, 256
  prices, 64
  repairs, 96
  safety, 236
Margin account, 355
Marginal utility, 32
Marijuana, 187
Markdown, 73
Market economy, 382
Markup, 64
Marriage
  car insurance, 146
  common-law, 226
  legal requirements, 244, 245
  legal rights, 225–227, 229
  women, 225–227
Mass, 95, 98
Mass transit, 130, 196, 228, 236
Maternity benefits, 190, 191
Maturity of bonds, 349
Maximum earnings credit (Social Security), 207
Maximum payments (Social Security), 209
Measures, metric, 95, 97–100
Meat
  grades, 85, 231
  inspection, 84, 86, 230, 231
Mechanical jobs, 256
Mechanization, 251, 255, 392
Mediator, 392
Medicaid, 190–194, 214, 215
Medical, *See* Health
Mental
  handicap, 250
  illness, 180, 194
Merchandise
  bought on credit, 52
  damaged, 52, 74
  repossess, 60
  returning, 90, 91
  seals of approval, 86, 87, 89
Metabolism, 183

Method of payment, 274
Metre, 98
Metric system, 95, 97–100
Middle income families, credit, 46
Mileage, 138
Milligram (mg), 95
Millilitre (ml), 98
Millimetre (mm), 98
Mineral resources, 233
Mineralogy, 160
Minkus Stamp Journal, 343
Minimum
  balance in checking account, 274
  income, 200, 209
  insurance, car, 142
  resale prices, 65
  standards for housing, 237
  subsistence level, 26
  wages, 392
Mining, 362, 363, 378
Minorities, 251, 252
Minors, 226
Misdemeanor, 229
Misleading advertisement, 91
Mobile homes, 288, 290, 306–310
  park directory, 310
Mobility
  car, 130–157
  mass transit, 130
  suburbs, 130, 131
Model airplane making, 160
Model car, 138
Modular house, 301
Mole, 95, 97
Mondopoint sizes, 99
Money, 9–62, 266, 267, 385, *Also see* Spending
  activities, 42
  circulation, 236
  devaluation, 386
  discussion, 42
  goals, 33
  needs and wants, 30–33
  plans, 33, 34
  records, 34–36
  resources available, 30
  review, 42
  sharing responsibilities, 39, 41, 42
  terms, 42
  values, personal, 15, 16
  working wife, 41
Money orders, 271–273
Monthly statement, 223
Moody's Investors Service, 351

Mortgage, 48, 49, 51, 52, 233, 267, 268, 288, 310–314, 320
  chattel, 51
  FHA, 310–313
  home improvement, 310
  insurance, 321
  mobile home, 310
  second, 313
  veterans (VA or G.I.), 310–313
Motorcycle, 148, 174
Mt. Trashmore, 371, 379
Moving, 310, 316, 317
  fees in mobile home park, 310
Municipal bonds, 357
Muscular dystrophy, 180
Music, 160–162
Mutual
  fund, 356
  savings bank, 313

N

NADA Used Car Guide, 131
Napoleon, 218
National
  banks, 235
  Bureau of Standards, 151, 232
  income, 384
  parks, 169, 234, 235
Natural
  fibers, 115
  resources, 231
Need
  basic, 30–33
  car, 131, 133
  clothing, 105–108, 113
  consumer, 237
  credit, 54
  energy, 372
  food, 182, 183
  housing, 288
  life insurance, 327–331
  shopping, 74, 76
Net earning, 351
New York City, 362, 374
New York Times, The, 345, 367, 371
Newspaper
  advertising, 65–67, 72
  bond prices, 354
  stock prices, 353
Newsweek, 345
Ninety-day account, 49
Nitrogen, 378
No-fault insurance, 148
Noise, 376, 377
No-load fund, 356
No-passbook account, 281
Nonforfeiture values, 335, 336

Nonrenewable insurance, 320
Nonstore retailers, 68
Nonsurgical health care, 191
Nonworking time, 158–160
Notes
  Federal Reserve, 236
  government, 236, 357
Numismatic News, 343
Nurses, 246, 248, 330
  aids, 246
  practical 230
  registered, 246
Nutrition, 83, 180

O

Obesity, 181–183
Obligations, co-signer, 225
Occupational Outlook Handbook, 243, 256
Occupational Outlook Quarterly, 241, 251
Occupational safety, 197, 233, 235
Occupational Safety and Health Act (OSHA), 197
Occupations, 242–265, *Also see* Jobs
Odd lot, stock, 355
Odometer, 138
Office jobs, 251, 254, 255
Office of Education (U.S.), 233
Oil, 138, 139, 372, 379
On-the-job training, 248
One-purpose credit cards, 50
Open
  accounts, 49
  dating, 83
  spaces, 362, 365–367
Open-end
  funds, 356
  mortgage, 311
Operating costs, car, 148–153
Operator, job, 251, 256, 291
Opportunities, equal, 251, 252, 392, 394, 395
Opportunity cost, 33
Options
  mortgage, 311
  stock, 392
Optomism
  economy, 387
  individual spending, 18
Ordinance, 376
Outlets, electric, 304, 377
Outstanding balance, 51, 223
Overbuying, 80
Overdrawn account, 274, 275
Overhauled engine, 136

Oversupply, manpower, 242
Over-the-counter drugs, 79, 80, 188, 189
Overuse of credit, 29

P

Packaging
  drugs, 197
  Fair Packaging and Labeling Act, 81
  food, 81, 82
  Food and Drug Administration, 232
  metric, 100
  sizes, 82, 83, 100
  waste, 371
Packing, 123–125, 316
Painting, 160, 303, 341
Pans, 371
Paper money, 266
Parent benefits, *See* Social Security
Parents Magazine, 87, 89
Parking contract, 228
Parks, 169, 234, 235, 308
  mobile home, 308
  national, 169
Part-time
  education, 249
  job, 249
Partially unemployed insurance, 211
Pass, employee, 269
Passbook, 53, 281–283
Patient rights, 189, 190
Pawnbroker, 53, 54
Paycheck, 33
Payee, 275, 276
Payments
  bills, 271
  car, 48, 141, 142
  credit, 51, 52, 58, 223
  down, 51, 300
  health care, 190–194
  life insurance, 322, 338
  method, 47, 274
  plans, 49
  Social Security, 209, 210
  unable to meet, 60, 61
Payroll
  deductions, 273
  tax, 389
Peak spending periods, 47
Peers, influence spending, 16, 17
Pension, 200, 202, 203, 255, 323, 324, 392, *Also see* Social Security
Percentage

of house owned, 312
  rate, 221, 222
Permanent care label, 118–121
Permanently reduced benefits, 204
Permits, 389
Personal
  appearance, 123, 126–128
  check, 271–279
  improvement, 94
  property, 221
  products, labels, 79–81
  protection, 179–240
  services, 255
  values, 16
Pessimism
  economy, 387
  individual spending, 18
Phosphate, 368
Photography, 160, 162, 163
Physical
  fitness, 163, 184–186
  life insurance, 320
Physicians, 252
Pipes, house, 304
Placement office, 208, 259
Plaintiff, 229
Plans
  career, 241–359
  clothes purchases, 105–110
  education, 242–265
  floor, 297
  health, 190–194
  housing, 288–319
  spending, 39, 41, 42
Playground, 310
Pledge, 52
Points
  credit rating, 58, 59
  mortgage, 313
Policy
  car insurance, 142
  life insurance, 325, 326
  public, 378
Pollution
  air, 362, 363, 372–376
  airplane, 374, 376
  car, 374
  fertilizer, 378
  water, 173, 368, 369
Ponce de Léon, 180
Popular Mechanics, 79
Popular Science, 79
Population, 289, 364
Postal Service, 96, 235, 271–273
Poultry, 84, 86, 231
Power, 235, 237
Practical nurse, 246, 330

Prefabrication, 300, 301, 303
Preferred stock, 349
Pregnancy, 189
Preliminary contract, 313
Premium
  car insurance, 142
  life insurance, 326, 335
Prepayment
  credit contract, 57
  health insurance, 190–194
  mortgage, 311
Prescription drugs, 186, 194
President's Committee on Consumer Interests, 237
President's Council on Physical Fitness and Sports, 184
Preventive health care, 194
Price
  bicycle, 163–165
  car, 140–142
  comparison shopping, 65
  freeze, 392
  repairs, 89, 90
  sale, 73, 74
  setting, 64–66
  trading stamps, 76
Prime rate, 54
Priorities, 15
Private sales, 74
Problems
  consumer, 52, 87–95
  credit, 60, 61
  repairs, 88–90
  returns, 90, 91
Producers, 65
Products, safety standards, 236
Professional associations, 96
Professional Numismatic Guild, 343
Professions, 252, 253
Profit, 64
Progressive tax, 390
Promissory notes, 266, 349
Promotions, sales, 76, 77, 82
Property taxes, 387, 388
Prosecutor, 96
Prospectus, 237, 356
Prosperity, 250, 299
Protection
  consumer, 223, 230
  health, 180–199
  jobs, 255
  legal, 218–240
Public
  accomodations, 228, 229
  assistance, 200, 213–215
    Aid to Dependent Children (ADC), 213, 214

Cuban Refugee Program,
214, 215
Child Welfare Services, 215
carriers, 228, 236
Health Service, 232, 233
Publications, government for
consumers, 168, 232, 243
Purchasing power, 384
Purification of water, 173

Q

Quality
clothing, 67, 113
price, 65
Quart, 98
Quarter of coverage, Social
Security, 201

R

Race discrimination, 251, 252,
392, 394, 395
Racing saddle, 165
Radiation, 233
Radio, 65, 66, 237
Railroad retirement, 193, 211
Range of package sizes, 82, 83
Rape, 229
Rates
add-on, 221
annual percentage, 221, 222
bank accounts, 53, 266
car insurance, 145–147
credit, 57, 58
discount, 221
electricity, 237
Federal Reserve, 236
gas, 237
interest, 53, 267
moving, 316
public transportation, 236
Social Security, 201
telephone, 237
Rating, credit, 57–59
Rayon, 115
Real estate, *Also see* Home and
Housing
investment, 345–347
jobs, 253, 256
taxes, 298, 387, 388
Rebuilt parts, car, 136
Receipt, 47, 271, 275
Recession, 256, 351, 383
Recipes, metric, 99, 100
Recommended dietary
allowance, 182
Reconcile check statement, 277,
278
Reconditioned engine, 136

Record
credit, 58, 59, 61
musical, 161, 162
Recovery, 383
Recreation, 158–178, 231, 250,
291, 300, 310, 371, *Also see*
Lesiure and specific
activites
activities, 178
backpacking, 166–178
bicycling, 163–166
camping, 166–170
children, 291
discussion, 178
facilities, 174, 231, 234, 297,
300, 371
fishing, 172, 173
handicapped people, 170
hobbies, 160, 161
housing, 160, 310
jobs, 250, 255
music, 161, 162
photography, 160, 162, 163
problem solving, 178
review, 177
senior citizens, 159, 161
skiing, 170–172
spending, 160, 177
tennis, 173, 174
terms, 177
vehicles, 174–176, 362, 364
Recycling, 30, 106, 107, 368,
370, 371, 378
Redeem
bonds, 284, 349
stock fund, 357
Reduced benefits, Social
Security, 204
Reevaluation, 316
References, 96, 243
Refund, 90, 223
Regenerated fibers, 116
Register
check, 277
securities, 237, 351
Regulatory agencies
federal, 96, 235–237, 383
state, 237, 238
Rehabilitation
land, 378
vocational, 208, 213
Reinstate
debt, 61
life insurance, 335
Remanufactured parts, 136
Remodel house, 291, 292, 304
Renewable insurance, 320
Rent

car, 50, 154, 155, 228
housing, 46, 54, 220, 221,
295–297
Repair
car, 137, 140, 147, 248, 250
clothing, 122, 227, 228
equipment, 88–90
estimate, 90
household, 220, 250
roof, 303
services, 90
warranty, 77, 78
Repayment plans, 54, 61
Replacement warranty, 77, 78
Repossession, 60
Resale prices, 65
Research, energy, 372
Reserve banks, 236
Resources
community, 30, 31
natural, 233, 378, 379
personal, 29, 30
recreation, 233, 234
reusing, See Recycling
transportation, 130
Responsibility
baggage, 228
driver, 154
marriage, 225–229
Restaurant inspection, 237
Reston, Virginia, 365, 366
Restrictions, mobile home park,
310
Restrictive endorsement, 269
Resume, 260, 261
Retail Coin Dealers Association,
343
Retailers, 49, 50, 52, 65, 67–73,
253
Retirement, *See* Senior citizens
Reusing, *See* Recycling
Revenue bonds, 357
Review, *See* specific topics
Riders, insurance, 327
Riding, *See* Car, Bicycle,
Motorcycle, Snowmobile,
Mass transit
Risks
assigned, 147
credit, 53, 54
sharing, 320
Rights, 225–229
Road test, 138–140
Robbery, 229
Roof, 288–319
Round lot, stock, 355
Route, airline, 236
Rummage sale, 72

Rural population, 289
Rusk, Howard A., 196
Revolving charge account, 49

S

Safe deposit box, 267, 284, 285
Safety
  bicycles, 165, 166
  car, 151, 154
  consumer rights, 230
  drugs, 154, 195
  food, 195, 232
  hotel guest, 229
  labels, 236
  motorcycle, 174, 175
  packaging, 197
  snowmobile, 176
  standards, 196, 197, 236
  swimming, 195
  tires, 151
  water, 195, 367
  worker, 197
Sales, 52, 65, 72–77, 90, 92–94
  contract, *See* Contract
  credit, *See* Credit
  tax, 389
Sanitation, food, 233
Savings, 279–285, *Also see* Bank
  bonds, 273, 283–285
Savings and loan associations,
  53, 268, 313
Schools, *Also see* Education and
  Jobs
  correspondence, 93, 94
  influence on value of house,
  293
  private, 247
  Social Security benefits for
  students, 205, 206
  technical, 247
  vocational, 245, 247
Seals of approval, 84, 86, 87, 89,
  165
Seasonal
  sales, 73
  workers, 211
Seat belts, 154, 196
Second mortgage, 313
Seconds, goods, 95
Secretary, 254
Securities, 236, 237, 347–358,
  Also see Stocks and Bonds
Security deposit, 52, 220, 221
Sedan, 133, 134
Seersucker, 115
Selecting
  clothing, 110–118
  investment fund, 356, 357

Selective tax, 389
Self-employment, and Social
  Security, 207
Self-medication, 79, 80
Self-regulated economy, 383
Self-service stores, 66
Semiskilled, 245, 246, 257
Senior citizen, *Also see*
  Medicaid, Medicare, Social
  Security, Supplementary
  Security Income Program,
  Veterans, and Welfare
  annuity, 323, 324
  health insurance, 193, 194
  housing, 292, 293
  leisure time, 159, 160
  mobile home parks, 310
  plans, 255
  railroad workers, 193
  recreation, 159, 161
Separates, clothing, 107
Septic tank, 218, 300, 378
Series EE and HH bonds, 283
Serving size, 83
Service, *Also see* Shopping and
  Warranty
  community, 160
  jobs, 250, 251, 253, 255, 256
Settlement
  credit, 60
  life insurance, 334
Sewage, 218, 231, 237, 300, 304,
  305, 368, 369, 378
Sew-ups, 165
Sex discrimination, 392
Shares
  credit union, 284
  savings and loan association,
  268
  stock, 347
Sharing
  alternative to buying, 30
  risk, 320
  responsibilities, 39, 41, 42
Sharkskin, 115
Shipping jobs, 254
Shock absorbers, 137, 138
Shoes, 99, 107–109, 227, 228
Shop foreperson, 392
Shopping, 63–178, *Also see*
  specific topics
  activities, 102, 103
  bargains, 72–76
  discussion, 101, 102
  facilities, 67–73, 172
  problem solving, 101
  problems, 87–95
  recreation, 158–177

repairs, 88–90
  returns, 90, 91
  review, 100, 101
  terms, 101
  time, 64
  trends, 72
SI metric system, 95
Sickness, *See* Disability and
  Health leave, 255, 392
Siding, house, 303
Signature
  card, 281
  check, 276, 277
  loan, 52
Signs, 66
Silhouette, 111
Silk, 115
Single purpose credit card, 50
Singles, housing, 288–290, 294,
  295
Site
  camping, 169, 170
  mobile home, 308
Sizes
  bicycle, 165
  car, 131
  clothing, 67, 88, 98, 113
  metric, 98–100
  packages, 82, 83, 100
  sewing, 83
Skiing, 170–172, 371
Skilled jobs, 246, 247, 251, 256
Skin, 79, 80, 127, 128, 186
Sleeping areas, 377
Slowdown, work, 392
Small
  claims court, 96, 223, 225, 229
  loan company, 57
Smallpox, 180
Smoking, 186
Snacks, 181
Snow tires, 152, 153
Snowmobile, 176
Social patterns, 17, 18
Social Security (FICA), 190,
  192–194, 200–210, 215, 233,
  273, 293
Sodium, 83
Solid waste, 362, 368–371
Sound-absorbing, 377
Sources of information, 78, 95,
  96
Space, housing, 300, 302
Special
  education, 250
  endorsement, 269
  sales, 74, 92
Specialty

car, 133, 135
store, 68, 69
Spectorsky, A. Z., 26
Speedometer, 99
Spending, 10–25, 34–38, *Also
see* specific topics
activities, 24, 25
discussion, 24
problem solving, 24
review, 23
terms, 24
Spoilage, 231
Sports, 20–22, 133, 135,
163–178, 180–185, *Also see*
specific topics
Spraying, 195
Stages of life, 48, 288
Stain resistance, 117
Stamps
collecting, 340, 342, 343
food, 196
labels, 79–87, 89, 99, 113,
118–121, 236
tax, 314, 390
trading, 76
Standard and Poor, 351, 356
Standard of identity, 81
Standards
American Standards Institute,
87
health, 392
houses, 237
international, 232
living, 300
National Bureau of, 232
safety, 196, 197, 233, 235, 236
weights and measures, 232,
237
work, 233, 235, 392
State
car
inspection, 137
insurance, 142
consumer representation, 237,
238
Department of Education, 247
employment agency, 208, 247
food inspection, 86
jobs, 255, 256
regulations, 53, 142, 237, 238
retirement programs, 200, 201
unemployment insurance, 211
Statement
bank, 277, 278
credit, 59, 60, 223
of identity, 81

Station wagon, 133, 135
Steam engine, 374
Steering, 138–140
Stenographer, 254
Stereo Review, 162
Sterilization, 194
Stevenson, Gloria, 244, 245
Steward, shop, 392
Stock company reports, 336, 357
Stockholm Conference, 379
Stocks, 237, 267, 285, 325,
347–349, 353, 355, 357, 392
Stopping payment, 275, 277
Storage, 122, 123, 296, 306
Stores, 51, 52, 64, 66–73, 76, 77,
90, 91, 163, 164
Straight life insurance, 322
Strike, 391
Strip mining, 362, 363, 378
Stripes, 111
Students
credit, 47
Social Security benefits, 205,
206
spending, 34–38
Style
clothing, 74, 111, 112
life, 291, 328
Subcompact car, 131, 132
Sublet, 321
Subsidy, airline, 236
Substance, 95
Suburb, 130, 131, 289
Subway poster, 66
Sulphur dioxide, 373
Summer job, 259, 260
Supermarket promotions, 66, 76,
77
Supplementary Security Income
Program (SSI), 213–215
Supply
food, 364
money, 236
water, 237
Surgery
elective, 194
insurance, 191
Survey
real estate, 314
sales fraud, 93
Surviving divorced wife, Social
Security benefits, 202
Suspension, car, 137
Swap, *See* Trading
Swimming, 161, 185, 195, 310
Synthetics, 368

T
Tabulating operator, 255
Tapes, 161, 162
Tariff, 386
Taxes, 46, 61, 211, 271, 272,
293, 298, 311, 312, 314, 316,
337, 385–390
estate, 389
excise, 389
gasoline, 389
income, 61, 271, 272, 388, 389
property, 388
sales, 389
unemployment, 211
Teachers, 252
Technical
school, 247
workers, 253
Technology, 180, 250
Teenagers, *See* Youth
Telephone
jobs, 254
rates, 237
shopping, 66, 72
tax, 389
Television, 65, 66, 72, 237, 371
Temperature
car, 139
metric, 95, 97
Tennis, 173, 174
Termites, 303
Term insurance, 329
Terms, *See* specific topics
Textile labels, 118–121
Theft, 229
Thirty-day accounts, 49
Thrift
account, 267, 268
attitude, 11
shop, 71, 72
Tile, 377
Time
clothing care, 118
costs, 30, 64, 74, 141
homemaker, 160
measuring, 95
working, 72, 158–160, 392
Time magazine, 345
Tires, 137, 151–153
Toaster, 371
Ton, 98
Tools, 274
Townhouse, 297
Trade
balance of, 386, 387
international 386, 387

skilled, 246, 247
Trade-in, 222
Trading
alternative to money, 30
stamps, 76
stock, 349, 350
Traffic, 130, 196, 228, 236, 297
Trailer, 288, 290, 306
Training, job, 208, 213, 243, 245,
254, 256, 262, 263, *Also see*
Jobs
Transmission, 137, 139, 140
Transportation, 130–157,
163–166, 174–176, 196, 228,
236, 256
automobile, *See* Car
bicycle, 163–166
motorcycle, 174–176
jobs, 256
mass, 130, 196, 228, 236
Trash, 237, 362, 368–371
Travel
credit, 47, 50
jobs, 130, 131
wardrobe, 123
youth, 20
Travelers checks, 267, 271–273
Treasury
bills, 357
Department of, 211, 235
notes, 357, 358
Trends
checking accounts, 279
clothing, 104, 105
jobs, 254
shopping, 70–73
Social Security, 209, 210
young people, 19–21
Triacetate, 116
Trucks, 133, 135, 256, 257, 376
jobs, 256, 257
noise, 376
Trusts, 209, 211, 267, 268
Truth-in-Lending Law, 44, 57,
221, 223
Tuberculosis, 180
Tweed, 115
Typhus, 180

U
Underweight, 182
Underwriters' Laboratories (UL),
86, 89
Unemployment, 200, 210–212,
242, 256
insurance, 200, 210–212

Uninsured motorist, 144
Unions, 200, 201, 390–392
Unit pricing, 66
United States, 168, 191, 195,
204, 205, 211, 231–237, 260,
343, 377, *Also see*
Commission, Federal, and
Government
Civil Aeronautics Board
(CAB), 236
Consumer Advisory Council,
237
Environmental Protection
Agency, 377
Federal Aviation Agency
(FAA), 236
Food and Drug Administration
(FDA), 80, 81–96, 195, 230,
232, 233
Geological Survey, 168
Office of Education, 233
Postal Service, 235, 343
Public Health Service, 232,
233
Veterans Administration (VA),
237
United States of America
Standards Institute, 87, 89
United States Savings and Loan
League, 268
United States Stamp Catalog,
343
Unsecured loan, 52
Unskilled work, 251, 256, 257
Urban
development, 233
housing, 288, 292
population, 289
Utility
commission, 372
diminishing marginal, 32

V
Vacations, 255
Vaccines, 180
Value, assessed, 388
Van, 133, 135
Variable annuity, 325
Vending machines, 68, 70
Venereal disease, 189
Verification check, 269
Veterans Administration (VA or
G.I.), 196, 211, 237,
310–313, 336, 337
health care, 196
life insurance, 336, 337

mortgage, 310–313
Vibration, 377
VISA, 50
Vitamins, 188
Vocational
rehabilitation, 208, 213
schools, 245, 289
Volume, 98
Voluntary labeling, appliances,
373, 374
Voucher, paycheck, 268, 269

W
Waiver, life insurance premium,
335
Wage
earner, 29, 200, 392
freeze, 392
minimum 392
Wall Street Journal, The, 230,
351
Walls, 377
Wants, 30–33
Wardrobe planning, 105–110,
123
Warnings, safety, 236
Warrants, stock, 355
Warranty, 67, 77–79, 137, 138,
140, 222
car, 136–138, 140, 222
battery, 138
housing, *See* Housing
seals, *See* Seals
Washing, 369, 371
Waste
sewage, 218, 305, 368, 369,
378, 379
solid, 237, 362, 368, 370, 371
Water, 173, 195, 235, 237, 304,
305, 367–370, 378, 379
skiing, 171, 172
Webster, Norman, 371
Weight
individual, 182
metric, 98
package, 95
Weights and measures, 232, 237
Welfare
Aid to Dependent Children
(ADC), 213, 214
Child Welfare Services, 215
Cuban Refugee Program, 214,
215
General assistance, 215
Public assistance, 213–215
White-collar jobs, 250, 251, 256

Whole life insurance, 322, 323, 330
Widow, *See* Women
Widower, Social Security benefits, 202, 209
Wiesenberger, Arthur, 357
Winter driving, 152, 153
Wire-ons, 165
Wiring, 304
Withdrawals, savings, 281, 283
W-2 form, 388
Women
  homemaker, 337
  jobs, 251, 252
  life insurance, 337
  legal rights, 226, 227
  Social Security, 202, 206, 207
  working, 36, 37, 41, 206, 207, 244, 245, 254–257

Wool, 115
Work, *Also see* Jobs
  time, 72, 158–160, 244, 245, 392
  underemployment, 211–213, 215
Work credits, Social Security, 203
Worker's Compensation, 192, 200, 212, 213
World Health Organization, 365
Wright, Robert A., 367
Writing a check, 275–277

X

X-ray technician, 253

Y

Yard sale, 72
Yield to maturity, bonds, 353

YMCA, 160
YWCA, 160
Your Price Authority Blue Book, 131
Your Social Security, 203, 204
Youth
  credit, 23, 46, 47
  employment service, 259
  housing, 288, 290–292
  leisure, 158
  market, 23
  patients, 189, 190
  spending, 19–23
  workers, 257–259

Z

Zoning, 219, 299, 300, 365, 377